CHICAGO PUBLIC LIBRARY
P9-EMH-258

The
Chicago Public Library
C
P L
AVALON BRANCH LIBRARY
8828 SO. STONY ISLAND AVE.
CHICAGO, IL 60617
Call No.
Branch
Form 178

# MARTIN LUTHER KING, JR. AND THE CIVIL RIGHTS MOVEMENT

Edited by David J. Garrow

A CARLSON PUBLISHING SERIES

# Direct Action and Desegregation, 1960-1962

## TOWARD A THEORY OF THE RATIONALIZATION OF PROTEST

James H. Laue

PREFACE BY DAVID J. GARROW

CARLSON
*Publishing Inc*

BROOKLYN, NEW YORK, 1989

**Library of Congress Cataloging-in Publication Data**

Laue, James H.
Direct action and desegregation, 1960-1962 : toward a theory of the rationalization of protest / James H. Laue.
p. cm. —(Martin Luther King, Jr., and the Civil Rights Movement ; 15)
Bibliography: p.
Includes index.
1. Afro-Americans—Civil rights—History—20th century. 2. Afro-Americans—Civil rights—Southern States—History—20th century. 3. Civil rights demonstrations—United States—History—20th century. 4. Civil rights demonstrations—Southern States–History—20th century. 5. Direct action. 6. Southern States—Race relations. 7. Afro-Americans—History—1877-1964. I. Title. II. Series.
E185.61.L35 1989
323.1'196073075—dc20 89-9867
ISBN 0-926019-09-0 (alk. paper)

This book was written as a doctoral dissertation at Harvard University in 1965. It has been edited, proofread, typeset and indexed for publication here.

Typographic design: Julian Waters

Typeface: Bitstream ITC Galliard

The index to this book was created using NL Cindex, a scholarly indexing program from the Newberry Library.

For a complete listing of the volumes in this series, please see the back of this book.

Printed on acid-free, 250-year-life paper.

Manufactured in the United States of America.

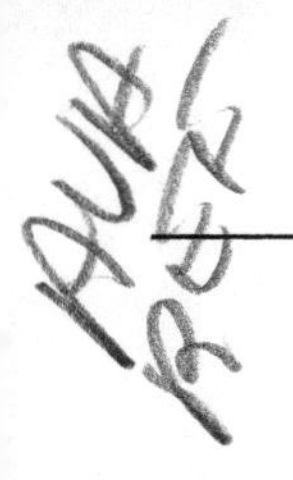

To all
who took their bodies off the line
long enough to help me with this project.

# Contents

## *C. THE THEORY*
## *The Rationalization of Protest*

# List of Figures

# Series Editor's Preface

James H. Laue's *Direct Action and Desegregation* is one of the most—and perhaps simply *the* most—valuable historical sources for understanding the rich interplay of what in retrospect were undeniably the two most important years of the post-World War II black freedom struggle, namely the twenty-four months beginning with the onset of the southern student sit-in movement on February 1, 1960, in Greensboro, North Carolina.

Many summary treatments of the black freedom struggle, and particularly the 1954-1965 period, may unfortunately leave the general reader insufficiently aware of how truly crucial the early phases of black student activism were to the entire subsequent course of the civil rights movement and to all of American political life throughout the 1960s. The onset of the sit-ins, the founding of the Student Nonviolent Coordinating Committee (SNCC), and the evolution of black student attitudes towards older activists and other civil rights organizations during events such as the 1961 Freedom Rides and the 1961-1962 protest campaign in Albany, Georgia, represented three of the most influential occurrences in the black freedom struggle and in the burgeoning of youthful activism that so dramatically distinguished the decade of the 1960s from that of the 1950s.

Jim Laue's 1965 manuscript, based heavily upon his own extended 1960 and 1962 research trips across the South and his intimate participant/observer presence at any number of now-historic movement meetings and conferences, is as rich a discussion of that crucial two year period as any we are likely to ever have. Especially in Chapter Four, concerning the 1960 sit-ins, and Chapter Six, concerning the pre-history and early development of the Albany Movement, Laue has provided us with descriptive accounts that are and will remain of timeless historical value. While most any reader, and particularly oral historians and sociologists, will likely also be notably impressed by the perceptive and sensitive discussion of participant/observation that Professor Laue provides in Chapter Two, readers who are not social movement sociologists should nonetheless not skip over the extremely rich material, particularly on SNCC and on the Southern Christian Leadership Conference (SCLC), that is contained in one of Laue's more theoretical sections, Chapter Eight. Although his typological discussions of Weber and Parsons will be of specific interest only to scholarly specialists, some chapter titles and introductory references ought not to obscure the very valuable historical materials and discussions that occur throughout the entire manuscript.

In part because Professor Laue's manuscript, as a Harvard dissertation, has never been available in a microform edition (as most other universities' dissertations are), it has never been extensively used even by many published scholars of the American civil rights movement. I am very pleased that Carlson Publishing's eighteen volume series on *Martin Luther King, Jr., and the Civil Rights Movement* will bring James Laue's important work to the much wider audience it has long deserved.

David J. Garrow

# Preface 1989

Thanks to the initiative of publisher Ralph Carlson, I have completed, in the relative safety of my study, the somewhat frightening requirement of carefully reading and analyzing something I wrote nearly a quarter of a century ago. The experience was both humbling and exhilarating.

Looking at the beginnings of the civil rights movement from this distance first made me sense the scope of historic racism in the United States and the enormity of the accomplishment of all those who "put their bodies on the line" to redirect that history. But I quickly found myself drawn to the more personal and subjective parts of the dissertation, which reminded me so vividly of the people, the crises and my participant observation research experience in the movement—which unquestionably were the most significant influences shaping my life and vocation today. As Andy Young, one of my mentors and heroes in the movement of the 1960s, said in response to my question about what he thought of northern whites who came down to get involved in the movement: "It's fine. Once you get shot at in a foxhole down here, you get religion—and you never lose it."

Young—the former Congressman and United Nations Ambassador and now the Mayor of Atlanta—is like the rest of us who were part of this movement: the commitment to social change and racial justice got stamped in through the experience, and informs our thinking, politics and personal values for the rest of our lives. That, indeed, expresses the major paradox which is at the heart of the theoretical perspective in my dissertation: that while the forces of rationalization and bureaucratization inevitably co-opt and constrain the charismatic idea, the process is never totally successful when the idea deals with life and death and identity issues, and has recruited committed adherents who never forget. The personal is not ultimately packageable and predictable. As I modestly reminded Max Weber in his language in the last paragraph of my dissertation, when a phenomenon like the sit-in movement becomes the "official business" of a rationalizing social system, it is at best futile to hope for the "complete elimination" of ". . . love, hatred, and all purely personal, irrational, and emotional elements which escape calculation."

Which parts of the dissertation, if any, are most useful to modern scholars, activists and policy makers—the theory, the narrative of the movement in its first two years, the method, the treatment of issues, the example of the people involved? The readers and history will have to judge.

### *The People*

The commitment of the hundreds of persons with whom I worked in the movement made the most lasting impact on my life. People and their rights are, after all, what the movement was and is all about. They learned, through the movement, the fear and potentials inherent in putting your body on the line. They learned skills—in organizing, public speaking, confronting injustices, controlling their own fears and behavior, honing and applying healthy skepticism.

Where are they now? Virtually everyone I know of is still involved in some work for social justice and social change: Andy Young as Mayor of Atlanta; Jim Forman writing and organizing in Washington, D.C.; Julian Bond having served a distinguished political career and continuing to lecture and write on social issues; Will Campbell ministering to socially marginal whites in the South and inspiring would-be Christians with his writing; Jim Lawson continuing his ministry in a large Los Angeles parish and through his work in the World Council of Churches and elsewhere; Connie Curry directing the poverty program in Atlanta; Charles Gomillion still writing about racial injustice well into his 80s; Tom Hayden serving in the California legislature with a strong track record in human rights and environmental matters.

Others are gone: college presidents Herman Long and Vivian Henderson, the quietly inspiring Ella Baker, former Urban League director Whitney Young—and, of course, Martin Luther King, Jr., who was killed six years to the day after my April 4, 1962 interview with him. But, of course, their work lives on and continues to serve as a model for our lives.

Many movement leaders I did not interview also continue their commitment in their mid-life incarnations. Marian Wright Edelman of Spelman is the influential founding director of the Children's Defense Fund in Washington, the leading advocate in the nation for children's rights. Marion Barry is the two-term mayor of Washington.

Structures and institutions are important, to be sure. But the persons involved are the essence. They are ends in themselves, and they are the object of the civil rights movement's means. I hope they are still alive to the readers of this manuscript.

*The History*

In trying to organize a description of the antecedents and early days of the civil rights movement of the 1960s, I chose to focus on a significant early protest and move in concentric circles from a community (Montgomery, chapter 3) to a region (the South, chapter 4), to the nation and national policy implications (chapter 5), and back to a community for a new and not always successful phase (Albany, chapter 6). The settings in chapters 3, 4 and 5 provide the context for an analysis of the development of the three most significant movement organizations: the Southern Christian Leadership Conference beginning with King, Abernathy and the Montgomery bus boycott in the late 1950s; the Student Nonviolent Coordinating Committee, formed to coordinate and extend the lunch counter sit-ins in 1960; and the Congress of Racial Equality (CORE), the organizer of the Freedom Rides.

I suspect these sections will provide the most attractive reading for social historians and students of social movements. In re-reading them, I was captured by the detailed step-by-step accounts of events and interactions that nursed the movement into being and effectiveness. Of special interest today is the wavering but ultimately helpful response of the federal government to the Freedom Rides, for it reflects the importance of the role of a transcendent power or guarantor of First and Fourteenth Amendment rights in the success of social protest.

*The Issues*

All the major issues treated in the dissertation are of course with us today—racism, social change, co-optation of protest, minor reform versus structural change, the organization of social movements. The civil rights movement produced or facilitated significant social change. The Civil Rights Act of 1964 and the Voter Rights Act of 1965 have made lasting impacts on institutional practices and political leadership patterns. Tens of thousands of persons trained in the movement continue to work with, within, and outside the system for change today. Yet we still have with us Forsyth County, Howard Beach, skinheads, homelessness, declining numbers of blacks in higher education and countless other indicators that the work is far from finished. The critical question is whether the vision and techniques of the 1960s movements have been so blunted through Weberian rationalization and sophisticated establishment responses that they can never again be effective in promoting basic change in the United States.

Jim Lawson knew about the requirement for structural change and the dangers of cooptation, and taught me in our 1962 interview:

> Most of us work simply for concessions from the system, not for transforming the system . . . But if after 300 years, segregation is still a basic pattern rather than a peripheral custom, should we not question the "American way of life" which allows segregation so much structural support?

*The Theory*

The theory developed in the dissertation is built around Weber's concepts of charisma and rationalization, Parsons' four functional problems of social systems, and the use of stages for organizing the flow of historical events. It attempts to provide a framework to understand what happens to social movements as they are caught in a tug between spontaneity and systematization, between success and stagnation, between movement and program. The concepts, flow and interrelations are summarized in the master chart following the index.

In some ways the theoretical contribution is the most universal and long-lasting, but it did not hold my attention after all these years as well as the historical narrative and descriptions. I encourage some computer-wise reader to try to develop better graphics to illuminate the theory—both its structural elements and its intended dynamism (which now is imprisoned in Aristotelian categories on the printed page).

In my present incarnation as a conflict resolution practitioner and scholar, I was shocked to find my definition of conflict employing the concept "specifically as a major adaptive mechanism to external systems" in the theoretical framework (p. 191). I do not use such language anymore. I knew then that Parsons was heavily criticized as an apostle of functionalism and its implication for system maintenance, but I found his four functional problems useful for analyzing the inevitable changes that occur in social movements. I still find the framework useful, but would not begin a discussion of the concept of conflict with the notion of "adaptive mechanisms." The point, of course, is that conflict often is the engine of social change, the mechanism for getting the mule's attention so behavior may be modified toward social justice.

In any case, my early studies of Weber have been crucial to my present analyses of "the ravages of success" I now see in the conflict resolution "movement." Weber lives, and is extremely helpful in preparing for and fending off the ravages of success.

*The Method*

My favorite quote from all the interviews conducted for this dissertation came from SNCC director Jim Forman over ribs at B.B.'s on Auburn Avenue in 1962. In responding to a question about the development of the movement, he said:

"Come on Laue . . . you know this stuff!"

Of course he was right, based on what he knew of me as a friend and participant in the movement. My interviewing and scholarly roles were secondary. "You're right," I said. "But I have to get you to say it for the dissertation."

I found the sections on participant observation compelling because they relate so closely to the work I do today as a mediator—observing, synthesizing, informally interviewing, and facilitating understanding and relationships. Of special interest to readers involved in qualitative research or epistemological pursuits will be pages 23-33 on participant observation and pages 51-54 on exploratory research. I see a continuity in my development as I reflect on those sections, especially the second reference which proposes precisely the research metaphor we employ in mediation and conflict resolution practice—the dialogue.

*A Personal Postscript*

My adult "career" (more a vocation, to be sure) has carried me from a small minority-less Wisconsin town to activism in a clear-cut moral cause, to analysis and development as a scholar, to work as a third party claiming to help resolve important social and racial conflicts. My participation in the civil rights movement clearly was the most important formative influence. The moral questions were clear. The people (at least the good guys) were attractive and committed. The combination of risk and incredible leaps in learning was irresistible.

I was told by an adviser at Harvard some time after my dissertation was completed and accepted that I had been viewed as something of a risk and an unorthodox candidate, for I seemed "strongly committed" to the movement and was not doing a "straight empirical or hypothesis-testing dissertation." When I turned up in jail for testing lunch counter segregation in Miami in August 1960—on Harvard research money—more explanation of the validity and nuances of participant observation was in order. Later I looked tame, though, in the face of SDS-ers in the sociology doctoral program who regarded even "theory" and "data" as establishment tools.

So my own odyssey has been one of pushing the edges to advance social justice. The activist background prepared me—as it did a surprisingly large group of my mediator colleagues—to understand power and powerlessness in the pursuit of constructive change through mediation. My dissertation field work and writing prepared me well for my post-movement step in 1965 to the Justice Department's mediation agency, the Community Relations Service, just in time for Selma. I was in the next room at the Lorraine Motel in Memphis on April 4, 1968, when another of my heroes from the movement was killed. My work in the 1970s and 1980s in complex policy disputes in the growing movement for conflict resolution was molded by these experiences. Now I understand better the then-curious allusions of Tom Hayden, fellow movement sociologist Marty Oppenheimer (whose dissertation also is published in this series) and others to Trotsky, Marx, socialism and other phenomena that seemed peripheral to the central message of the civil rights movement: that oppressed blacks are fighting for their rights, and naturally we should help them.

As I write this, I am preparing to leave for South Africa tonight for three weeks. The purpose: work on racism and conflict resolution. This chance juxtaposition helps keep things in perspective.

James H. Laue
March 30, 1989

# Acknowledgments

The many persons who have contributed to this dissertation are, for the most part, listed in the appendices which follow the last chapter. But several of them deserve special acknowledgment here.

Dr. Gordon W. Allport and Dr. Thomas F. Pettigrew of the Department of Social Relations at Harvard University provided the inspiration from which this project grew and much of the technical assistance which helped to bring it to completion. With their aid, I secured grants from the Taconic Foundation, the Laboratory of Social Relations and The Society for the Psychological Study of Social Issues to carry out the research. I am especially grateful to Dr. Allport for a thorough reading and helpful criticisms on the second draft. Dr. Florence Kluckhohn and Dr. Richard Mann of the Department of History at Harvard joined in the Committee which helped me design the project in 1961 and 1962.

My wife, Mariann R. Laue, has helped in vital ways at every stage—coding, tabulating, proof-reading, typing, etc. I have appreciated even more her good counsel, her patience and stabilizing influence during the completion of the writing. Without her faith and encouragement, the project could not have come to fruition.

I was fortunate to have Judy Beckley as typist for the final manuscript. Mrs. Ann Ray, Jane Redmon and Ernestine Williams gave invaluable typing assistance, and Mrs. Mary Chapnick excellently drew important charts. The Community Relations Service of the U.S. Department of Commerce, Washington, D.C., encouraged the project, and graciously granted use of typewriters and office space during the final phases.

The subjects of this study deserve re-acknowledgment here: I am grateful to all who took their bodies off the line long enough to help me with this project.

For assistance in the 1989 publication of this manuscript, I am especially grateful to my wife, Marianne R. Laue, for her precision editing, to my mother, Jane H. Laue, for her interest in and support of my work over the years, and to Ralph Carlson, for his initiative and painstaking work in bringing this project to fruition.

# A. Introduction

## Direct Action and Desegregation

ONE

# Statement of the Problem

## Spontaneous Protest and Institutionalization in American Race Relations

> . . . That is the destiny of every new idea. It is crystallized in formulas so that it may be propagated. It is intrusted to a body of interpreters so that it may be preserved. That body is prudently recruited, sometimes specifically paid . .
>
> Silone[1]

> I first became involved in The Movement when at the age of five I learned I was a Negro.
>
> James Forman
> Executive Director,
> Student Nonviolent
> Coordinating Committee

The lunch counter sit-ins which grew into a social movement in the American South in 1960 were, for thousands of persons, an idea whose time had come. They were like a new discovery, an awesome and illuminating notion whose social expression revamped carefully-laid life plans and altered the institutional structure of a whole nation. And the revamping and alteration continues, for individual lives, for the social structure—and, in some cases, for American values themselves.

This study traces the start, rapid growth and institutionalization of the sit-in movement in the United States from February 1, 1960, to February 1,

1962. A theory is developed to explain how spontaneous social protest is "crystallized in formulas" and "propagated"—in Weberian terms, how it is *rationalized*. The theory is applied to direct action and desegregation during this period, and from it interpretations and predictions are made about the situation after 1962.

The analysis reveals that the tempo and pattern of the desegregation process in the United States have altered radically since 1960 because of the widespread application and success of direct action techniques. As a direct result of these protests, more actual desegregation of public accommodations took place in the two years from February 1960 to February 1962 than in the previous two decades:

1. Thousands of lunch counters and other facilities in approximately 150 southern cities dropped racial barriers.[2]
2. Over 7,000 Americans willingly went to jail.
3. Upwards of 100,000 persons actively participated in the protests, many thousands more supported the efforts in boycott, and millions more were touched by mass media reports on "the closest thing to a student revolution this country has ever seen."[3]
4. New organizations arose and existing groups were revitalized on a nationwide scale. Millions of dollars from individual, organizational, state and federal sources became involved.
5. Almost 75 state and local biracial committees were established.

Rarely do such institutional changes occur in so short a time.

The cultural impact of this action is also manifested in the various mass communications and art media. "Anything"-in has become a standard part of academic and liberal vocabularies. The word "sit-in" appeared in dictionaries as early as 1962.[4] The wires and local newspapers have carried innumerable feature articles on the "re-awakening" of American college students. A good example is a *New York Times* series in 1962 which began, "Before the day ends American college students will have picketed something or someone, engaged in a sit-in somewhere or marched someplace."[5] The National Broadcasting Company's series of "white papers" on both sit-ins and Freedom Rides has been widely viewed.[6] And in addition to dozens of jail-produced "freedom songs" which have become a part of American folk and protest literature, Tin Pan Alley has been caught up by direct action with a little rock-and-roll ditty called "I'm Gonna Sit-in Until You Give In ('til you give me alla your love)."[7]

The culture-wide impact of the direct action protests should become clear in a variety of contexts as the analysis unfolds, so I will add to the present documentation only the widespread feeling among this study's informants that the sit-ins heralded a new political consciousness and effectiveness for American college students.[8] "For the first time," said Bruce Galphin (a race relations reporter, former campus activist and world traveler), "a student movement in the United States has played a part in influencing tradition and the government as European and Latin American student revolutions have been doing for years."

## *a. HISTORICAL AND THEORETICAL PERSPECTIVES*

The history of spontaneous rebellion against slavery and segregation is as old as these two institutions of involuntary servitude themselves—as old, that is, as the history of man. In the American case, uprisings against slavery began before captured Africans ever set foot on North America; nearly 60 shipboard slave revolts made it into the historical record in the 18th and 19th centuries, and Herbert Aptheker's documentation of American slave revolts leaves no doubt about the protest legacy spawned by the western plantation system.[9]

But the deeper meaning of this kind of protest stems from the millions of instances of daily revolt in the histories of all suppressed peoples. In the American South of the early 1800s, travelers' reports are full of stories of tool breakage, stealing, running away and general slowdown by the slaves.[10] This daily rebellion provided the life-stuff from which black revolutionaries like Nat Turner and Denmark Vesey fashioned their group protests against slavery.

And so it is with the open revolt against segregation today. Although the segregated system has become firmly embedded in the institutional structure of American society through nearly a century's exercise of legal and extra-legal sanctions, Negro Americans daily rebel. "Every doorsill becomes a crisis situation," as one student sit-in leader put it.[11] At times these personal rebellions have fused into spontaneous mass protest. And then the process seems to retreat to the low ebb of the cycle—back to the millions of formally unconnected daily revolts—as the unifying force is surrounded by its own and society's structures.

This study, then, is conceived as an attempt to (a) *interpret the origins and growth of the direct action movement from 1960-62*, and (b) *develop a general sociological theory to explain and predict the processes of protest and rationalization in racial patterns*. The theory is built on five basic ideas: Max Weber's concepts of *rationalization, charisma* and the *three types of legitimate authority*, and Talcott Parsons' typology of the *four fundamental imperatives* within *the social system*.

The argument is organized in three parts, each containing several chapters. This introductory section clarifies definitions, assesses the relevant literature, and offers a tentative statement of the theory and an analysis of the study's design and methods, with a theoretical note on interviewing "elites."

Section B deals with the basic factual and interpretive data from which the theory develops—nonviolent direct action against segregation in the United States from February 1, 1960, to February 1, 1962. An attempt is made to develop this material in terms of its own internal logic, which is seen as consonant with the larger theory of socio-racial change proposed in the final section.

Section C outlines the elements of a theory of rationalization, applies the theory to the direct action movement, and offers conclusions and predictions. An underlying theme is the inherent paradox involved in the attempt to structure the ultimately unstructurable—protest.

Before attempting a tentative statement of the theory, there are several questions to be confronted and definitions to be made: (1) What do we mean by prejudice, discrimination, segregation, desegregation and integration? (2) What is "nonviolent direct action?" (3) Are the direct action protests a "social movement?" This brief section attempts to set questions like this in a coherent sociological framework which will lend itself to clarification and expansion as the analysis develops.

### *Some Basic Definitions*

Since many of the terms which appear in a variety of contexts throughout the dissertation have become almost second-nature in race relations terminology, it is best to explicitly define the most important of them here. Central to the exposition are the concepts of minority, prejudice, discrimination, segregation, desegregation, integration and protest.

According to Louis Wirth, a *minority* is ". . . a group of people who, because of their physical or cultural characteristics, are singled out from the others in the society in which they live for differential and unequal treatment, and who, therefore, regard themselves as objects of collective discrimination."[12]

The writings of Gordon W. Allport and Robin Williams, among others, have clarified the sometimes hazy distinction between prejudice and discrimination. *Prejudice* is an attitude—a positive or negative prejudgment of a person or thing or idea based on an overgeneralization from insufficient evidence. It is not subject to change with the introduction of new evidence.[13] *Discrimination*, on the other hand, is a form of behavior—"the unequal treatment of individuals considered to belong to a particular social group."[14] Thus we find that prejudice generally is manifested in discriminatory behavior, but that such behavior does not always imply prejudice on the part of the discriminator.

*Segregation*, then, is the societal counterpart of individual discrimination. When discrimination against certain minority groups is approved and enforced by the dominant group—either legally or by common custom—the result is segregation. Segregation is thus an institutionalized form of discrimination.[15]

A distinction should be made between desegregation and integration. *Desegregation* refers to the simple removal of legal and custom-enforced barriers to equal participation in the society. It is, in a sense, "bringing the system back to zero," evening up the opportunity of all component groups for "another start." *Integration*, however, is a psycho-spiritual as well as sociological concept. It implies the harmonization and unification of diverse groups and individuals in a completely functional system, above and beyond mere removal of barriers to equal participation. In addition, integration implies a societal consensus that members of *all* its subgroups share this right to participation, and that these members do, in fact, participate on a full and open basis.

*Protest*—the process on which this dissertation centers—may be defined on several institutional levels. First and foremost it is that process which has crystallized from the day-to-day rebellions of minority members, as described above. In this sense it is a profoundly individual matter. But protest also refers, on the collectivity level, to group attempts to secure goals through a wide variety of tactics ranging from an unorganized, spontaneous sit-in to a complex and coordinated movement. This kind of protest may involve attacks on various institutions within the society; in the case of nonviolent direct action against segregation in the United States, the protest is aimed at social, economic, political and religious institutions, as well as less formal matters of local custom.

James Q. Wilson deals with protest in still another sense which is relevant to the present topic.[16] Within the context of bargaining theory, protest is seen as the exclusive use of "negative inducements" (threats) that rely for their effect on ". . . sanctions which require mass action or response." Mass nonviolent direct action fits this definition, for as a threat-in-reserve, it has become the major catalyst in Negro-white power relationships in many southern communities today.

*What is "Nonviolent Direct Action"?*

From the beginning of the sit-ins in February of 1960, they have been identified as a "passive resistance" movement, or "civil disobedience," or as "nonviolent direct action." In these pages the protests are most often referred to as *nonviolent direct action*; thus a word of clarification is in order.

The phrase "nonviolent direct action" encompasses both the philosophy and the method of the protests under study. Passive resistance is most closely identified with Gandhi's work in South Africa and India in the first half of the twentieth century.[17] Leo Kuper presents a useful distinction of types of passive resistance in his study of *Passive Resistance in South Africa*.[18] One type works at the level of a society's power relations; he calls it "Change by Embarrassment of the Rulers." Here, the success of protest depends directly on mass participation by the subordinate group, which embarrasses the dominant group and thereby causes its leaders to initiate specific changes in the social structure. Kuper's second type of passive resistance is a classical expression of Gandhi's *Satyagraha*—"Conversion by Suffering." Under this system, nonviolence is regarded as an expression of strength, its efficacy relying on the moral superiority of the soul, and soul-force as against body-force. If the motivation is pure, *Satyagraha* brings about social change via a change of heart in the rulers. The redemptive power of unmerited suffering activates a searching of the conscience in the power group, and ultimately leads to a change in the evil system.

This typology is subsumed, however, by nonviolent direct action as practiced in the current American protests and analyzed in this study. For the resistance has, from the beginning, employed both types of protest, purposely embarrassing local southern "rulers" by their actions, and with equal consciousness voluntarily submitting to suffering in an attempt to bring about social change.

The American protests have also involved civil disobedience—a deliberate breaking of laws felt to be unjust. But this is only one facet of the resistance, for local law-breaking has always been accompanied by economic and political pressures in the total effort. In addition, Will Campbell points out[19] that the protest has often been directed at customs which are not actually laws.

The Congress of Racial Equality cites the threefold power inherent in the kind of nonviolent direct action it espouses: "(1) the power of active goodwill and non-retaliation; (2) the power of public opinion against an injustice; (3) the power of refusing to be a party to injustice, as illustrated by the boycott and the strike."[20] And both the Student Nonviolent Coordinating Committee and Martin Luther King's Southern Christian Leadership Conference formally subscribe to nonviolence as a worthy ideal for all of one's thought and action. This excerpt from the Statement of Purpose of the SNCC constitution is representative:

> We affirm the philosophical or religious ideal of nonviolence as the foundation of our purpose, the presupposition of our faith, and the manner of our action.
>
> By appealing to conscience and standing on the moral nature of human existence, nonviolence nurtures the atmosphere in which reconciliation and justice become actual possibilities.[21]

For our purpose, then, the concept of nonviolent direct action will include *all* of these dimensions, for they all have been in evidence in the phenomenon under study and their use is being exemplified and extended with each passing week. Nonviolent direct action can best be viewed as *active non-cooperation with segregation* in whatever form or location it appears, based on the ideal of social change through voluntary suffering and the need for crisis to bring direct communication between dominant and subordinate groups.

Wilson elaborates a fourfold classification of the types of protest;[22] these types are encountered many times and in many specific forms in the following pages:

*Verbal*—mass meetings, denunciatory statements, pamphleteering, etc.

*Physical*—picketing, sit-downs, marches, violence, etc.

*Economic*—boycott, strike, selective buying, etc.

*Political*—voting reprisals, including voter registration in many Deep South areas, etc.

### *The Elements of a Social Movement*

The sit-ins were a "movement" before any social scientist defined them as such. Leslie Dunbar, who did more than anyone to fix the label "sit-in" on the lunch counter demonstrations in the early days, makes the point well:[23]

> Almost from the beginning the sit-ins have been referred to as a 'movement.' That both participants and observers felt this way about them is noteworthy, because the name 'movement' does not catch on unless people sense that it does apply. No one ever speaks of the 'school desegregation movement.' One accomplishment, then, of the sit-in was to achieve, almost from the start, this recognition.

The aim here is to sift through the various meanings of "social movement" in the sociological literature and make a tentative assessment of the accuracy of attaching this label to the direct action protests. There are four criteria for a "movement":

(1) *Broadly Based Participation*. The geographical-numerical requirement is generally the starting point in consideration of social movements. The direct action protests meet this criterion. Within three months after the "trigger incident" on February 1, 1960, the sit-in demonstrations had spread to more than 100 cities in every southern state, and had stimulated sympathy action in every major city in the United States (and in many smaller college and university towns like Oberlin and Antioch, Ohio, and Columbia, Missouri).[24] The most conservative informed estimates[25] of total *active* participation in the protests from February 1, 1960, to February 1, 1962, exclusive of those who passively participated by cooperation with a boycott, range from 100,000 to 125,000 persons. And even more important, the demonstrations have been broadly based *within* communities, drawing all

social, occupational and educational levels of the Negro population into action at one time or another. Thus, the criterion of a broad structural base is met on the basis of the total social system, as well as on all levels *within* the subsystems of "the Negro community" within protest cities.

(2) *"We-Feeling."* Given the broad participation in direct action during this period, an equally important criterion is a sense of group identity and solidarity on the part of the actors—a strong "we-feeling." The sit-ins had this from the beginning. Even though the action was spread over a whole nation, civil rights organizations and the mass media provided a system of communication that nurtured this kind of group cohesion. Participants in the spring and summer of 1960 referred to "the sit-in movement" as a matter of course. For a period following the Freedom Rides in May and June there was some momentary semantical shuffling as to whether the Rides, too, were a "movement." But this was soon resolved, and now everyone connected with the direct action protests speaks simply of "the Movement"—a term which encompasses everything from the first sit-in to current voter registration efforts in the Deep South. By 1961 "the Movement" already had its sacred days and sacred events and places: participants share a common feeling of purpose when they refer to May 17 or February 1, and mere mention of Greensboro, Birmingham or Selma today carries with it a whole host of meanings which never are verbalized. Discussion about these cities is carried on with the assumption that everyone is familiar with the particular events, personalities, suffering and social change associated with direct action there. The strong in-group/out-group distinction is further reinforced with a growing repertoire of jokes and songs which were at first only directed at segregation and segregationists, but increasingly turn their focus on Negroes formerly in the in-group who are thought to be "sell-outs." This process receives extended treatment in chapter 8.

(3) *Common Ideology*. Goals, targets, tactics, developing organizational structure—all are sustained by a unifying ideology. The sit-ins early recruited members and carried throughout the South on the strength of a dedication to absolute noncompromise with segregation and to the technique of nonviolence. Some "movements" have to search for years for that unifying and comprehensive set of principles and goals which lends cohesion to otherwise uncoordinated efforts. But the sit-ins had this from the beginning in the ideal of nonviolence and in the person and event of Martin Luther King and the Montgomery bus boycott of 1956. Chapter 3 tries to show how the presence of this ready-made ideological support gave the students

the impetus which carried their sit-ins to movement proportions in a very short period of time.

(4) *Broadening Focus*. If a bit of broadly based and self-conscious protest against existing forms is to become a movement, its focus must constantly broaden until it includes revolution or at least major reform in some aspect of the social order.[26] The sit-ins focused on one particular facility which was commonly segregated in the southern United States—the dimestore lunch counter. In this sense it provided an easily visible and vulnerable rallying point. But given the ideological commitment to total integration and nonviolence—whose broader implications were understood by only a few in the early days—the protests soon filled themselves with the necessary structure of targets and tactics to work at these broader goals. Thus, as the original goals are either abandoned or achieved, and the opposition perfects its tactics, a movement's continuation and growth depends on the ability of the leadership to supplant these aims with more comprehensive goals.[27]

So, the quotation marks around the word "movement" now may be dropped—for purposes of clarity and convenience as well as theoretical relevance. The data (nonviolent direct action against segregation in the United States from February 1960 to February 1962) *do*, in fact, justify use of the concept of social movement within the limits of the criteria just offered. The term will be used interchangeably with "the protests," "the demonstrations," and "the effort" or "the revolt," as we already have done.

### *Social Movements Theory*

The theory of social movements being developed here differs in several important ways from the theories put forth in the past. My essential grievance with much previous work on "social movements" is that the definition offered and the actual "movements" studied are broad enough to include just about any kind of collectivity which persists for a period of time. Scholarly treatises in the name of "social movements theory" have been turned out on phenomena ranging from birth control and prohibition to repeal, the Urban League, the D.A.R., the Rotary Clubs, group health, the Ku Klux Klan and the Southern Tenant Farmers' Union! We are further told that Christian Science, technocracy, Moral Re-armament, CORE and the Shakers also qualify as social movements.[28] The structural and temporal boundaries of social movements theory need tightening—or any club, organization or religious faith may be included. This study attempts to overcome such problems by specifically defining the structure, scope and time periods involved.

Social movements theory is viewed here as a part of the larger study of social change. In assessing previous work in the field, several representative articles, chapters and books are examined. These, in turn, have drawn on other sources which cannot be dealt with at length here. None is viewed as totally sufficient to deal with the direct action movement; rather all are used in developing a more general theory of the protest-rationalization cycle in American race relations patterns. Since sociology is, ideally, a cumulative endeavor, these sources are viewed in chronological order in an attempt to trace the development of common themes.[29]

(1) C. A. Dawson and W. E. Gettys' 1935 outline of the four stages through which all social movements pass is representative of the kind of analysis American sociologists have undertaken in this field.[30] The emphasis is basically temporal, with no apparent attempt to trace structural development in terms of any unified theoretical perspective. But the basic formulation of the temporal succession of the movement seems sound in the light of general theory. Movements persistently drive toward organization and solidification, following early stages of (a) social unrest and (b) popular excitement. Stage (c) is thus labeled "the stage of formalization," and final phase (d) is called "the stage of institutionalization." Dawson and Gettys' work seems more than adequate to this point but, like much movement theory, the actual elaboration and diffusion of the movement's units within a whole range of social systems and subsystems during formalization and institutionalization are left unclear. This project's developing theory attempts to answer this need.

(2) Two articles by Paul Meadows in the 1940s add depth to an understanding of social change, but also leave a number of serious questions unanswered. Meadows' 1941 study offers a three-stage theory of "Sequence in Revolution."[31] "Revolution" is only quantitatively removed from "movement" in the Meadows system, the former distinguished by its quest for a totally new set of symbols in the social order[32]—that is, a new cultural order. The first stage is "incubation," a pre-crisis situation in which the action of the prospective revolutionaries is characterized by withdrawal responses. In the second or "action" phase, the revolutionaries create crises by the use of predominantly approach responses. The final or "adaptive" phase is seen as a post-crisis period in which accommodative responses guide the actions

of the former revolutionaries. Meadows' emphasis on *crisis* is perhaps the most lasting contribution of this formulation; the notion of crisis and how it is perceived and dealt with in a number of relevant social systems is central to the argument of this study. But Meadows' system is logically inconsistent at the point where he introduces "structuralization" in the "action" phase of the sequence—for in any such generalized ideal-typical analysis, the polar concepts of "action" and "structure" must be represented in separate stages or phases.

Meadows' 1946 contribution[33] is disorienting not because of any theoretical proposition advanced, but because of its cataloguing of the various kinds of social phenomena which have been called "social movements" (see page 14). The list includes service clubs, organizations, religious sects and churches, political ideologies, hate groups and other diverse forms of normative patterns, collectivities and social action.

(3) Rudolf Heberle outlines the major focus of his 1951 book *Social Movements* in a 1949 article entitled "Observations on the Sociology of Social Movements."[34] His perspective encompasses several specifications which are especially important in the study of direct action. First is his observation that social commotion becomes a movement only when it expands its program to encompass all relevant related issues. Although I cannot agree on the order in which he relates these factors, I find that the differentiation between a *movement* and its *program*—and the dynamic processes of exchange between them—is a most necessary part of a coherent theory of protest and rationalization. This issue is taken up again in chapters 7-9. A second major contribution of the Heberle approach is the emphasis on the "informal groups" which develop within the movement and help sustain it. He suggests that the movement can thus take the place of *Gemeinschaft*-like groups in a heterogeneous society where such communal ties are generally fleeting and unsatisfying. In the present study on direct action, informal structure is often seen as more important than formal and stated structural characteristics in determining direction and tactics, and in mediating meaning in social protest. Finally, Heberle's delineation of criteria for a social movement seen incomplete. He sees three requirements as minimal: a we-feeling, comprehensiveness of aims, and orientation toward a "new social order." His omission of the geographical-numerical order is crucial, for without this dimension, the theory admits many types of collectivities no larger than, say, a localized band of radicals whose "movement" actually never gets out of the "underground" stage.

(4) The most frequently quoted and comprehensive source of social movements theory today is Herbert Blumer's chapter in the College Outline Series' *Principles of Sociology*. Most relevant to our purposes are two sets of distinctions he makes: that between "general," "specific," and "expressive" movements, and that of "reform" and "revolutionary" movements. Both need clarification in the light of more recent research and theoretical reformulation.

Blumer's tripartite division of types of social movements would do much to help clear up the fuzzy boundaries of the field if it were strictly heeded. By *general social movements* he means broad and pervasive changes in values, which take the form of groping and uncoordinated efforts with neither established leadership nor recognized membership. "Cultural drift" is a good synonym, he suggests. Here are classified such expressions as the labor movement, the youth movement, the women's movement and the peace movement. *Specific social movements* develop out of general dissatisfaction and hope generated by social movements. They have a well-defined objective or goal, and are quick to form a body of traditions, a guiding set of values, a philosophy, sets of rules and a general body of expectations. Here Blumer stresses the increasing organization and solidification of purpose which characterizes the life history of a social movement. He sees five means through which a movement is able to grow and become organized: agitation, development of *esprit de corps*, development of morale, formulation of an ideology, and development of operating tactics. *Expressive movements*, finally, are defined negatively: their characteristic feature is that they *do not* seek to change the institutions of the social order. Rather, the tension and unrest out of which they emerge are released through some type of expressive behavior rather than in concerted social action. Religious movements and fashion movements are seen as the prototypes here.

Blumer adds a very brief qualification that specific movements may merge, but does not carry the point beyond this. This is the crucial issue for validation of this kind of a typology, I believe, for elements of all three "types" are found in varying degrees in *every* movement—and particularly in the direct action protests. Nonviolent direct action *does* have a specific rationale all its own—but this characteristic cannot be separated from its expressive component, which is especially prominent because of the socially subordinate nature of the protest population. This leads to Blumer's distinction between reform and revolutionary movements: both are classed as specific movements, but one seeks to change some specific phase or limited area of the existing social order, the other seeks to reconstruct the entire social order.

Again there are theoretical difficulties when reform movements are said to encompass middle class participants doing something *for* the depressed classes, while revolutionary movements recruit directly from the underprivileged classes. For a number of reasons which are treated in chapters 7 and 8, this kind of distinction becomes meaningless in a highly differentiated class structure. Looking only at the case in point, from the beginning the direct action movement has drawn participants in varying degrees from *all* racial and class levels.

Many aspects of Blumer's analysis will come in for extensive treatment as the theory emerges, so only three brief disagreements are raised here before moving on. First, there is serious question about the contention that "a social movement, of the specific sort, does not come into existence with . . . a structure and organization already established." One can say, rather, that it depends on the *content* of the particular movement itself. For highly rationalized modern society now has a ready-made structure of voluntary associations waiting for the birth of any new idea with movement proportions—and the movement's character is shaped from the beginning by this framework.

Second, Blumer's feeling that "in the beginning a social movement . . . has no clear objective" is of doubtful applicability if the "broadening of focus" criterion is valid. In the case of the direct action protest, for instance, the demonstrations early took on movement proportions specifically because there was a clear objective (desegregation of lunch counters) at the beginning. In fact, the objectives were clearer then than two years later.

And finally, in outlining the characteristics of reform as opposed to revolutionary movements, Blumer fails to make the crucial distinction between *normative order* and *the existing social structure*. A reform movement is seen as accepting the existing mores and using them to criticize the social defects it is attacking, while a revolutionary movement always challenges the existing mores and proposes a new scheme of cultural values. Without this culture-social system distinction, any theory is incapable of determining whether the prevailing social order is, in fact, an accurate and undistorted representation of the underlying value patterns.

(5) Perhaps the most comprehensive—albeit introductory—recent treatment of the field of social movements is C. Wendell King's *Social Movements in the United States*, published in 1956.[35] King's work draws

heavily on Blumer and on a wide range of studies of individual social movements. His most important advance over the other works above is his explicit attention to external as well as internal influences on the life history of the movement—and the reciprocal effects on the total society. But still he has not made the theoretical leap to a consideration of subsystems within the movement, a step which is deemed crucial in this project's study of direct action.

Some other lasting contributions of King's volume to the understanding of movements include: (a) an excellent analysis of the goal confusion and subsequent search for meaning engendered by mass society; (b) a discussion of the process of selection and integration of cultural innovations; and (c) a typology of movement functionaries (leaders, bureaucrats and agitators) which proves useful in analysis of the direct action protests. Yet King's writing shows no systematic application of general sociological theory; worthwhile leads raised in one section are not followed up in the same terms in the appropriate later phases. And he has an understanding of charisma which is quite foreign to the one employed in this study; it is not seen in the universalistic terms which Weber intended, but rather as some kind of situational component in various types of social action. One reads, for instance, "*If* the movement is founded by a charismatic leader . . ."[36] But for Weber, Parsons and the present study, a charismatic ideal (or its semantic equivalent) embodied in a leader or leaders is *the* indispensable element in initiating any social movement.

Finally, King's interpretation of the "incipient" phase of a movement is too limited. He contends that at this early stage, the movement exists only in the minds of a small nucleus who are organized only informally and in terms of primary relationships. Again this criterion does not hold for the direct action protests (and probably for a growing number of social movements), mainly because of the temporal telescoping effect of the mass media. The *idea* of a "sit-in movement" had existed in the minds of many and diverse persons with no relationship at all for years.[37] And when it first burst into the open, there was an *immediate* mass following—a phenomenon running contrary to King's theory of the long and tedious growth process in all such movements.

(6) It is instructive to examine the treatment of social movements in a currently popular introductory sociology text; Broom and Selznick's *Sociology: A Text with Adapted Readings* fulfills this requirement.[38] The topic is covered under "social change" and "political movements." In a summary

under social change, the we-feeling and common ideology criteria are met, in addition to what the authors call "an orientation toward action" (which would appear to be inherent in the very word, "movement"). The broad base and broadening focus requirements are not mentioned. Then the authors postulate three stages in the life of political movements: emergence from social unrest, solidification through organization, and transformation into institutions. This simple and concise treatment seems to fairly represent the perspective of American sociology on this phenomenon; its extremely general nature warrants no further elaboration or criticism here.

(7) Two extremely important recent works are Lewis M. Killian and Ralph Turner's *Collective Behavior*,[39] and Neil J. Smelser's *Theory of Collective Behavior*. Killian and Turner draw together in a socio-psychological framework most of the important contributions to the study of collective behavior until 1957, including a useful re-working of Blumer's approach. Smelser "activizes" Parsonian categories, explains the crucial distinction between "norm-oriented" and "value-oriented" movements, and provides the most comprehensive bibliography on collective behavior and social movements to date. Their relevance to the theory of rationalization is so great that discussion of their contributions is reserved for the theory building section in chapter 7.

### *b. TENTATIVE STATEMENT OF THE THEORY*

The purpose of this study is to develop a general sociological theory to explain and predict the processes of protest and rationalization in racial patterns, based on interpretations of the origins and growth of the direct action movement from 1960-62. The basically evolutionary and functional system which emerges has its main roots in the general theory of Max Weber and Talcott Parsons, but is also informed by the material covered in the last section. The new level theoretical synthesis is approached via five analytical conceptions at the very foundation of sociology: *rationalization*, *charisma*, the *three types of legitimate authority*, the *four functional imperatives* and *the social system*. The task, then, is to understand and predict the rationalization of solutions to the four functional imperatives within interrelated social systems.

### *The Stages of Rationalization*

A major thrust in this study is the attempt to apply the broad outlines of Weber's foremost theoretical concern—the process of rationalization—to the emergence of direct action protests and their institutionalization in American race relations. The process of rationalization is only vaguely defined in Weber's work, since it was implicit in all he wrote. If we were to choose one absolute in his system—that is, one untestable, *a priori* assumption of the order of "God" for theologians or emanationism for the Hegelians—it would be rationalization. This process for Weber is the significant and distinguishing feature of western culture.

A precise definition of rationalization is thus hard to come by from Weber's work alone, since his whole system is predicated on the assumption that the process does, in fact, operate. We come closest to a formal delineation of the process in the essay on "The Social Psychology of the World Religions."[40] Here Weber concedes that "rationalism" (which I understand as the ideal end-point toward which the process of rationalization is moving) may have many different meanings. "It means one thing," Weber begins, "if we think of the kind of rationalization the systematic thinker performs on the image of the world: an increasing theoretical mastery of reality by means of increasingly precise and abstract concepts. Rationalism means another thing if we think of the methodical attainment of a definitely given and practical end by means of an increasingly precise calculation of adequate means . . . 'rational' may also mean a 'systematic arrangement.'" Later in the same essay (p. 298), Weber distinguishes between *substantive* rationalization and *formal* rationalization, the former referring to a patrimonial administration in which rewards are dispensed "in the manner of the master of a large house upon the members of his household," and the latter describing an essentially rational-legal form of administration operating on universalistic principles.

These meanings, though diverse, "ultimately . . . belong inseparately together," says Weber.[41] For the common theme in all of them is *the tendency for social action to differentiate into systems for attaining the commonly agreed-upon goals of the actors by means of an increasingly precise calculation of available and adequate means*.[42] This, I believe, is the common basis of meaning in Weber's wide implicit application of the rationalistic assumption. Rationalization is "the process of change underlying the shift from traditional to modern society;[43] it is ". . . the substitution for the unthinking acceptance of ancient custom, of deliberate adaptation to situations in terms of self-interest;[44] it is the "disenchantment of the world."[45] *It is the drive toward logical consistency of systems of thought and action.*

The process of rationalization is open itself to measurement, elaboration and systematization in terms of general sociological theory. This is one of the tasks left to modern sociology in the Weberian legacy: the theoretical spelling out of the *extent* of rationalization and *directions* which rationalization can take. Gerth and Mills suggest that these aspects of rationalization can be measured "negatively in terms of the degree to which magical elements of thought are displaced, or positively by the extent to which ideas gain in systematic coherence and naturalistic consistency."[46] The emphasis in this study leans toward the "positive" mode of analysis—developing a theory about the transformation of spontaneous social protest into a structured system of action. In the words of G. H. Mead, "That is the problem, to incorporate the methods of change into the order of society itself."[47]

Inherent in the Weberian assumption of universal rationalization are the notions of *movement* and the *temporal dimension*. But what is the *structure* of this movement, of this temporal succession? Can we delineate ideal-typical stages through which the rationalization of action moves? Marking out the analytical boundaries of such stages is the first task of the present study. Two other important Weberian contributions—*the three types of legitimation of authority* and the notion of *charisma*—are employed as a starting point, for it appears that these elements of Weber's work combine into a logically consistent system which does not violate the spirit of his work.

Four analytically distinct stages are delineated in the process of rationalization:

Stage I—Traditional Control
Stage II—The Charismatic Breakthrough
Stage III—Routinization
Stage IV—Rational-Legal Organization

By combining Weber's concept of the process of rationalization with his major orientations toward the problems of social change (charisma) and social control (the types of authority), we hope to reach a synthesis in this temporal dimension which will yield greater analytical power than previous theories. In fact, the use of this approach provides a logically coherent temporal framework within which to vary the structural aspects of the theory—the four functional imperatives. The formal elaboration of this approach to the process of rationalization appears in Chapter Seven.

### *The Four Functional Imperatives*

But *what* is being rationalized? In this study, one answer is proposed: the *solutions* to the four functional imperatives.

After over two years of immersion in the direct action data, I found that Parsons' functional paradigm[48] is a particularly powerful analytical framework in dealing with this kind of sequential or cyclical phenomenon. It facilitates comparison of elements within and between *stages*, as well as within and between *social systems*.

Following Parsons, our frame of reference is *goal-oriented action* organized in a social system and subsystems. The "four functional imperatives" as used here shall refer to *those environmental and situational exigencies to which each social system must adapt to maintain its boundaries*. The four imperatives are ranged along two axes, one dealing with allocation and integration of the units and energy within the system (internal) and the other concerned with maintenance of the system's boundaries *vis-a-vis* other systems (external). The internal problems are pattern-maintenance (or latent integration) and integration, and the external problems are goal-attainment and adaptation. Any system, to maintain itself, must effectively solve the various subproblems arising from these imperatives.

### *The Social System*

A social system shall be defined as (a) a plurality of actors with (b) a shared set of values and (c) a system of rewards which enable these members to maintain certain distinct patterns of interrelationships.[49] The system is oriented toward boundary-maintenance and maintenance of the functional interdependence of its units. As rationalization proceeds, this basic task of self-preservation is implemented by an increasingly more complex organization of the solutions to the four functional imperatives.

A major shortcoming of previous work dealing with social protest and its effect on/and incorporation into society, has been the lack of systematic attempts to distinguish between various social systems involved. The nature and boundaries of the social systems studied here are clearly specified. The theory of rationalization is applied systematically to one system—the direct action protest movement itself. Brief comment is offered on three subsystems—the Congress of Racial Equality, the Southern Christian Leadership Conference and the Student Nonviolent Coordinating Committee.

Analysis of rationalization in the protest system itself is carried through the functional imperatives in each of the four stages. The process is organized in the following manner in a master chart at the end of the book.

| | Traditional Control | The Charismatic Breakthrough | Routinization | Rational-Legal Organization |
|---|---|---|---|---|
| L | | | | |
| I | | | | |
| G | | | | |
| A | | | | |

Within this outline, we shall be trying to specify in a particular theoretical context what Weber meant by rationalization. In the process, the analysis may offer one possible direction for a problem voiced by Parsons some fifteen years ago: that Weber failed ". . . to carry through a systematic functional analysis of a generalized social system of action."[50] Parsons' work has spoken directly to this need; the present study may be seen as an attempt to synthesize Weberian and Parsonian analyses both to understand the rationalization of protest systems and to improve prediction in intergroup relations.

The built-in paradoxes of the rationalization of protest remains. Direct action is inherently opposed to stable structure; its major norm consists of creating crises which demand resolution. Thus, a very specific level of prediction at this point is impossible, for the prime motivation of the nonviolent direct actor is to "beat" the predictors (be they southern policemen or sociologists) in an attempt to create the most dramatic crises possible. Direct action in the desegregation process—and protest in general—contains this constant check against perfect internal rationalization. For this reason, the theme of the sociological paradox is found at many points during this study.

TWO

# Design and Method

## Exploratory Action Research

'If . . . people accept you, you'll learn the answers in the long run without even having to ask the questions.'

I found that this was true. As I sat and listened, I learned the answers to questions that I would not even have had the sense to ask if I had been getting my information solely on an interviewing basis.

William Foote Whyte[1]

My research on direct action and desegregation during the past five years has involved many different methods, among them participant observation, interviewing and documentary analysis. In this chapter, use of these techniques in this project is reported, with an explanation of why I think they were appropriate in the light of the project's design, and an assessment of some of the problems of this approach.

### *a. THE BASIS: PARTICIPANT OBSERVATION*

"The experience of *my own behavior*," writes Peter Munch,[2] "is the ultimate source of my knowledge that human action has 'meaning.' And as my own experience is the only experience that I can ever perceive by direct sensation, it is ultimately the *only source* from which I can have empirical knowledge of even the existence (let alone the nature) of mental conditions and events in other persons."

The logical extension of this position into the realm of social scientific research is the technique of participant observation: "*a conscious and systematic sharing, in so far as circumstances permit, in the life-activities and, on occasion, in the interests and affects of a group of persons. Its purpose,*" continues Florence Kluckhohn, "*is to obtain data about behavior through direct contact and in terms of specific situations in which the distortion that results from the investigator's being an outside agent is reduced to a minimum.*"[3]

Modern social scientists generally have avoided making themselves the direct and participating instruments of observation this interpretation would suggest, choosing instead second and third-hand reports *about* human experience in the form of interviews or questionnaires or content analysis. Reasons for this are many: the attempt to build and maintain objective standards of research, the growing sophistication in quantification afforded by the standardized forms of empirical data-collection and analysis, protection from involvement with the subjects on any other basis than the research problem, ability to maneuver around subject defenses, and the discipline's structure of reinforcement for quantitative research.

*Appropriateness of Participant Observation for this Project*

In addition to use of the more standardized research methods (as described later in this chapter), I tried to serve as an instrument for directly observing certain forms of social behavior while participating in the behavior as fully as possible in much of this project. Research on the early stages of the direct action movement seemed to lend itself naturally to the technique of participant observation for several reasons:

(1) The phenomena under analysis are occurring in society *now*, in an ever passing present which waits for neither segregation nor science. In this case, the social scientist is not dealing with a controlled laboratory experiment with specific structural and temporal limits. The standard hypothesis-testing procedures cannot keep up with a young social movement on which there exists little prior research. At this stage, both the internal logic of social change and the sociologist's own sensitivity are violated if he forces himself to exclude relevant data for the sake of testing a carefully worked-out hypothesis whose validity is common knowledge to everyone connected with the movement. A movement does not hold still out of respect for available sociological methods.

(2) The direct action movement, like all such phenomena, is action-oriented and demands high commitment from its constituency. This, coupled with a developing numbness to the constant probing of the press, has meant

that the movement's internal structure could be studied most accurately and comprehensively only from the inside—by one who is accepted within the limits of role structure deemed "safe" by movement leaders. It was possible to obtain more than cordial press release type data by participating to some degree in the movement, as I hope to demonstrate at many stages throughout this study.

(3) One of the most important sources of data about social change is the interpretation of the innovators about their own actions. Particularly in the case of a self-conscious social movement, the innovators are eager to define themselves and their movement through conversations with persons they respect and trust. From the beginning of this project, the use of participant observation maximized the opportunities for the researcher to engage in this kind of dialogue with movement leaders. Such discussions proved invaluable as a source of ideas for further testing in the present research and in the development of the formal theory presented in Section C.

*Some Further Assumptions*

There are three assumptions about the nature of man, experience and truth which are at the base of this study and its methods. They are stated explicitly here to put the project's findings and theory in proper context:

(1) Each man has a set of meanings by which he explains and is able to function effectively in his particular universe. The sociologist generally brings a radically different orientation to the life-situation than the layman. Statements about social reality established through sociological research therefore tend to be of a higher order of generality (and thus of scientific utility) if they are the product of a *two-way* communication between researcher and subject. The social scientist may avoid making naive conclusions and save much time by checking his findings through dialogue with subjects as much as is feasible. One discussion with a critically marginal member of the subject-group may eliminate much exhaustive and unproductive testing, and free the researcher's time to explore higher level problems.[4]

(2) The most complete form of sociological datum is that gathered via the *direct experience* of the sociologist, namely, "an observation of some social event, the events which precede and follow it, and explanations of its meaning by participants and spectators, before, during and after the

occurrence."[5] Such a research assumption places the burden on the sensitivity of the sociologist as an instrument of observation. It also eliminates at least one step between the actual unit of behavior under study and a record of this behavior in the researcher's mind or notebook. For, as Munch points out,[6] between the interviewer and the social action he studied is *another* unit of social action—that of the respondent's perception, symbolic translation and reporting of the event. Thus, participant observation can greatly reduce the errors inherent in the process of recording social action for sociological analysis, by reducing the number of transactions necessary. The researcher now has to contend only with his own biases in the observation-to-meaning stage.

(3) The final assumption is that sociological truth is not to be found solely in the sheer numerical weight and statistical complexity of arrangement of objects, statuses or types. Statements like "The term *raw data* is used synonymously with *nonquatified data*," are common in leading texts on method.[7] It is important to stress that quantification is only part of the analytical process—the part which comes *after* the researcher has *decided* (on other than scientific grounds) that the action he is studying *can* be symbolically transformed into numbers, percentages and/or probabilities, and still in any way meaningfully represent the "raw" data of human interaction. David Riesman has observed that "in a survey of elites . . . not every individual counts one."[8] I have tried to value each informant as much for the *quality of his interpretations* as for the quantitative weight he adds to the sample size.

It is especially important that these assumptions be made explicit, since this project aims at understanding the *internal development* of a social movement, and building from this understanding a general theory capable of explanation and prediction. Norbert Elias writes:

> For while one need not know in order to understand the structure of molecules, what it feels like to be one of those atoms, in order to understand the functioning of human groups one needs to know, as it were, from inside how human beings *experience* their own and other groups, and one cannot know without active involvement.[9]

The most difficult methodological problem of this project, then, has been the balancing of the need to know from the inside with the need for objective detachment. A comprehensive understanding of the role of the *informal social structure* in the development of the movement could only come from close day-to-day contacts on the inside. Yet these data could only be translated into sound analysis through periods of conscious withdrawal from involvement. The tension between involvement and detachment in research is explored in detail below.

### *The Participant Observer's Insight Process*

Many of the facts and interpretations presented in this study are not backed by exhaustive numerical documentation. Some of them are sociological truths known to all within the direct action movement. Many of the interpretations represent a synthesis of the thinking of the people within the movement, arrived at via many hours in dialogue. Others are the result of drawing analogies and inferences from the behavior of different persons who were occasionally hostile to one another but not to me. These, then, are the three basic processes involved in the participant observer's process of insight: *socialization, dialogue,* and *inference-by-analogy.*

*Socialization*. The marginal sociologist, as one can accurately call the participant observer, always has his feet in two cultures—the sociological and that of the system(s) under study. He is, in effect, using the values, norms and attitudes he learned during his sociological socialization to assess his more recent socialization into the subject-culture. His is a "conscious and systematic sharing" of the total life of the system. Rather than repressing his subjective reactions to the socialization process, he turns them into tools in the insight process. If, for instance, he develops a polemical stance in the course of his work, he does not try to cast it aside as a threat to objectivity, but rather asks, "What effect has immersion in the life of this particular community had on my attitudes toward X variable?" Rather than dismissing the polemic out-of-hand, he uses the sociologist's causal framework to discover its etiology, and thus taps those elements in the system which could lead to the development of such a stance. Thus *the researcher's feelings are treated as part of the data*, rather than being set aside as "improper" or "irrelevant" in an attempt at objective detachment.

*Dialogue*. A second element in the insight process is the ongoing dialogue of the observer as he constantly measures his interpretations of what is going on with those of non-marginal participants. He takes an active part in the ideological life of the system while hypothesizing, juxtaposing and synthesizing as best he can. He can only do this on any significant level because he has a legitimate place within the role-structure of the group—because he is *accepted*. His understanding of the *meaning* of behavior to the actors reaches higher levels as he actively compares the meaning he derives from his *own* participation with that of the full-time members. Much of his activity is informal hypothesis-testing, which takes place every day during his life in the system. An idea may be formulated, tested and discarded within a few minutes in a group discussion with members of the system. In my own case, some hypotheses spun in the relative seclusion of Cambridge were forced to become sophisticated or die—for attempting to test such notions in a statistical fashion after the intensity of dialogue had proven them to be sterile academic artifacts, would be a waste of time.

*Inference-by-Analogy*. How do we perceive the *meaning* of a social action? Munch argues that the process is basically the same as that by which we perceive the meaning of a sentence.[10] In the case of the sentence, there is first a stimulus emitted by another person, which makes a sense impression on the receiver. Then comes the immediate assumption on the part of the receiver that this particular action is symbolic of ideas or volitions or attitudes, and the empathic feeling that, "If I were he, I would have these particular ideas, volitions and attitudes if I were emitting that kind of a stimulus." The final step is the conclusion that these qualities are actually present in the other person. This is almost entirely a process of inference—and we go through the same process of stimulus inference when we attribute meaning to the actions of others. Weber believed that "inference by analogy from the observer's own experience is the most important source of understanding" of the meaning of social action for other persons.[11] An observer sensitive to this process, then, can study the dynamics of group life directly by analogy from his own socialization, all the time extrapolating his behavior in an attempt to form laws, and checking his own impressions against those of other members of the system who can bring a fresh, extra-sociological framework to the problem.

Thus the participant observer is in a good position to understand cultural, social and personality structures because he is directly experiencing the impact of symbolic and institutional forces on his own personality as he is inducted into the system. By becoming a role-incumbent, the observer actually experiences the accompanying covert behavioral transactions, and often is able to determine the nature and degree of the gap between covert and overt behavior in others.

Taking into account all of these elements, the insight process of the participant observer can be schematically represented as follows:

THE PARTICIPANT OBSERVER'S INSIGHT PROCESS

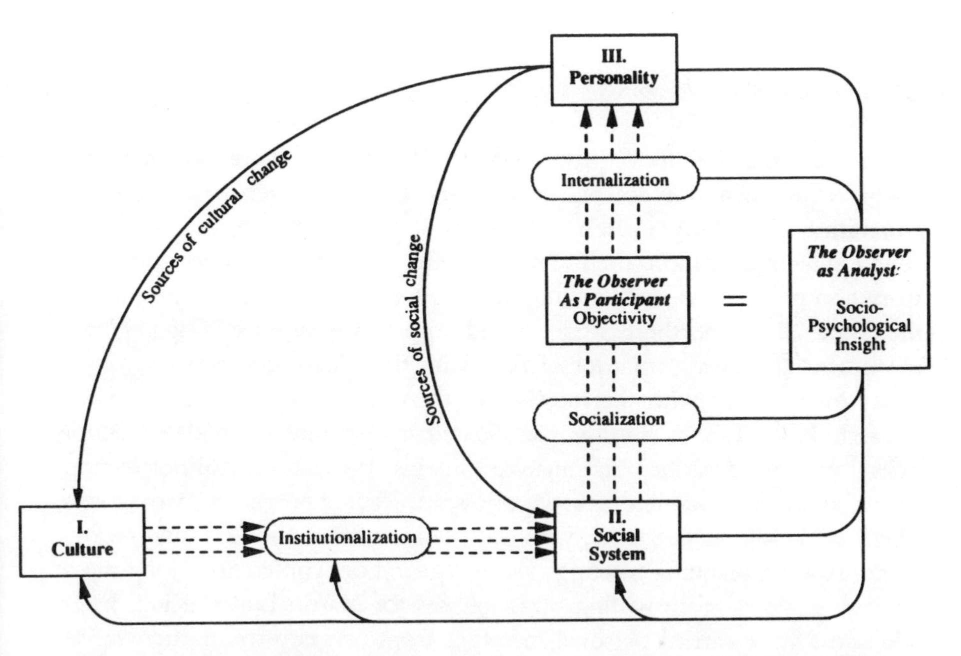


The general temporal direction of the diagram is counter-clockwise, beginning in the lower left or Culture cell. The observer plugs in between phases II and III, and brings his sociological framework to bear on the process of his socialization into the system under study. By "learning" (or "identifying with") the attitudinal structure of a new group, he is also "learning" the social structure and values. By maintaining a half-a-room away perspective on himself and resisting complete internalization, the observer gains insight on all three systems which, in turn, feeds back into the whole process for further refinement.

Dollard's canon that ". . . a scientist's first loyalty is to his data . . . He must seek them where they can be found and grasp them as they permit,"[12] is especially applicable to action research in race relations. But the insight paradigm here proposed can keep the data from running away with one, and give systematic yet necessarily flexible framework for analysis.

## *The Movement and Doctoral Dissertations*

Two recurring methodological problems of participant observation are the difficulties of role-legitimation for the researcher, and his role conflicts. The forms in which these problems were present in this project, and the ways I attempted to deal with them, are described below.

### *Legitimation of the Researcher's Role*

In the direct action movement, from the beginning, there has been one major requirement for acceptance into the role-structure: a demonstrated commitment to desegregation. "Demonstrated commitment" to the direct action elites means more than "I'm with you in spirit and I want to write a story about you." As early as June of 1960 sit-inners were complaining to me about all the northern students and reporters who were "bugging" the movement and taking up a lot of time with their naive questions.

My involvement with the movement, then, has always had more than a research basis. I have directly participated in virtually every direct action behavioral unit described and analyzed in this dissertation: pamphleteering, sit-ins, kneel-ins, wade-ins, picketing, boycott, leading nonviolent workshops, arrest and jail, negotiation with city and store officials, fund-raising, demonstration-planning meetings, voter registration, conferences, long-range strategy sessions—even writing press releases for Martin Luther King, Jr. In addition I have carried personal messages from one city to another, served as chauffeur for students in need of a quick ride, composed and sent telegrams for the organizations, been granted access to confidential files. In short, here is a case of the sociologist being socialized into the movement—learning its values and prohibitions, its rigid norms and behavioral nuances as a consciously marginal researcher. My only "failing" in the eyes of the direct action innovators is that I did not go on a Freedom Ride; I was invited by CORE to be a member of the original team, but Ph.D special examinations took precedence.

In short, a simple *demonstrated* commitment to desegregation was all that was needed to legitimize my role with the direct actionists. But this was not part of a "research technique" or "design"; it was and is a part of life itself. The subsequent benefits in research access are invaluable, but they are secondary to the more general orientation. It is simply a matter of relating to the "subjects" openly and freely as total human beings in every phase of life, rather than consciously restricting and manipulating the relationship to encompass only those attributes relevant to the study at hand. From this openness comes acceptance and a sense of the powerful in-group structure which binds the direct action protests into a cohesive movement. In at least five southern cities I visited as a nomadic researcher between 1960 and 1962, I was boarded at a moment's notice by the Negro community, sometimes very late at night, on the basis of one criterion: I was in the movement.

I found after a while that my status as sociologist became less and less relevant in the informants' judgment of me. All of them knew from the beginning that I was a researcher from Harvard, but this did not matter in their placing of me in a legitimate role context. What mattered was my status as Jim Laue, friend and participant. Everyone knew that I would be recording ego-threatening information from, for instance, my observation of heated planning meetings and witnessing of minor power struggles. But this knowledge made no difference. At the Atlanta SNCC conference in October, 1960, a special closed session of the 13 elected SNCC representatives was planned with Dr. King. I was the only "observer" allowed in the meeting—white, at that. Another sit-in sociologist asked me that day: "How do you con yourself into these secret meetings?" It was not possible to answer him in his terminology, for the notion of "conning" does not reside in the participant observation framework.

There are other examples of how access was gained to innumerable "secrets" of the informal movement structure—how I became one of only a few persons outside the Greensboro Negro community to learn the well-guarded details of how the first sit-in originated there in 1960, or how I uncovered the dynamics of the "great conspiracy" (as one leader called it) which turned SNCC from direct action *per se* to voter registration in 1961. This raises the question of how such legitimation is diffused. The old adage, "It's not *what* you know, but *who* you know," (sociological translation: particularistic ties are more important than universalistic ones) is indeed applicable. On two different occasions the chairman of SNCC paused in important strategy sessions to introduce me to the staff members I did not already know. With tongue-in-cheek he said, "This is . . . ah . . . Doctor Laue from Harvard, who is writing the definitive study on the movement," and instructed the brothers to get to know me and give me all the help they could. And many times, strong friendships and research relationships began by my saying something like, "Will Campbell in Nashville said you'd be a good man to talk with about . . ." William Foote Whyte's account of his experience in "Cornerville" is sound: "I found that my acceptance . . . depended on the personal relationships I developed far more than upon any explanations I might give."[13] As his chief informant, Doc, told Whyte many times: "Just tell 'em you're my friend, that's all that counts."[14]

*Role conflict.* In such a situation, role conflict in inevitable. The kind of conflicts which developed within me were not of the participant observer's standard "how can I satisfy my own personality needs and still be a marginal observer?" type. Instead they arose within the social system as a result of my close friendships with members in a number of informally competing groups. My marginality had, in fact, made me a source of communication and reconciliation between the competing groups and individuals. But questions like "What do the rest of the people in the movement think of me?" were very hard to handle. If a strong antagonism did, in fact, exist, I offered a straightforward explanation of some of the sociological and psychological factors leading to personal and organizational competition in social movements.

In addition to the Harvard status and personal commitment to the movement (especially the arrest and probation), my acceptance was based on a willingness to discuss and constructively criticize any facet of the movement with any of the "inside" individuals and organizations. In a sense, it could be dangerous *not* to be open with me since I was on a first-name basis with leaders of almost all factions in the movement, and therefore in a position to hear negative information about competing persons and organizations.[15] Each wants his own contributions well understood.

My attendance at two parties best illustrates the kinds of role conflict engendered for the marginal sociologist in such life-and-research situations. One was a going-away party on the last night I was in Atlanta in April of 1962, given by members of the Southern Christian Leadership Conference staff. The inevitable freedom songs and stories began early in the evening, and soon we were singing one verse which began, "Martin King's our leader . . . " The smiles were barely suppressed on the faces of the five or six persons there who were in close enough touch with the student group to know their hostility toward King, his power and his organization. I had sung the same verse at an SCLC conference of Mississippi delta Negroes for whom Martin King was, indeed, the symbolic leader. But in this more sophisticated context the role conflicts of some of the "marginals" present—including myself—were intense.

At another party, virtually all of the SNCC staff members were together shortly after the release of two field secretaries from a Louisiana jail on $7,000 bond for "criminal anarchy." It was clearly a cathartic session permeated by the unspoken spirit that here were gathered the most militant and dedicated of all the direct action protestors—the students. The singing, the anti-segregation jokes and the tales of suffering for the cause reached an almost unbearably painful level when someone suggested we do some role-playing. The leaders of the various adult protest organizations—including King and SCLC—were thoroughly discredited as "moderates" by the students' portrayals. The U.S. Attorney General was given the works ("Well, you boys and girls know I'm with you in spirit"), and so were leading targets like the governors of Alabama and Mississippi and the Louisiana jailer. Early in the game I was invited to take the role of a top official in one of the direct action organizations—a man despised by many of the students. What shall I do? My performance would have to be sufficiently rough on the man to fulfill the gleefully rising expectations of the group. After a moment, I suggested to the executive secretary of SNCC, "No, *you* take him and *I'll* play Malcolm X." This move put me in a much safer position—but even then not totally comfortable, for Minister Malcolm, too, was a good friend. Even more, the new militantly nationalistic strain in the student protest group meant that any portrayal of a Muslim leader would have to be carefully balanced between acceptance of Muslim militancy and rejection of black supremacy. This I did successfully enough, it seems, to resolve a potential crisis in my marginally supportive position *vis-a-vis* the total movement.

### *b. RESEARCH CHRONOLOGY*

Sociological theory does not develop as a strictly logical or rational process; it is born and matures as an attempt to organize the confusing welter of man's experiences in social life. Since this project's attempt at theory-building is directly dependent on matters of time and sequential experience, it is necessary to sketch a brief chronology of the research upon which the final report is based.

*February 1960 to April 1962.* My interest in the sit-ins began to crystallize in February of 1960, shortly after they had begun, as a result of participation in Gordon W. Allport's Social Relations seminar on intergroup conflict and prejudice. Between 1960 and 1962 (the period covered in this study), the movement claimed the large portion of my research time and energy, including two extended research trips of two months each, over a dozen shorter trips to conferences and meetings, a series of papers, articles, speeches, discussions and debates, participation in Boston and national CORE activities, and constant communication with informants throughout the nation.

From February 1 until early June 1960, I followed the emerging sit-in movement in the South through the media, personal contacts, and communiques from groups like CORE and the Southern Regional Council. I concentrated on the supporting effort in Boston via participant observation.[16] My first extensive research trip[17] lasted from June 18 to August 28. In the course of the summer I became acquainted with officials of CORE, SCLC, the NAACP, the Southern Regional Council, SNCC, and various academicians, race relations consultants for church organizations, and members of local protest groups. I attended the Race Relations Institute at Fisk University in Nashville, the CORE national convention in St. Louis, a CORE nonviolent training workshop in Miami, and several SCLC workshops in Atlanta. In addition, my travels took me to Knoxville and Chattanooga, Tennessee; Greenville, South Carolina; and Greensboro, North Carolina, for extended stays, as well as shorter stops in other cities. The friendly acceptance I received at my first stop in Nashville was to set the tone for the rest of the research; I met many persons there who were to become close friends and key informants. I also experienced my first of two bomb scares in Nashville and learned—for purposes of rapport and safety—when to say "colored" and when to say "Negro."

I was socialized very rapidly, learning the Negro college students' techniques for dealing with tense situations. While at first they could endure the bumbling *faux pas* of the outsider, this tolerance did not last long as my socialization progressed. I was taunted by students in Nashville, for instance, for being naive about police techniques and for being afraid to talk back when our mixed group was confronted by a policeman. "You should have told him you were Negro," one told me. "That works every time!" I soon learned to let nothing faze me, to act in the most difficult situation as though I had been through all of this before.

Participation in and concurrent analysis (including much after-hours note-taking) of nearly every behavioral phase of the movement took a good deal of my time. So did the conducting of interviews with student leaders and combing of files at the Southern Regional Council and other agencies. After some anxious integrated trips through Georgia and the Carolinas, more picketing, another bomb scare, and attendance at the funeral of the Imperial Wizard of the Ku Klux Klan, I ended up in Miami for the CORE action institute, where 18 of us were arrested for sitting-in at a super store in suburban Miami. This meant an overnight jail stay, a hearing, trial, judgment of guilty, and probation for a year. I was to find later that the Miami incident provided an important status as the movement increasingly emphasized "putting your body on the line" for would-be insiders. By this time, too, I had picked up the bulk of the dozens of movement songs I have since shared with participants in many cities.

During the 1960-61 academic year and until February of 1962 the research continued through participation in Boston area civil rights activities, a number of speeches and seminars, attendance at several conferences in the South, following media and organizational reports, and correspondence with friends in the movement. After spending the fall preparing prospectuses, the final field data were gathered in a research trip from February 19 to April 9, 1962. The major part of the time was spent in Atlanta—the nexus of the civil rights communications network in the South. The tracking down of informants also led me to Albany and McIntosh, Georgia, Nashville, Montgomery, Jackson, Washington, D.C., New York and New Haven. It is significant that this second long research trip took me more into Deep South areas than did the journey of 1960—for the direct action movement itself had moved progressively from the Border South into the Deep South.

The Deep South's impact on my personality gave me a better understanding of the motivations of the protestors, I believe. Taking a drink of Colored water at the Jackson airport in 1962 became an act of self-assertion calculated to maintain my personal autonomy against the segregated system. Talking to a knife-wielding, brick-throwing gang of white teenagers after a sit-in in Nashville profoundly affected some long-held theological considerations about the nature of man. And visceral reactions return each time I think of the Delta Negroes—militant by Mississippi standards—who were actually afraid to talk to me because of my skin color. Words passed between us, but the oppression phobia prevented any real communication.

*April 1962 to Present: Compilation and Analysis*. A good part of April 1962 was spent reading interviews, coding, filing, and drawing up (and rejecting) chapter outlines. This process of constant data processing, revision and synthesis has continued to a lesser degree throughout the entire writing, of course. But the crucial point came at the beginning of May 1962 when the theoretical structure fell into place. Two years of following the data where they may lead had prepared me for the moment of truth; I spent a day filling in cells and tables in the outline as fast as I could write when the working synthesis of Weberian and Parsonian theory was ready for the test. I found that long-held implicit hypotheses had, indeed, directed my research in service of the development of a theory of rationalization. The implications of my work had been as unspoken for me as were the specifics of the process of rationalization for Weber. Interpretations of the data further developed in 1963-64 through two years of college teaching at Roanoke, Virginia, and Atlanta, attendance at various conferences and the March on Washington, two research trips to Albany, Georgia, and continuous work in local civil rights situations in an advisory capacity.[18]

The outline of this study, then, has evolved from the confrontation of several years of direct experience in the movement with a developing knowledge of the theoretical legacy of academic sociology. Here, as in all research, the principle of indeterminacy has applied—I could not be in more than one place at once. Whenever I concentrated on a particular informant, geographical area or type of datum, all others were excluded for that moment. The structure of this dissertation is conditioned by at least two unavoidable limitations imposed by the necessarily chronological nature of research:

(1) The *order of experience* is virtually impossible to control in such research. I have watched the movement develop from the successive vantage points of Boston, the middle South, Wisconsin, the Deep South, the middle South again, etc. Thus my conception of the *development* of the protests subtly conforms to the conditions surrounding my own induction into the movement. As in any research, my perspective is limited by the fact that I started from one academic stance, one geographical locale, one visceral commitment. The struggle for a universalistic outlook never ends.

(2) Most important, the *order of informants* structures one's outlook on the research phenomenon in almost imperceptible ways. In the early stages of the last long research trip, for instance, I was suggestible due to my long absence from direct day-to-day contact with the movement and the subsequent need for structure. Therefore, the first informants in Nashville in February filled this semi-void with orientations which influenced the remainder of the research. My long dialogues with the Rev. Will Campbell of the National Council of Churches are the best example. I had long

respected Campbell as one of the most knowledgeable and committed of all direct action insiders. As my first informant on the final field trip, his suggestions and interpretations gave me much-needed handles on the data—handles at which I could only grasp in the previous months of research-in-absentia. Our discussion of original sin, for instance, reinforced the study's concentration on bureaucratic aspects of the movement. The personal and organizational in-fighting, the need for impersonal bureaucratic structures to (a) further one's own ends, and (b) help check the selfish motives of others—all of these things I had known in the movement were logically consistent with the neo-orthodox notion that man is, indeed, self-centered and self-seeking. Had not Nashville been the first stop (which it was solely for geographical reasons), this outlook which has so profoundly shaped the dissertation may have gotten lost in the late-March rush to finish the field work in time.

### c. *THE INTERVIEWS: A NOTE ON INTERVIEWING ELITES*

In addition to hundreds of hours of direct participation, dialogue and informal interviews over the past several years, I have structured the data in 45 dialogue-interviews with movement leaders, participants and observers. They were conducted in February, March and April of 1962, ranging from one-and-one-half to five hours in length. For comparative purposes, there are 11 interviews with student leaders in the early days of 1960. Only a small portion of these earlier interview data are included in this limited study.

Since the interview data came from a highly selective sample of informants, it was impossible to do a pre-test in the standard manner. The 1960 interviews and the two years of experience in the movement prior to February 1962 served as a rough equivalent. From these experiences I learned some of the difficulties of asking questions which allow for the necessary tension between structure and freedom—structured (i.e., informed) enough to prevent my classification as a naive northern white liberal social scientist, yet open enough to encourage a broad freedom of interpretation.

Even more important, I found that I could only write meaningful questions because I was enough of an insider to be able to partially answer them. During the course of my involvement in the movement, variables were constantly being constructed from experience, tested, recast, and re-tested until a comfortable formulation was reached.

### *The Sample*

Informants were all "elites"—they came to their position in this study as a result of their expertise in the growing direct action protests against segregation in the United States. The sample is thus *purposive* or *focused* (and, therefore non-probability): informants were selected on the basis of the researcher's prior knowledge of their position in the movement.

A basic assumption underlying this kind of sample is voiced by Selltiz, *et al*: ". . . that with good judgment and an appropriate strategy one can hand-pick the cases . . . and thus develop samples that are satisfactory in relation to one's needs."[19] But the assumptions need not be even this complicated, for the informants simply *are*, by every relevant measure, the major leaders, spokesmen and observers of the direct action movement for the time period under study.[20]

Beyond the nucleus of civil rights leaders and acknowledged experts on the movement, the sample was constructed in snowball fashion. After each interview, I asked, "Who else do you think I should talk with about these questions?" More often than not, the potential informants were already on my list from previous experience in the tight in-group structure of civil rights workers in the South. And on several occasions, informants suggested other sources of information before the interview dialogue was over.

The 45 interviews came from representatives of three groups, differentiated in terms of the relationship of their occupational role to the movement. The three groups:[21]

Student Leaders — 13
Adult Leaders — 8
Indirect Leaders and Observers — 24

*Student Leaders*. Thirteen of the 15 persons who were staff members of the Student Nonviolent Coordinating Committee at the time of the interviews are included in this group. One other was in jail, and the final member was inaccessible due to geographical reasons. The term Student designates a position in the role structure of the movement but does not necessarily conform to the standard educational definition of the word. (One informant, for instance, was 27 at the time of the interview, another 33. Both remain in the movement as students as this report is completed.) Technically, most of the students are civil rights professionals, having dropped out of school to devote full time to the movement. Some important characteristics of the student group are:

*Age* — 11 of the 13 were between 20 and 29 years old.
*Sex* — 12 males and one female.
*Race* — 11 Negroes and two whites.
*Educational Level* — one had not finished high school, two had completed their sophomore year in college, four had college degrees, five had done graduate study, including two M.A.s and one B.D. Most had been in the upper half of their college class, but only two in the top 10 percent.
*College Major* — six social science, three each natural science and humanities, three other.

Only one of the 13 had not been in jail; most of them had been in jail at least several times, and one held the movement record of 26 (27 before the interviews were completed). By mid-1964 some SNCC workers had passed the 60 mark.

*Adult Leaders*. Included in this category are eight representatives of the civil rights groups commonly known within the movement at that time as "the adult organizations"—the Congress of Racial Equality, Dr. Martin Luther King, Jr.'s Southern Christian Leadership Conference, and the National Association for the Advancement of Colored People. While the NAACP is not a direct action organization *per se*, it has taken active roles in several capacities in the nonviolent protests, as outlined in chapter 8.

*Indirect Leaders and Observers*. The third and largest group is composed of:

intergroup relations agency personnel — 9
social scientists — 7
consultants for religious denominations — 3
free-lance activists — 3
newsmen — 2

Many of them have had major parts in the spread and continued effectiveness of the movement, but their occupational roles specifically designate them as "outsiders." The very nature of their formal "outside" status gives them considerable influence with the media and public officials, even though it is generally known that they are deeply committed to the movement. The best example is the role of the Southern Regional Council, whose research reports and press releases at every stage of the protests (and particularly in the first few months after February 1960) lent substance to the efforts and helped crystallize the image of the demonstrations as a full-fledged social movement.

For purposes of analysis, the Adults and Outside Observers have been grouped into one category, which is referred to as simply Adults. They were administered the same interview schedule (see below), and generally were lumped together by younger protestors as "adults" (i.e., non-students). It seems clear from the interpretation in Section C of this study that *rejection of adult authority* was the crucial distinguishing feature of student protestors.

These two main groups—Students and Adults—offer, in effect, a partial control situation. By comparing their responses, an attempt is made to:

(a) discover and interpret bias arising from participants' ego-needs;

(b) infer the functions and meaning of the movement at two levels of participation, and thus

(c) gain a more comprehensive picture of the total phenomenon through integration of these dimensions.

### *The Instruments*

The interview-dialogues were structured around two schedules, *Form 1* for the Student leaders and *Form 2* for Adult participants and observers. Both forms ask for three kinds of data: *personal information, facts* and *interpretation*. On many items the informant's selection and presentation of facts provide valuable clues to his own interpretive framework.

*Form 1* consists of 46 open-ended items, two pre-coded items each containing several parts, and 33 census items, many with pre-coded responses. The items are arranged in the following general categories:

I. General Impression — 9 items.
II. On Nonviolence — 8 items.
III. Leadership — 5 items.
IV. On the Student Nonviolent Coordinating Committee — 5 items.
V. On Non-Student Participation — 11 items.
VI. The Forms of Protest — 4 items.
VII. Your Own Participation — 4 items.
VIII. Personal Information - 33 items.
IX. Future of the Movement — 2 items.

*Form 2* consists of 35 open-ended items and one pre-coded item containing several parts, arranged in the following categories:

I. General Impressions — 9 items.
II. On Nonviolence — 5 items.
III. Leadership — 6 items.
IV. On the Student Nonviolent Coordinating Committee — 4 items.
V. On Non-Student Participation — 8 items.
VI. The Forms of Protest — 4 items.
VII. Future of the Movement — 2 items.

The complete interview schedules may be found in the Appendix. Results from specific questions are reported throughout the dissertation as one basis for interpretation and construction of theory. Comments on the general format follow:

I. General Impressions

Both forms begin by asking informants to discuss the nature of their recruitment to and involvement in the movement.[22] Then they are given the first of several opportunities—this one completely unstructured—to discuss what seem to them to be the major changes in the movement during its first two years since Greensboro. Section I asks this in a number of ways on both forms: "In what ways does the movement seem different to you now than it was in the beginning in 1960?" "What has been the biggest change in the movement since it began?" "Have there been any big 'turning points' . . .?"

II. On Nonviolence

Section II elicits information about the informants' understanding of nonviolence (including the reading and workshop background of student participants) and their perception of its place as a motivating ideology in the movement. The "technique vs. way-of-life" dichotomy, already firmly crystallized at this point, is also explored here.

III. Leadership

Since the whole direct action protest is in the deepest sense a rebellion against the institutionalized leadership of the Negro community in America, Section III asks informants to discuss leadership in the movement. Here the perception of the movement's most important leaders is recorded, the Student-Adult conflict is explored and leadership changes since Greensboro are charted.

## IV. On SNCC

In many ways, SNCC is the institutionalized symbol of the youthful revolt which grew into the sit-in movement. Section IV of both forms asks informants to discuss whether SNCC "speaks for the student movement," whether (and how) its members and functions have changed since 1960, and what kind of changes its role may undergo in the future. The differing images of SNCC elicited from the wide range of informants are one of the best indicators of the levels and degree of interorganizational conflict and consensus throughout this study.

## V. On Non-Student Participation

The nature of the movement's self-conscious identity is explored in both forms in Section V. Much of the data for the inter-systemic comparisons drawn in this study come from this section in which informants are asked to consider the student movement's relationship to civil rights organizations, "adults" in general, "the white community," "the Negro community" and such specific groups as Negro college administrators, the federal government, local white businessmen and the national offices of the chain stores.

## VI. The Forms of Protest

In a more structured attempt to chart the changing form of the movement, Section VI asks whether the "forms or kinds" of protests differed in February 1962 from the earlier period of the movement. An especially useful item—formulated, as were most of the others, on the basis of what prior research experiences had indicated were relevant variables—asked whether there were "spontaneous" demonstrations in various cities today like those which took place in the first few months of the sit-ins? Or is everything organized?"

## *Form 1*, VII and VIII
## Student Participation and Personal Information

After the major substantive and interpretative parts of *Form 1*, Student informants were asked to focus on their personal involvement. Items in Section VII asked them to discuss how the movement has affected their "outlook on life," which event in the movement was most important for them and how long they expected to stay actively involved in the movement. Standard census-type data were gathered in Section VIII, in addition to specialized information on travel and educational experiences, their reactions to the 1954 Supreme Court school desegregation decision, the forms of their participation and their arrest and jailings record. The last item, as indicated in Section C, has an important bearing on the stratification system of the movement.

### *Form 1*, IX, and *Form 2*, VII
### Future of the Movement

Completing the movement from the *general* and *abstract* to the *specific* and *personal*, the schedule calls for predictions from both Students and Adults concerning the course of the desegregation process and the movement itself in the next five and 25 years. The rationale here is two-fold: first, to bring together the predictions of many of the most knowledgeable persons in the desegregation area as an aid to sociological prediction and, second, to gain some measure of an optimism-pessimism dimension for this same group of elites.

The unstructured format contained a number of methodological pitfalls and unique advantages. Among the problems were:

(a) great expenditures of time in the actual interviewing process, often necessitating several call-backs to complete the schedule when informants got "hung up" on some questions;

(b) forcing of data to develop categories in coding after the field work;[23]

(c) difficulty in formulating comparative generalizations about specific variables;

(d) inability to control the interview situation as much as would be desirable—especially the researcher's own participation in discussing important issues relating to the questions; and

(e) tendency to over-identify with the informants because of the personal-conversational nature of the interview.

Among the advantages which made this kind of interviewing especially useful in the present project are:

(a) the loose funnel approach beginning with "General Impressions" and a conversation "On Nonviolence," was helpful in drawing informants' thoughts to the issues at hand without pre-structuring their orientation—a must in this kind of exploratory action research at the early stages of a complex social movement;

(b) flexibility of administration and a conversational setting which allows for extended and intensive consideration of issues defined as important by the informants;

(c) a structural safeguard against violating the complexity and unity of the data;

(d) the chance to get the "feel" of the data in their complete form and context contributes to developing adequate codes in a way that is impossible if the answers are pre-coded; and

(e) the data are retained in their complete context (i.e., the original interviews, in this case ranging up to 45 hand-written pages per interview) to be drawn on for qualitative support during the analysis.

The brief part of the schedule calling for pre-coded responses in section V asked the informants to rate a number of groups (including those mentioned on page 61) on a seven-point scale ranging from "strongly in favor of" to "strongly opposed to the goals and methods of the protest movement." Informants were allowed to split answers for goals and methods, but a surprisingly small number—one of the 13 students and six of the 32 adults—chose to do so.[24]

The interview schedules are thus seen as supporting the major thrust of this project—the development and clarification of a particular facet of social change theory. The interviews provide *data* to be synthesized into *variables*, which in turn are related in a body of *theory*.

### *The Approach*

It cannot be emphasized strongly enough that the interview data contained in this report represent only a small part of the total relationship of the author and the informants. In every case, the "interviews" more closely resembled dialogues or the intense discussion of friends with similar concerns. Because of this context, in many cases I knew in general what information and interpretations would be forthcoming from informants before the questions were posed, but it was necessary to ask them for purposes of systematization.

There was a mixture of formal procedure and informal friendship in most of the interview settings. Five of the 13 sessions with the SNCC members were held in various informal home settings, and 15 of the 32 Adult interviews were held in the homes of the informant-friends, usually accompanied by a meal and other activities ranging from a country-and-western singing session with Rev. Will Campbell in Nashville to a backyard baseball game with Rev. Wyatt Walker of SCLC in Atlanta.

Each interview began with the following statement:

> This is a guide sheet for questions to be asked of leaders and observers of the direct action protest movement against segregation. Many of the questions do not call for specific answers, but rather are to be used as guides to more general discussion topics. The purpose is to determine the important characteristics of the movement's organization and leadership. This material will be used for a doctoral dissertation at Harvard University. I will appreciate permission to quote interpretative statements in the dissertation.

Questions were asked in order as they appear on the interview schedules. Often I found our orientations were so similar that informants anticipated the next area of discussion. That all of the informants were "elites" or "experts" called for an interview approach radically different from standard techniques. *The approach that developed was a natural outgrowth of the quality of the relationship already existing between the researcher and his informants.* Its major characteristics:

(a) recognition of common ideological and personal commitments;

(b) mutual trust, a first-name basis;

(c) a mutual sense of responsibility—theirs to follow their commitments to action, mine to convey their activity accurately and fairly to the world;

(d) a constant interplay of "inside" information with interpretation, hopefully pushing us towards ever higher levels of synthesis of understanding of the movement; my use of information and interpretative orientations at strategic times was a major part of the interview situation—my way of telling them I could not be satisfied with "press release responses," but rather demanded their deepest honest insights on a situation we both knew well.[25]

But here as in other kinds of research, a delicate balance must be maintained; many informants perceived me as knowing too much—so much, some of them felt, that the interview itself was a needless ritual. Some sample quotes from the interview schedules:

> "I haven't talked with as many student leaders as you have, but . . ." (Dunbar).

"I'm not telling you anything you don't know . . ."[26]

"We had a faction. You know about that? OK. We'll go on . . ."[27]

If there was an incident most accurately symbolic of the problems of an elite interviewing an elite, it was the exchange which took place in my session with James Forman, Executive Secretary of SNCC:[28]

*Forman* [after a lengthy explanation of the developing structure of his organization]: "Come on! You know all this."

*Laue*: "Yes, but I have to get *you* to say it."

In many cases I *did* know the answers to the questions of sociological fact and interpretation I was asking. Participant observation—simply *living* in the system with a sociological eye towards its functioning—gave me these answers. And the fact that the more formal interviews often added little to my knowledge of these persons and the relevant situations is a testimony for the efficacy of participant observation as a valid and reliable source of data and interpretation *in itself*. It is hoped that these two approaches complement one another in this study.

## *Coding and Analysis*

No attempt was made at coding the 1,031 handwritten pages of open-ended interview data until all of the interviews had been read three times. In these first readings, important quotes and interpretations were recorded and synthesized under the general outline of the report which was developing. Notes about possible coding categories were made. This was completed within one month after the field work ended.

Based on an immediate sense of the data which was gained from the three readings, the basic outline and argument of the dissertation had taken form. Within this context, the final coding categories were constructed (see the Appendix for complete codes and tabulations). The categories were based on several criteria—some of them intuitive, some logical:

(a) the sense of relevance of materials which comes only after living with a project (and collecting various kinds of data on it) for several years;

(b) a "natural" criterion—the triple reading of the interviews, which pointed up many possible codifications which could be developed directly from the data; and

(c) the theory of rationalization being developed by this project.

Some of the categories are purely descriptive, some analytical; both are considered necessary for this kind of theory-building. For question I.2 on both forms, for instance ("What do you think were the most important factors in the start and rapid spread of the sit-in movement at this time?"), the following categories were developed:

a. "tenor of the times," "inevitable" (including Montgomery, etc.)
b. college competition
c. mass media communication
d. television
e. tokenism
f. 1954 decision
g. changing leadership
h. Greensboro dynamics
i. personal frustrations
j. role of students
k. relative deprivation

Most of these response categories are clearly descriptive, but *relative deprivation* (k), for example, is an analytical or explanatory variable, based on the coder's judgment that an understanding of relative deprivation appears in some form in the informant's response. Responses (a), (g), (i) and (j) also have an analytical component. In short, every effort has been made to translate the informants' language to that of the analytical sociologist, for it was assumed (and validated many times in the course of the field work) that most of the informants are, of necessity, constantly making analytical judgments about the movement and their part in it in the course of their normal activity. It is the special task of the sociologist of in-process movements to build these semantic bridges between the activists and the analysts.

After code construction was completed (including nine pages of codes for *Form 1* and seven pages for *Form 2*), the interviews were coded directly to 3 x 5 cards.[29] Each card has an identifying tag consisting of the interview number and coded position of informant. The Student (*Form 1*) and Adult (*Form 2*) decks are further identified by red and black marks respectively.

Thus the interview labeled "b 18A" with a blue mark is readily identifiable as a leader of an adult direct action organization.

An early coding decision was to record *all* responses applicable for each question *in the order given*. This was one of many attempts to overcome the major disadvantage of using unstructured questions—the tendency to force and distort data in the translation from qualitative response to quantitative symbol on the code card. Another effort in this direction is the coding of an asterisk (*) beside any response which contains a unique or especially powerful interpretation, to refer the analyst back to the original data as often as possible.

Next came the compilation of marginals, first tabulated by hand on check sheets, then typewritten duplicate in a 19-page packet for the Students and a 12-page set for Adult informants.

The fourth phase—following code construction, coding and marginal tabulation—was analysis of the data. While analysis of interview data is, in reality, a never-ending process that takes place from the moment researcher and informant sit down to talk, it was at this stage that quantitative techniques were *formally* applied in an effort to get the full power from the material.

Techniques of statistical analysis in this project are not complex. The aim was not complicated manipulation of abstractly defined variables in hypothesis-testing, but rather the translation of observational and informant data into a comprehensive theory of rationalization which itself defines variables and specifies their relationships.

The nature of the sample precluded the use of even the standard nonparametric or distribution-free statistical tests of significance. The minimum assumption which must be made for valid use of nonparametric methods is, according to Siegel, *independence*—that ". . . the selection of any one case from the population for inclusion in the sample must not bias the chances of any other case for inclusion."[30] Or, as Peatman puts it, "The general condition for [the] safe use [of distribution-free methods] in significance testing is that of RANDOMIZATION."[31] Ours is, as described earlier, a *purposive* or *focused* sample, with informants selected specifically because of the particular position they occupy in the phenomenon under study. Thus, I have attempted to get at the numerical significance of the interview data through the use of simple comparative measures such as percentages. It should be reiterated that the use of quantitative measures is intended only to support the validity of observational and informant interpretations which provide the major thrust of this report.

### *d. DOCUMENTARY ANALYSIS*

A further attempt to explain the rationalization of direct action protest is made through several forms of documentary analysis:

(1) the growth of new publications stemming from the movement is taken as a direct indicator of growing rationalization as defined by our theory;

(2) many major "Statements of Purpose" and other important mailings from SNCC for the period under study are analyzed to determine how the student organization views its role (basically as communicator, coordinator or initiator?); and

(3) the *Southern Patriot* (a civil rights monthly of the Southern Conference Education Fund, now in its third decade of publication) is analyzed to determine 1960-62 changes in its reporting on the movement and the major organizations involved.

Sources of data for these analyses are widespread. The first is dependent on my keeping up with the various publications through scanning periodical indexes and the publications themselves, through multiplication of mailing lists on which my name appears, and through the help of researcher-friends who know my interest. Sources for part (2) are self-explanatory—I am on several mailing lists of all the major civil rights organizations, and further personal contact has helped me obtain a copy of virtually everything SNCC has ever published for public and civil rights in-group consumption.

Research on the *Patriot* was done in the files of the Southern Regional Council in March and April of 1962.

### *e. SUPPLEMENTARY AND SUPPORTIVE DATA*

The research methods and approaches explained above cannot be separated from the *context of sources* in which they become meaningful—that is, against the background of materials which tell the story of the direct action protest movement from the standpoint of the participant and not the sociologist. Most of the sources listed here have not been subject to the intensive analysis of those in the previous section, but they have been important as day-to-day mechanisms of contact with the movement and a constant source of new ideas for analysis. They fill several filing cabinets and include:

(1) *Mailings, newsletters, pamphlets, policy statements, appeals for funds, regular publications* (such as *The Crisis* and *CORElator*), etc. from the American Civil Liberties Union, Americans for Democratic Action, American Friends Service Committee, American Jewish Committee, Anti-Defamation League, Center for the Study of Conflict Resolution, Church Peace Mission, Commission on Christian Social Concerns of The Methodist Church, Committee for Nonviolent Action, the Congress of Racial Equality, Council for United Civil Rights Leadership, Council of Federated Organizations (COFO in Mississippi), Episcopal Society for Cultural and Racial Unity, Fellowship of Reconciliation, Highlander Folk School, NAACP, National Catholic Conference for Interracial Justice, National Conference of Christians and Jews, National Conference on Religion and Race, National Council of Churches, National Student Christian Federation, National Urban League, Northern Student Movement, Southern Christian Leadership Conference, Southern Conference Educational Fund, Southern Regional Council, Southern Student Freedom Fund, Students for a Democratic Society, Student Nonviolent Coordinating Committee, Student Peace Union, Tocsin, Tuskegee Institute, United Church of Christ, U.S. National Student Association, Voter Education Project, War Resisters' League, World University Service, YM and YWCA, and numerous local biracial committees and human relations councils, to name the most important sources.

(2) *Professional journals* in the behavioral sciences which are now carrying more and more material relevant to the direct action protests, and *books* which are now appearing at a rapid rate as public and professional interest crystallizes around the growing civil rights crisis in America.

(3) *Audio-visual materials* such as phonograph records of many of the organizations listed above (including several on the March on Washington), tape recordings of mass meetings and strategy sessions done by other social scientists, and all the other songs expressive of the movement.

(4) *Mass media reports*, especially from *Atlanta Constitution*, *Christian Science Monitor*, *New York Times*, and *Washington Post*; *Afro-American*, *Amsterdam News*, *Atlanta Inquirer*, *Atlanta World*, *Mississippi Free Press*, *Muhammad Speaks*, *Norfolk Journal and Guide*, and *Pittsburgh Courier*; *Commentary*, *Correspondence*, *Current*, *Dissent*, *Ebony*, *Jet*, *Life*, *The Nation*,

*New Freedom*, *New Republic*, *Newsweek*, *New University Thought*, *The Reporter*, *Time* and *U.S. News and World Report*.

(5) *Personal documents* including diaries from student participants, personal letters from movement participants and leaders (one while on a chain gang in South Carolina, for instance[32]), even "love letters"—my daily long letters to my fiancee during the two months of field research in 1962. The letters have served as a perspective-giving running account of the research—its successes, problems and reorientations as the project developed. They have been most useful as a record of the day-to-day development of the theory which at once orients and results from this research.

A less structured but equally important source of supportive data alluded to in the Research Chronology has been my attendance at various conferences and meetings before and during the period of analysis of data. Some of the specific methods listed in this section were conceived and contacts made through my attendance at such gatherings as the National Conference on Religion and Race in January 1963, the March on Washington, a conference of direct action leaders in December 1963 on "Revolution, Nonviolence and the Church" and the annual conventions of SCLC and CORE. The renewal of contacts with key informants was valuable for keeping in touch with the movement.

In addition, my on-going discussions with fellow sociologists have guarded against overlooking the obvious in the data and have constantly suggested new analytical dimensions.[33]

## *f. TOWARD A DESIGN FOR EXPLORATORY ACTION RESEARCH: THE DIALOGUE*

Kurt Lewin defines action research as the systematic study of ". . . the conditions and effects of various forms of social action," concerned with either "general laws of group life" or "diagnosis of a specific situation."[34] This project is best described, I believe, as *exploratory action research*—a concentration on the early stages of the form of social action under study.

Exploratory action research has several characteristics:

(1) the phenomenon under study is contemporary;
(2) it often involves some elements of interpersonal or intergroup conflict;

(3) therefore research design and findings may be influenced by ameliorative agencies such as social work and intergroup relations; and

(4) since the phenomenon is in-process, transitory and in the formative stages, the researcher can use standardized research methods only to a limited extent.

Each of these conditions presents several problems to be overcome in the course of turning out sophisticated sociological research. An example of each: (1) the researcher does not have the perspective (and thus the predictive ability) of the historical, experimental or survey researcher, whose universe, variables and time-span are under more rigid control; (2) first-hand data from participants may be hard to obtain due to suspicion of "outsiders" (including sociologists);[35] (3) there is a compelling tendency to phrase research problems in applied rather than pure terms, and to take actively involved agency personnel as a reference group competing with that of the profession; and (4) statistical hypothesis-testing of the relationships between precisely defined variables from bodies of well-developed theory is very difficult.

But the action researcher, accepting these limitations, can make the best of the situation by capitalizing on the unique possibilities of his role. His special calling could be to (a) define variables and thus (b) build theory through promoting *Verstehen*—a systematic and insightful understanding of the action phenomenon. By providing and constantly clarifying this kind of understanding, the action researcher can help later researchers avoid some of the problems of static hypothesis-testing which inevitably creep in when research is removed from its natural context.[36]

In short, *all* theory is developed from life experiences, regardless of how vague, long ago, submerged or translated they may be. The process involves *observation*, informal *quantification*, then insightful *generalization*. This project has been a conscious attempt to design and order certain kinds of life experiences in a way which will facilitate this theory-building process.

Based on the experience of the project, a number of guidelines may be suggested which can aid the action researcher.

(1) *Elites as Informants*—Elites are one of the best sources of data in action research. This category may include active leaders, consultants, and observers—who are or become, by the nature of their role, *cosmopolitan*. Their activity forces them to get the Big Picture, to think in strategic and

long-range terms. Each elite synthesizes the phenomena into distinct perspectives, then the sociologist can synthesize the various elite perspectives.

(2) *The Dialogue as Research Tool*—The sociologist must get beyond a surface or professional relationship with the elite to elicit the level and kind of data needed for sophisticated sociological analysis. This is realized best through some form of the *dialogue*—the intense, open, and honest personal interchange directed at achieving even higher levels of knowledge or interpretation of the phenomenon under study.[37] We may summarize the material devoted to the dialogue in this chapter as follows:

(a) the researcher maintains a total openness with informants, discussing critically the problems of such research—over-involvement, subjectivity, the philosophy of sociology and social research, etc.;
(b) the researcher allows for a considerable expenditure of time and energy with each informant, thus limiting him to a small number (hence the "purposive" or "focused" sample);
(c) the researcher must have a prior high-level knowledge of the phenomenon under study (often arrived at through participant observation) as a basis for the respect necessary to engage in creative dialogue;
(d) the researcher must maintain (and warrant) an aura of responsibility and trustworthiness in his relations to the informant and the data;
(e) since the informants may be elites in other senses than the sociological, permission is asked to list their names in the project report and to quote specific passages.

If all of these conditions are met,[38] the researcher gains access to the inside experience and knowledge of those in the best position to know. Further, he is able to tap this experience at its deepest level because he is free to discuss and challenge in the dialogue. In the dialogic interview the researcher resists the temptation to force data or accept simplistic responses; if a question is not meaningful to an informant, the researcher probes until there is a common understanding. Such an approach allows two seemingly contradictory responses of one informant in this study to stand: "the students realize they have to accept adult help" and "now the students have the attitude they can do it alone."[39] The method tries not to force informants into being "rational" or "consistent" for the sake of earlier data-processing.

The researcher is also unconcerned if the interview-dialogue has to be conducted in more than one sitting (some in this project took three sessions to complete). In fact, he is grateful to be allowed access to his informant-friend's thought processes on several different occasions in hopes of gaining even more possible interpretations.

The researcher who relates to his informants in this way is, of course, taking many risks. The greatest of these is peculiar to his role as "marginal communicator," as discussed earlier in this chapter. He becomes a source of synthesized information which is available to none of the informants individually. For this reason he may be sought out as both an information-giver and weapon to be used against other factions within the social systems under study. In several instances, my informants seriously hampered my attempt at data-gathering because *they* were quizzing *me* about my interpretations of latest developments.

In short, the dialogic design for data collection in action research asks for full personal involvement on the part of the researcher as well as the informant. Not only do elites demand the feeling they are being listened to as *persons* and not as numbers,[40] but the researcher needs constant reminders of his responsibility to his deeply-involved activist subjects.

Under the kind of circumstances outlined in this chapter, the sociologist may start bridging the wide and often defensive gap between social activist and sociological analyst. Perhaps then the growing group of activist elites may be willing to eagerly *share* rather than jealously surrender vital data for the analytical mill.[41]

# B. The Data:

## Nonviolent Direct Action Against Segregation in the United States, 1960-1962

PREFACE

# Pre-1960: A Community Rebels

It's like waiting for a bus, man. You know where you're going all the time, but you can't get there 'til the right vehicle comes along.

Negro sit-inner
North Carolina, 1960

Historians of race relations in twentieth-century America no doubt will mark two mid-century dates as turning points in the desegregation process: 1954 and 1960. On the surface, 1954 can be seen as a *legal* turning point, and 1960 as a *personal* turning point in the drive of Negro Americans for equal opportunity to achieve the goals of their society. Recognizing that any such demarcation of "periods" or "phases" set off by "turning points" is at best oversimplified, this section attempts to chart the *changes in direction*, *strategy*, and *attitude* which accompanied the genesis and growth of the direct action movement against segregation. The focus is on the first two years of the movement, February 1, 1960 to February 1, 1962.

This section relies primarily on observation and description to convey the sense of the changes that have taken place with the advent of direct action. But the description is couched in a consciously analytical framework to facilitate the development of theory in the next section. By focusing on changes in "direction, strategy and attitude," for instance, we are making analytical distinctions between action at three system levels—*culture* (direction: goals and values), *social system* (strategy: new norms and institutional patterns for implementation) and *personality* (attitude: newly crystallized aspirations and motivation).

In short, the last decade has seen the thrust for desegregation in America turn into a full-scale social movement, with the initiative for innovation transferred from the hands of a relatively few professionals to the militant personal action of persons of every color and class level. The days of "leave it to the NAACP, the courts and the government" are over. The nation has seen a turn to personal responsibility for change on the day-to-day level. We have seen a move from ***professional action*** to ***militant personal action*** in a day when human relations are becoming ever more professionalized. It is the goal of this section to explain how such a major change in life-style of hundreds of thousands of persons could take place in so short a time.

# THREE

# Pre-1960: A Community Rebels

You are as good as anyone.
Mrs. Martin Luther King, Sr.

I don't care how long I have to live with this system, I will never accept it.
Rev. Martin Luther King, Sr.

As far back as I could remember, I had resented segregation.
Dr. Martin Luther King, Jr.[1]

There have never been "good race relations" in the United States. Roughly translated, this Chamber of Commerce cliche has meant something like "Things have been quiet around here . . . the Nigras know their place." Rather the statements of the M. L. King Family of Atlanta are closer to the reality: there is, in fact, a constant revolt on the personal level, passed on from generation to generation. From time to time it has found group channels—slave revolts, protest organizations, direct action demonstrations, the sit-in movement.

The history of direct action until 1960 was one of formally unconnected demonstrations in many parts of the country which never found a unifying focus on a regional or national level. There had been many rebellions on a sub-community level. Not until Martin Luther King and the Montgomery bus boycott in 1955-56 had an entire Negro community mobilized for direct action against segregation. The events leading up to Montgomery are examined first.

## *a. THE ROAD TO MONTGOMERY: GANDHI AND THE PACIFISTS*

The legal strategy culminating in the 1954 Supreme Court decision against public school segregation was, of necessity, conceived and carried out by professionals—persons with specialized training who could devote full time to the desegregation struggle. Much the same was true in direct action. Low educational levels, lack of economic and political power, and the resulting scarcity of articulate and militant Negro leadership had necessarily kept the drive for equal rights in the hands of a few skilled professionals. The mass direct action that did take place was sporadic, short-lived and elicited continuing commitment from only a few.

Many of these few could be classed as professional pacifists, whose personal commitment had led them to full time work with nonviolent strategies for social change in labor, race and international relations. Their commitment was, in most cases, a profound and deeply thought-out synthesis of the civil disobedience of America's Henry David Thoreau and the *satyagraha* ("Soul-Force" or "Truth-Force") of India's Mohandas Gandhi. Since half of this study's Adult informants (16 of 32) said they first had heard of nonviolent direct action in connection with Gandhi,[2] the analysis begins with this tradition.

Thoreau published his essay, "Civil Disobedience," in 1849, followed by "Slavery in Massachusetts" in 1854—both of which considered nonviolent possibilities of overcoming unjust governments. He decries those ". . . who are in opinion opposed to slavery and to the war, who yet in effect do nothing to put an end to them; who . . . sit down with their hands in their pockets, and say that they know not what to do, and do nothing."[3] Here the basis for activism is clearly set.

Thoreau also gave us a modern western rationale for nonadherence to an immoral law: "The only place which Massachusetts has provided for her freer and less desponding spirits, is in her prisons, to be put out and locked out of the state by her own act, as they have already put themselves out by their principles."[4]

Nonviolent direct action first attained large scale philosophical and practical acceptance in the early twentieth century under Gandhi in Africa and India. Gandhi's application of "passive resistance" met its first test in 1906 when the Transvaal government tried to implement a registration act for all Indians. The rapid rise to power of this mode of action is reflected by the unprecedented and personally dangerous pass-burning by more than 2,000 Indians in Johannesburg in 1908.[5] Gandhi's return to India in 1915 and his leadership in the relatively peaceful liberation of the country from British rule in 1947 were important as models for American pacifism.[6]

The running dialogue between East and West regarding morally acceptable remedies for civil injustice and spiritual separation has a long history. Thoreau and Emerson originally borrowed heavily from the *Bhagavad-Gita* and some of the Hindu *Upanishads*. And Gandhi echoed Thoreau (not to mention St. Paul) when he wrote that the prisoner's soul is free. He studied "Civil Disobedience" during his second long stay in jail, calling it a "masterly treatise" which left a "deep impression" on him.[7] Thus Thoreau in Massachusetts borrowed from Gandhi's India and repaid the debt with words that reached Gandhi in a jail cell. The dialogue continues today as demonstrators read Gandhi and Zen, CORE gives its annual "Gandhi award" to an outstanding civil rights leader, CORE, FOR and SCLC explicitly credit Gandhi in their statements of philosophy and support the distribution of Gandhian literature, and the "Gandhi Society" (formed by SCLC in 1963) keeps alive an awareness of the debt owed Gandhi by the American civil rights movement.[8]

How, then, could this catalytic form of action come to the American South? It could come in massive form only as a result of (1) basic structural changes accumulating over some period of time in the social system and (2) long-term recruitment of participants through grass roots education and activism.

### *Basic Structural Changes*

For several decades, the South had been experiencing major modifications of institutionalized patterns in several systems: economic (especially communication and transportation), political, educational and religious. The social system process of structural differentiation (which is shown in Section C to be closely linked to rationalization) has its counterparts at the cultural and personality level in the detraditionalization of values and attitudes. These changes affect all levels of the social system, i.e., in this case, the minority and protesting groups as well as the total community.

The development of the direct action protest movement over the whole South would not have been possible without the necessary technological conditions for its spread, tolerance of innovation in the total system and strong motivation of the protestors—all of which are linked to enabling structural maturations in the social systems. Some of these structural preconditions are listed below, and their implications are more fully discussed in Section C:

(a) *Urbanization* and *industrialization* in the emerging South, and the nationalizing effect of interstate economic activity.
(b) *Governmental and legal developments*, including court decisions.
(c) *Migration*, rural to urban, South to North, for both Negro and white (including travel and service in the armed forces).
(d) *Improvement of Negro education*, including theological training.
(e) *Growth of nationalism* and anti-colonialism.
(f) *Television*.

Most informants, both Student and Adult, viewed the development of the movement in the light of structural conditions instead of situationalism, even though they could not express it in sociological terms. The most frequent responses to the question, "What do you think were the most important factors in the start and rapid spread of the sit-in movement at this time?" were codable as "tenor of the times," "inevitable," etc. To be assigned this code, a response had to indicate some awareness of the sweeping institutional changes which made a southern mass direct action movement a possibility in 1960 when it was not in, say, 1930. While this question is geared specifically to the argument of chapter 4, the responses are included here as important background materials:

Figure 1

MOST IMPORTANT FACTORS
IN START AND SPREAD OF SIT-IN MOVEMENT
(I.2, both forms)

| | *Students* (n = 13) | *Adults* (n = 30) |
|---|---|---|
| "Tenor of the times," "inevitable," (including Montgomery), etc. | 7 (54%) | 18 (60%) |
| mass media communication | 6 (46%) | 3 (10%) |
| 1954 decision | 5 (38%) | 9 (30%) |
| relative deprivation | 5 (38%) | 9 (30%) |
| personal frustrations | 3 (23%) | 10 (33%) |

| | | |
|---|---|---|
| role of students | 3 (23%) | 4 (13%) |
| college competition | 2 (15%) | 7 (23%) |
| Greensboro dynamics | 1 ( 8%) | 2 ( 7%) |
| television | 0 ( 0%) | 3 (10%) |
| changing leadership | 0 ( 0%) | 2 ( 7%) |
| tokenism | 0 ( 0%) | 2 ( 7%) |
| other | 3 (23%) | 2 ( 7%) |

Note that almost half of the students mention the importance of the mass media, and that 38% of the Students and 30% of the Adults name the 1954 decision—all on a free recall basis.[9] The same proportions of Student and Adult informants phrase their answers in a sociologically relevant framework of relative deprivation, which is treated more fully in Section C.

### *History of Nonviolent Education and Activism in America*

The emergence of a full-scale nonviolent social movement in 1960 was made possible, then, in the context of numerous structural changes which may be called enabling maturations. But the transformation of structural readiness into specific social action was accomplished through an accumulation of attitudes and strategic skills over a long incubation period at the grass roots level. This accumulation may be analyzed in terms of the basic operationalizing devices for the two components—(a) nonviolent conferences (attitudes) and (b) direct action projects (strategic skills).

*Conferences*. It is, of course, hard to separate philosophical education in nonviolence from the education which comes from participation in demonstrations, for planning sessions have always accompanied demonstrations. In addition, there have been formal and informal discussions of nonviolent methods of resolving America's racial problems for many years. Certainly the Niagara Movement and other groups which led to the founding of the NAACP in the early 1900s dealt with such issues.

It is difficult to document the number and impact of conferences and meetings which dealt with these issues, but it is safe to say that there must have been hundreds of these and other educational gatherings prior to 1955 and Montgomery. They occurred with increasing frequency in the 1940s and 1950s, reaching an ever-expanding group of potential recruits to direct action. Some seemingly important and representative contributions to the education of Americans in nonviolence are listed below:

| | |
|---|---|
| 1915 | Fellowship of Reconciliation founded. |
| 1923 | War Resisters League founded. |
| 1928 | Howard Thurman and Benjamin Mays meet with Gandhi to discuss application of *satyagraha* to American racial problems.[10] |
| 1936 | A. Philip Randolph organizes National Negro Congress (one of a growing number of such groups exploring various approaches to the problem).[11] |
| 1941 | Randolph conceives March on Washington Movement, involving thousands of Negroes and whites in planning for massive direct action.[12] |
| 1942 | MOWM announces plans to employ Gandhian civil disobedience tactics against racial segregation.[13] CORE organized. |
| 1943 | Fellowship of Reconciliation and War Resisters League sponsor institutes on "Race Relations and Nonviolence" in New York; St. Louis; Indianapolis; Columbus, Ohio; and Pittsburgh.[14] |
| 1946 | Two-month interracial workshop on pacifism in Chicago. Pacifist Institutes on Nonviolence and Race Relations in West Chester and Pittsburgh, Pennsylvania[15] |
| 1948 | Randolph promotes formation of League for Nonviolent Civil Disobedience Against Military Segregation.[16] |
| 1952 | SCEF sponsors Youth Conference in Columbia, South Carolina, with Negro and white delegates from 48 colleges and universities in 18 southern and border states . . . "one of the first integrated student meetings ever held in the South."[17] |

It is significant that at this point in *recorded* materials, the emphasis shifts from institutes and conferences to direct action projects.[18] By the mid-1950s interracial conferences which included discussion of direct action techniques were occurring with some frequency in all areas of the country, sponsored by such groups as CORE, FOR, SCEF, local NAACP chapters and national church groups. The extensive literature of these and other groups also contributed to the growing dialogue on nonviolence during the two decades preceding 1960. A powerful educator has been the annual Race Relations Institute, sponsored by the United Church of Christ each summer at Fisk University in Nashville since 1945. Equally important were many conferences at Highlander Folk School in Tennessee, where Miles Horton and Septima Clark brought Negro and white adults and young people together for what was, for most of them, the first time in an equal-status situation.

Such grass roots nonviolent educational endeavors, then, have both resulted from and/or hastened the maturation of the structural changes prerequisite for the full-scale social movement that was to develop in 1960.

*Projects*. The road to Montgomery has been paved most recently by the labor movement, peace strikes and other activities in a legacy of direct action protest which is older than even most of today's direct actionists suspect. Many different protest techniques have been employed over the years, as noted in chapter 1, each emerging as it became less dangerous and potentially more successful. So when public accommodations became a source of strain, the method ideally suited to ameliorating discrimination in this area—direct action—was applied.

The application of direct action to discrimination in public accommodations has increased as it became appropriate and safe during the 1940s and 1950s, culminating in the sit-in movement. But there is evidence that this form of protest is as old as public accommodations restrictions. Some examples of the relatively few recorded direct action protests against American racial discrimination help put the current movement in perspective:

| | |
|---|---|
| 1868 | Mrs. Catherine Brown, a Negro, refuses to move to a segregated railroad car in a trip from Alexandria, Virginia, to Washington, D.C., is bodily removed from the train, sues and wins her case before the U.S. Supreme Court.[19] |
| 1871 | Negro Robert Fox refuses to move from white section of streetcar in Louisville, Kentucky, is thrown off, triggering full-scale "ride-in" which wins right for nonsegregated use following local court denial of this right.[20] |

1875 One man sit-in by Negro at the Metropolitan Opera House in New York City.[21]

[Alan Westin and C. Vann Woodward note a number of such incidents involving public accommodations from 1866 to the early 1880s, after the Federal Civil Rights Act of 1866 with its "equal benefits of the laws" clause had set off a flurry of enforcement suits—which were to be repeated with the 1947 Journey of Reconciliation, the 1961 Freedom Rides and the 1964 testing of the Federal Civil Rights Law. See below.][22]

1917 8,000 NAACP members stage New York march in protest against post-World War II "Red Summer."[23]

1940 Howard University students conduct unsuccessful sit-ins at lunch counters in Washington, D.C.

1942 More than 100,000 Negroes attend MOWM protest rallies in several large cities including New York, Chicago and St. Louis.[24] Threatened March on Washington brings establishment of President's Committee on Fair Employment Practices five days before the marching date.[25] Five hundred New York MOWM members hold silent parade on June 25 protesting execution of Negro sharecropper and other "violent mob acts of Southerners."[26] CORE founded after sit-in campaign at segregated restaurant in Chicago, carries on protests in several cities during 1940s and 1950s.[27]

1947 FOR and CORE sponsor Journey of Reconciliation through the Middle South to test Supreme Court decision barring discrimination in interstate travel. Members beaten, arrested and serve time on chain gang.[28] More than 1,000 University of Chicago students picket to end discrimination in Medical School and other facilities.[29]

1948 Randolph initiates civil disobedience campaign against military discrimination in March; four months later, President Truman creates Fair Employment Board and President's Committee on Equality of Treatment and Opportunity in the Armed Services.[30]

1949 Palisades, New Jersey, swimming pool desegregated after two-year nonviolent campaign.[31]

1950 Student demonstrators arrested at lunch counter in Washington, D.C.[32]

| | |
|---|---|
| 1952 | Amusement park in Cincinnati desegregates after nonviolent demonstrations.[33] |
| 1953 | Lunch counters desegregated in St. Louis after four-year campaign of sit-ins and picketing by CORE; shorter CORE campaign desegregates lunch counters in Washington, D.C.[34] |
| 1954 | Lunch counters desegregated in Baltimore after CORE direct action campaign.[35] |

. . . All of which did not seem to fall into place as nicely as it does now—since Montgomery and Martin Luther King.

## *b. MARTIN LUTHER KING AND THE CHARISMATIC BREAK-THROUGH OF NONVIOLENCE*

Before any full-scale social movement can develop, its philosophical bases must be at least partially legitimated in the host system. Until this legitimation takes place, the seemingly disparate pieces of any protest with movement potentialities cannot coalesce. In the Montgomery bus boycott in 1955-56 the necessary elements of nonviolent protest came together and crystallized to provide a symbolic focus for later action. The Rev. Dr. Martin Luther, King, Jr., was the man through whom this synthesis was accomplished.[36]

### *The Montgomery Bus Boycott and Related Developments*

Rosa Parks should have known better. She was no young woman. She had lived a long time under the laws of the state of Alabama and the city of Montgomery. She knew that when the bus driver told her and other Negroes to get up from their seats and move to the back of the bus to accommodate white passengers getting on, she should move. But somehow on December 1, 1955, she could not bring herself to do it. Rosa Parks would go to jail. She would pay the fine. And though she did not know it, she would set a city of 50,000 Negroes walking and trigger off a new form of Negro protest that would bring into prominence a new and dynamic leader.

Mrs. Parks' arrest was not the cause of the city-wide bus boycott by Negroes that was to follow, only its precipitant. The bus service in Montgomery had long been something that particularly annoyed Negro patrons. Though they were the major source of the bus line's customers (about 75 percent), they were continually subjected to the indignities of segregation. There were no Negro bus drivers, and many of the white drivers were rude, even abusive:

> It was not uncommon to hear [the bus drivers] referring to Negro passengers as 'niggers,' 'black cows,' and 'black apes.' Frequently Negroes paid their fare at the front door, and then were forced to get off and reboard the bus at the rear. Often the bus pulled off with the Negro's dime in the box before he had had time to reach the rear door.[37]

Word of the arrest of the quiet seamstress aroused the Negro community of Montgomery. Negro leaders consolidated existing factions and called for a boycott of city buses on Monday, December 5, the day of the trial. Word spread through mimeographed hand-outs and the pulpits on Sunday. Mrs. Parks was convicted and fined $10, the boycott was nearly 100 percent effective, and the protest movement was on.

The Montgomery Improvement Association was formed, and King was chosen president. Young (26 years old), southern-born (Atlanta) and highly-educated (B.D. at Crozer, Ph.D in social philosophy at Boston University), he had just come to Montgomery as pastor of the Dexter Avenue Baptist Church. Thus, King was not yet deeply entangled in the complex factionalism of local Negro leadership, and was able to unify and sustain the protest through his preaching at mass meetings. His major message was non-cooperation with the evil system: "He who accepts evil without protesting it is . . . as much involved in it as he who helps to perpetrate it."[38]

The MIA mobilized and informed the Negro community for an essentially negative and non-agressive protest. Little face-to-face confrontation with whites was needed at this stage; Negroes simply extended the already existing racial separation an important economic notch further. King combined the teachings of Gandhi and the more familiar Christian ethical mandates into a philosophy of direct action for social change:

> As I delved into the philosophy of Gandhi my skepticism concerning the power of love gradually diminished, and I came to see for the first time its potency in the area of social reform . . . Prior to reading Gandhi, I had about

> concluded that the ethics of Jesus were only effective in individual relationship . . . But I [soon] saw how utterly mistaken I was.
>
> Gandhi was probably the first person in history to lift the love ethic of Jesus above mere interaction between individuals to a powerful and effective social force on a large scale.[39]

Further, King set the tone which was to motivate the pronouncements and actions of many future sit-inners: ". . . protest courageously, and yet with dignity and Christian love . . . and you will inject new meaning and dignity into the veins of civilization."[40]

The demands of the MIA were simple and direct: (1) a guarantee of courteous treatment, (2) passenger seating on a first-come, first-served basis, with Negroes seating from the back, and (3) hiring of Negro bus drivers on predominantly Negro routes. Week after week Negroes stayed off the buses. With the strategic help of experienced pacifists like Glen Smiley of the FOR, Bayard Rustin of the War Resisters League, Ella Baker, Rev. James M. Lawson, Jr.,[41] and longtime local leaders like E. D. Nixon, King's charismatic inspiration was harnessed and infused into a cohesive social movement.

The protest grew, and violent opposition grew. But King's power as a leader and his Christian-Gandhian commitment kept the movement nonviolent despite a growing sense of retaliatory bitterness. The story of how King quelled an angry and armed mob of Negroes which had formed after the bombing of his home is well known to many Negro Americans as a first symbol of his special powers of leadership.

Harassment, both official and non-official, were part of the pattern of opposition over the long months of the boycott. Many Negroes had their homes bombed. There were threatening letters and telephone calls. One day King was trailed by city policemen and finally arrested for "going thirty in a twenty-five mile zone," then released on cash bond. Later, MIA leaders, King included, were arrested and convicted for "conspiracy to prevent the operation of a lawful business, without just cause or legal excuse," then released on appeal. Finally, the city started action against the motor pool, as a "private enterprise operating without a license" and a "public nuisance."[42]

All these tactics failed for Montgomery segregationists, for on November 13, 1956—less than a year after the boycott began—the U.S. Supreme Court affirmed the decision of a lower federal court and declared Alabama's state and local laws requiring segregation on buses unconstitutional.

Here, then, were the necessary elements for the genesis of a broad-based social movement: a simple and understandable goal (first-come, first-served on bus seats), a religiously sanctioned philosophy (Gandhian nonviolence rooted in Christian love), a strategy of action (the boycott, which gave Negroes all over America the image of *people* with whom to identify in their aspirations), a charismatic leader (Martin Luther King, Jr.,—a living symbol of the middle class goals for which many Negroes had nearly given up striving), and a new-found sense of the power of mass action (who ever thought *we* could make Mr. Charlie jump like that?!). Negroes had proven it could work on a community-wide level, and the Montgomery success was soon to spark other protests.[43]

Here an existing organizational structure was to aid in the regional and national diffusion of the ideal and practice of nonviolence. The FOR printed a colorful illustrated comic book called "Martin Luther King and the Montgomery Story" and distributed it to virtually every Negro school and college in the country. I confidently estimate that more than 90 percent of southern Negroes over 10 years old know of Martin Luther King and Montgomery, largely via this mechanism, which tells in the closing pages how to initiate and organize a nonviolent campaign. Most of the hundreds of direct action protesters I know also are familiar with King's autobiographical account of the boycott, *Stride Toward Freedom*, published in 1958.

Montgomery, then, established once and for all the morality and practical effectiveness of the ethic King preached. The seeds for a system-wide social movement were thus planted in a local movement, which reached its limited goals and soon took on the institutional form of the Montgomery Improvement Association. From 1956 to 1960 similar Improvement Associations were organized in other southern cities, including Tallahassee, Florida, Shreveport, Louisiana, Nashville, Tennessee, and Mobile, Alabama; they provided the leadership for bus boycotts and other direct action protests on a local basis.[44] In 1957, King and some of his associates in the Montgomery boycott established the Southern Christian Leadership Conference. Its growth and emergence as a major civil rights organization is analyzed in chapter 8.

If sociologists had today's perspective in the late 1950s, we should have been able to predict the inevitable development of a South- and nation-wide protest movement. The Montgomery mood had taken hold. On May 17 in 1957, 1958 and 1959—the anniversary of the 1954 school desegregation decision—King and A. Phillip Randolph led tens of thousands of Negroes and whites on "prayer pilgrimages" to Washington, D.C. And there were many local demonstrations, the details of which are only beginning to surface in academic circles. A sampling:

1956 — Beginning of a four-year boycott of an Orangeburg, South Carolina, milk company which refused to extend credit to a Negro mother whose bleeder baby eventually died. South Carolina State students led boycott, joined by faculty; several expelled. Boycott lasts until February 1, 1960, when Orangeburg students are one of first South Carolina groups to follow lead of Greensboro sit-inners.[45] Autherine Lucy blocked in attempt to enroll in University of Alabama.

1957 — Seven Negroes convicted of trespassing while seeking service at white ice cream counter in Durham, North Carolina.[46] Atlanta University students ordered out of white section in Georgia legislature and out of downtown public library. Library quietly desegregated in 1958.[47]

1958 — More sit-ins and stand-ins in white section of Georgia legislature. CORE-sponsored sit-ins gain equal lunch counter service in Charleston, West Virginia.[48] NAACP Youth Councils in Oklahoma City launch sit-in drive that opens 56 lunch counters in Oklahoma and Kansas.[49]

1959 — Morgan State College students stage semi-successful series of sit-ins at Baltimore lunch counters.[50] YWCA at University of Texas leads three weeks of sit-ins at restaurants in Austin.[51] CORE leads lunch counter sit-ins in Miami.[52] Rev. James Lawson (FOR representative and Vanderbilt Divinity student) conducts nonviolent workshops and leads sit-in tests at Nashville department store lunch counters in November and December.[53]

And as late as January 1, 1960—just one month before the beginning of the sit-in movement—King led 1,600 Virginians in a prayer pilgrimage for public schools at the capitol in Richmond. The same day more than 800 Negroes and whites protested segregated facilities at the Greenville, South Carolina, airport.[54]

Continuing in the educational tradition mentioned earlier in this chapter, several significant conferences were held post-Montgomery, pre-Greensboro. Three of the most important meetings were a Southwide Institute on Nonviolent Resistance in July of 1959,[55] a CORE Action Institute in Miami in September,[56] and the 18th Ecumenical Student Conference on the Christian World Mission, sponsored by the National Student Christian Federation in Athens, Ohio, during Christmas vacation, 1959. The theme of the latter conference brought both King and Lawson as speakers. Several informants besides King and Lawson were at Athens, and one who later worked for SNCC estimated that 75 percent of the first-wave sit-in leaders of one month hence were there.[57]

By the 1950s, the accumulation of structural changes was emerging as a major desegregation variable; southern business and political leaders were beginning to realize that overt racial tensions could not be tolerated if outside capital were to continue to flow in. By 1960, Little Rock, for instance, had gone almost three years without attracting a single new industry after the school desegregation flare-up in 1957—a sharp contrast to the pre-crisis average of five large new plants per year since 1950.[58] It soon became clear that racial conflicts (including direct action demonstrations) must not be allowed to come to the surface for exposure to the national media for any length of time. Thus, many white decision-makers were, step-by-step, becoming tuned to the necessity of rapid resolution of overt racial problems.

## *A Theoretical Note on Changing Negro Leadership*

An important corollary effect of the Montgomery boycott was the influence of King's militant leadership on the growth of long latent militancy in other southern Negro leaders. The emergence of such militancy in a number of communities was a basic internal prerequisite for a Southwide protest movement.

There is evidence that such leadership had been developing for some time. The Rev. J. Metz Rollins, a leader of the 1958 Tallahassee bus boycott, points out that "there has been a power struggle in almost every Negro community in the South during the past few years before the decks were finally cleared for action."[59] King's role at Montgomery undoubtedly quickened the leadership struggle taking place in other Negro communities, manifested in the protests which emerged in various southern cities after 1956, as described above.

The parties to this Negro leadership struggle have been described by sociologists as "accommodation" and "protest" leaders[60] or "moderate" and "militant" leaders.[61] The most important distinguishing characteristic of the new leader is his *source of legitimacy*, which differs markedly from that of the old leader. The legitimation of the protest or militant leader is based on the acceptance of the Negro community and rejection by the white community.[62] His greatest source of power is ". . . located in the refusal to cooperate with the processes of segregation and discrimination."[63] In contrast, the position of the accommodationist or moderate is based on the acceptance of *both* white and Negro communities. Lewis Jones has called this phenomenon (which clearly was the predominant pattern of white/Negro leadership interaction until the late 1950s) *intercessory leadership*;[64] the Negro "leader's" role often was reduced to carrying messages back and forth between the communities, and "keeping things quiet over there" in exchange for various sanctions. But more and more the white man has found it impossible to call and get things straightened out.

Formal documentation of the movement away from intercessory leadership among Negroes is found in several sources. Killian and Smith's study of the 1958 Tallahassee bus boycott shows that the old leaders of the Negro community were replaced almost overnight by new leaders ". . . who clearly reflect the protest motive rather than any spirit of accommodation. These Negro leaders have widespread political support, and the extent of their influence is widely conceded by the old leaders whom they displaced."[65]

Pettigrew and Campbell's finding that protest leaders are "young, mobile, educated and not deeply rooted in the community"[66] also was borne out in the Tallahassee study. In another community, the top seven Negro leaders were found to have a shorter length of residence than most Negroes of comparable statuses.[67] And it is clear that King's lack of longstanding entanglement in Montgomery Negro leadership struggles greatly enhanced his other favorable attributes and made him an immediate success as a unifying leader.

This shift in leadership patterns could occur only because certain structural changes were taking place. Pettigrew, Campbell and the Monahans noted at least two of these changes above: increasing mobility and better education. Even most important has been the growth of an economically independent class of Negro professionals. Lewis Jones emphasizes that "salaried Negroes working under whites are being replaced in the leadership structure by Negroes whose economic well-being depends on *Negroes*." Jones concludes that the gradual wearing away of the old order is symbolized by the fact that even top NAACP leaders in many southern communities today are doctors and lawyers, rather than the school teachers and preachers of the past.[68]

### *Summary: The Personalization of Charisma*

Amid all these developments, then, it was the person of Martin Luther King, Jr., who carried the ideal of nonviolence into the consciousness of Negro America. After the year-long boycott resulted in a Supreme Court order banning segregation in intrastate transportation, nonviolence for Negro Americans was no longer an abstract principle, no longer a mystical and little understood practice of some disgruntled Hindus on the other side of the world. It was a *person*—an individual combining youth, vigor, educational achievement, leadership ability and a religious aura. It was a *person* who suffered *with* the lay community for the just cause—not an organization or a court decision of some highly educated professionals who stood outside and argued *for* the cause.

This is what I mean by *the charismatic breakthrough of the ideal of nonviolence*. The charisma of this idea had to be embodied in an individual before it could be identified with, and thus understood and legitimated. With Montgomery, the notion of nonviolence had "broken through" into Negro consciousness as a way of thinking and acting for the long-floundering desegregation effort.[69] Its use as a protest strategy had been *legitimated*. It was here and now . . . and in the deepest American South it had worked. Negroes had proved to themselves, their white friends and the segregationists that they could organize, lead, sustain and carry through to victory a protest involving all strata of the community. Thus with the Montgomery boycott, the ideological basis for a widespread nonviolent movement against segregation had taken its place along with the structural bases.[70]

# FOUR

# The Sit-Ins (1960): A Region Revolts

One of these days I'm gonna say, goddam it, 'Nawsuh!'
—from an old Negro poem[1]

It just griped me, man, being persecuted.
—Atlanta sit-in leader[2]

Before 1960, the rebellion had been localized. The sit-ins of 1960 expanded it to a regional level. What before was only a series of loosely connected systems with vaguely similar goals and methods, became with the sit-ins one self-conscious system perceiving itself as a South-wide movement made up of many interrelated parts.

The 1960s have seen direct action protests spread through concentric circles of awareness and action until at the middle of the decade few persons or institutions can escape daily confrontation with "The Problem" and "those _____-ins." The sit-in movement can be viewed as the second stage of a three-phase process of the nationalization of nonviolence. First it was a single community. Then a regional movement with coherence between a number of communities arose. And only a year later the movement began its final stage of nationalization with the Freedom Rides, which evoked participation from the entire nation and deeply involved the federal government.

This chapter deals with the crucial and focal year in the desegregation process, 1960—the year direct action became a movement.

## *a. THE SIT-IN MOVEMENT SWEEPS THE SOUTH*

The majority of Negroes still live on a close-to-subsistence income; the average nonwhite family cash income in 1960 was $62 weekly compared to $112 for the typical white family.[3] By 1960, however, Negroes were getting a bigger share of America's expanding economy—but not enough. Census records show, for instance, that while the social and economic status of some Negro Americans is rising rapidly, that of white Americans is rising even faster, thus making the gap wider and wider.[4]

It is in the context of these conditions that we view the start and rapid spread of the sit-in movement in the spring of 1960. The direct action protests are, indeed, a "revolution of rising expectations."[5]

The trigger incident for the sit-in movement has been elevated nearly to the status of a holy event . . . everyone connected with the movement today knows it "began" on February 1, 1960, when four North Carolina A & T freshmen took seats at a segregated Woolworth lunch counter in Greensboro, were refused service and remained 45 minutes until the store closed.[6]

How did they get there? Social structural developments dictated that this would happen sometime soon, somewhere. It happened in isolated instances before, as shown in chapter 3. That it happened in 1960 in Greensboro is due to a combination of situational and personal factors within the maturing structural context: a local white merchant who catered to Negro clientele had urged various students to engage in such activity, the students' personal frustration had been mounting, and their family background had prepared them for such a bold piece of deviance. Ezell Blair, the most articulate (and thus the informal leader) of the four, says of his parents, "They taught me civil rights." Both his parents are secondary teachers with M.A. degrees, and both are extremely active in church work, the NAACP and other civil rights activities. "As long as I can remember," he concludes, "they told me never to take a seat on the back of the bus."[7]

Blair told me that 21 students were back the second day, in alternating shifts lasting from 10 a.m. until closing time. Already three of the sit-inners were white college students—an indicator of things to come.[8] By the end of the week, over 200 students were involved.

On February 8, Durham and Winston-Salem Negro students began sit-ins and picketing, and the sense of "movement" was on its way. By February 11, the protests were already expanding their base of popular support when High Point, North Carolina, high school students sat-in. On the 12th, Rock Hill, South Carolina, became the first sit-in city in a Deep South state. By the end of February, sit-ins had occurred in 30 cities in seven states (including Deep South Alabama and South Carolina), and the action focus had broadened with a sit-in at a library in Petersburg, Virginia.

A little over two months later, on April 11, the first Mississippi demonstration brought the total cities affected to 78 in all 13 southern states. The rate of expansion of the movement regressed as spring examinations approached, but found new life in participation by high school students during the summer. A complete chronological list of protest cities during the spring of 1960 appears in the Appendix.

Numbers are more important at the beginning of a social movement than in later stages, for it is during the charismatic phase that the phenomenon must clearly establish itself as a movement. The best estimates I have been able to draw together[9] place the number of southern participants in the movement at somewhere around 50,000 during the initial phase in the spring of 1960. Thousands more soon were involved less directly as Negro adults were asked to boycott and were forced by the circumstances to provide legal aid, bail money and negotiating teams. Northern support and sympathy demonstrations blossomed almost overnight, as shown in part c of this chapter.

Some 2,000 demonstrators were arrested in the first wave of the movement that spring—a precursor of the mass arrests which were to become commonplace in the desegregation struggle. More than 100 students were expelled from Negro colleges for participating in demonstrations, and a dozen or more faculty members at Negro colleges had lost their jobs for their roles in the protest before the spring term ended.[10] The political institutions reacted almost immediately: most southern states passed some form of "trespass" bill amounting to an anti-sit-in law before April 1. Georgia was the first—on February 18, before any sit-ins had occurred there.

Success came rapidly, for in most cities where early sit-ins took place, some segregation customs already had been weakening for at least a decade. The first desegregation of lunch counters resulting from the movement came in San Antonio, Texas, on March 15.[11] Nashville[12] lowered lunch counter barriers on May 10—a symbolic breakthrough because the city was the scene of prolonged demonstrations, many arrests, rather unorthodox legal procedures, community bitterness and the first sustained Negro boycott. By June 1, 11 cities had desegregated some facilities as a result of the sit-ins; some 200 were to follow during the next two years.

So, within a few months, a spontaneous, uncoordinated, grass-roots revolt had grown into a full-scale social movement which years of careful strategy by civil rights professionals had not been able to accomplish.[13] It is clear from chapter 3 how societal conditions in America have been pointing toward increasing rationalization and democratization, but how can one explain the swiftness and intensity of the protest's growth at this particular time and in this particular place? At least five factors must be considered:

(1) *Personal and Situational Readiness*. Long-term changes in structural conditions, social, economic and educational levels (and therefore aspirations) and in the process of protest itself produced the state of psycho-social readiness to protest among young Negroes. It will be remembered that one-third of our Adult sample and nearly one-fourth of the Student sample mentioned growing "personal frustration" as a reason for the start and rapid spread of the sit-ins at this time.[14]

One can only get the feeling of how intense was (and is) this readiness by listening to protestors' animated descriptions of their relationship with the movement. "All you needed in this movement was a body and some discipline," commented one participant.[15] "Your relationship with the movement is just like a love affair," said another. "You can't explain it. All you know is it's something you *have* to do."[16] The vehicle analogy is accurate: "It's like waiting for a bus, man. You know where you're going all the time, but you can't get there 'til the right vehicle comes along."[17]

(2) *Demographic Factors*. The early spread of the movement is roughly consonant with two important demographic predictors of desegregation trends—urbanism and Negro/white ratio.[18] It is significant that the initial protest occurred in a city close to several other urban areas; 11 of the first 15 sit-in cities are in the Piedmont region, within a 100-mile radius of Greensboro. Urbanism and the accompanying breakdown of traditional values (and another urban phenomenon—the existence of colleges and chain stores!) seem to be determinants of sit-in spread during the early charismatic phase.[19] A charting of populations of the early protest cities is revealing:[20]

Figure 2

PROTEST CITIES BY POPULATION, FEBRUARY—JUNE, 1960

| Population | Number and % of Total of Protest Cities | |
|---|---|---|
| over 50,000 | 46 | 58% |
| 25,000-50,000 | 12 | 15% |
| 10,000-25,000 | 16 | 20% |
| under 10,000 | 4 | 7% |

Of the four cities under 10,000, two are the seat of Negro colleges (Hampton, Virginia, and Tuskegee, Alabama).

The sit-ins which took place during this period while the protest was establishing itself as a movement also conform to predictions[21] concerning Negro/white ratio; nearly 80 percent of the early demonstrations took place in the mid-South and border states where Negroes make up less than 30 percent of the population.

Figure 3

SIT-IN CITIES RANKED BY STATE'S DENSITY OF NEGRO POPULATION FEBRUARY — JUNE, 1960

| Percent Negro Population | State | Number of Cities Involved in Protest |
|---|---|---|
| Less than 20 percent | Florida | 12 |
| | Texas | 6 |
| | Tennessee | 5 |
| | Kentucky | 2 |
| | West Virginia | 2 |
| | | 27 |
| 20 – 29 percent | North Carolina | 18 |
| | Virginia | 10 |
| | Georgia | 4 |
| | Arkansas | 2 |
| | | 34 |
| 30 – 39 percent | Alabama | 4 |
| | Louisiana | 3 |
| | | 7 |
| 40 – 49 percent and over | South Carolina | 8 |
| | Mississippi | 2 |
| | | 10 |

The only exception to this low ratio, non-Deep South pattern was South Carolina, where proximity to the origin, recent industrialization (largely in textiles) and the existence of several Negro colleges probably were important variables.

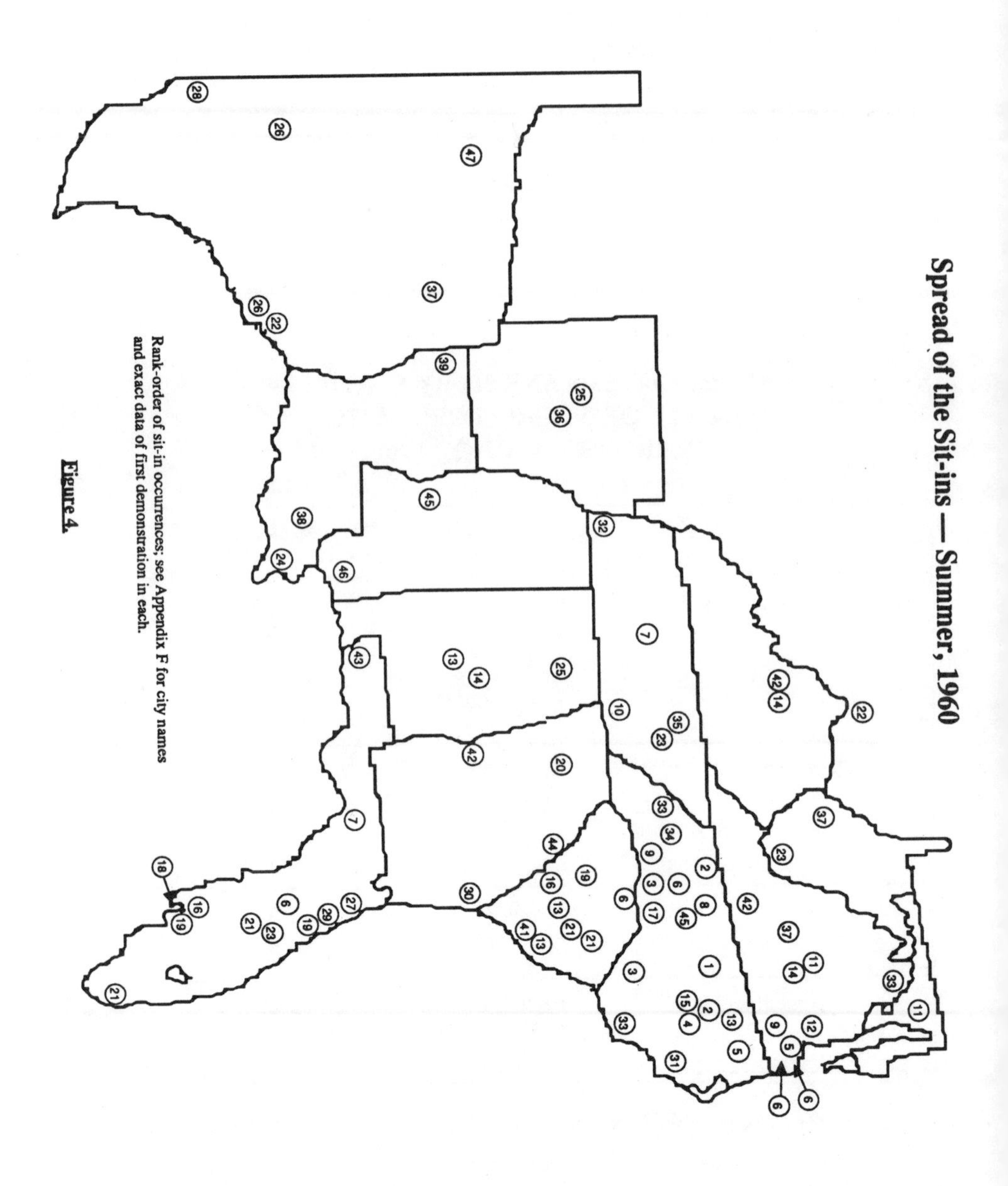

Spread of the Sit-ins — Summer, 1960

Rank-order of sit-in occurrences; see Appendix F for city names and exact data of first demonstration in each.

Figure 4.

Figure 4 on the preceeding page showing the rank-order of sit-in occurrences from February 1 to June 1, 1960, offers demographic perspective on the variables discussed in this section.

(3) *Mass Media*. The growth of a movement of such broad scope in so short a time clearly was not possible without some mechanisms of rapid and efficient communication. Radio, television and newspapers spread the word quickly. Many eventual sit-inners first heard of Greensboro this way, and six of the 13 Student informants saw "mass media communication" as an important factor in the early rapid spread of the sit-ins.[22] The strong support from northern colleges, civil rights groups and church organizations which developed almost immediately was only possible because of this kind of instantaneous communication (see section c of this chapter).

Two variations on this theme should be noted. First, the sense of movement which grew early was given an invaluable boost by the Southern Regional Council, whose image as an objective research organization gives it respectable access to media channels. As early as February 25—barely three weeks after Greensboro—the SRC had published a special report entitled, "The Student Protest Movement, Winter, 1960,"[23] which, among other things, (a) firmly called the demonstrations a "movement," (b) consciously reiterated the term "sit-in" instead of "sit-down,"[24] (c) presented background material on previous direct action campaigns, and (d) said boldly that ". . . the sit-ins mark a new trend in the Negro attack on segregation, adding to legal suits the use of economic pressure and direct action."[25] As today's perspective reveals, rarely has a social scientist interpreted such a sweeping phenomenon so well, so fast and on so little available evidence as did SRC Research Director Leslie Dunbar in that initial report. With "the movement" thus established for the "outside world," SRC continued to issue authoritative reports on the diffusion of the protest and its moral, legal and economic implications.

Ella Baker observes a second, quite uncontrolled (and uncontrollable) variable—that of the fairly stable world situation in early 1960.[26] There was no Berlin Wall, no Cuba, no Vietnam to vie for the big media space and headlines. There were no severe domestic crises; the 1959 recession was past and the 1960 elections were still months away. Thus the media had space and energy to follow the sit-ins in depth and detail. This was especially important for northern newspapers (many of whom dispatched special reporters to cover the movement), but affected the southern press as well.

(4) *College Competition*. Dunbar believes the crucial factor in diffusing the early sit-ins was the presence of a group of Negro colleges close to each other[27] and many informants have mentioned the role played by competition between Negro colleges. Thomas Pettigrew noted it on a research trip through the South in the spring of 1960, and I have observed its operation during all of my field trips from 1960 to the present. Inter-school (and therefore, inter-community) competition is built into the college situation in a way that does not hold true for, say, local NAACP chapters. So the response of Negro students to Greensboro was almost always phrased in terms of "keeping up" with the other students. "When students came to me to talk about their protest plans," recalls Tuskegee Dean Charles Gomillion, "I asked them, 'Where are you going to sit-in here?' [in predominantly rural Macon County, Alabama], 'We *have* to go,' they said. 'What will other colleges think of us if we don't?'"[28]

One commentator has suggested with a good deal of seriousness that the vehicle for diffusion through competition was the simple fact of a basketball schedule:

> The news from Greensboro was spread rapidly by the press and radio; more effectively, it spread along the basketball circuit. Most of the schools involved in the early weeks were athletic rivals; basketball games were occasions for the transfer of enthusiasm. A & T played five games in two weeks and students at each of the five schools were shortly involved in the sitdowns.[29]

(5) *Professional Diffusion*. Among the few civil rights workers who could be said to be "waiting" for something like Greensboro were Gordon Carey (CORE Field Director), James McCain (CORE Southern Field Director), Herbert Wright (NAACP Youth Secretary), Rev. James Lawson (FOR Southern Field Representative), and Dr. Martin Luther King, Jr. of SCLC. All were involved in support of the sit-ins within two weeks after the four freshmen took their seats.

Carey, McCain and several aides came to Greensboro in response to a call for help in nonviolent training from local NAACP President, Dr. George Simpkins, who had recently read a CORE pamphlet on nonviolent direct action. Close-to-life training situations were set up, with potential sit-inners subjected to verbal and physical abuse to see whether they could "take it" before going on actual demonstrations. King visited briefly from Montgomery, bringing technical advice and inspiration.[30]

Within a week, Wright was dispatched to the South to set up training institutes similar to those being conducted in Greensboro. His strong advocacy of direct action, while contrary to the stated national policy of the NAACP at that time, was a catalyst in the early diffusion of the movement.[31] On February 10, Carey called Lawson in Nashville and was told that demonstrations were already scheduled to begin the next day.[32] In fact, Lawson had led sit-in tests at department store lunch counters two months earlier, and Nashville students were planning to resume protests during Brotherhood Week (later in February) before Greensboro speeded up the timetable.[33] Lawson's deep understanding of Gandhian ethics and his long experience in direct action made Nashville a focal point for training workshops, one of which was carried in a nationwide television special in March 1960. Since then, Nashville has contributed more than its share of first-line leaders to the South-wide protests.

Professionals were helpful in many other ways. Late in February, CORE called for a nationwide boycott against discriminatory chain stores. The NAACP, after a long internal policy debate, threw the support of its nationwide network of local chapters behind the boycott in an important turning point on March 17.

Thus it was that professionals were catalytic at first; none of them could have "come down" and started a movement, but their experience played a big part in channeling the charisma generated by spontaneous social protest. Section C of this study shows that professionals see themselves as the major movers in later stages of this (and any other) movement after conscious organization sets in.

### *b. THE ORGANIZATION OF PROTEST*

Conscious organization set in early in the sit-ins. No spontaneously-generated phenomenon can sustain itself for long without some form of organization, for the charisma of the ideal wanes and the opposition learns. Perhaps organization came early here because the intensity was so great, and the overturning of traditional status relationships so startling and complete. "We used to burn up with the kind of intensity it's impossible to sustain," commented James Gibson, an early Atlanta participant and later Executive Secretary of the Atlanta NAACP branch.[34]

The growth of committees and organizations to guide the protest in local areas was immediate: the Greensboro Citizens' Association, the Nashville Nonviolent Movement, and the Committee on Appeal for Human Rights in Atlanta, for example. From the start there was need to get material and make signs, for transportation, to raise bail money, to talk with the press, to plan information and recruitment meetings and training sessions. How to contact sympathetic whites? What to do if offered a negotiation?

*The Raleigh Conference and the Student Nonviolent Coordinating Committee.*

From the beginning, the sit-ins were self-consciously more than a disconnected series of local protests. So when the call went out for demonstrators to come together during Easter vacation for a "Youth Leadership Meeting" in Raleigh, North Carolina, there was an immediate and enthusiastic response. Here, then, is perhaps the most important single juncture of the movement's organizational career, the first movement-wide sacred event—the "Raleigh Conference."

Here, as at other points, one person is largely responsible for the particular direction the movement took. Ella J. Baker, then Executive Director of the Southern Christian Leadership Conference, conceived of the meeting and coordinated it through the SCLC organization. Some movements have to search for a guiding set of principles, but this one had them ready-made and articulated through the person of SCLC President Martin Luther King, Jr. Miss Baker knew this, and the Raleigh Conference was the way to unify the young movement around this cohesive force.

More than 200 students and supporting adults (Negro and white, North and South) attended the Raleigh meeting. The brochure that brought them was a simple one-page mimeographed sheet—a primitive model of the slick paper calls to commitment which were to develop as the movement rationalized. The wording was succinct and to the point; here again, many civil rights workers had known what was needed for a long time, and finally one of them was presented with a chance to implement. Several parts of the call to Raleigh are important enough to be reproduced in full here:

TO STUDENT LEADERS:

YOUR OPPORTUNITY

* TO SHARE experiences gained in recent protest demonstrations,

AND

* TO HELP chart future goals for effective action

*WHY THIS MEETING?*

Recent lunch counter Sit-ins and other nonviolent protests by students of the South are tremendously significant developments in the drive for Freedom and Human Dignity in America.

The courageous, dedicated and thoughtful leadership manifested by hundreds of Negro students on college campuses, in large cities and small towns, and the overwhelming support by thousands of others, present new challenges for the future. This great potential for social change now calls for evaluation in terms of where do we go from here. The Easter week-end conference is convened to help find answers. Together, we can chart new goals and achieve a more unified sense of direction for *training and action in Nonviolent Resistance*.

*WHO WILL ATTEND?*

Representation is invited from all areas of recent protest. However, to be effective, a leadership conference should not be too large. For this reason, each community is being asked to send a specified number of youth leaders. Adult Freedom Fighters will be present for counsel and guidance, but the meeting will be youth centered.

Five years later, this call seems uncanny in its comprehensiveness. Here was the first crystallization of the ideology which has become second nature to all participants now: *Freedom*, *Human Dignity*, *potential for social change*, *Freedom Fighters*. The literature distributed to participants in the Raleigh Conference further structured the language of protest and showed the students the religious, philosophical and historical context with which their actions had continuity. An example is the "Statement to the Press by Dr. Martin Luther King, Jr.:"

> This is an era of offensive on the part of oppressed people. All peoples deprived of dignity and freedom are on the march on every continent throughout the world. The student sit-in movement represents just such an offensive in the history of the Negro peoples' struggle for freedom. The students have taken the struggle for justice into their own strong hands. In less than two months more Negro freedom fighters have revealed to the nation and the world their determination and courage than has occurred in many years. They have embraced a philosophy of mass direct nonviolent action. They are moving away from tactics which are suitable merely for gradual and long term change.
>
> Today the leaders of the sit-in movement are assembled here from ten states and some forty communities to evaluate these recent sit-ins and to chart future goals. They realize that they must now evolve a strategy for victory. Some elements which suggest themselves for discussion are: (1) *The need for some type of continuing organization*. Those who oppose justice are well organized. To win out the student movement must be organized. (2) *The students must consider calling for a nationwide campaign of "selective buying."* Such a program is a moral act. It is a moral necessity to select, to buy from those agencies, those stores, and businesses where one can buy with dignity and self respect. It is immoral to spend one's money where one cannot be treated with respect. (3) The students must seriously consider training a group of volunteers who will *willingly go to jail rather than pay bail* or fines. This courageous willingness to go to jail may well be the thing to awaken the dozing conscience of many of our white brothers. We are in an era in which a prison term for a freedom struggle is a badge of honor. (4) The youth must *take the freedom struggle into every community in the South without exception*. Inevitably this broadening of the struggle and the determination which it represents will arouse vocal and vigorous support and place pressures on the federal government that will compel its intervention. (5) The students will certainly want to *delve deeper into the philosophy of nonviolence*. It must be made palpably clear that resistance and nonviolence are not in themselves good. There is another element that must be present in our struggle that then makes our resistance and nonviolence truly meaningful. That element is reconciliation. Our ultimate end must be the creation of the beloved community. The tactics of nonviolence without the spirit of nonviolence may indeed become a new kind of violence.[35]

This statement, too, demonstrates the internal continuity of the movement and the powerful role of this conference and King's ideology in shaping the course of the protest. Each of the five suggestions he makes here has been implemented in many ways in the movement—not necessarily because he made them, but because they represent a correct analysis of what had to be done to effectively challenge segregation in America. The Freedom Rides and the 1964 Mississippi Summer Project, for example, were both conceived *later and independently of King and this conference* to "place pressure on the federal government that will compel its intervention."

Other conference material quoted excerpts from King's *Stride Toward Freedom*, Richard Gregg's *The Power of Nonviolence* and from some of Gandhi's *satyagraha* campaigns.

The Student Nonviolent Coordinating Committee was voted into existence at the Raleigh Conference, and representatives were elected from the southern states and the District of Columbia. Its stated organizational purpose was ". . . to coordinate activities, analyze the status of the movement and map plans for the future. It is self-directing, but welcomes the participation and assistance of supporting and observer groups."[36] A year later, SNCC had this to say about its goals and activities in a release entitled "The Raleigh Conference and the Formation of the Student Nonviolent Coordinating Committee:"

> The Student Nonviolent Coordinating Committee . . . was commissioned to work toward the coordination of the student movement. At its monthly meetings, the Committee was to evaluate the progress made in the various protest areas; to discuss, develop, and suggest strategy to these local areas; to work with supporting organizations outside the South and all groups laboring in the field of civil rights and human relations; to speak on behalf of the student movement whenever the need and opportunity arose. In short, the Committee was to aim at its title—*coordination*, on all fronts.
>
> Toward this end, our efforts have been directed. We have served as a clearing house for students who were expelled from schools because of their participation in the protests. We have sent out information about the movement and the Committee to many organizations. Efforts have been made *to establish a network of contact across the entire South*, by letters, by the newsletter, and through the work of our field personnel. The public has been kept aware of our actions and reactions through press releases. We have labored on the political front, sending delegates to the Washington, D.C. demonstrations for FREEDOM NOW and the platform committees of the Democratic and Republican National Conventions.
>
> We have received great response from all over the nation. It is our belief, and certainly our hope, that we have helped to fulfill the wishes of the Raleigh Conference. [emphasis added]

SNCC's self-conception during the first year of its existence, then, was largely one of the coordinator, as the title implies. Subcommittees on coordination, communication and finance were established, and the state representatives met every month to pool ideas and experiences. Observers were allowed in these meetings, and by the August meeting they outnumbered the delegates. The one full-time staff person during this period was Jane Stembridge, a native white southerner in theological training at Union Seminary in New York City. Office space and equipment were furnished by SCLC, and for some time the press and others often mistakenly labeled SNCC a "chapter" or "youth group" of SCLC.

During the first "breather"—summer, 1960—the annual institutes and conferences dealing with race relations found themselves devoting almost all of their time to the sit-ins. Perhaps the three most important were the annual NAACP convention in St. Paul, Minnesota, the annual Race Relations Institute at Fisk University in Nashville, and the annual CORE convention in St. Louis; I attended the latter two. All of these meetings dealt with ways of relating to the sit-in movement. A number of sit-in resolutions were hotly debated at St. Paul.[37] Time and again at Fisk, discussion group members exclaimed, "We can't seem to talk about anything but the sit-ins!"[38] Every session seemed to get around to the movement. And delegates to the annual convention of CORE—the archetypical direct action organization in America—spent most of the convention time discussing the rapidly expanding work of the organization and its field secretaries as a result of the sit-ins.

The summer was important in another way, as SNCC representatives went to both National Party Conventions, spoke to their platform committees, and played a major role in both parties' adoption of the strongest civil rights planks in history. In fact, both parties condoned nonviolent demonstrations, with the Republicans adding a clause about the rights of the individual businessman.

Demonstrations continued during that summer—most of them extensions of spring activities in cities where desegregation objectives had not been obtained. By December, approximately 90 cities had been involved, and by February 1961 (the first anniversary of the movement), there had been demonstrations in more than 100 different southern cities.

But by mid-summer 1960, attention was turning to number of successes rather than number of cities where demonstrations had occurred.[39] Several cities (including Greensboro on July 25) desegregated lunch counters during the summer quietly while many student leaders were away. A Southern Regional Council report on August 1 showed that 27 cities had desegregated some facilities as a result of the sit-ins. By October 1 the number had jumped to 94 cities—partially reflecting a meeting of U.S. Attorney General William Rogers with national chain store managers in June, in which he reportedly urged desegregation in as many cities as possible. By November, there were 115 cities, 126 by December 1, and almost 140 by the first anniversary of the movement. In many of them, demonstrations had not occurred; the possibility of direct action had been enough to move the local decision-makers to action.

The large increase in success cities in October and November reflects another important aspect of the complex relationship between protest, organization and the media. A second south-wide conference was sponsored by SNCC in Atlanta in October,[40] and the chain stores timed a press release on lunch counter desegregation to hit the papers at that time. A joint statement from Woolworth, Kress, Grant and McCrory-McClellan said that "... in some 75 percent of the southern communities affected by integration there had been no form of protest,"[41] wistfully hoping to dispell further demonstrations.

### *The Atlanta Conference and SNCC*

On the surface, the Atlanta Conference (some called it the "Second Raleigh Conference") of October 14-16, 1960, dealt with "Nonviolence and the Achievement of Desegregation."[42] But, for the sociologist, more than anything else the conference demonstrated the problems of routinization facing the movement. Money to help sponsor the conference was donated by a labor group only on the condition that a particular civil rights leader considered too far left would not be asked to speak.[43] Internally, there was an attempted take-over by several of the representatives who had been elected at Raleigh. The attempt was thinly veiled by loose adherence to rules of parliamentary procedure—forcing motions, not recognizing opposing factions who wished to speak, etc. A disproportionate share of the conference's formal meeting time (at least 70 percent is a conservative estimate) was spent on matters of internal organization rather than ideals and program. The informal underground caucuses, some of which I attended, took even more time on such matters.

The organizational problem was clearly seen by two of the major speakers, Ella Baker and Rev. James Lawson, who pleaded with the 300 participants and observers early in the conference to "keep the movement and action foremost," and "not to get bogged down in organization."[44] Further, two of my most knowledgeable and inside informants—both SNCC advisors and backers—spent most of their energy at the conference trying to guard against what they saw as a conscious attempt of SCLC to take over SNCC as a part of its growing program.[45]

SNCC entered a new phase.[46] The group of Raleigh-elected representatives who had been in power throughout the summer succeeded in getting themselves re-elected at the Atlanta Conference, and a mild form of organizational paralysis set in until a new charismatic event—the Freedom Rides—presented itself in May of 1961. The worst fears of Miss Baker, Miss Stembridge, Lawson and Miss Constance Curry (Director of the U.S. National Student Association's Southern Project and a close guide and confidant for SNCC) had been realized: *organization* had overpowered *ideals*. Projects and programs were conceived, but SNCC learned that, charismatically, you can't go home again. You cannot "start a movement," they learned—you can only hope to develop programs which capitalize on a movement which has begun.

Monthly meetings of the executive committee of SNCC were held in an attempt to mold scattered local protests into the full-scale and sustained movement they remembered from the spring. But the goals were getting more diffuse, the area deeper south, and the opposition tougher.[47] SNCC sponsored a nationwide "Election Day Action Project" on November 8 to ". . . call attention to the denial of voting rights in the South, and to the need for meaningful civil rights action."[48] But response was small and generally unnoticed in the press.

Another attempt to ignite a sweeping movement "like the good old days of 1960" took place in February 1961. Celebrating the first anniversary of the movement, several hundred students were arrested and started a short-lived "jail-in" phase by refusing bail. It began in Rock Hill, South Carolina, when Thomas Gaither (then a CORE Field Secretary after being a student leader the year before) and seven students refused bail after being sentenced to 30 days on the chain gang for a lunch counter sit-in. SNCC sent out a call for jail-inners. Several hundred came to protest, including weekend busloads from as far away as Nashville, and some were arrested. Seventy students went to jail in Atlanta on February 1 in a sympathy jail-in, but came out in two weeks when they found that the white decision-makers and the mass media were forgetting about them. The original Rock Hill group served its time. Gaither sent his "greetings and best wishes" to the CORE council meeting on February 11th and invited all council members to join him in the York County Prison Camp.[49] Several students in New Orleans and Tallahassee served short jail terms in April, but the possibility of a mass "jail-in" movement was gone.

But local efforts (many of them unreported, to be sure) continued on the motivational coattails of spring 1960.[50] Several boycotts were in process, the most effective in Savannah and Atlanta.[51] Attention turned to theatres on the first anniversary in Nashville, Hampton, Virginia, and other cities, a move initiated by students at the University of Texas. In other areas, a January 22nd "ride-in"[52] tested a bus desegregation announcement in Savannah. On March 2 the second largest number of arrests in a single outing until Birmingham 1963 took place in Columbia, South Carolina, when 187 marching students were taken into custody.[53] The incident barely rated a mention in the national press. In early April, Mississippi experienced its first sit-in (1960 action had occurred at a beach in Biloxi), provided by nine Tougaloo College students in a Jackson public library.

CORE continued the demonstrations in Louisiana and voter work in South Carolina where its main southern thrust has been concentrated since 1960, and SCLC continued to grow organizationally as it pointed toward voter education activities. Year-old court cases keep NAACP lawyers busy.

The movement temporarily seemed to have diffused into a series of local actions, with the national and regional civil rights groups desperately trying to find a unifying handle. They found it soon in the Freedom Rides, the subject of chapter 5.

### *c. A DIFFUSION OF POLITICAL AWARENESS*

Before turning to a consideration of the Freedom Rides, it is necessary to look at an important side-effect of the sit-ins without which the Freedom Rides would not have been possible. We shall call this phenomenon *a diffusion of political awareness*. Southern author and integration worker Anne Braden says it best:

> The sit-ins brought back the life-blood of citizen participation that had been scared out of our parents by the witch hunts and McCarthyism.[54]

This increasing awareness of opportunities for political participation began with northern student support of the sit-ins almost as soon as they had started. It rapidly spread upward and outward—to adults, church and labor groups, political and civic organizations. Six of my Adult informants two years later were saying that, as a result of the sit-ins, American students were beginning to take the lead in social change and revolutionary movements, and thus getting more in line with their counterparts in European, Latin American and Middle and Far Eastern universities.[55]

Tens of thousands of college students from San Diego State to Harvard joined sympathy picket lines, formed activist organizations, raised money for bail and fine fees, and helped set up scholarship funds for expelled sit-inners in the spring of 1960. Analysts of the collegiate culture like David Riesman, with whom I have discussed this at length, agree that the new political activism of college students of the 1960s was brought to the surface largely by the impact of the sit-ins. The celebrated campus apathy of the 1950s is gone. West Coast students protested House Committee on Un-American Activities hearings in the much-publicized San Francisco demonstrations of May 12-14 . . . Student protests of U.S. policy regarding Cuba increased . . . Campus peace groups grew—all from a latent (if not dead) start after the sit-ins reawakened political activism.

It is impossible to record all of the local student groups formed from the impetus of the sit-ins, but one may point to the Progressive Students League at Oberlin, the Ann Arbor Direct Action Committee, Boston's Emergency Public Integration Committee (EPIC), Students for Integration at the University of Minnesota, and Slate Political Party in the Berkeley area as representative examples. And on a national level, Students for a Democratic Society has become a major force in university politics since its inception by sit-in inspired activists.

The story of EPIC in Boston during 1960 is perhaps representative of the nature and development of sit-in support groups in other cities.[56] It was formed late in February 1960 to coordinate the activities of groups and individuals who desired to support the sit-in movement. Organized and populated by students, EPIC recruited adult groups and approached a 50/50 student/adult membership ratio by the end of the spring. Members picketed 18 Boston area Woolworth stores, obtained more than 10,000 signatures on a "Don't Shop at Woolworth's" petition, initiated a letter-writing campaign to Woolworth's main office, sponsored a rally featuring Harry Belafonte which raised $10,000, and engaged in many other supportive activities for the southern protest. More than 600 Boston area citizens actively worked in EPIC and 6,000 attended the rally. A list of participating groups indicates the wide appeal of this kind of activity:

*Students From:*

Harvard, Brandeis, Massachusetts Institute of Technology, Boston University, Tufts, Northeastern, Wellesley, Radcliffe, Cardinal Cushing College, Emmanuel, Eastern Nazarene, Simmons, Holy Cross, Episcopal Theological Seminary, Cambridge School of Weston.

*Community Groups:*

Interdenominational Ministerial Alliance of Greater Boston, Boston NAACP, Greater Boston CORE, International Ladies Garment Workers Union, International Union of Electrotypographers, United Packing Workers, America Veterans Committee, Fellowship of Reconciliation, Roxbury Elks Club, AFL-CIO.

Political activity on these campuses and within these groups has not been the same since EPIC—a fact which holds true for nearly every urban area college community in the United States.

Local support from latent sources in the South also came rapidly. Church women were especially active—a phenomenon reminiscent of the role of the Association of Southern Women for the Prevention of Lynching 30 years earlier.[57] On February 18 the Greensboro Council of Church Women wrote the local Kress and Woolworth managers assuring them that the white women of Greensboro would "support a policy of equal service."[58]

The participants from virtually every Negro college in the South were joined almost immediately by white students. Without systematically surveying such participation, I knew of white involvement in the first months of the sit-in movement from Agnes Scott College, Duke University, Emory University, Fisk University, University of Florida, the Florida State University, Georgia Tech, Greensboro College, Huntingdon College, Loyola University, Mercer University, University of North Carolina, University of Oklahoma, Peabody College, Randolph-Macon Woman's College, Scarritt College, Southern Methodist University, Stetson University, University of Texas, Tulane University, Vanderbilt University, University of Virginia, Wake Forest College, and Woman's College of the University of North Carolina.[59]

On March 7 the North Carolina Human Relations Council wrote to lunch counter managers in the state citing examples of peaceful desegregation in Salisbury, Fayetteville and Chapel Hill, and urging them to follow a similar policy.[60] And in Nashville the call for a biracial committee to work out plans for desegregation drew immediate public support from the local chapters of such groups as the American Association of University Women and the League of Women Voters.[61]

It is easy to see, then, from the most cursory look at the response of student and local community groups, that many persons and organizations had been "talking and ready" for a long time. Nearly every major religious group, for instance, had a firm pronouncement on desegregation before 1960.[62] A structure of acceptance through voluntary associations had been building for many years, and there is no question that these groups have been rejuvenated by the sit-ins and subsequent activism.[63]

To get a clearer picture of the structure of support into which the movement so rapidly fell, one may look at the various political, labor, religious, student and civic groups and publications which explicitly approved the sit-ins *before May 1, 1960*, via resolution, financial aid and/or direct participation:[64]

— Board of Managers of United Church Women (church women urged to support merchants who desegregate, give money to movement, promote biracial committees).
— Board of Social and Economic Relations of the Methodist Church.
— *Presbyterian Outlook*.
— National Student Christian Federation.
— Division of Racial Minorities and Division of Christian Citizenship of the Protestant Episcopal Church.
— 127 of 180 faculty members in Arts and Sciences and 14 of 15 in Divinity at Vanderbilt University (especially relevant because of the expulsion of sit-in leader James Lawson, a Methodist minister and B.D. candidate).
— United Presbyterian Church.
— Board of Home Missions of the Congregational Christian Churches (offers to serve as clearing house for contributions to the movement).
— Department of Christian Social Relations, Women's Division of Christian Service, The Methodist Church.
— U.S. National Student Association, and a student conference sponsored jointly by USNSA and the Taconic Foundation.
— American Association of University Professors in annual meeting.
— World University Service (Board of Trustees endorses and offers to help relocate expelled students).
— Young Adult Council.
— Americans for Democratic Action, Campus Division.
— American Youth Hostels.
— YMCA of the United States.
— Liberal Religious Youth.
— Lisle Foundation.
— Youth Division, NAACP.

— National Council of Catholic Youth.
— National Scholarship Service and Fund for Negro Students.
— North American Student Cooperative League.
— Students for a Democratic Society.
— United Christian Youth Movement.
— Workmen's Circle.
— Young Christian Workers.
— Young Democratic Clubs of America.
— Young Republican National Federation.
— State Human Relations Councils (in all southern states where they exist; most offer aid in reconciliation, too).

It should be remembered that this list does not include the many established civil rights groups and human relations agencies which supported the movement from the first days with advice, leadership training, and financial support. Such a listing is only intended to be suggestive of the number and scope of voluntary associations which supported the sit-ins almost immediately. And many groups joined later, including for instance, the National Federation of Canadian University Students, who supported the 1961 jail-ins.

From February 1, 1960, to May 1, 1961, then, a "new" form of social protest was introduced, became a movement, brought almost instant support and success on several planes and was well on the way to full legitimation. "The students," said Ella Baker, an observer of the last 30 years of the desegregation process from the inside, "have the first real revolution in this whole struggle."[65]

FIVE

# The Freedom Rides (1961): A Nation Reacts

This rebellion marks a lessening of hope and faith in the process of the courts, of elections, of Congress, and of education . . . No one should expect this kind of [protest] to disappear . . .

—Walter Lippman[1]

It is somewhat disconcerting to walk into a men's room under the eyes of TV cameras, and to have two policemen follow you.

—a Freedom Rider[2]

These reactions of a noted political analyst and a Freedom Rider indicate something of the social etiology, motivation, goals and effects of the Freedom Rides—the second phase of the direct action movement of the 1960s. The turn to direct action as a major mode of protest has marked, in Lippman's words, a "lessening of hope and faith" in the institutionalized processes for redress of grievance and social change in America. And a walk into the men's room was not only disconcerting for southern custom, laws and law-enforcement; it called the federal government and the nation to confront anew the relationship of federalism and individual civil rights.

In this chapter the Freedom Rides are viewed as the focus of the direct action movement during its second year and the symbol of new directions which are still shaping the course of the protest.

## *a. THE FREEDOM RIDES OF SUMMER, 1961: SYMBOL OF THE MATURING PROCESS*

For some months prior to the spring of 1961, the movement was undergoing a broadening of focus—a major precondition of the transition from reform to revolution.[3] Direct actionists had moved rapidly from the lunch counters to parks, pools, theatres, restaurants, churches, libraries, museums, art galleries, laundromats, golf courses, beaches, courtrooms, jails and other local facilities. Desegregation had come somewhere in all of these services and accommodations during the first year. One of the logical next moves was to a broader-than-local focus: interstate transportation facilities.

Too, the civil rights organizations had been playing an ever-expanding role in the movement with their legal, financial and leadership assistance. The February, 1961, Rock Hill arrests which began the attempt at a jail-in movement, for instance, were the result of a local CORE Action Institute in December of 1960.[4] SCLC and the NAACP continued action projects and boycotts, SNCC was growing as a force for initiation as well as communication, and all the organizations had started programs of nationwide support for intimidated and displaced Negroes who had registered in Haywood and Fayette counties, Tennessee.

It is in this context of a broadening focus and growing *organizational involvement* that the Freedom Rides took place. The Rides began as an organizational project and developed into a new phase of a mass movement—a reversal of what happened with the sit-ins, which were spontaneously combusted as a mass movement and soon routinized under programs of the civil rights groups. One perceptive informant notes in response to charges of "organizational agitation" in the Freedom Rides that only the first Ride was *not* spontaneous. Unexpectedly, then, a project "caught on," and the organizations' search for a motivational and fund-raising focus was over for a while.[5]

### *A Chronology of the Freedom Rides*[6]

The Rides caught on quite unexpectedly. They began quite unobtrusively in a bus-riding conversation between CORE staff members Gordon Carey and Thomas Gaither in the winter of 1961.[7] Carey broached the subject at the CORE Council Meeting in Lexington, Kentucky, in February 1961. I recall the way it was buried in mountains of organizational business ranging from "Disaffiliations" to "Report on Associated Drygoods Corporation Project,"[8] and how it got a favorable but not enthusiastic response. To all of us, it seemed like another appropriate application of the direct action approach.

CORE later told the purpose of the "Freedom Ride, 1961," with an innocuous statement linking this project to the 1947 Journey of Reconciliation. It went on:

> The *Freedom Ride* will differ from its predecessor in three important respects. First, it will penetrate . . . into the Deep South. Second, it will challenge segregation not only aboard buses but in terminal eating facilities, waiting rooms, rest stops, etc. Third, participants who are arrested will remain in jail rather than accept . . . bail or payment of fines . . .
>
> The main purpose of the *Freedom Ride*, like the Journey 14 years ago, is to make bus desegregation a reality instead of merely an approved legal doctrine. By demonstrating that a group *can* ride buses in a desegregated manner even in the Deep South, CORE hopes to encourage other people to do likewise.[9]

Like the 1947 Journey, the 1961 Ride was testing southern compliance with a Supreme Court ruling. Late in 1960, the Court had ruled in *Boynton v. Commonwealth of Virginia* (364 U.S. 454) that discrimination against interstate travelers in terminal facilities—whether or not owned by the carrier—violates the Interstate Commerce Act.[10] There was another important tie to the 1947 protest trip: a participant in both was James Farmer, newly named director of CORE in February 1961. Farmer eventually was to spend more than a month in a Mississippi prison and further establish the national reputation of CORE as a leading militant direct action organization.

CORE carefully recruited an interracial, interregional team of 16 for the initial Ride. All knew the dangers involved. Although some were experienced protestors, all underwent rigorous training sessions in nonviolent philosophy and methods before the Ride. The project was to begin in Washington, D.C., on May 4 and culminate with a rally in New Orleans on May 17, the anniversary of the 1954 school desegregation decision. "I will either spend May 17," said Farmer, "in New Orleans or in a Mississippi jail." In time, he was to keep both appointments.

Elaborate preparation was made along the route. Gaither traveled the entire route arranging for mass meetings, housing, legal aid, etc. He enlisted the help of several local NAACP chapters and other Negro groups, and unknowingly opened the way for the Negro community mobilization that was to characterize the next phase of the movement.

Since the Freedom Rides represent such an important turning point in the maturation of the movement, a condensed chronology of those several crucial days follows:[11]

| | |
|---|---|
| March 13 | CORE publicly announces Freedom Ride. |
| April 28 | CORE writes to President Kennedy, informing him of plans. |
| May 4 | Ride begins in Washington; arrives in Richmond. |
| May 7 | Arrival in Danville, Virginia; dispute over restaurant service settled quietly at Trailways terminal. |
| May 8 | Arrival in Charlotte, North Carolina; arrest of one Rider for trespass while seeking shoe shine at Union Bus Terminal. |
| May 9 | Arrival in Rock Hill, South Carolina and attack in Greyhound terminal; white waiting room at Trailways terminal closed when bus pulls in. |
| May 10 | Defendant in Charlotte trespass case acquitted. Two riders arrested in Winnsboro, South Carolina, and released after several hours; charges dropped. |
| May 12 | Arrival in Augusta, Georgia; use all facilities. |
| May 13 | Travel through Athens, Georgia, where all facilities used; arrival in Atlanta where restaurant closed at Greyhound terminal. |
| | Court of Appeals of the Fifth Circuit directs a lower court to "obliterate" the distinction between interstate and intrastate passengers at the train terminal in Birmingham. This was one of many stations in the South with one waiting room for all interstate passengers, and a second for Negro intrastate travelers. |
| May 14 | Some Riders served at Trailways station in Atlanta. Entire group (minus Farmer, who temporarily leaves ride upon word of the death of his father in Washington) leaves for Birmingham, riding in Trailways and Greyhound buses. |
| | Department of Justice advises Birmingham police it has received warnings of planned violence there. Mob prevents passengers from getting off Greyhound bus in Anniston, Alabama. Slit tires go flat six miles south of Anniston, men following in automobiles prevented from boarding disabled bus by a state |

law-enforcement officer on bus. Bus is destroyed by incendiary bomb. Newsphoto of flaming bus circulates widely. All passengers removed, and 12 admitted to hospital, mostly for smoke inhalation; they later resumed ride to Birmingham.

On Trailways bus, Anniston mob beats one Negro and two white Riders. Bus continues to Birmingham, where Riders and newsmen attacked by hostile natives.[12] Rider James Peck of CORE national staff severely beaten, requiring 50 head stitches. No arrests at either Anniston or Birmingham. Despite warnings of probable trouble, no police are on hand in Birmingham, and none arrive until ten minutes after fighting begins. (It is Mother's Day. When Birmingham Police Chief Bull Connor is asked why there were no policemen at the Trailways station to avert violence, he explains that most of the men are off duty visiting their mothers.)[13]

May 15 — Greyhound drivers refuse to take group to Montgomery; Riders fly to New Orleans.

Alabama Governor John Patterson issues his first statement, advising Riders to "get out of Alabama as quickly as possible." U.S. Attorney General Robert Kennedy asks the state to provide police protection; the Governor first agrees, then changes his position. The Governor later says, "We may even take out all the terminals and let them stop at telephone poles.[14]

May 16 — CORE Riders stay in seclusion in New Orleans. In Birmingham, federal arrests begin for violence of the 14th.

May 17 — Riders meet at church in New Orleans, then disband, ending original CORE-planned ride.

But Nashville students, led by many who were active in the sit-ins the year before, arrive in Birmingham to carry on Freedom Rides. Policemen meet bus, escort into city, arrest 10 Riders and take five sympathizers (Birmingham Negroes) into protective custody.

May 18 — Riders stay in jail. The five Birmingham Negroes released. Attorney General Kennedy tries unsuccessfully to reach Governor Patterson by telephone.

May 19 — Connor carries most Riders to Tennessee line by car in early morning. They are back in Birmingham by bus in the afternoon, joined by about 10 others, where they unsuccessfully seek bus service to Montgomery.

Alabama court enjoins CORE and followers from further "freedom rides," patrolmen read order on incoming buses. Governor is unavailable by phone to President and Attorney General, but Justice aide confers with Governor.

May 20 Governor says "We are not going to escort these agitators." At 8:30 a.m., waiting Nashville Riders finally taken on Greyhound bus to Montgomery. FBI advises local police of possible violence, is assured that local authority sufficient. Bus arrives; no uniformed police on hand, "race riot involving hundreds" breaks out. At least six Riders beaten; most severely beaten is James Zwerg, white, who lies in street for an hour awaiting Negro ambulance.[15] News photographers attacked, beaten, kicked, their equipment smashed. "A Negro—not a Freedom Rider—was set afire by some of the mob after they had poured kerosene over him."[16] Justice department official knocked unconscious. Police arrive about 10 minutes after fighting begins.

After again failing to reach Governor, U.S. Attorney General orders federal marshals to Montgomery, and obtains Federal District Court injunction against Ku Klux Klan, National States Rights Party and other individuals interfering with "peaceful interstate travel by bus." President John Kennedy appeals to state and local Alabama officials for order.

May 21 Federal marshals continue to arrive.

Dr. Martin Luther King, Jr., cuts short speaking tour and flies to Montgomery to address Negro mass meeting at a church. Young white mob forms, pens Negroes in church all night after bitter rioting. Governor proclaims martial law in Montgomery. Deputy U.S. Attorney General Byron White confers with Governor, who angrily denounces federal intervention.

American Nazi Party announces plan to send "hate bus" from Washington to New Orleans.[17]

Alabama Associated Press Association condemns "breakdown of civilized rule" in Alabama, praises Public Safety Director Floyd Mann as "the one notable [exception]." Mississippi Governor Barnett wires offer of support to Governor Patterson.

| | |
|---|---|
| May 22 | 800 National Guardsmen on duty. More federal marshals ordered in. Montgomery Ministerial Association calls for "all necessary steps" to prevent further mob violence.<br><br>"Hate bus" leaves Washington.<br><br>Federal agents arrest four men in Anniston bus-burning.[18] Additional students from Nashville, New Orleans and New York begin arriving in New Orleans as spirit of mass protest grows. |
| May 23 | "Hate bus" escorted through Montgomery by federal officers, reaches New Orleans.<br><br>Montgomery quiet as National Guardsmen patrol city. Governor blames Sunday night riot on federal marshals.<br><br>Justice Department officials in continuing telephone contact with Mississippi officials.<br><br>King, Farmer, Montgomery minister Ralph Abernathy and Nashville students Diane Nash and John Lewis hold press conference, announce Ride will continue regardless of cost.<br><br>A few more students arrive in Montgomery.<br><br>In Montgomery: Rotary Club demands withdrawal of federal marshals; Chamber of Commerce calls on local law enforcement agencies to "maintain and preserve" law and order; Junior Chamber condemns "agitators" and regrets failure of local police; Alabama legislature convenes, unanimously commends Governor for proclaiming martial law, denounces Freedom Riders and federal intervention.<br><br>Louisiana legislature commends Governor Patterson; Governor Barnett has Mississippi National Guard on stand-by alert. |
| May 24 | Some Riders eat breakfast at terminal, then heavily protected and escorted by National Guardsmen, leave for Mississippi. The rest come on a second bus later in the morning. Changing of the guard takes place at Mississippi line; 27 arrested seeking service in Jackson with no disturbance, charged with breach of peace and refusal to obey an officer.<br><br>Additional Riders arrive in Montgomery, including professors and students from the North. |

Justice Department asks in Federal District Court for injunction to prevent heads of Birmingham and Montgomery police departments from interfering with interstate travel.

Attorney General issues appeal for a "cooling-off period." Civil rights organizational officials promptly say "no."

Greyhound Corporation orders disciplinary action against Montgomery employees who had refused food service to Negroes.

In New Orleans, "hate bus" passengers jailed for "unreasonably" alarming the public.

In LaGrange, Georgia, five men attempting to organize resistance to latest Freedom Ride bus are arrested.

May 25 Montgomery Negro leader shot in wrist from passing car.

Latest group of Riders arrested while eating at Trailways terminal in Montgomery, including Rev. Wyatt T. Walker of SCLC, Abernathy and Birmingham minister Fred Shuttlesworth.

May 26 King announces in Atlanta a "temporary lull but no cooling off" in the Rides.

Police Chiefs in Birmingham and Montgomery under subpoena to produce records of their activities.

In Montgomery, northern professors and students post bail.

In Jackson, the 27 are convicted, fined $200 each, given 60 days suspended jail sentences. Police dogs on duty in front of courthouse during trial.

Roy Wilkins, Executive Secretary of NAACP, dissents from "cooling off" request.

May 27 Americans for Democratic Action vice chairman urges Riders to disregard "cooling off" plea.

A "Freedom Riders Coordinating Committee" is formed in Atlanta, composed of representatives of CORE, SCLC, SNCC and the Nashville Nonviolent Movement.

May 28 — Seventeen Riders arriving from Montgomery and Memphis arrested in Jackson white waiting room. Again, the arrests are cleanly handled with no violence.

May 29 — Trial begins in Montgomery on federal charges against Birmingham and Montgomery police heads. Martial law ends.

In Jackson, 19 of the first group of Riders are put to work at a prison farm. The 17 who arrived May 28 are convicted on breach of peace charges and sentenced to 60 days or $200; they choose jail.

In LaGrange, Georgia, three of those arrested May 24 are convicted and two bound over to a higher court.

Attorney General Kennedy requests the Interstate Commerce Commission to ban by regulation segregation in interstate bus terminals (which had already been accomplished in theory by earlier ICC rulings and the Supreme Court's Boynton decision).

June-July[19] — CORE, SCLC, SNCC and the Nashville Nonviolent Movement mobilize more Riders from North and West Coast for Rides to Jackson in an effort to focus the effort on a symbolic hard-core area. Many Negro Riders are veterans of southern sit-ins, while most of the whites are non-South young people.[20] More than 400 are arrested in Jackson under a cut-and-dried procedure which allows for no mob violence (and little exercise of constitutional rights on the part of the Riders).

More than 300 spend from a week to two months in Parchman Prison and other Mississippi jails, however, and the reports of beatings, torture and other mistreatment there are unparalleled in their brutality up to this point in the movement.[21]

Ten rabbis and ministers are arrested at Tallahassee airport in July.

Labor, educational and religious groups raise money for court costs.

August 5 — City of Jackson informs CORE that all Freedom Riders released on $500 appeal bonds (about 150) must appear in person in Jackson on August 14 for individual trials or forfeit the bond.[22] This is one of a series of moves by Mississippi to financially break CORE and the movement. NAACP and other groups organize legal support.

August 14 — CORE succeeds in getting most defendants to Jackson to save appeal bonds, but spends thousands of dollars to do it. First of many Riders convicted as expected [but ". . . a Supreme Court ruling on unsegregated transportation service on February 26, 1962 . . . makes the . . . convictions unlikely to stand."[23]].

August 15 — Interstate Commerce Commission begins hearings on Attorney General Kennedy's request for a ruling banning segregation in terminals and terminal-related facilities.[24]

Sept. 22 — ICC issues order banning segregation in interstate terminal facilities, effective November 1.[25]

October 16 — Three major railroads serving the Deep South announce end of segregation in both trains and terminals.[26]

November 1 — ICC order becomes effective. Tests show compliance in most areas except Mississippi, parts of Louisiana, and southern Georgia. Federal government obtains injunctions against all tested facilities in Mississippi and Louisiana, resulting in at least temporary desegregation.

### *Importance of the Freedom Rides to the Movement*

There is no question that the Freedom Rides marked an important turning point in the direct action movement which, for several months before the Rides, had been floundering in organizational attempts to regain the mass charismatic base of the protests. To the unstructured question, "Have there been any big 'turning points' in the course of the movement?", 54 percent of the Student informants and 40 percent of the Adults replied, "the Freedom Rides." No other phenomenon was mentioned by more than 17 percent of the Adults (five of 30 noted the advent of economic pressure from the adult community as significant). Forty-six percent of the Student informants spontaneously mentioned the events surrounding the change in SNCC's format in the summer of 1961 (see chapter 8), but this, too, was directly stimulated by the Freedom Rides.[27]

More than any other event or series of events, then, *the Rides represent a major transition from the early spontaneous and charismatic activities of the sit-inners to the more difficult, dangerous and complicated planned projects of the last few years*—in the words of the direct actionists, "getting down to the knitty-gritty."

As noted early in the chapter, the Freedom Rides were representative of the maturation of the direct action movement because they attacked broader and more complicated problems than local lunch counters and because they involved more intense organizational support and participation. The foregoing chronology makes it clear that there were many other ways in which the developing directions of the protest came together in the *kairotic* events of the Rides. Most important was the planned and direct challenge to the federal government, which is treated in the last section of this chapter. Other elements symbolic of the maturing movement may be summarized as follows:

(1) *The "nationalization" of the Movement*. The national mobilization of conscience which had begun in Montgomery and grown in 1960 reached full bloom with the Freedom Rides. There was greater-than-ever participation by non-southerners and whites, by clergy and academicians of national note. With the polemic removed, segregationist charges of "outsider" were technically correct; "After all," writes critic-participant Thomas Kahn, "who else would use interstate transportation if not the people from out of state?"[28]

With national involvement, new-found channels of communication and pressure on southern officials opened up.[29] The Minnesota Attorney General, for instance, asked his counterpart in Mississippi ". . . to investigate reports [that] Minnesotans were 'incarcerated like felons'" and that the privacy of young women Freedom Riders ". . . was invaded because they are under constant supervision of male prison guards."[30] And the international proportions of the Rides were magnified with the story in July of an Indonesian exchange student who Mississippi officials refused to arrest "as a courtesy because he was a visitor to this country."[31]

It has also been argued (even among deeply committed agency personnel) that the Freedom Rides were not healthy for the civil rights movement because of the mass influx of only situationally-committed demonstrators. Many were northern and west coast whites, some of whom bore uncertain characterlogical and ideological credentials. Public opinion poll data from June 1961 showed an almost 3-1 disapproval of the Rides in a nationwide sample.[32]

A major latent function of this nationalization has been the activation of civil rights activities in the North and West by non-southern Riders whose own commitment was intensified by the stressful situations of Ride, trial and jail. And money was poured in to the civil rights organizations by newly-sensitized persons who could not participate directly.[33]

(2) *Development of "Hard-core Professionals."* This form of action required deeper commitment than the earlier sit-ins. There were naturally fewer participants, and those who did take part knew they faced almost sure physical and/or mental harassment. The barriers were more rigid, the strategies more complex—and this is more true every day in 1965 as the movement reaches more rigid racism and more complex and subtle forms of segregation. The deeper commitment by a relatively small group of actionists was indicated early when the Riders and their organizations immediately and unanimously rejected the Justice Department's call for a "cooling-off" period after the Montgomery violence. Had they not taken this stand, an unhealthy precedent would have been established: segregationists would know that any time they wished to slow down the drive for desegregation they need only turn to violence to enlist the aid of even the federal government in their cause.

(3) *Shifting Focus to the Deep South*. The local and national reaction to the Freedom Rides was instrumental in decisions by the civil rights groups to carry the protest squarely to the most recalcitrant and dangerous areas of the nation. As early as August 1960, I had heard SNCC militants eager to move as an organization to Alabama and Mississippi.[34] Yet it was not possible until something like the Freedom Rides "penetrated daringly . . . into these two citadels of caste," as Leslie Dunbar wrote during the summer of 1961. "This is likely to be a telling defeat for Alabama and Mississippi," he concluded, "just as it would be for any tyranny whose fearsome myth of invincibility had been defied, and the defiant not destroyed."[35] He was right, for since then the movement has found its spiritual and financial lifeblood more and more in the rural Deep South confrontation.

(4) *Confrontation of Southern Community Factions*. The Freedom Rides broke the charade of silence and with it the monolithic hold of the racist ethos on many Deep South communities. The events of May 1961 were too brutal, too shocking, for any but the most callous to keep quiet. Crisis forces people to take stands—or at least to bring latent positions out into the open. The various pronouncements listed under May 23 in the chronology in this chapter are an example. "Only a few newspapers, such as

the *Alabama Journal*," notes the Southern Regional Council,[36] "defended or did not criticize Governor Patterson and the Birmingham and Montgomery police." The *Birmingham News* editorialized that "We asked for federal intervention—and we got it." It added that "We the people—the newspaper people, the lawyers, the bankers, the executives, the labor leaders, the clergy, and the average householders, workers and businessmen" permitted "intolerance and brutality to take over . . . We the people have let gangs of vicious men ride this state now for months."[37] The Rides led most southern papers to comment—many for the first time in such circumstances—"Our politicians have led us to this!"[38]

Freedom Rider and Union Seminary theologian Robert McAfee Brown saw another side of this process. The real purpose of the Rides, he writes, is to give encouragement to southern [white] "liberals." "They cannot, for local reasons, engage in Freedom Rides or even openly approve of them, but they can perhaps pick up and build upon whatever a Freedom Ride may have done to loosen segregation patterns in their own towns."[39] And often another phase of the "loosening" process aids the movement: "We created a climate in Mississippi where it's at least possible to keep an office open," says Diane Nash Bevel.[40]

Encouragement to the local Negro community is at least as great a by-product. This has been true particularly in Albany, Georgia, and in Jackson, Mississippi. I have observed the positive responses of Albany Negroes to outside help on several occasions. And former CORE Field Secretary Thomas Gaither reports that before the Freedom rides he could get only one Jackson Negro family to agree to house a Rider, but that since 1961 there are literally hundreds of Negro homes in Jackson where a pro-integrationist visitor of any color may be housed.[41] In short, as Laue writes, crisis brings stand-taking within both Negro and white communities where previously it may not have been "necessary, permitted, and/or safe."[42]

(5) *Mobilization and Cooperation of Civil Rights Groups*. Since 1960, organizational conflict has been intensified among the civil rights groups as they competed for an ever bigger share of the civil rights contribution dollar and for recognition in the swift success of direct action. The Freedom Ride crisis brought a temporary halt to the in-fighting as the major organizations (CORE, SNCC, SCLC and NAACP) mobilized people, money, legal aid and publicity in record time after the Alabama violence and move to Mississippi. The Freedom Ride Coordinating Committee was short-lived, however. The organizations refused to relinquish their autonomy,[43] and

formal cooperation after June was minimal until the unifying crisis of Birmingham, 1963, and the March on Washington.[44]

Even more significant in demonstrating the intricate linkages between civil rights groups is the entrance of the Nashville students after the original CORE Ride had been abandoned. When they came to Montgomery, and sparked the Rides to movement proportions, the protest had gone full-circle—for they had been trained and inspired by Rev. James Lawson, who was still acting under inspiration he received working with King and the bus boycott in Montgomery in 1956.[45]

### *b. THE FREEDOM RIDES AND THE FEDERAL GOVERNMENT*

The sit-ins were addressed to local custom and to the hopefully guilty consciences of segregationists. While the Freedom Rides may have shaken up these constituencies, the real target was the federal government and its powers of enforcement in the area of civil rights. The Rides' deepest significance as a symbol of things to come in the movement lies in their bold challenge to American federalism.[46]

The Freedom Rides were, from the beginning, conceived as an attack on clearly unconstitutional state laws and a challenge to the federal government to enforce the considerable powers it already possessed in the area of civil rights. This was CORE's aim—to effect a rapid mobilization of the federal powers which already existed. This aim was realized through:

- the considerable intervention by the Department of Justice on an informal level;
- the attempts at communication by the President and the Attorney General;
- the sending of marshals;
- the nationwide publicity which put further pressure on the federal government to protect the rights of American citizens (some of them semi-notables) wherever they travel within the United States;
- the ICC ruling on interstate terminal facilities and its subsequent enforcement.[47]

Not only did the Freedom Rides confront the federal government with a demand for immediate enforcement of civil rights protections, but they served as the first of many motivational barbs which were to move the Department of Justice to action in hopes of *avoiding* similar crises situations.[48] It was a clear case of avoidance learning in which the federal government learned along with Deep South communities that the best way to avoid a severe racial crisis is to promote *some* desegregation before *all* is demanded. Thus, the Justice Department turned more diligently to prosecution of voting cases (there were other reasons involved, as we shall see) in hopes of persuading the direct actionists to turn their attentions in this direction. To some degree, the Department succeeded, as outlined in the next chapter.

---

Other things happened in 1961, to be sure.[49] But just as the importance of 1960 is symbolized by several months of sit-ins, so do the Freedom Rides serve as a focus in understanding the trends established in 1961. Of the other protests taking place in 1961, many were in some way tied to the resonant chord struck in persons and organizations by the Rides.[50] James Farmer could write truthfully upon his release from Parchman Prison in July that "The last few months have revolutionized the civil rights scene."[51]

There certainly was a revolution in the growth and prestige of CORE and other civil rights groups.[52] But perhaps the biggest change of all was not one of organization or technique—but one of attitude, in the intensified commitment and determination of men like Farmer and King, and of thousands of Americans who were only "with you in spirit" before. More than anything else, the Rides and their reactions made people see the difficulty and danger of the desegregation process as it rushed toward more difficult barriers. If the hard-core problems of the deepest of Deep South rural areas were to be attacked, *now*, there would have to be an intensification of commitment, a sharpening of strategy, a new ability to patiently outsmart fast-learning segregationist community leaders. In short, the sit-ins had made it look too easy; in 1961, the movement learned that Deep South defensive traditionalism was different from Border South moderation.

Thus it was that the movement learned from the Freedom Rides that the road ahead would be longer, harder, more hostile and more violent than anyone dared to imagine.[53]

SIX

# Albany and Beyond

It was too late. We had delivered the idea that would disrupt the system . . We mocked the system that teaches men to be good Negroes instead of good men.

—Charles Sherrod of SNCC[1]

This is a Deep South city, with a hundred-year history of Negro silence and white complacency which has now been shattered for all time.

—Professor Howard Zinn[2]

The Freedom Rides "delivered" many ideas to many people—to the federal government, to southern Negroes and some whites, and to the nation at large. But the most important message of the Rides came as a feedback to the civil rights leaders and organizations themselves. It was the realization that, *without a carefully planned, concentrated, sustained attack, the movement would not come in force to the rural Deep South for many years*. In Sherrod's words, the idea that would disrupt the system of segregation could not have been delivered to the rural Deep South without this realization.

Since this moment of truth, the major efforts of the movement have been directed toward cracking the tight white political structure in the Deep South.[3] This task has provided the unifying goal around which were built new organizational structures both locally and nationally, new techniques of community mobilization and change, two federal civil rights laws, and a new sense of cooperative "movement" for a strengthened cause against an entrenched system.

Even the institutional forms which these new directions were to take came from the impetus of the Freedom Rides. "We got the idea of mobilizing the whole community," said SNCC Field Secretary Charles Sherrod, "from the way the people responded in Jackson. Local folk stood up against the system as they never had before—many [more than 50] went to jail with the Freedom Riders."[4] Sherrod and others knew that only through involving the total class spectrum of the Negro community in sustained political action could the system be broken in the Deep South.

But how to prepare for this action? James Forman, who assumed the job as SNCC Executive Secretary in the crucial period of fall, 1961, knew how. A student of revolutionary history and contemporary African movements, Forman points out that ". . . a small, disciplined group of revolutionaries has often been able to accomplish more than large democratic groups."[5]

But neither Sherrod nor Forman—who were to play such important roles later—initiated the internal changes in the movement which led to mobilization for extensive political action in the Deep South. Rather it was a former Vice President of the U.S. National Student Association, Howard University Negro student Tim Jenkins, who conceived and operationalized "the takeover"[6] of SNCC that changed it, in his words, "from an amorphous movement to an organization."[7]

## *a. ALBANY REALLY BEGAN IN NASHVILLE*

The catalyst for change in SNCC, and, therefore, eventually the whole movement, was a "Special Southern Student Leadership Seminar" organized by Jenkins and held in Nashville July 30 to August 26, 1961. "We made a calculated attempt to pull the best people out of the movement," said Jenkins, "and give them a solid academic approach to understanding the movement. What we needed now was information, not inspiration."[8]

### *The Seminar*

Early in the summer, Jenkins had prepared a seminar prospectus in collaboration with Professor Harland Randolph of Ohio State University, whom he had met through national NSA politics. New World Foundation and its director, Vernon Eagle, agreed to support the seminar for $10,000—an investment which has brought desegregation returns higher than anyone had predicted. The content of the seminar reflects Jenkins' desire for a higher level of social, political and economic sophistication of student direct actionists. The central theme was *Understanding the Nature of Social Change*, including, among others, the following topics:

> Fundamental Values Involved in Human and Civil Rights, Human Rights and the International Situation, Minority and Majority Group Relations, Learning Theories in Determination of Behavior, Social Status, Psychiatric Analysis of 'Sexual Taboos,' Community Sources of Influence and Power, Anti-Semitism in the South and the Nation, Groups to the Right and Left, Government Sources of Influence and Power, Adjustment of Communicative Symbols to Various Audiences, and Principles and Types of Communication.

The final week of the seminar was devoted to development and presentation of critical papers by the 30 participants.[9]

The list of consultants shows the seriousness and sophistication of the seminar. Among them were Dr. Kenneth Clark of City College of New York, SRC President James McBride Dabbs, Assistant U.S. Attorney General John Doar, Howard University sociologist Dr. E. Franklin Frazier, labor lobbyist Herbert Hill of the NAACP, Howard historian Dr. Rayford W. Logan, Dr. Herman Long (Director of the Fisk Race Relations Institute), author Lillian Smith and Dr. Hans Spiegel of the Community Tensions Center of Springfield College.

Among the participants were all but three of the SNCC staff members as of spring 1962—and all of these three were involved in similarly important phases of the movement at that time.[10]

It could be argued that this seminar or a functional equivalent was necessary to help SNCC mature with the movement. The development of sophisticated leadership and initiation skills was a necessity if the movement were to continue. Three factors are important here.

First, since late in November 1960, the students' disenchantment with King's leadership was growing too fast to be contained. Although this feeling existed all throughout the summer of 1960, it came to a head when, during a SNCC Executive Council meeting on November 26, 1960, the members watched King's ill-fated television debate with *Richmond News Leader* Editor James Kilpatrick. Unprepared, King's retreat to vague ethical generalities was no match for Kilpatrick's superior oratorical legalism. "It was almost in the cards that he would muff it," says former King aide Ella Baker, who was with the students at the time, "for he had not forced himself to analytically come to grips with these issues. The students were sitting there in front of the TV, waiting for him to 'take care' of Kilpatrick. Finally some got up and walked away. Their criticism of King, which finally broke openly to the surface, forced them to be healthily critical of themselves and their goals and purposes."[11]

A repeat of this situation took place in connection with the Freedom Rides, when the students became angered at King's indecisiveness. "I called him from Montgomery for advice," recalls Diane Nash Bevel. "There were people in jail, legal issues to deal with, negotiations, money problems—and all he could say was, 'Yes . . . yes, you have a problem there.'"[12] "They came back from the Freedom Rides," concludes Ella Baker, "with the terrible feeling that the angel has feet of clay."[13] —And, one might add, the firm realization that leadership skills had to be built from within the student group.

Second, even after more than a year in the movement, most of the student leaders had little knowledge of orderly procedure and few leadership skills. Rev. James Lawson said from the beginning that this was largely a function of the paternalism and lack of democratic training in Negro colleges.[14] Furthermore, the year of in-service training in the movement had been almost totally action-oriented, with almost no time devoted to reflection, writing and concentrated planning.[15]

Third, as indicated earlier, the progression of goals to more difficult types of discrimination in the recalcitrant Deep South necessitated more precise specification of targets and strategies and better long-range planning. In addition, the opposition was getting smarter all the time; police chiefs and other segregationist officials offered even stiffer challenges in an ever more complicated game.

### *The Direct Action-Voter Registration Cleavage in SNCC*

The seminar itself was only part of the takeover, which involved selling SNCC on the idea of concentrating on voter registration. Plans for a massive voter registration education program had been in the works since shortly before the Freedom Rides, led by several large foundations and the Justice Department under Robert Kennedy.[16] SNCC representatives were among those who discussed the matter with the Taconic Foundation and the federal government in June 1961.

But SNCC was fearful of selling-out to a conservative, go-slow stance symbolized by the Justice Department's call for a "cooling-off" during the Freedom Rides. It was widely believed among SNCC members that Justice and the foundations were making a calculated attempt to divert student energies away from direct action and into the safer and seemingly less spectacular business of registering voters. It was Jenkins, joined early by SNCC Chairman Charles McDew and Field Secretary Charles Jones, who convinced SNCC to turn toward a political program.[17] Jenkins first confronted the organization with the idea in the May 1961 meeting in Louisville; the Executive Committee was unimpressed. Support was growing by the time of the June meeting in Washington, for several of the members by then had been involved in discussions with Justice and the foundations. A sharp cleavage had developed, however, with Jenkins, McDew and Jones leading the voter registration wing and Diane Nash Bevel and Marion Barry leading the direct action faction.[18]

"This is the way we went to the meeting in Baltimore in early July," says Jenkins, "and we got them to accept our idea in spirit with the qualification that we come back with more specific plans at the August meeting. The three of us were successful in getting funds to do the research necessary to persuade the others, and the August meeting at Highlander after the seminar carried the day. The voter registration campaign was put on an equal footing with direct action. I would call it a successful power resolution and the saving of SNCC—for this prevented another organization from being started."[19]

So it was that the groundwork was laid for revolutionary internal changes within the student movement and revolutionary extensions into the basic structure of the American state.[20] In short, the change resulted in *the training of a small cadre of disciplined revolutionaries who could give strategic help to local protest groups lacking in leadership and organizational ability*. Jenkins sums up the rationale:

> We needed to develop the largest revolutionary program possible at this time . . . But there was no central theme in direct action, and we could only exploit the potential aroused in 1960 by going political. Otherwise the organization would die . . . When [the SNCC Executive Committee] saw all the people in Washington who would like to smash the southern bloc, they rapidly became appreciative of the power of the Justice Department and its potential to help and protect us in the political revolution. Only then was a political revolution through full Negro suffrage possible.[21]

So it was that SNCC changed, little over a year after its birth, from a "Coordinating Committee" for scattered and often spontaneous local direct action protests, to a small organization of staff professionals initiating local registration campaigns with the purpose of changing the political structure of the South and thus the nation. And Albany, Georgia, was first on the list.

## *b. THE MOVEMENT COMES TO THE DEEP SOUTH: THE MOBILIZATION OF ALBANY*[22]

Many other things happened in civil rights during the winter of 1961-62, but Albany is important as a symbolic focus of the movement's transition to a phase of *intensified community mobilization in the Deep South*. When the Albany Movement jelled in November and December of 1961, the patterns for Deep South protest for years to come had been established: "slowly developing anger and unpublicized dignified protest by Negro adults—a dramatic outburst of Negro students to bring the issues to public attention—and then a new synthesis of adult-student leadership marshaling the forces of the entire Negro community."[23]

### *A Detour: McComb*

One concentrated effort at mobilization was made prior to Albany—in McComb, Mississippi, beginning in mid-August 1961 under the direction of SNCC Field Secretary Robert Moss. More than 100 Negro high school students had been expelled, two Negroes sympathetic to the project were killed (one by a state legislator and the other by a McComb policeman), there were several dozen arrests, and numerous brutal beatings of potential registrants and Freedom Riders testing the ICC ordinance had taken place. Some voters were registered, but by the end of the year, the thrust of the voter drive in McComb had succumbed to police harassment of workers and head-turning to violence, destruction of Citizenship School headquarters and the lack of an educated and economically independent Negro population to sustain leadership and strategy.[24]

Voting workers had gone to McComb because facilities had been offered by the Pike County NAACP chapter and because it offered a semi-urban base for operations in the surrounding rural area in which Negroes make up more than 40 percent of the population. Two young SNCC field workers went to Albany under somewhat similar circumstances in October after one of them, Charles Sherrod, had surveyed voting potential in Southwest Georgia during the summer. Sherrod writes:[25]

> It stands out as the only metropolitan area of any prominence in Southwest Georgia.[26] It is the current crossroads of rural people in villages and towns within a radius of ninety miles. It was principally because of its location that

> Albany was chosen as the beachhead for democracy in *DEEP Southwest Georgia*.

Sherrod comes from Petersburg, Virginia, a B.D.-bearing Negro who had been active in the movement since 1960. With him from the beginning in Albany was Cordell Reagon of Nashville, who dropped out of high school to join the Freedom Rides the previous spring. These two men are largely responsible for what was to come in Albany.

### *In the Beginning—Grass Roots Organizing*

The story of the acceptance of the two SNCC workers into Albany is significant, for it has become the necessary pattern of operation in many rural Deep South areas. Too, it is a fine study in the intricacies of role-legitimation for the participant observer or social engineer:

> The population of Albany was in the first days of our stay here, very apprehensive. We had told many that our intention was to organize a Voter-Registration campaign . . . At the same time, it was known that we had little or no money. Further, there was doubt in the minds of many people as to who we really were.
>
> The first obstacle to remove, then, was the mental block in the minds of those who wanted to move but were unable for fear that we were not who we said we were. But when the people began to hear us in churches, social meetings, on the streets, in the pool halls, lunch rooms and night clubs, and other places where people gather, they began to open up a bit. We would tell them of how it feels to be in prison, what it means to be . . . in jail for the cause. We explained to them that we had stopped school because we felt compelled to do so since so many of us were in chains. We explained . . . that there were worse chains than jail and prison. We referred to the system that imprisons men's minds and robs them of creativity. We mocked the system that teaches men to be good Negroes instead of good men. We gave an account of the many resistances, of injustice in the courts, in employment, registration and voting. The people knew that such evils existed but when we pointed them out time and time again and emphasized the need for concerted action against them, the people began to think. At this point, we started to illustrate what had happened to Montgomery, Macon, Nashville, Atlanta, Savannah, Richmond and many other cities where people came together and protested against an evil system.[27]

Gradually the SNCC workers—living on a few dollars a week subsistence salary plus the growing good will and fried chicken of local

Negroes—established themselves as legitimate voting workers. "We're just like neighborhood boys . . . part of the common people," said Cordell Reagon after a short time in Albany.[28] Soon, writes Zinn, "they set up an office in a rundown little building two blocks from the Shiloh Baptist Church, registered voters, and through their enthusiasm and energy acted as a catalyst to a community which had already begun to stir."[29]

The most recent stirrings had concerned two racial incidents which occurred early in 1961. In January, a group of Negro leaders had asked the city commissioners to initiate the desegregation of certain city facilities. The commissioners never replied to the request. Then on February 6, segregationist editor James H. Gray of the *Albany Herald* (an outside agitator from Massachusetts who had segged his way to the chairmanship of the Georgia Democratic Party) editorially rejected the Negroes' requests ". . . both presently and also for the future." The Negro ministerial alliance had written to Gray asking for fair journalistic treatment, and to Mayor Asa D. Kelley requesting a hearing and proposing a biracial committee. There were no responses.

In February and March, rifle shots, egg-throwing, reckless driving through the campus and other activities by whites plagued Negro Albany State College, and Negro leaders felt that Gray's editorials had helped incite these and other incidents. The Dean of Students resigned in protest over the college administration's timidity in defending the students, and students staged a protest march on the President's office before going home for the summer.[30]

### *The Unifying Incident*

So the Albany Negro community was ready for the new ideas and militance of the SNCC workers. By late October the Youth Council of the local NAACP had begun to work with SNCC. Training workshops in nonviolence were held, and on November 1 several local students tested the ICC ruling on interstate terminals with the Youth Council's support. Sherrod describes with compassion just what took place in the heart of the Negro community at that time:

> At three o'clock, nine students approached the bus station, which is located only one block away from the predominantly 'Negro' business area. Upon seeing the neatly dressed students walk toward the station, a large number

> came from the pool room, lunch rooms, liquor stores, and other places . . . The stories of far away cities and their protests turned over in their minds. Was this a dream or was it really happening here in Albany? The students symbolized in the eyes of those who looked on, the expression of years of resentment—for police brutality, for poor housing, for disenfranchisement, for inferior education, for the whole damnable system. The fruit of years of prayer and sacrifice stood before the ageless hatchet-men of the South, the policemen, but the children of the new day stood tall, fearless before the legal executioners of the blacks in the DEEP South.
>
> The bus station was full of men in blue but up through the mass of people past the men with guns and billies ready, into the terminal they marched, quiet and quite clean. They were allowed to buy tickets to Florida but after sitting in the waiting room, they were asked to leave under the threat of arrest. They left as planned and later filed affidavits with the Interstate Commerce Commission. The idea had been delivered. In the hearts of the young and of the old, from that moment on, segregation was dead . . .[31]

This protest was the first unifying crisis for Albany, and on November 17, as Sherrod puts it, "a mass meeting of minds" took place and the Albany Movement was formed. Here was the beginning of the kind of class-cutting mobilization toward which the Nashville seminar was aiming. "Unify the community under local leadership and under a name which can encompass everyone," had been the advice of the new SNCC. Represented in the Albany Movement were the Negro ministerial alliance, the NAACP, SNCC and every other Negro organization in Albany—from the Federated Women's Club to the Lincoln Heights Improvement Association.[32] Said one Negro adult, "The kids were going to do it anyway . . . they were holding their own mass meetings and making plans . . . we didn't want them to have to do it alone."[33]

This unification was possible in Albany where it was not in McComb largely because of the existence of an economically independent Negro middle class and a Negro college to help furnish local manpower. But the crucially significant part of the Albany story was to come—the mobilization of a whole Negro community, across all class and occupational lines, into a militant group *willing to go to jail in the Deep South*. Montgomery had mobilized before, but then only for boycott of buses. College students (most of them economically free and many of them from outside the protest community), had gone to jail in the Deep South before, but never the maids, laborers, businessmen, ministers and teachers representing a whole community. The weeks to come brought this phenomenon in Albany and it said to the movement, the segregationists and the nation, "We are ready for the Deep South."[34]

Because the students had done their homework in the homes and meeting places of the Albany Negro community, the people were prepared for the events that shook the city and the movement. A chronology of the crucial happenings follows:[35]

| | |
|---|---|
| November 1 | ICC ruling first tested. |
| November 17 | Albany Movement formed. |
| November 22 | Three Albany State College students arrested in white lunchroom at Trailways bus terminal. Later, hundreds of students gather to take buses home for Thanksgiving holidays. Two more arrested, decide to remain in jail over Thanksgiving, later expelled from college without hearing. |
| November 25 | First mass meeting of Albany Movement attracts overflow crowd. Albany Movement President Dr. W.G. Anderson, Negro lawyer C.B. King and others speak. The Negro community is further unified by accounts of treatment by the five jailed students. |
| November 27 | Students' trial. At the call of the Albany Movement, more assemble in front of the City Hall, sing freedom songs while awaiting results. Led in prayer by newly-arrived SNCC worker Charles Jones, they march to church where 400 sign petition to college administration to reinstate expelled students. White businessmen decide to cancel annual Merchants Parade before Christmas. |
| November 28 | Gray editorial criticizes the march as "foolish." C. Jones responds in a published letter which won "sustained confidence in the 'Negro' community and cautious respect in the 'white.'" Growing frustration at the college as students who participated in march are fired from part-time jobs. |
| December 9 | Saturday. Negroes begin selective buying campaign against *Herald* advertisers because of Editor Gray's editorial policy. |
| December 10 | Sunday. Eleven Negroes and whites arrested by Chief Laurie Pritchett at Union Railway Terminal after ride from Atlanta. (Later Mayor Asa D. Kelley said, "That was our first mistake.") Several hundred Negroes watch. Why the arrests? Negro editor A.C. Searles said, "There was no traffic, no disturbance, no one |

moving. The students had made the trip to Albany desegregated without incident. Things had gone so smoothly I think it infuriated the chief."[36]

December 11 Mass meeting. Hundreds applaud the jailed persons, especially the three whites. SNCC Executive Director James Forman speaks. Plans made for direct action.

December 12 Trial of the 11; 400 Negro high school and college students march to City Hall in protest. 267 are arrested as they march peacefully, and 153 refuse bail. Mass meeting plans for another prayer vigil tomorrow.

December 13 Three different demonstrations take place. Local Negro real estate man Slater King leads prayer vigil of 70 to courthouse in morning; King arrested. 500 March to City Hall in afternoon, but none arrested. No word from mayor on trials of the others by 6:30 p.m., and hundreds more march; this time 202 are arrested. Chief Pritchett tells newsmen, "We can't tolerate . . . any . . . nigger organization to take over this town with mass demonstrations."[37] Mass meeting in evening.

December 14 Arrests reach 560; 300 remain in jail. Governor Ernest Vandiver sends 150 National Guardsmen to Albany. Wires and telephone calls to and from U.S. Attorney General. Sherrod and others beaten in county jails. Mayor calls Anderson and asks for bi-racial meeting. Negotiations begin.

December 15 Negotiations end at noon, with agreement on bus and train terminal desegregation and release of all Negro marchers, but disagreement on release of original Freedom Riders without bond. Evening: biggest mass meeting yet, with Dr. Martin Luther King, Jr., of SCLC, Ruby Hurley of NAACP and Richard Haley of CORE speaking at invitation of the Albany Movement. Speakers urge direct action, voter registration, boycott. Dr. Anderson tells meeting: "Be here at 7 o'clock in the morning. Eat a good breakfast. Wear warm clothes and wear your walking shoes."

December 16 Saturday. City commission balks at release of Freedom Riders without bond. Movement sends telegram setting 10 a.m. deadline after which demonstrations will resume. Further negotiations in tense atmosphere until early afternoon . . . no settlement. King and Anderson lead prayer march to City Hall in evening; 259 arrested, bringing week's total to 737.

| | |
|---|---|
| December 17 | Sunday. Quiet. *Herald* denounces outside agitators and rumors split in movement leadership. |
| December 18 | Negotiations resume and continue all day. Agreement on release of demonstrators on property bonds. |
| December 19 | Most demonstrators out of jail. By now 40 student demonstrators have been expelled from Albany State. |

## *The Fruits of Crisis*

Several important points should be noted about the events of this brief period in the life of the city of Albany, for they did more to alter the thinking of both races on their relations than the several previous decades. First, the role of historical accident and intersystemic challenge is illustrated in the December 10 arrests of the 11 "Freedom Riders." They had come in response to the stirrings of local Negroes, and having successfully used the terminal facilities, were preparing to leave when they were arrested. This move was a serious mistake for the segregationist chief, for within four days more than 500 Negroes (most of them local residents) had been arrested and the city was making an unprecedented request for a biracial negotiation. The city's challenge to the Negro community through these first arrests was the tip-over event for Negro patience, then the unifying effect of crisis was seen time and again.

These weeks produced only the first mobilization and the first of many crises for Albany. What was gained and what was lost in this first skirmish? On the surface, it would seem that Negroes only won the dubious right to pay property bonds when imprisoned for demonstrating—a long-established principle. Terminal desegregation was included in the package, but this was simply an echo of the ICC ruling which, technically, was already in effect. There was a promise for further negotiation, but little took place until the Civil Rights Law of 1964 made direct communication necessary on many levels.[38]

A crucial loss seems to have been the right of peaceful protest for redress of grievances. I have sat in Albany courtrooms several times and heard judges refuse to allow introduction of First and Fourteenth Amendment issues into a case. And Zinn rightly points out that the Albany police were praised even nationally for simply the negative police function of preventing violence against those exercising a constitutional right. "The purveyors of violence [in other Deep South cities] . . . have managed to lower the settlement terms for race crises . . . so that it becomes sufficient evidence of successful police action to have prevented violence."[39]

But to a man, those involved in the Albany Movement agree that there has been a significant victory in the minds of Negroes in deep Southwest Georgia. "We have freed the people's minds!" the students say over and over again. "We have seen the beginning of a new type of civic relationship in this community," said retired Negro railroader Marion S. Page on December 19 after the settlement.[40] And I have seen it in my two trips to Albany. The first time, in March 1962, Negroes on the streets even in the Negro sections kept their eyes to the ground rather than look in the eyes of an obviously outside white man. In September of the same year, after several more crises similar in pattern but smaller in scale than the first crisis, virtually every Negro I met even in the "white" downtown area looked me squarely in the eye with a firm and ready "Fine, fine . . . how you doin'?" reply.

This freeing of the minds has brought registration results, too. Reagon reported that by March 1962 (five months after he and Sherrod came to Albany), almost 400 Negroes had registered to vote for the first time. The figure has grown steadily since then.[41]

Paradoxical as it must seem to white segregationists, one of the best indicators of real progress in a city's race relations at this stage of the desegregation process is the "breakdown of communication." This may mean that literally, as the old story goes, when the white man yells, "Hey, boy!", the Negro no longer comes running. It is indeed a symbol of the breaking down of old status barriers. It results in an uneasiness of communication for whites who are unable to substitute dialogue for paternalism. A white merchant in Albany unknowingly said it most succinctly when he confided to me in September 1962 that before the agitators came, any Nigra in town could come up to any white man he knew, ask him for five dollars—and get it. That was real communication and good feeling, but now it is a thing of the past.

### *The March Through Georgia*

The NAACP had laid the groundwork for the Albany protests. SNCC student revolutionaries were the catalyst that molded the Albany Movement. SCLC provided the nationally-known charismatic leader and strategic know-how upon request. All of these groups plus CORE, SDS, the National Council of Churches and others have helped sustain the efforts since 1961.

The organizational trek to Albany has exemplified the growing importance of organized efforts by civil rights groups to extend the movement into remote areas of the Deep South. A long-range program and careful planning are necessary to even approach the massive structures of traditionalism in the Deep South, and this can only be accomplished through the concerted strategic and financial programs of large and professionally committed social systems—the civil rights, labor, student and religious groups.

Until mid-1965 and the federal Voting Rights Law, Albany remained a "beachhead in Southwest Georgia," with an ongoing voter registration program financed by the Voter Education Project (discussed later in this chapter) and staffed by SNCC and SCLC. Sporadic direct action campaigns continue today, and they all, in some way, have gotten their impetus from the organization-sustained projects. In the spring of 1962, a highly efficient boycott put the local intracity bus line out of business in two weeks, and it later reopened on a desegregated basis. Several white merchants who cater to Negro trade but hire no Negroes in responsible positions have also been put out of business by boycotts. (Testing of public accommodations facilities showed no desegregation until the Civil Rights Bill became law on July 2, 1964. The efficacy of direct action was attested to by a local official who said of the opening of facilities on July 3, "We're not going to give Martin Luther King any reason to come back."[42])

Albany was the first Deep South city since Montgomery to attract virtually all of the national civil rights organizations for help in carrying out a campaign on a specifically *local* issue—voting. A similar situation developed in Jackson when some of the groups (led by CORE) maintained an office to help stimulate local activities in conjunction with the Freedom Rides and the subsequent trials. But the pattern of community mobilization which was to emerge later even in Jackson (and, eventually in nearly every county in the Deep South), was developed in Albany. It has three general characteristics:

(1) The organizations do not come to a city or area strictly on their own, but only enter (a) when they are asked to come by local leaders who need help in strategy and program, (b) as a response to news of a local protest which indicates a community is "ready," or (c) on the basis of prior research into the potential of the area.[43] Note the sharp contrast between this carefully planned initiation of a desegregation *program* and the often

spontaneous, unplanned and uncoordinated outburst of a direct action *protest* in the early days of the sit-ins.

(2) There is a concerted effort to train local leadership to carry on the desegregation drive after the professionals have withdrawn their advice and support. As indicated by the ups and downs of the protest in Albany, Birmingham, Danville, St. Augustine, Selma and other areas, however, this goal has not always been reached.[44]

(3) The eventual aim of these programs is voter education and registration, for direct actionists soon learned the only hope for even token changes to filter down to the rural Deep South is a full-scale attack on voting discrimination. While only Negroes with relative independence of the white community could afford to participate in direct action, all ages and classes could take part in the less militant and less dangerous voting activity. "Citizenship schools" have always unified and implicitly trained Negroes for activism, for despite the one-time SNCC split over the issue, voter registration in the Deep South *is* direct action.

### c. *THE VOTE*

This chapter has focused on SNCC because this group is the major organizational product of the direct action movement. It was not the only civil rights group beginning to move into the area of voter registration in the Deep South, however. In fact, a number of local groups and the NAACP had been working for many years in voter registration, but with two important differences from the post-1961 activities: (a) they concentrated mainly on urban areas, and (b) they did not have the sense of "movement" generated by the direct action of 1960 and capitalized on by later protests. Further, the role of the federal government in promoting and protecting voting rights was just beginning to emerge under the Kennedy Administration in 1961.

Here again one can see the important role of a crisis event like the Freedom Rides. Most movement leaders I have talked with say the Riders were the catalyst which prompted the Justice Department to push harder for voting rights activity on the part of the civil rights groups, hoping to divert the energy generated into this less spectacular and more easily protected activity. SNCC's James Forman says it forcibly: "The Freedom Rides embarrassed the hell out of this country, and soon the government tried to turn us to voter education and registration with overtures of money for this kind of activity."[45] "But," says Negro social critic Louis Lomax, "friends of the President pointed out that the voter registration program would, in fact, aid [direct action] by making it possible for the money then being spent for voter registration to be diverted to other purposes . . ."[46]

The 1961 summer meetings with the Justice Department and the foundations were attended by the other major organizations in addition to SNCC: Roy Wilkins of the NAACP, Thurgood Marshall of the NAACP Legal Defense and Educational Fund, Whitney Young of the National Urban League, Dr. Martin Luther King, Jr., of SCLC, James Farmer of CORE and Dr. Leslie Dunbar of the Southern Regional Council.[47] All parties—the Administration, the civil rights leaders and the foundations—agreed on the rationale for a move to the political arena, and the Southern Regional Council solved the perennial problem of inter-organizational competition among the action groups by proposing to serve as administrator for the money.

*The Voter Education Project*

Never before in the history of American race relations had such a comprehensive voting program been proposed; such wide support from public and private sources was unprecedented. The Kennedy Administration's informal role in urging the Internal Revenue Service to give the project tax-exempt status was an unprecedented use of power in the area of protection and extension of voting rights. The Southern Regional Council, in applying for the ruling in letters dated December 14, 1961, and February 9, 1962, defined the objectives of the Voter Education Project (VEP):

> . . . to promote and to study and evaluate methods for teaching and encouraging exercise of the right to register and vote in areas in the South which, from the Council's past research, are known to be comparatively lowest in registration and voting. The work will necessarily largely involve the Negro population.
>
> . . . to develop educational programs which will be most effective in providing voters with the knowledge and will to register.
>
> . . . [to publish] a report, analysis and evaluation of the Project [recommending], on the basis of Project experience, the best methods of education designed to overcome low voter registration in the various geographic and cultural areas of the South.[48]

It is clear that the research aims were primarily of an experimental nature, and that recommendations were to constitute a large part of the research product. Here, then, seemed to be a respectable yet highly activist way to direct large sums of money into an intensive voter drive in the Deep South. The initial foundation allotment, for the two-year period beginning April 1, 1962, was nearly $600,000.[49] This sudden financial input substantially revitalized the direct action organizations (especially SNCC, whose summer shift to a voting emphasis had wisely prepared them for such a development), helped draw less action-oriented groups like the National Urban League more directly into the Deep South confrontation, called into existence local organizations specifically structured for voter registration—in short, generally expanded, intensified and professionalized the assault on voting discrimination in the South.

A VEP report listing the types of civil rights groups involved in the project is instructive, for it shows the diversified organizational structure within which the direct action movement had been adapting and through which it was helping implement its goals during the first two years (1962-64):[50]

> *national organizations* — NAACP, CORE, Urban League;
>
> *a regional organization* — SCLC;
>
> *a unique group*[51] — SNCC;
>
> *local organizations of long standing* — All-Citizens Registration Committee (Atlanta), Durham (North Carolina) Committee on Negro Affairs;
>
> *inexperienced groups* — Federated Organization for the Cause of Unlimited Self-Development (FOCUS in Baton Rouge);
>
> *ad hoc groups* [which VEP helped bring into existence] — Council of Federated Organizations (COFO in Mississippi), Jefferson County (Alabama) Voters Campaign; and
>
> *popular crusades* — the Albany Movement.

The movement seemed to be coming full circle early in 1962, then, as the first city to sustain a dangerous Deep South voter drive—Albany—now was eligible along with many other areas for extensive support and professional assistance in voting.[52]

*Resistance and Commitment: The Movement Matures*

In summary, since its inception the Voter Education Project has helped focus nationwide concern on the problem of voting rights in the Deep South through governmental and foundation involvement, SRC's reputation as objective and reliable, and the unquestioned constitutionality of Negro suffrage. VEP also helped dramatize the patterns of resistance met by voting workers in many areas. A VEP report of research on causes of low registration cited 10 such problems:[53]

(1) local governments' prohibition of Negro registration;

(2) governmental cheating (i.e., inequal administration of qualification tests);

(3) governmental restrictions against new registrations (poll taxes);

(4) governmental harassment in reprisal against Negro registration (e.g., capricious arrest of registration workers);

(5) private harassment, intimidation, violence, economic reprisal;

(6) Negro indifference and apathy;

(7) Negro alienation;

(8) Negro ignorance (inability to pass literacy requirements);

(9) Negro fear;

(10) area bias against democratic control, as in Virginia.

Facing these kinds of conditions in Albany and other Deep South areas, the movement necessarily has matured in its goals and strategies. The factors differentiating Albany from Montgomery clearly show this growth:

*Montgomery Bus Boycott*, (1955-56)

(a) Basically a negative, non-agressive protest—a "staying-away."
(b) Narrow, specific, essentially apolitical goals (desegregation of local buses), requiring only one protest technique—the boycott.
(c) Only movement leaders go to jail.
(d) An isolated community protest.

*Albany Movement,* (1961- )

(a) A positive, affirming protest, requiring direct confrontation by all protestors with the white community and its power agencies.
(b) Broad, revolutionary goals (attacking the whole political, economic and social structure), requiring a broad spectrum of techniques including voter registration, boycott and direct action demonstrations.
(c) Persons from all strata in the Negro community go to jail, involving a necessarily complex degree of community mobilization.
(d) Set against the background of a nationwide self-conscious anti-segregation movement, the protest rapidly takes on broader significance for its participants and is aided by a highly rationalized national organizational structure.

The characteristics of the Albany Movement are familiar to us in 1965 as those of protest and voting drives which have touched every Deep South state. It has been all but forgotten that the Albany Movement—despite its limited and uneven success—was the methodological basis for such well-known campaigns as the Mississippi Summer Project of 1964 and SCLC's SCOPE[54] in 1965, and virtually all of the less publicized projects like AEPAC[55] in east Tennessee and the Barbour County Voters League in Alabama.

From the perspective of a growing and rationalizing social protest system, then, Albany is the symbol of the movement's maturation through Deep South confrontation. Its impact is best summarized in the words of two SNCC workers who know it best from the inside:

*James Forman*:. . . The demonstrations have helped to solidify the Negro community for future power struggles, including . . . boycott of white stores by the Negroes. Without a doubt voter registration not only in Albany but in other Southwest Georgia counties will intensify.[56]

*Charles Sherrod*: So the superstructure is being shaken to the very foundations. The 'Negro'-'white' southern etiquette is being

> challenged. It is no longer a 'matter of fact' procedure for a 'Negro' to respond in 'yes sirs' or 'no sirs.' There is a continual questioning now of civil liberties, though such a term may be unknown to many of them. The people are slowly coming to . . . wonder if it is their right to say what they strongly believe even if this means letting the mayor or chief of police or 'bossman' know about it; *they are thinking*! Then there is also the thought that there is nothing wrong with walking in large numbers to a public place to pray in the open. *They are becoming. There are goals* . . . In a DEEP Southwest Georgia area where it is generally conceded that the 'Negro' has no rights that a 'white' man is bound to respect, *at last*, they sing, 'We Shall Overcome.' *There is hope*![57]

As Forman and Sherrod no doubt knew, they were now speaking not just for Albany, but for the whole movement, the South and the nation.

# C. The Theory

## The Rationalization of Protest

PREFACE

# The Movement After Two Years

In the final three chapters, a theory of the rationalization of protest is concurrently developed from, and applied to, the data of the direct action movement from February 1960 to February 1962. Predictions are made which should provide a number of testable hypotheses for future research in this and other social movements.

To facilitate the integration of theory and data, a brief review and summary of the movement's first two years is presented at the start of this section.[1]

Beginning with a four-man protest at a lunch counter in Greensboro, North Carolina, a southwide sit-in movement challenging discrimination in public accommodations erupted in the spring of 1960. Success was almost immediate, and by fall more than 100 cities had desegregated some accommodations—mostly lunch counters in variety stores.

From February 1, 1960 to February 1, 1962, nonviolent direct action came to bear the thrust of the desegregation effort; to a man, participants and students of the protest talked of a "movement"—symbolizing an internal cohesiveness of purpose never before seen in the process of desegregation in America. As a result of direct action, in those two years more actual desegregation of public accommodations took place than in the two previous decades.[2]

In numerical terms, some of the most important changes brought about by the direct action movement in 1960 and 1961 were:

(1) Thousands of lunch counters and other public accommodations[3] in approximately 150 southern cities dropped racial barriers.[4]
(2) More than 7,000 Negro and white Americans were arrested and most of them spent time in jail for (in most cases) nonviolently disobeying local discriminatory laws or customs.[5]
(3) Upwards of 100,000 persons—northern and southern, Negro and white—actively participated in the protests. Many thousands more

directly supported the efforts through boycott, and tens of thousands offered financial support through various civil rights organizations.[6]

(4) Latent pro-integrationist sentiment was activated through religious, labor and campus political groups, and a number of new politically activist organizations were formed.[7]

(5) In addition to the private energy and money activated, millions of federal, state and municipal dollars have become involved in investigation, enforcement, noncompliance and police action.[8]

(6) Between 50 and 75 southern cities established biracial committees to deal with racial problems where no legitimated forms of communication had existed before.[9] At least one state[10] created a state-wide interracial commission to facilitate resolution of intergroup tensions, and unofficial statewide Councils on Human Relations have, in nearly every southern state, gained status as informal race relations advisors to governmental officials.[11]

But since this dissertation is more concerned with the developing structure of the movement itself, some of the major *internal and substantive changes* which took place in 1960 and 1961 are now summarized. Briefly, the argument has been this:

(1) The sit-ins were born as an almost immediately mature movement in the spring of 1960, gaining widespread participation and support and early successes in desegregating public accommodations;

(2) By mid-1960, the charisma was waning, the movement was floundering, and initial problems of routinization of goals, leadership, techniques and structure were becoming acute;

(3) The CORE-sponsored Freedom Rides of May, 1961, unexpectedly provided a rejuvenating spark, and another phase of the movement (dangerous Deep South challenges calling for federal enforcement) was begun;

(4) By late in 1961, the movement-become-program was rationalizing its structure with some success, turning to revolutionary goals, and moving to implement these goals with voter registration and direct action in Deep South rural areas.

Adult and Student informants agreed in early spring 1962 that this movement-wide development had had important consequences for the internal structure of the protests. Some of their interpretations, presented below, provide a viable summary of important aspects of the first two years of the movement.

*Loss of Spontaneity*

Most persons connected with the movement have spent a good part of their time since 1960 trying to recapture the charisma and spontaneous success of the first few months of the sit-ins. So it is understandable that, in response to two different questions about the nature of the movement in early 1962 as compared to the early days in 1960, most of our sample of Student and Adult elites mentioned "loss of spontaneity" in one way or another. When asked "In what ways does the movement seem different to you now than it was in the beginning in 1960?", 64 percent of the Students and 55 percent of the Adults mentioned "loss of spontaneity." The percentages dropped to 50 percent and 41 percent respectively when the question was phrased, "What has been the biggest change in the movement since it began?"

Answers to these two questions were coded the same way, and there is consistency in the response patterns, with a few exceptions. In both forms of the question, a high percentage of the Student responses fall in the categories of "loss of spontaneity," "development of organizational structure," and "opposition tougher, Deep South now," while the Adults agree on spontaneity, structure and the "broadening of goals" of the protest in both question forms.

(See Figure 5 on the following page.)

Figure 5

HOW THE MOVEMENT SEEMS DIFFERENT FROM 1960
(I.4, both forms)
and
THE BIGGEST CHANGE IN THE MOVEMENT SINCE 1960
(I.7, both forms)

| | HOW SEEMS DIFFERENT | | BIGGEST CHANGE | |
|---|---|---|---|---|
| | *Students* (n = 11) | *Adults* (n = 10) | *Students* (n = 10) | *Adults* (n=27) |
| loss of spontaneity | 7 (64%) | 16 (55%) | 5 (50%) | 11 (41%) |
| opposition tougher, Deep South now | 6 (55%) | 4 (14%) | 3 (30%) | 3 (11%) |
| development of organizational structure | 4 (36%) | 16 (55%) | 4 (40%) | 7 (26%) |
| broadening of goals | 4 (36%) | 9 (31%) | 1 (10%) | 10 (40%) |
| development of strategies | 2 (18%) | 6 (21%) | 6 (60%) | 5 (19%) |
| development of philosophy, goals, values | 2 (18%) | 4 (14%) | 2 (20%) | 1 ( 4%) |
| more militant leadership | 1 ( 9%) | 1 ( 3%) | 0 ( 0%) | 4 (15%) |
| no movement now | 1 ( 9%) | 7 (24%) | 0 ( 0%) | 2 ( 7%) |
| organizational conflict | 0 ( 0%) | 5 (17%) | 0 ( 0%) | 9 (33%) |

Two responses on which there is virtually no Student-Adult agreement give us clues to their different perceptions of the development of the movement. First, in response to both forms, the Students mention fairly often (55 percent and 30 percent) the growing sophistication of the opposition and the fact that the thrust of the movement is taking them into the Deep South more frequently in 1962 than in the Border and Middle South-centered 1960 lunch counter sit-ins. Barely more than 10 percent of the Adults, on the other hand, list this toughening of the opposition as a significant change. Perhaps this indicates not only the more intense front lines involvement of the Students, but also their clearer perception of where the movement had to go from that point.

Second, not one Student mentions "organizational conflict" when asked about "differences" and "changes" in the movement, while 17 percent and 33 percent of the Adults mention on free recall the growing interorganization rivalry as a significant change. By every measure, the internal conflict is there, but only the Adults recognize it and/or are willing to talk about it.[12]

### *Leadership Changes: Withering Grass Roots and Blooming Professionals*

After two years, the direct action movement was facing a crisis in leadership. The Nashville Seminar training of summer 1961 was just beginning to bear fruit, and the movement sought in vain for the kind of grass roots production of spontaneous leaders which had marked the 1960 sit-ins. Student informants knew something was wrong, but generally were unable to articulate the problem in categories relevant to the current study; the question, "How has the leadership structure of the movement changed in the last two years?" failed to elicit any trend in responses.

But the Adult responses showed a pattern: 31 percent (eight persons) pointed to a "loss of grass roots leadership" as the biggest change in the movement's leadership since 1960, and 27 percent (seven persons, including only one overlap) saw the "emergence of institutionalized leadership" as the major change. Thus, almost one-half (14 informants) of the total Adult sample pointed out these significant changes in free recall. Further, one-half of this group went on to say that these changes had "hurt the movement."[13]

While the grass roots leadership was faltering in the post-charismatic second year of the movement, the growing professionalism of the remaining student leaders was affirmed by the informants. Eighty-three percent of the

Students and 72 percent of the Adults said that the student leaders of early 1962 were "more professional" than their counterparts of early 1960.[14]

### *Growing Student Receptiveness to Non-Students*

Since the movement was, from the beginning, a student revolt against Negro leadership and civil rights groups as well as segregation and its enforcers, I have continuously watched the changes in attitudes of student direct actionists toward "inside outsiders"—adults and civil rights groups. Fifty-four percent of the Adult sample said that the student leadership had become "more receptive to 'outside help'" during the first two years of the movement.[15]

Students were quick to perceive the "place" of outside help: "direct leadership," "financial-legal assistance" and "publicity" were named by 70 percent, 62 percent and 54 percent respectively as the points at which the civil rights organizations have played their biggest parts.[16] The Students were almost unanimous (85 percent) in naming CORE as the organization which had been "most involved in the movement," with 70 percent mentioning the NAACP and 54 percent SCLC.[17]

### *Changing Forms of Protest*

Eighty percent of the Students and 72 percent of the Adults said that the forms of protest early in 1962 were different from those of the first few months of the movement.[18] But only the Adults gave any clear indication of what this difference was, 52 percent of them listing the most frequent form of protest at that time as "mass demonstrations" and 35 percent "economic boycott." Other categories, which got sporadic mention in both samples, include "direct action with fewer participants," "legal approach," "voter registration drives" and "community mobilization approach."[19]

Significantly, there was a clear-cut feeling among informants in both samples that the concept of "spontaneous demonstration" no longer applied as it did in the early days of the sit-ins. Students and Adults answered the question, "Are there 'spontaneous' demonstrations in various cities today like those which took place in the first months of the sit-ins? Or is everything organized?" Forty-six percent of the Students and 60 percent of the Adults said, "no, 'everything is organized,'" or "not in the same sense."

Figure 6

ARE THERE 'SPONTANEOUS' DEMONSTRATIONS TWO YEARS AFTER THE MOVEMENT BEGAN?

(Forms 1 and 2, VI. 3)

| | Students (n = 13) | Adults (n = 30) |
|---|---|---|
| no, "everything organized" or "not in the same sense" | 6 (46%) | 18 (60%) |
| some, but not on the same scale | 4 (31%) | 4 (13%) |
| yes, spontaneous | 3 (23%) | 2 ( 7%) |
| always did have some planning | 0 ( 0%) | 7 (23%) |

*Summary*

In the first two years, then, the direct action protests evolved from:

(a) a spontaneously combusted movement to
(b) an ill-rationalized program to
(c) an organization-sparked movement (the Freedom Rides) to
(d) a rapidly-rationalizing revolutionary movement/program.

Major structural alterations were:

(a) a loss of spontaneity,
(b) a waning of grass roots leadership,
(c) the hesitating development of professional leadership,
(d) a necessary growing receptiveness of student militants to non-students and established civil rights groups, and
(e) development of new forms of protests.

The most important point for our discussion in this brief summary is the ever-present tension between *movement* and *program*, between *spontaneity* and *institutionalization*. The desire to remain spontaneous and charismatic is juxtaposed with the realized necessity for rationality in administering the movement/program; this paradox is the starting point for the development of theory in the final chapters.

SEVEN

# Dimensions of the Theory: The Stages of Rationalization and the Functional Imperatives

One of the most important aspects of the process of 'rationalization' of action is the substitution for unthinking acceptance of ancient custom, of deliberate adaptation to situations in terms of self-interest.

— Max Weber[1]

. . . That is the destiny of every new idea. It is crystallized in formulas so that it may be propagated. It is intrusted to a body of interpreters so that it may be preserved. That body is prudently recruited, sometimes specifically paid . .

— Ignazio Silone[2]

This chapter is an attempt to construct a theoretical perspective to explain and interpret the rationalization of social protest. The theory was developed from the analysis of a specific body of data—the direct action protest movement, as outlined in Section B of this paper and summarized in the preceding pages. It is intended as a contribution to a general theory of social development, change and institutionalization.

*Rationalization* is defined as *the tendency for social action to differentiate into systems for attaining the commonly agreed-upon goals of the actors by means of an increasingly precise calculation of available and adequate means.*[3]

It is assumed that rationalization is a natural process in the life history of social systems, with development proceeding through orderly stages as the system changes in size and duration. The end goal of the process of rationalization is pure *rationality*—social behavior which is ". . . purposefully directed toward explicit empirical objectives and planned in accordance with the best available scientific knowledge."[4] The ideal typical structural form toward which rationalization and rational social behavior drive is, in Weber's terms, the rational bureaucracy, whose characteristics are specified later in this chapter.

The general term *protest* now may be defined for purposes of theory construction as *responsible deviance*[5] *which uses threats and promises enforced by collective action, including withdrawal as well as aggression, to elicit concessions from the relevant enforcers of social control.* The concept of protest as used in this study thus encompasses social movements, reform and revolutionary movements, as well as localized political action whose goal is to win concessions from decision-makers when other appeals have failed.

Construction of theory proceeds, after some preliminary assumptions and qualifiers, from four basic sociological concepts in addition to *rationalization*, as noted in chapter 1: *charisma* and *the three types of legitimate authority* (Weber), and *the social system* and *the four functional imperatives* (Parsons).

## a. ASSUMPTIONS, DEFINITIONS, QUALIFICATIONS

More precise meanings of rationalization and its implications can emerge only after certain assumptions, definitions and qualifications are made clear. Discussed in descending order of generality, they deal with the nature of systems, the social system, social development and change, and competition and conflict.

### On System

The most general assumption underlying this analysis is that behavior is organized in a series of systems and subsystems. A system as here defined has five components: units, interaction, patterning, boundaries and temporality. A functioning system, then, is one in which recognized *units* (be they statuses, rabbits or planets) *interact* with one another in a *patterned* way (as contrasted to random or erratic behavior) within defined *boundaries* during a specific *time* period.[6]

## *The Social System*

The behavioral sciences analyze human action as it is organized into three systems—culture, social system and personality.[7] While all three approaches are important for understanding social interaction, this study focuses on the *social system*, which is defined as a *problem-solving plurality of goal-oriented personalities organized in institutional patterns*. This definition has the advantage of explicitly linking action at the social system level with *culture* (the shared heritage of values which specifies *goals* in society) and *personality* (the organization of cultural cognitions, cathexes and evaluations in the individual, internalized through socialization in a social system). Thus, men are seen as goal-seeking organisms who can reach their goals only through organized group efforts designed to solve certain problems. These problems, as defined and developed later in the chapter, involve not only goal-attainment, but also making provisions for the maintenance of the system's basic beliefs and for its smooth internal and external functioning.

## *Social Development, Social Change and Rationalization*

Perhaps the most crucial distinction to be made in determining the place of the present study in the development of general theory, is that between *development* in social systems and *change* in social systems.[8] *Development* refers to *natural* (i.e., predictable) *modifications which take place within any social system as it exists through time and responds to various inherent, internal and external exigencies*—chief among which are population growth and ideological and technological diffusion from other systems. An analogy for these general changes may be made with the general transformation undergone by an animal as it grows and responds to inherent, internal and external stimuli.[9] Furthermore, just as in biological organisms, social development has its own unique directionality: *a movement toward increasing rationality in the arrangement of social relations*.[10] Weber clearly meant rationalization as a *developmental* concept, not a variable to be manipulated in studies of social change; rationalization is the natural course of development in all societies.[11]

Increasing rationality usually occurs with sheer passage of time in a subsystem existing *within* an already highly rationalized society[12]—as is the case with the direct action protest movement within American society. The degree of rationality of the host system sets the general limits of alternative goals, strategies and organizational forms available to emergent subsystems.[13]

*Social change*, then, takes place within a context of social development and, in terms of our formulation, is largely dependent on the current state of rationalization in the system at large. *Social change* shall refer to *significant variations from developmental patterns which are not predictable or extrapolable from prior knowledge of the established patterns.*[14] These variations are of four general types: alterations in the *rate, direction, intensity* and *scope* of the developmental process,[15] usually occurring at the subsystem level and diffusing upward, downward and laterally in the total system.

Significant change may occur in three ideal-typical ways,[16] or a combination of them:

(a) through "drift" at a series of seemingly unrelated levels in connection with seemingly unimportant issues which, through neglect of the system's decision-makers, crystallizes into wider effects;

(b) through "quiet change" engineered by the system's decision-makers and enforcers of social control; and

(c) through conflict and crisis-creation by subsystems which force negotiation and concessions by the enforcers and decision-makers.

Modes (a) and (b) often lead to (c), which usually involves more actors more intensely and therefore brings about more rapid and lasting change at cultural and personality levels as well as in the social system. Quite obviously, this third mode of change is paramount in the present analysis.

Thus, the theory of the rationalization of protest is viewed as a contribution to theories of *social development* as well as theories of *social change*. In this framework, rationalization is the major process through which social systems inevitably move toward rationality as they grow in size and mature structurally—the major process, that is, of *development*. Rationalization theory is an effort to systematize the form and sequence of this process. Social change, on the other hand, takes place *within* the context of ongoing social development, so to predict social change, one needs to know precisely the content of social development and the laws which govern it. By taking a step in that direction, the theory of rationalization may facilitate the prediction of social change.[17]

### *The Constancy of Competition and Conflict*

The other major condition of this model which must be noted before proceeding with the theory is that competition is present in all social systems at all times. *Competition* is defined as *the process whereby system members oppose one another in seeking the scarce rewards they have learned to want, while suppressing antagonistic feelings toward competing actors*.[18] Social systems teach most of their members, that is, to avoid awareness of the constant competition which is a component of all social interaction.

Competition exists in all systems at all times, and is managed to a greater or lesser degree by various mechanisms of social control and group integration.[19] When these mechanisms no longer can satisfy a large proportion of the competing actors (i.e., convince them that their needs are being adequately met), *conflict* arises. *Conflict is intensified competition of which a substantial proportion of those involved are aware*. All systems strive to maintain a low level of tension and often deny that any real competition exists, but various kinds of precipitating events function to bring latent opposition to the surface in the form of conflict.[20]

In the model being developed here, competition and conflict are as essential to the smooth functioning of the social system as the basic equilibrating processes of institutionalization and social control. Every social system represents a precarious balance between the two principles of *change* and *stability*, of *spontaneous behavior* and *institutional patterning*, of (in Weber's ideal-typical extremes) *charisma* and *bureaucracy*. Society as a dynamic balance of competing and conflicting elements is indeed the natural state of affairs. A competitive state which surfaces as conflict and eventually produces a crisis situation often has a clarifying and cathartic effect on the system and its long-suppressed components. In this sense, competition and conflict, while appearing to be disequilibrating forces in the short-run, contribute to the long-range equilibration of the system.[21]

Society as the dialectic is the key to our understanding of conflict, then, for the opposition of two or more unreconciled entities is the growing edge of social change—and thus of the persistence of society itself. One of the basic assumptions of this model now may be restated: certain kinds of changes (conceptualized as "development" or "process" or "cycle") are inherent in the nature of social systems, and they mature through situations of conflict.

The theory developed in this chapter sees the two general processes of *institutionalization* and *change* as dependent on one another and, in fact, providing the basic stuff out of which the other—and ultimately, society itself—is formed and maintained. In this framework, any social system consists of the interaction of these two master processes involving competition, conflict and cooperation in various states of intensity and relationship.

As always, it seems, Max Weber said it first and best: ". . . conflict cannot be excluded from social life . . . 'Peace' is nothing more than a change in the form of conflict or in the antagonists or in the objects of the conflict, or finally in the chances of selection."[22] Every social situation, then, is a kind of precariously institutionalized stand-off. This paper's theory attempts to explain how the competitive elements which have broken through into certain kinds of conflict situations are reinstitutionalized at a higher level of consensus (or stand-off) through *the rationalization of protest*.[23]

### *b. GENERALIZABILITY OF THE THEORY OF THE RATIONALIZATION OF PROTEST*

The preceding section has indicated, in general, the place of the current study in general theory. In short, the following specifications already have been made:

Figure 7

THE PLACE OF THE PRESENT STUDY IN GENERAL THEORY

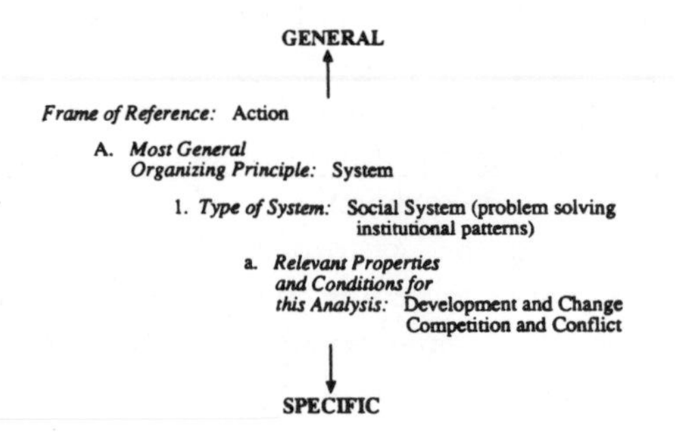

As figure 7 indicates, this study focuses on several important properties of social systems. Further, the argument proceeds from analysis of manifestations of these and other properties in a particular kind of social system—*the protest system*.

This analysis assumes that protest systems differ from "normal" social systems in degree only, not in kind, for protest is latent in every social system. When protest comes to the surface, certain sociological processes are accentuated and others suppressed. Development of the theory centers on contributions of the protest process to systematic stabilization and change, as generalized from a particular social system (the direct action protest movement) and three of its subsystems (CORE, SCLC and SNCC).

The literal generalizability of the theory developed in this chapter is limited to situations of intergroup conflict[24] with the following specifications:[25]

(1) *The conflict reaches proportions of a "movement" or at least some form of "collective behavior."* A "movement" has been defined as a collective phenomenon involving (a) a common ideology specifying goals, (b) broad-based (i.e., stratum-cutting) participation, (c) a we-feeling, and (d) a broadening focus of goals and strategies. Collective behavior is a more generic term, referring to the activities of groups formed in times of "social unrest"[26] and ". . . governed by emergent or spontaneous norms rather than formalized norms."[27] Thus collective behavior is properly viewed as an exploratory, reality-testing activity by emerging social groups—as compared to the more rigidly patterned behavior of formal groups in highly institutionalized settings. The most common form of collective behavior cited by sociologists may be loosely categorized as crowds, mass behavior, the behavior of publics and social movements.[28]

(2) *The conflict occurs at an intrasocietal level.* The theory of the rationalization of protest does not purport to deal with international conflict situations or those which are otherwise compounded by such variables as basic cultural differences, language barriers and wide geographical separation of actors. In the intrasocietal setting, conditions are more conducive to accurate communication which tends to (a) lessen the probability of conflict arising and (b) act as a catalyst mechanism in speeding up the process of conflict resolution. Even though we are dealing with essentially "local" theory, many of the general principles developed here no doubt are extrapolable to situations of international conflict.

(3) *The conflict occurs within a highly differentiated society.* The present analysis is limited to social systems which are already well along in the

process of rationalizing their economy and other institutional patterns.[29] Two conditions of a highly rationalized society are crucial for this analysis of protest: a high degree of mobility and the existence of sophisticated forms of mass communication. The importance of these conditions will be noted later in connection with the *relativizing* processes which play a crucial role in mobilizing social unrest for the take-off phase of protest. The exposure to value and behavioral alternatives afforded by high mobility and mass communication also is a major reason for the theory's contention that rationalization of intergroup protest situations inevitably leads toward rational-legal organization instead of traditional patrimonalism.

While limiting generalizability, these qualifications also can aid in clarifying the analysis of change. In connection with (1), for instance, I believe that concentration on the processes of institutionalization and change in times of collective excitement and crisis can sharpen our understanding of the general nature of the processes, for crisis often brings out latent social patterns which operate beneath the surface in "normal" times. Extrapolation from intrasystemic processes to intersystemic and total system processes (2) is a productive and accepted principle in small groups research, and we are beginning to learn from applying the same strategy in more complex research settings. And (3), the world's societies are so rapidly rationalizing that concentration on theories of the rationalization of protest in already highly differentiated systems could give us ready-made models of analysis just waiting for emerging societies to reach the specified conditions for study. These research advantages compound themselves when we take note of the generally low incidence of "collective behavior" (1) in pre-rational societies (3) where more primary group channels of expression and change usually absorb conflict before it reaches an overt mass action stage.

### *c. THE RATIONALIZATION OF PROTEST, I: ANALYSIS OF THE ELEMENTS*

The process of rationalization is, for Max Weber, *the* significant and distinguishing feature of western culture. It is implicit in his work, and only vaguely defined, as pointed out in chapter 1. The theoretical part of this study was conceived in response to the fact that Weber, one of the foremost social theorists of all time, nowhere precisely defines his most general working assumption. An initial attempt is made here to construct the general structural and temporal dimensions of the process of rationalization.

In beginning theory construction,[31] the definition of rationalization is repeated: it is *the tendency for social action to differentiate into systems for attaining the commonly agreed-upon goals of the actors by means of an increasingly precise calculation of available and adequate means.* Rationalization is thus seen as a natural process in the life history of social systems, with development proceeding through orderly stages as the system changes in size and age. Inherent in Weber's concept is the notion of *change through time*; there is a sense of movement, of directionality, of inevitability.

So now we raise in detail the questions first posed in chapter one: *How* do social systems change through time? and *What* is changing? Or, translated into the framework of this study: *How does rationalization proceed?* and *What is being rationalized?* The task of this paper is to begin to construct an answer to these questions which is both theoretically sound and empirically operational for research.

The form for an answer to the first question comes from Weber himself. The temporal nature of rationalization is analyzed as operating through four stages which are designated as the Rationalization Cycle. These stages represent a systematic unification of two important Weberian concepts which never were pushed to their logical limits by their author: *the three types of legitimate authority* (traditional, charismatic and rational-legal) and an important intervening variable (*the routinization of charisma*).[32] As outlined in chapter one, the four analytically distinct stages are:

The Rationalization Cycle

| I. | II. | III. | IV. |
|---|---|---|---|
| Traditional Control | The Charismatic Breakthrough | Routinization | Rational-Legal Organization |

The conditions of each stage are analytically derivable from the preceding stages, and the whole process cycles as innovations are absorbed and rationalized at ever higher levels of generality. Thus, what was Stage IV during one cycle may be considered "Traditional Control" (Stage I) from an opposing charismatic orientation.

An answer to the second basic question, "What is being rationalized?", comes from Parsons' formulation of the four functional imperatives[33]—those environmental and situational exigencies to which each social system must adapt to maintain its boundaries. To "maintain its boundaries" does not imply a static social system model, driving relentlessly toward perfect equilibrium. Rather it is equivalent to the notion of "preserving its existence as a system"—which usually involves drastic changes in the organization of the system as it continuously adapts to never-ending environmental challenge, as well as internal and external conflict.[34] Solutions to these and other systemic problems, then, never are ultimate. The four imperative needs which any social system is constantly trying to satisfy are:

(a) *Pattern-Maintenance* (or Latent Integration) — maintenance of the system's value patterns;
(b) *Integration* — providing for allocation and integration of units and energy within the system;
(c) *Goal Attainment* — providing facilities for achieving goals derived from the value pattern; and
(d) *Adaptation* — providing mechanisms through which the system may successfully relate to external systems, both physical and social.

Thus, the major theoretical argument of this paper is that Weber's basic underlying assumptions about social structure, process and change can be given systematic coherence and research utility by formalizing the process of the *rationalization cycle*, which involves four different yet interrelated solutions to the four basic functional needs of all social systems. This model as applied to the rationalization of protest within the systemic limitations outlined in part b of this chapter, is elaborated and presented in chart form on the fold-out at the end of the book.[35]

*Explanation of the Eight Basic Elements of the Rationalization Paradigm: The Four Stages and LIGA*

The theory of rationalization charted on the preceding pages should be viewed first and foremost as a study in the *development and change of social systems through time*. For this reason, the four Stages of Rationalization are placed along the horizontal axis at the top of the chart, and particular cells are identified first by the stage in which they appear and secondly by the problem solution they represent. In fact, one can only refer to the *structure* of a society by first locating it *in a particular time period* and with reference to *the total time dimension*.

*Four Stages of Rationalization*. In this context, the four stages of the rationalization cycle are defined as follows:

### Stage I: Traditional Control

As used here, Traditional Control is not to be confused with what Weber meant by "traditionalism" in any of its several specific forms.[36] Rather it means *the given state of social organization* at which the analytical framework enters—the antithesis of the new order envisioned in the ideology which activates Stage II. Social unrest and tension are latent in the social system, to be sure, but the prescribed and historically effective mechanisms of social control are still in effect and are unable to maintain equilibrium. In this way, the given conditions *are* "traditional" in the Weberian sense, however, for a significant proportion of actors unquestioningly[37] accept the going norms as "the way things are" (and, to a large extent, "should be").

In the particular phenomenon under study here (intergroup conflict in a highly differentiated society), the traditional control against which the Stage II elites are rebelling is based on discrimination due to certain stereotyped ascribed characteristics—notably race. In this sense, white America's paternalistic system of racial social control seems very much like the type of traditional authority Weber calls "patrimonialism."[38] In short, the given state of affairs retains a sufficient emphasis on ascription to promote some degree of latent dissatisfaction among achievement-oriented minority group members.

It should be remembered, too, that the Traditional Control of Stage I is enforced by the society at large, and not the protest systems under study. Thus the components specified here for Stage I refer to the adaptive state of the undeveloped protest system in relation to the total system. Latent protest systems are not sources of control in themselves but, functionally speaking, control is maintained *through* them because they have more-or-less passively *adapted to* the larger control system rather than *acting on it*.

### Stage II. The Charismatic Breakthrough

When the balance of activities in the latent protest system shifts from passively *adapting to*, to actively *acting on* the larger system of control, the process is said to have entered Stage II.[39] The Charismatic Breakthrough represents the stage of intense social innovation. The notion of charisma—that exceptional and spontaneous quality of "the gift"—is used to describe this stage specifically because it encompasses such a wide range of meanings. Above all it is a *source of moral authority*—an ideal which demands of its followers an attitude of reverence and respect. As such, it is a revolutionary force[40] which proposes a new moral order and elicits from followers a sense of duty and obligation in conforming to the demands of the new code.[41]

Stage II is referred to as a "breakthrough" because, in an almost literal sense, the charismatic ideal breaks through into the consciousness of a significant number of actors and presents itself as a viable course of action in resolving a particular dilemma. When this occurs, there is a breakthrough in another sense—the transformation of competition into overt conflict as latent sentiment for change is organized around the newly emergent charismatic solution.

We have been speaking of "the charismatic ideal" instead of "the charismatic leader" purposely. Charisma is too often associated with a person, while Weber's intention was that charisma be considered ". . . a *quality*, not necessarily only of persons, but of a 'supernatural' order."[42] Thus, particular individuals are only the *means* which bear the gift, the *forms* in which the charismatic ideal is embodied.

It is during this stage that the social system is, in Parsons and White's terms, "short-circuited" by elite innovators who mediate the charismatic ideal directly to personalities without the necessity of a fully rationalized institutional structure for enforcement.[43] The Charismatic Breakthrough, in effect, creates crises within the total system which have to be resolved (i.e., rationalized) either through *ad hoc* or established channels to maintain system boundaries. Parsons has stated clearly the relationship between charisma and rationalization:

> It is necessary . . . that new, relatively unrationalized . . . 'material' should be introduced into the system from the outside. By thus reducing the general level of rationalization of the system, the process of rationalization itself could, as it were, get a new start... In Max Weber's scheme . . . one of the theoretical functions of the concept of *charisma* was to serve as the conceptualization of the source of new orientations on which the process of rationalization was then conceived to operate.[44]

## Stage III. Routinization

"By its very nature," wrote Weber, "the existence of charismatic authority is specifically unstable."[45] Elaborating on the volatile temporality of charisma, Parsons adds that "For the message [of the charismatic innovator] to become embodied in a permanent everyday structure, to become institutionalized, it must undergo a fundamental change."[46] Routinization, then, involves the specification of goals and formalization of means which is necessary if the charismatic ideal is to be implemented.[47]

Charisma must, in Weber's words, ". . . come into the permanent institutions of a community" if its program is to be even partially effective. But when this happens, ". . . it is the fate of charisma . . . to give way to powers of tradition or of rational socialization."[48]

Thus at least two meanings emerge, depending on which system is the focus of analysis. In one, the emphasis is on the routinization of the innovation system itself. This process, which may be called *internal routinization*, is the focus of the present analysis. The second meaning is *external routinization*, focusing on the diffusion and acceptance of the Stage II innovations in the total system.

The protest system as well as the host systems are *disequilibriated* in Stage II; Stage III may be seen as the phase of *re-equilibration*.[49] For at this point, the drive toward rationalization is encouraged as the protest system faces problems of goals succession (L), leadership succession and membership recruitment (I), need for more sophisticated tactics as the opposition grows in its ability to handle once-successful forms of protest (G), and day-to-day economic exigencies (A). If solutions to these kinds of problems cannot be found and routinized, the charismatic fervor of Stage II dissipates. Routinization, then, is the tip-over point on which the protest totters between moving ahead to institutionalization of its goals and means (both internal and external) or falling back to charismatic slogans which once were a source of inspiration but no longer move the system and its members.

## Stage IV. Rational-Legal Organization

Stage III contains the beginnings of institutionalization of means and ends—which is formalized in Stage IV. Building on Weberian theory, Stage II innovations can be structured and elaborated in the direction of either substantive rationality (roughly equivalent to traditionalism) or formal rationality (roughly equivalent to rational-legal organization). Protest systems involved in intergroup conflict within highly differentiated societies inevitably strive toward formal rationality or a rational-legal form of social organization.[50] Minority group protest is directed *against* a system of traditional patrimonialism in which particularistic considerations rule supreme, and *toward* the ultimate goal of a highly rational social system governed by universalistic rules impartially administered without regard to ascribed characteristics—especially race.

Indeed, historical evidence leads to the conclusion that once economic rationalization is proceeding at a rapid rate in the social system, there is no other direction the entire system can go but away from ascription and toward achievement as the basis of stratification.[51] Viewed in the context of the social consequences of economic rationalization, the trend to rational-legal organization may be expressed another way: the broad exposure to different values and persons afforded by increasing mobility and mass communications technology hastens the development of democratic universality and the demise of tribal particularism. Only a rational-legal form of organization can administer a society whose ethnocentrism has begun to crack (or at least become more inclusive) due to exposure to alternatives.

The ideal-typical structural type around which a rational-legal system is organized is, of course, bureaucracy—the antithesis of spontaneous, sporadic, unorganized charisma. The development of bureaucracy is discussed below under integrative problems.

*The Four Functional Imperatives*. The answer to the crucial question, "*What* is being rationalized, and *how*?", is necessarily complex; the man dealing with such a query is attempting to explain no less than the whole trend of historical development itself. But at this stage—when conceptualization of the process of rationalization is still in early and unsophisticated forms—any attempt to answer this question must limit itself to the most basic elements of the problem, hoping to adequately systematize them as an outline for further rationalization of the theory itself.

The present study has chosen to focus on what seems to be the most general problem of social systems—the Hobbesian problem of order and orderly change. Thus, our conception of the *content* of the rationalization process is grounded in those basic processes through which a system maintains itself while undergoing continuous change. As noted on page 152 of this chapter, the processes are labeled the four *functional imperatives* (pattern-maintenance, integration, goal attainment and adaptation), and refer to those environmental and situational exigencies to which each social system must adapt to maintain itself.[52] Focusing on the concept of function in a study of development and change is appropriate if it is in fact, as Parsons contends, ". . . the link between the structural and the dynamic aspects of the system."[53] By studying changing functions as they relate to time and to one another, the content of the process of rationalization may be delineated.

Each of the functional imperatives, then, represents a *category of problem-types* to which the system must constantly furnish solutions. Within each of the imperatives are specified three problem-types called *priority problems*, for their solution is of highest priority for the continued adaptation and functioning of protest systems.[54] They are:

(1) *Content and basic structure of the solutions* — the system's evaluative orientations toward L, I, G or A exigencies and the framework within which the solutions are organized (all feeding back to, and dependent on L).

(2) *Range and relevance of the solutions* — the systems in which they are involved, scope of applicability, etc.

(3) *Dominant mechanisms employed in the solutions* — the major means of implementing the solution at various system levels, largely prescribed by solutions at levels 1 (content-structure) and 2 (range-relevance).

The imperatives from which the problems arise now are explained in descending order of generality, from basic groundings to specific facilities:

### (1) Pattern-Maintenance

Culturally and historically derived solutions to problems of meaning determine the orientation of actors to situations. In Parsonian shorthand this imperative is called the "L" function, for "latent integration"—a reference to the fact that value patterns must be maintained in the latent form of attitudes which predispose actors to appropriate responses. Basic values underlying the social and personality systems reside in this category. Norms, institutional structures, mechanisms of social control, attitudes—all are *based on* and *derived from* the patterns of value orientation of the system. And if the system is to continue to exist and pursue its goals in a coherent fashion, these patterns must be maintained.

Smelser's summary of the L function emphasizes its priority among the four imperatives and points out a more specific kind of problem it solves in the process of maintaining cultural values:

> Every social system is governed by a value system which specifies the nature of the system, its goals, and the means of attaining these goals. A social system's first functional requirement is to preserve the integrity of the value system itself and to assure that individual actors conform to it. This involves socializing and educating individuals, as well as providing tension-control mechanisms for handling and resolving individual disturbances relating to the values.[55]

In short, if a social system is to maintain a given state of equilibrium even within the broadest limits, it must elicit a high degree of commitment to its values from most of its members. Changes in the *kinds* and *intensity* of commitment are both the root and result of social change.

In this study, the L imperative is designated simply as Ideology, since this is the form taken by the value pattern in protest systems. *"Ideology"* in this analysis shall refer to *a system of empirically oriented beliefs interpreting the present situation of a collectivity in terms of its (a) history, (b) goals and (c) teleological possibilities, and (d) usually containing within it at least some prescription of the means for realizing its aims.*[56] The crucial importance of ideology for protest systems cannot be overstressed. In protest systems, firm ideological bases may, as Hadley Cantril and others have suggested, lead the members into a microcosm which ". . . becomes a small world in itself, commanding the total allegiance of its members and providing a totality of values and gratifications . . ."[57]

## (2) Integration

Solutions to the integrative problem maintain order in the system among its component parts in their day-to-day interaction with one another and the system at large. Some division of labor is necessary in any social system to carry out the specialized tasks as defined in L, and the energy and units involved in this differentiation must be smoothly allocated continuously for the system to mesh.

The structural focus of the integrative problem is on the internal organization of the system, including leadership and the organization of norms and statuses into institutional patterns. The processual focus has to do with such basic ongoing phenomena as symbolic cohesion, recruitment and socialization of new members, control of deviance, and the succession of mechanisms to handle these exigencies. Informal structure—which often is more important than formal structure in maintaining internal cohesion in groups operating under constant high tension—also is treated as a part of this imperative.

### (3) Goal-Attainment

Provision of structural facilities for attainment of the hierarchy of goals specified in L is the function of the third imperative. While pattern-maintenance and integration are basically oriented toward the internal stability of the system, both goal-attainment and adaptation are processes whereby the system relates to the given situation and the external environment. That is, the needs and desires of the system and individual actors as defined in the value system must be translated from symbolic abstractions into operational mechanisms for successfully dealing with external elements (i.e., elements not under continuous control of the system).

Collective goal-attainment behavior operates in response to perceived mandates derived from the meaning of the situation (L). As the meaning of the situation changes, goal-attainment mechanisms also change. As explained below, G units are the first to follow L changes in the definition of the situation as man, the goal-oriented animal, immediately seeks to optimize gratification. Thus the problem of organization of motivation for "right" behavior is dealt with in the L-G interchange.

### (4) Adaptation

The system must not only provide means for attaining goals in specific situations, but also more general ways of successfully relating to external systems. It must provide, in Parsons' words, ". . . disposable facilities independent of their relevance to any particular goals."[58] Adaptive facilities are "disposable" in the sense that they may be used in a number of alternative ways in the process of allocation between the system and subsystems. Since a certain minimum level of successful transactions between the system and other relevant systems is necessary for continued existence, this paradigm speaks of the adaptive imperative as "Relation to Other Systems."

Theories of collective behavior, conflict and social movements have, for years, been dealing with adaptive interchanges between systems without specifying the process as such. By explicitly recognizing this problem, the theory of rationalization hopes to facilitate the task of sorting out components and functions in relation to their respective systems.

As the analysis proceeds, the adaptive cell will emerge as important for rationalization in another way: after the total process reaches a certain stage, the internal development of protest systems is activated largely in response to inter-systemic challenge. The two major sources of this challenge, analyzed in detail below, are (a) the everyday economic exigencies of sustained group life which catch up with the most charismatic of movements, and (b) challenge from opposing systems.

### *A Note on Interpretation*

The movement of the chart through time is, of course, from left to right within the 16 cells marked off by the parallel lines. Two structural linkages are assumed without specific markings on the chart. *A causative element is assumed in all left-to-right horizontal relations*, since the problem solution in the lower number stage contains within it at least some of the preconditions of the solution to the same problem in the following stage. *Some interdependence is assumed between elements in all within-stage solutions*, since certain conditions must be met in *all* the problem areas before *any* can move on to higher level resolutions. Each condition may be said to exist *because* of all the others in that stage; a balancing or reciprocal causation operates. That is, a given state of each is necessary to maintain a given state of the others.[59] In the short-hand of the chart, some causation is assumed for each solution in temporal succession: I ⟶ II ⟶ III ⟶ IV; and an important degree of interrelationship is assumed for the solutions within each stage:

L
I
G
A

Thus are illustrated two of the three basic directions of boundary interchanges in such a paradigm—*horizontal* (within problem, between stages) and *vertical* (within stage, between problems). The third is *diagonal* (between problems and stages). Within these three directions, there are five logical types of linkages in the rationalization process, which operate between whole cells as well as between priority problems in different cells:

(1) *Implied Causation* ( → , horizontal). Left-to-right ("push") causation for *all* solutions in temporal succession through the four stages.

(2) *Implied Interdependence* ( ↕ , vertical). Functional interrelationship between elements in *all* within-stage solutions.

(3) *Push Causation* ( , diagonal). Left-to-right causation linking (a) total imperative cell in early stage to different imperative cell in later stage (example: III.L.2.b to IV.I.2a) or (b) primary element in one imperative cell to secondary element in another cell (example: I.G.1a to II.I.3).

(4) *Pull Causation* ( and , horizontal and diagonal). The coming fulfillment in a later stage is anticipated by the system, which thus "reaches back" to pull the problem to the higher level solution (examples: IV.I.3 pulls III.I.3, and L pulls I at every stage).

(5) *Feedback* ( , horizontal and diagonal). Information and/or energy from later stages of rationalization are fed back to (and stored in) earlier problem solutions, thus changing the emerging character of the solution in the next cycle (example: IV.L to I.L).

These five types may not be the most important linkages for every model of social system change, but this analysis hopes to demonstrate that they are the major causal and relational interchanges for the rationalization cycle. The most crucial interchanges for the rationalization of protest systems are marked in red on the chart; readers are invited to refer to these markings often to study the logic of the linkages proposed in this theory. Several conditions should be remembered in interpreting the paradigm and these relationships:

(1) A combination of linkages may exist between any two elements in the chart. For example

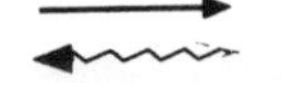

represents the common combination of causation and feedback between two variables.

(2) Left-to-right causation (Implied Causation) and vertical reciprocal relationships (Implied Interdependence) are assumed throughout the chart, so an especially important interchange is indicated when

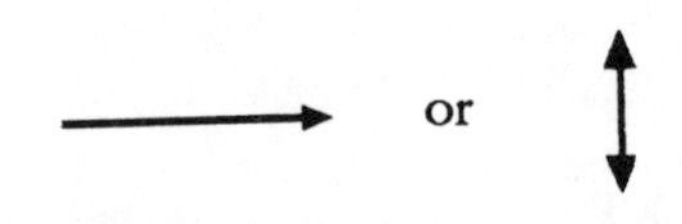


lines appear in the chart.

(3) The *'s in cells I.L, II.L and II.G, III.A and IV.I indicate the most crucial problem(s) at each of the four stages. Logically, then, the *-cells participate in the largest number of significant interchanges in each stage.

(4) L pulls I and G pulls A at every stage. A recent Parsons-White formulation of social change dynamics[60] sees the value consensus (L) and achievement mechanisms (G) breaking through to a new level in what rationalization theory labels Stage II. The breakthrough is accomplished by elite innovators who translate new values into action, and thus short-circuit the usual

A G
L I

route of institutionalization. At the early stages of the breakthrough, A and I are not yet differentiated out of the new L — G synthesis. This process, which would be represented as

$A \quad G_2 \qquad\qquad A_2 \quad G_2$
$L_2 \quad I_1 \quad \longrightarrow \quad L_2 \quad I_2$

in the classical four-fold diagram, is symbolized by the type of Pull Causation in which the new L definition reaches back and pulls the earlier I mechanisms to catch up (i.e., become institutionalized), and the new G mechanisms pull the earlier A mechanisms to the new institutionalization. The crucial interchange here is between II.A and III.A, for it is at this point that the adaptive mechanisms must be institutionalized so the system can free itself from previous dependence on elites and move more autonomously toward full rationalization.

(5) L and A.3.b are the focal problems for the entire process. The L components are, in the most profound sense, both dependent and independent variables in relation to the rest of the system. The rationalization cycle does not take off until a certain redefinition of L has taken place, yet the redefinition only occurs when certain kinds of institutional and environmental strains have accumulated after entering the system through the external adaptive processes of challenge conflict, crisis and the like (A.3.b). It is assumed for purposes of the rationalization chart that the changes in solutions in I, G and A-type problems at all stages feed back to L. And it is clear that the developing ideology pushes from the inside for the resolution of each external adaptive stage—which kicks off the next phase and, in time, another cycle.

(6) *Cycling* is the most general of all the dynamic processes involved in rationalization. It refers to the fact that *the four stages occur over and over again in sequence as the process by which innovations are absorbed by the system*. Each time an innovation is introduced into the system, the current level of social organization is challenged to incorporate or reject it. When elite innovators take up the cause of the innovative ideal and challenge the host system, competition with the former L may be transformed into conflict. If it attracts attention and support, the process moves into Stage II, and another cycle of rationalization is on its way. Therefore, when we speak of *the rationalization cycle*, we refer to phenomena on two levels: (a) *micro innovation*, in which the process operates as described above in absorbing the never-ending flow of innovative strains introduced into the system;[61] and (b) *macro process*, referring to the never-ending drive toward rationality of systems throughout their entire existence. Thus, the total life history of a social system which exists (i.e., maintains its boundaries) for, say 500 years, may be characterized in terms of the *macro process* of rationalization,

while its day-to-day and month-to-month operation is seen as an interrelated series of rationalizations of *micro innovations*.

*Temporal Succession of Priority Problem Solutions: Description and Explanation of the Chart*

The components of the theory now are presented in within-problem succession through the four stages. Again it should be noted that the components are analyzed in within-problem order instead of within-stage order to emphasize movement over structure.

## IDEOLOGY

*L.1. Content and Structure* (nature of assumptions, values, goals.)

I. *particularistic, exclusive* — small group of "chosen" holding ideology variant to total system defensively gravitate toward self-righteous ethnocentrism (even though it may be contrary to stated values) to reinforce and affirm deviant identity.[62]

II. *divergent modification* — sharpening and clarifying of ideology in attempt to differentiate growing protest system from outside world, prove uniqueness, and thus provide *raison d'etre* and convince followers.[63]

III. *democratic modification* — boundaries of the "chosen" broaden as the ideology is subjected to external and internal dialogue; reciprocal exposure of media prompts growing openness and breakdown of exclusivity.[64]

IV. *universalistic, democratic rationality*[65] — intense conflict eventually promotes dialogue and hastens the shift from local to cosmopolitan orientation in the protest system, consonant with the breakdown of ascription which is a major part of the rationalization process in society at-large.

*L.2.a. Range of Appeal*[66]

I. *narrow; specific subgroups* — the demands of the ideology are great, requiring a particular ascribed status and/or intense commitment for membership; therefore the appeal is small.[67]

II. *focused* — range of appeal now centers down around specific groups and situations which can respond to the call of the newly emergent charismatic ideal.

III. *expanding* — successes and exposure via the media in Stage II aid in recruitment, and the appeal expands as ideological content democratizes.

IV. *wide, differentiated* — wide-scale institutionalization of the ideology can take place only if it can appeal to a differentiated spectrum of class, racial and geographical interests; wider (including "middle class") appeal is a correlate of the emerging universalistic character of the ideology.[68]

*L.2.b. Range of Intensity*

I. *latent* — intensity may be high within the restricted and immature protest system, but it is dormant in relation to the host system since it has not yet found access to channels of expression.

II. *high* — the achievement possibilities opened up by emergence of the charismatic ideal crystallizes motivation into intense commitment to the ideology.

III. *waning* — as the range of appeals expands, the intensity becomes more diffused; worldly ideologies by definition cannot maintain high intensity.[69]

IV. *low* — the ideology now is routinized and the motivation of actors now more directly tied to organizational structures than values.

*L.3. Dominant Maintenance Mechanisms* (orientation of appeal for maintenance of ideology).

I. *ideal-centrism* — commitment to the ideology maintained through appeals to its inherent rightness.

II. *existential-centrism* — rightness of the ideology now is self-validating as individual actors experience new sense of meaning from following divergently modifying charismatic ideal.

III. *movement-centrism* — Stage II divergent modification (L.1) now sustains ideology as intensity and successes in goal-attainment lag; commitment ensured through appeals to rightness of the protest system as members need constant reinforcement for maintaining variant societal role.

IV. *rationality-centrism* — appeal to rational, efficient and practical reasons for maintaining ideology and commitment to it, although ideological content still may be rooted in and supported by charismatic referents.[70]

---

## INTEGRATION

*I.1. Internal Organizational Structure* (norms, statuses, patterns, institutional subsystems).[71]

I. *fragmented, undifferentiated* — organized around traditional relations of small staff; (a) little specialization, (b) primitive authority hierarchy, (c) informal administrative rules, (d) emphasis on efficiency secondary, (e) selection and promotion based on nepotism and length of service, (f) little differentiation of personal and professional roles.

II. *small, undifferentiated; surface cohesion but latent instability* — organized around informal cohesion of the chosen and their relation to emergent charismatic ideal; (a) little specialization, (b) authority hierarchy undeveloped, centering on charismatic leader, (c) growing need for rational rules, but informal emphasis remains, (d) no formal emphasis on efficiency, since success level high in charismatic phase, (e) selection and promotion based on commitment to ideal, (f) little differentiation of personal and professional roles.

III. *expanding, differentiating, unstable* — drive toward higher-level re-equilibration is hampered by conflict as individuals are unable to continue to subject personal goals to ideal goals; (a) growing specialization, (b) hierarchy developing, including formal administrator role, (c) number and complexity of formal rules grow to check personal ambitions and reinforce emphasis on ideal goals, (d) efficiency emphasized as system tries to meet everyday integrative exigencies, (e) selection and promotion based on technical competence as well as nepotism and length of service, (f) growing differentiation of personal and professional roles.

IV. *differentiated* — rational bureaucracy institutionalized; (a) highly interdependent division of labor based on functional specialization, (b) well-defined hierarchy of authority,[72] (c) precise system of rules, (d) efficiency a major organizational goal, (e) selection and promotion based on technical competence, (f) institutionalized impersonality.

*I.2.a.* *Bases of Recruitment of Members and Leaders*[73]

I. *narrow* — participation appeals to a select group, limited by the content of the ideology, lack of wide publicity in the media and lack of immediate prestige and other highly valued rewards.

II. *situationally broad* — the excitement of action engendered by intense commitment draws recruits in each local charismatic situation from among groups with the least stable positions in the system.[74]

III. *expanding* — successes and exposure via the media in Stage II, and the democratic modification of ideological content in Stage III, make protest more "respectable" and thereby broaden the range of social positions from which members may be recruited.

IV. *wide, differentiated* — the institutionalization and growing "respectabilization" of the protest system means that members now are recruited from a differentiated spectrum of class, racial and geographical levels.[75]

*I.2.b.* *Dominant Leadership Roles*[76]

I. *all-purpose professional* — primitive division of labor with limited goals and a small staff means that, like the small family business, "everybody does everything."

II. *charismatic* — the charismatic leader in Stage II is the pivotal figure in the rationalization cycle; although other leadership types are latently active, the whole tone of the protest at this and later stages is set by the Stage II elite innovator.[77]

III. (a) *administrator*, (b) *adaptor* (from Stage I.) — the first major differentiation of leadership roles takes place; charismatic leadership is dormant at this stage, and roles (a) and (b) are differentiated out of Stage I all-purpose professional role; *administrator* directs internal and external development of the protest, while *adaptor* role is called forth by increasing needs for negotiation and bargaining relationships with subsystems and external systems.

IV. (three sets of differentiated roles from Stages II and III): (II). *symbol, ideologue* — the mature protest must furnish both a continuing powerful *symbol* with whom participants and potential recruits can identify, and a viable ideology for meeting the growing range and complexity of problems;[78] the initial carrier of the charismatic ideal usually is able to fulfill the first role in a moderately successful movement (because he has established himself in Stage II), but often a professional writer-revolutionary takes over the *ideologue* function (although conceivably one person may handle both roles).

(III.a) *strategist, bureaucrat* — as the protest approaches rationality, the administrator role which emerged in Stage III splits into two roles; the *strategist* is the policy-maker and major decison-maker for the mature protest system (although his role may not be apparent on the surface), and the *bureaucrat* is responsible for administering the policies of the strategist and serving as a liaison to rank-and-file membership.

(III.b) *propagandist, agitator, fund-raiser* — the adaptor role of Stage III differentiates into three roles: the *propagandist* devises suitable methods of representing the ideas of the symbol-ideologue and the policies of the strategist to external systems (usually through the media) and subsystems (usually through a house organ, retreats, conferences, etc.); the *agitator* is responsible for furthering the goals of the protest through continuing challenge of the target institutions and/or values of the total system; the *fund-raiser* takes responsibility for provision of physical sustenance out of the hands of others in the system, thus freeing their time for more intense pursuit of the ideal and organizational goals.

*I.2.c.* *Dominant Membership Roles*

I. *nominal supporter* — if a formal organization exists at this stage, the dominant membership role calls for minimum involvement and financial support, while the all-purpose professionals carry out the program.

II. *unspecialized functionary* — called to participation-as-duty by the charismatic ideal and/or leader, members perform tasks as situational needs demand.

III. *multi-speciality functionary* — system needs at this stage call for the performance of many roles by members in the transition to rationality; the roles to be differentiated out in Stage IV are latently active here.

IV. *bureaucrat, agitator, active supporter, nominal supporter* — membership roles in the rationalized protest system complement leadership roles; the *member-bureaucrat* is responsible for the everyday efficient operation of the organization through carrying out the policies outlined at the strategist and leader-bureaucrat level; the *member-agitator* is usually a member of a "field staff," working with the leader-agitator and helping implement the goals at the grass-roots action level; the *active supporter* is the lowest status participant (i.e., has the fewest decision-making prerogatives), and is usually an unpaid volunteer in contrast to the paid full-time workers above him in the status hierarchy; the *nominal supporter* maintains much the same role as his namesake in Stage I, now responding to the calls of the fund-raiser for financial support with minimum personal involvement.

*I.3. Dominant Integrative Mechanisms* (orientation of appeal for maintenance of internal social control).[79]

I. *tradition-centrism* — integration maintained through appeals for devotion to the small, personal, exclusive ingroup.

II. *ideal-centrism* — integration of rapidly expanding system maintained through inner-directed devotion to the ideal, sense of moral duty to respond to charismatic call.

III. *success-centrism* — control mechanisms become autonomous as the system turns in on itself and become a deviant subculture;[80] integration maintained through appeals to successes of Stage II and attempts to replicate them; complementary conditions at this stage are (a) a tendency toward authoritarian control[81] and (b) growing emphasis on informal group structure.[82]

IV. *rationality-centrism* — integration maintained through appeal to ideals of practicality and efficiency as bureaucracy emphasizing rational-legal norms emerge.

---

## GOAL ATTAINMENT

*G.1.a. Nature and Structure of Internal Goals*[83]

I. *ideal-centered* — nature and structure of internal goals largely determined by the ideology within existing limits of social systems; minimal emphasis on internal goals because (a) large proportion of energy necessarily devoted to simply maintaining existence as definable latent protest system, and (b) participants bound by the high proportion of experiences shared by all in undifferentiated group.

II. *latent* — internal goals unimportant at this stage, since the newly emerged charismatic ideal directs commitment and action toward abuses in the total system.

III. *movement-centered* — need to meet everyday economic exigencies displaces energy (which was directed toward external goals in Stage II) to expanding internal goals: ". . . the dominating orientation of leaders and members shifts from implementation of the values the organization is taken to represent . . . to maintaining the organizational structure as such."[84]

IV. *subsystem-centered* — multiplication and diversification of goals is a correlate of rationalization, and provisions for reaching these goals are increasingly parceled out to subsystems; differentiation of bases of appeal and recruitment also lead to the growth of subsystems.

*G.1.b. Nature and Structure of External Goals*

I. *ideal-centered* — limited range and influence of the latent protest system keeps societal goals idealistic (and often unrealistic since there is little chance to test them against the realities of Traditional Control).

II. *norm-oriented: reform* — focus of goals is at social system level, with the object being ". . . to restore, protect, modify or create norms,"[85] as specified in the ideology; this is the "honeymoon" period[86] in which success is rapid and highly reinforcing.

III. *situation-oriented* — goals now are oriented both to normative change and value change, but the honeymoon is over and the system experiences a "technique lag" as it unsuccessfully tries to apply Stage II strategies to new and more complex situations; reform goals may become secondary to the immediate need of creating situational successes to validate continued existence of the protest system.

IV. *value-oriented: revolution* — if the protest reaches this stage, its goals have broadened and rationalized so they necessarily include an attempt ". . . to restore, protect, modify, or create values" as well as norms;[87] in terms of the consensus which existed under the given Traditional Control of Stage I, the goals of Stage IV are revolutionary; growing political sophistication as expanding scope of protest necessitates approaching total system at the level of formal control.

*G.2. Range of Goals*

I. *situational* — ideologically, goals are broad, but in practice they are tied to local situations which happen to come to the attention of the small group of all-purpose professionals.

II. *focused, specific* — targets become focused in specific situations which have high intensity participation by new recruits; often the particular location in which the goal is being pursued is selected through accidental reinforcement instead of conscious choice.

III. *expanding* — as the range of intensity wanes (*III*.L.2.b), the range of goals expands with the differentiating bases of recruitment (*III*.I.2.a.); as more and more structural components of the given Traditional Control of Stage I are challenged, the protest system comes to challenge basic values, as well.

IV. *wide and diffuse* — the democratizing ideology (*III*.L.1 and *IV*.L.1) now calls for basic changes in all remnants of ascriptive values and norms; the wide and differentiated bases of membership recruitment also demand support for a broad range of goals.[88]

### *G.3. Dominant Achievement Mechanisms*[89]

I. *localized protests: responding* — the small group of professionals responds to local challenges to Traditional Control and capitalizes on local initiative and/or community readiness for change by supplying strategic help.

II. *spontaneous mass-appeal demonstrations: communication* — the protest itself is no longer under control of a particular professional group and the initiatives for action and scope of the protest are largely determined by recruits who feel morally bound to respond to the newly articulated charismatic ideal; the excitement of overt challenge to norms has a mass appeal and releases latent hostility; internally, attempts are made to sustain and spread the protest through diffusing information of local situations and successes to potential protest areas.

III. *planned mass-appeal demonstrations: coordination* — in an effort to sustain the charisma and immediate successes of Stage II, the growing organizational leadership plans large demonstrations and attempts to coordinate local efforts; use of threat (to demonstrate if demands are not met) and promise (not to demonstrate if demands are met) in bargaining with external systems; "technique lag" (see *III*.G.1.b) hampers efforts as continued application of Stage II strategies fails to bring desired results and prevents discovery of more sophisticated methods.

IV. *disciplined long-range programs: initiation-coordination* — rational planning is institutionalized, and protest demonstrations now are seen as one part of a long-range program initiated and coordinated by the highly differentiated organizational structure described in *IV*.I; unrealistic hopes for reinstatement of the immediately successful mechanisms of

Stage II are displaced by devotion to disciplined planning and implementation.

---

## RELATION TO OTHER SYSTEMS[90]

### *A.1. External Organizational Structure*[91]

I. *latent, fragmented, situational* — rational principles and mechanisms for relation to external systems are undeveloped; adaptive exigencies are resolved *ad hoc*.

II. *diffuse, undifferentiated, unsophisticated* — the charismatic character of action at this stage is antithetical to highly rational organization, thus the structure for relating to external systems is considered unimportant; institutionalized principles and techniques have not emerged (and are not felt to be necessary) at this stage.

III. *expanding, differentiating* — this is a crucial problem in the most crucial cell for the system at this stage; movements cannot live by charisma alone, and several types of external challenges force the system to organize adaptive facilities, including (a) day-to-day economic needs (which spur development of fund-raising machinery), and (b) growth of counter-movements (which prompts rationalization of strategies).[92]

IV. *differentiated, sophisticated* — as the protest system relates to an ever-wider constituency of subsystems and external systems, the external organizational structure must, of necessity, become more complex and comprehensive; new facilities are needed to provide for high level negotiation, continued fund-raising, public relations, etc.

### *A.2.a. Range of Relevant Systems*[93]

I. *narrow, specific* — particularistic ideology (L), narrow range of goals (G), small membership under intense commitment and action demands, limited financial resources and underdeveloped structural facilities (I and A) keep the range of external relations small.

II. *situationally broad* — although the range of social subsystems affected by Stage II action may not be wide in terms of the total system, it is relatively broad in each *local* situation; the excitement of action engendered by intense commitment to the charismatic ideals appealing to actors on many system levels.

III. *expanding* — successes and growing exposure via the media expand the effect of the protest;[94] its influence now is felt through the actions of peripheral supporters in widely-scattered geographical areas; relevance is also extended through growing mailing lists for newsletters, direct appeals for funds, etc.

IV. *broad, differentiated* — it is now necessary for the protest system to maintain relations with a widely differentiated group of systems, ranging from small factions and organizations which have developed within to total system political leaders and news media.

*A.2.b.* *Rate of Desired Change* (in relevant systems)

I. *slow* — small membership, limited financial resources, underdeveloped structural facilities and unrationalized techniques keep the number of successes low—and, therefore, the rate of desired change in relevant systems is slow and sporadic.

II. *growing* — rapid increase in successes due to "coming of age" of the charismatic ideal, heightened participation by intensely-committed recruits, opposition's lack of sophisticated techniques for combatting the new form of protest.

III. *rapid* — heightened action at Stage II "catches up" with the total system as negotiation over demonstration-produced crises results in large number of successes at this stage.

IV. *waning to moderate* — the charismatic ideal and the goals it specifies are now institutionalized at a higher (more general) level in the total system than in the Traditional Control of Stage I; the rate of change levels off to a moderate pace, which is slower than Stages II and III, but faster than Stage I—and more stable (due to highly rationalized adaptive mechanisms) than any of the other stages.[95]

*A.3.a.* *Dominant Adaptive Mechanisms to Subsystems*

I. *latent* — the internal organization of the pre-take-off protest system is small and undifferentiated, with few or no important subsystems.[96]

II. *communication* — information diffusion within the emerging protest system relates subsystems to one another and reinforces their identification with The Cause ("it's bigger than any of us separately"); hearing of others involved in the same deviant activity reinforces the rightness of the ideal and binds subsystems more closely to the emerging total system.

III. *coordination* — a system-wide voice emerges from efforts at internal communication and now attempts to coordinate the protest in the name of necessity, efficiency and practicality; first attempts at coordination often lead to internal conflict as each faction's version of the charismatic ideal is not yet sufficiently secularized to permit rational organization.

IV. *initiation-coordination* — initiation of externally-oriented action on a movement-wide level necessitates precise coordination between subsystems (local protests and organizations); action is initiated *vis-a-vis* subsystems in the form of directives, calling of conferences, growing interchangeability of personnel in various locations, etc.

### A.3.b. *Dominant Adaptive Mechanisms to External Systems*[97]

I. *competition; challenge*[98] — *competition* (the process whereby actors oppose one another in seeking the scarce rewards they have learned to want) is constant in every system, and a continuous mode of adaptation between systems even though it may not be formally recognized or acknowledged; *challenges* (open and public presentation of demands and grievances) by various subsystems including the latent protest system are successfully resisted and/or absorbed by the Traditional Control mechanisms of the host system and overt conflict is prevented.

II. *conflict; crisis* — traditional mechanisms of control are unable to manage the increasing frequency of challenges, and competition breaks through into *conflict* (intensified competition of which a substantial proportion of those involved are aware); with awareness of competition comes polarization of opinion, and the lines of opposition are more clearly drawn than ever before;[99] the tip-over point for the success of the protest system is the emergence of *crisis* (definition of the situation by the enforcers of Traditional Control as serious enough to demand rapid resolution).

III. *confrontation; communication* — once the total system decision-makers have defined the situation as a crisis, the protest system has something to bargain with: the threat to create further crises if demands are not met, and/or the promise *not* to do so if concessions are given; this situation promotes *confrontation* (the realization on the part of the dominant group that the subordinate group has legitimate demands which must be dealt with), and thus *communication* (direct, face-to-face negotiation between the protest system and external systems, each bargaining from a position of power).

IV. *compromise; change*[100] — that *compromise* (victories and concessions for all systems involved) is inevitable was known by total system leaders when they defined the situation as a crisis . . . all that is left to be decided in Stage IV is how much and what form; *change*, then, refers to total system acceptance of at least some of the demands of Stages I and II which, by definition, means increasing emphasis on rationality and achievement and decreasing emphasis on ascription.

Perhaps the most succinct summary of the foregoing specification of the elements of rationalization would be: *as charisma routinizes, organization rationalizes*. That is, a certain balance of unrationalized energy with rational organization is needed to sustain any system of social action—and especially protest systems. Portrayed graphically, the relationship between charisma and organization in a successful protest system appears as follows:

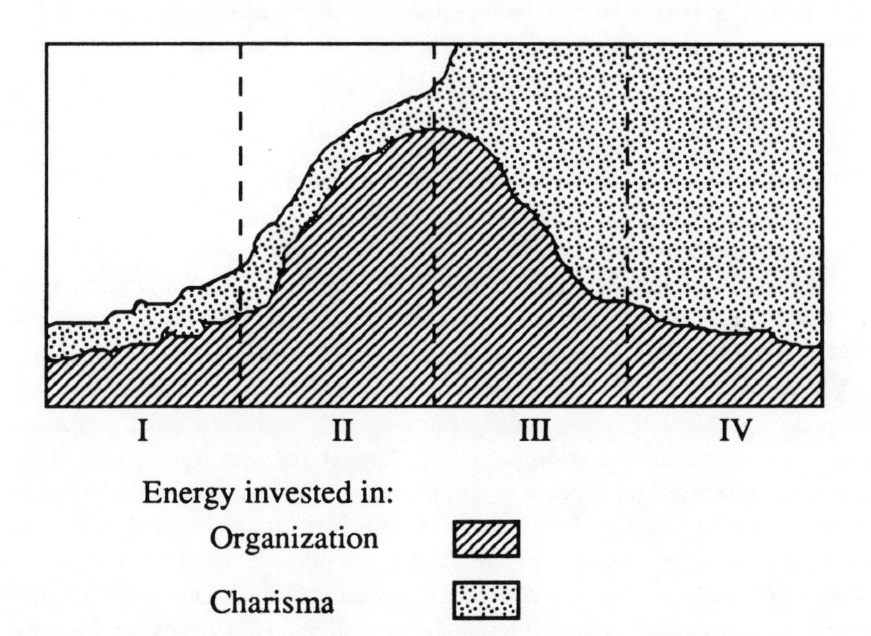


Before the Charismatic Breakthrough in Stage II, neither charismatic energy nor organization are up to full efficiency. During the charismatic stage, organization is virtually nonexistent, but as the charisma is routinized ("wears down") in Stage III, organizational structures must rationalize ("build up") to compensate and sustain the protest.

### d. THE RATIONALIZATION OF PROTEST, II: INTERRELATIONSHIP OF THE ELEMENTS

In further analyzing the interrelationships between elements in the rationalization paradigm, it should be remembered that the stages and problems which make up the structure of the analysis are ideal types. The theory suggests that these categories explain the *dominant* structures and processes in the rationalization of protest against which specific empirical cases may be measured. A "perfectly" rationalizing protest system would solve priority problems in exactly the form and sequence prescribed by the paradigm. The particular case being studied in this project—the direct action protest movement—thus is viewed in chapter 8 as approximating the rationalization process to a greater or lesser degree in its various components.

#### *Differential Significance of Problems and Problem-Stages*

The rationalization chart is arranged with the most "powerful" imperatives at the top;[101] latent integration is the most *general* problem any system has to solve to maintain its existence—and therefore, the most *significant* problem for the life of the rest of the system. The other internal imperative (integration) and the two external imperatives (goal attainment and adaptation) deal with progressively more specific and situational exigencies which are rooted in the continuous solutions at the first level. In addition, adaptive exigencies are especially significant in any study of extensive social development and change, for it is here at boundary interchanges and systemic linkages that sources of change are introduced and mediated to the system. Therefore analysis of the direct action movement deals largely with adaptive problems (especially A.3.b., Dominant Adaptive Mechanisms to External Systems) and the relation of their solutions to those at the integrative level.

Further, at each of the four stages of rationalization, at least one of the functional imperatives is more important than the others; that is, *the thrust of the system at that point depends more on effective solutions to some problems than others*. As noted earlier, the symbolic indication of this phenomenon in the paradigm is the greater number of important boundary interchanges in which the significant cell or cells are involved. The most important imperatives at each stage are indicated by an asterisk (*) in the upper left corner of the cell.

At Stage I, problems of latent integration are central. The latent system is directed mainly toward the maintenance of patterns which are at least slightly variant from the dominant values of the host culture. External challenges, both ideological and structural, constantly remind the latent protest system of its variances, and an inordinate amount of energy may be invested simply in maintaining the corporate identity within the boundaries of Traditional Control.

The Charismatic Breakthrough at Stage II thrusts two imperatives to the front—L and G. The charismatic ideal has, in an important sense, broken away from the Traditional Control of the past, and elite innovators are attempting to implement the ideal with appropriate mechanisms—namely spontaneous mass appeal demonstrations in the case under study.

Solutions to integrative and adaptive problems "catch up" to the new L-G consensus only after the charismatic ideal, the elite leadership and the dominant achievement mechanisms have begun to undergo the process of institutionalization. The A imperative begins the process first, and proceeds more rapidly toward full institutionalization than the I imperative, because this is the level at which the protest system is on the "front lines." Solutions to day-to-day intersystemic challenges from opposing systems, from personality needs and from immediate economic exigencies must be met first if the protest system is to remain in existence. Only if these kinds of adaptive mechanisms are institutionalized can the system free itself from overdependence on elites and move toward full rationalization. For these reasons, the adaptive imperative is viewed as the most significant cell at Stage III.

Thus, innovative mechanisms conceived in L and tested in G must become institutionalized in A before full internal rationalization can take place. Internal stability can come only after external stability is assured. The I imperative, then, becomes the focal point of development in Stage IV—Rational-Legal Organization. Only when the charismatic ideal becomes rationalized and programmed at this stage is the system prepared for initiation of another cycle of change and institutionalization at a higher level.

The L-G pull toward change through the stages of the rationalization cycle may then be charted as follows:

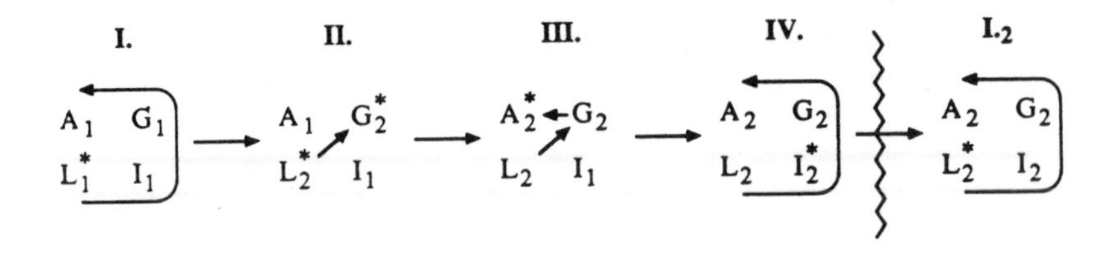


After stabilization of adaptive mechanisms has taken place in Stage III, the normal flow of control within the system is reestablished *at a higher level of value consensus*. That is, the binding force of innovation, conflict and change on antagonists within a total system reconstitutes L in a new stage of Traditional Control which is more democratic, more rational and less ascription-oriented than the previous L.

*Boundary Interchanges and Stress Points*

The important contribution of certain boundary interchanges[102] to the movement of rationalization through four stages has been described earlier in this chapter and illustrated by arrows on the fold-out chart at the end of the book. At various points in the process, the effects of important interchanges combine to form what we shall call *stress points*—crucial junctures between stages, problems and problem-stages which help shape the future content, direction, and intensity of systemic development and change. These junctures also may be called choice points, for it is here that alternative paths present themselves most dramatically to the system's decision-makers. Rational consideration of the consequences of stress-point decisions contributes to increasing rationality.

Theoretically, at stress points the developing process of rationalization could go "either way"—back to ascriptive traditionalism or forward toward achievement-oriented rationalism. But the specifications of rationalization theory make it clear that the usual course is toward the latter.[103] From the point of view of *social development*, then, stress points indicate those functional junctures which have to be successfully negotiated by the system before it can proceed further toward the end goal of rationality. If priority problems at these points are not effectively solved, the system becomes stalled and lapses back toward patrimonialism, where it marks time until another charismatic breakthrough takes place.

There are two master processes around which the major stress points cluster—*leadership succession* and *goal succession*. Both processes consist of the subprocesses of *expansion, displacement* and *substitution* within a context of *increasing differentiation*. The specifics of these processes have been dealt with in the explication of the rationalization chart, and now the analysis must turn to their more general role.

Stress points are a useful conceptual tool for analyzing the structural characteristics during the most crucial periods of the two succession processes. When the process of succession becomes magnified at certain points in the life of the system (and thereby more on public display for its enemies), leaders and members are challenged to clarify principles and goals. Too, they must rethink strategies more in the light of their practical effectiveness than their charismatic righteousness.

Succession and subsequent differentiation in both leadership and goals come largely in response to extra-systematic challenges and exigencies inherent in the process of rationalization. Expanding membership and waning ideological intensity pose one set of problems, the need for everyday operating funds another, and the growing sophistication of the opposition still another. A system which is not flexible enough to expand, displace and/or substitute leadership roles and goals in the face of such a wide range of changing problems soon dies.

*Leadership Succession*. Stage-to-stage changes in leadership roles as outlined earlier, show the succession process more clearly when charted as follows:

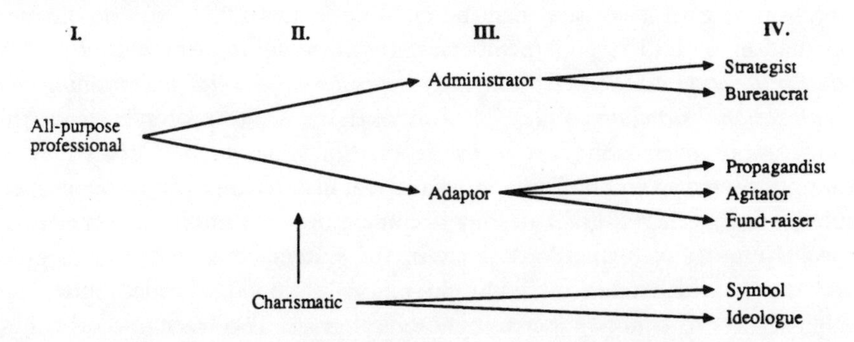


Here the basic process of differentiation (the splitting of one role into two or more) is seen as Stage III as the system growth engendered by Stage II charismatic innovators creates the need for two roles where the all-purpose professional alone once served. Further growth and routinization promotes the differentiation of the three existing roles into seven as the system enters the final stage of rationalization.

Each Stage interchange thus presents an occasion for a crisis in leadership succession. The system must successfully institutionalize the new roles demanded in these specifications (whether through rational specification or in reaction to a perceived succession crisis) to move into and through each Stage. Succession thus is viewed as a natural and necessary process, not as ". . . a mere loss of organizational effectiveness, a crisis from which the organization has to recover"—for often it is the process through which "needed innovations are introduced to counteract earlier deterioration . . ."[104]

As the protest system rationalizes, it is likely that occupants of some leadership roles will be recruited from more established and "respectable" levels of society; after all, the fund-raiser (Stage IV) is less a deviant role than the adaptor (Stage III), and the ideologue (Stage IV) a much more institutionalized role than the charismatic innovator (Stage II). Established leaders and administrators may be recruited from such diverse fields as religion, labor, politics and education.

Another important problem presents itself in the substitution dimension of succession: effective replacement of a particular leader can take place only if his role has been sufficiently rationalized to tie followers to him for basically technical rather than charismatic reasons.[105] Logically, then, the problem of leadership *replacement* becomes less acute as a system moves closer to rational-legal organization.

*Goal Succession*. Sheldon Messinger's classical statement of the nature and direction of goal succession may be cited again here: ". . . the dominating orientation of leaders and members shifts *from the implementation of the values the organization is taken to represent . . . to maintaining the organizational structure as such*."[106] But when applied to protest systems, this formulation covers only part of the story. For while *internal* goals may be turning toward an emphasis on organizational maintenance (displacement and substitution), *external* goals steadily become more revolutionary as they drive toward rationality (expansion). That is, the systematic clarification of goals and means which takes place during rationalization drives ideologues and other leaders to conceive increasingly radical goals. Too, each success brings the desire for more. And the only way the protest system can get "more" in the face of stiffening opposition is to rationalize internal organization to stabilize channels of funds, recruitment, ideas and strategies. Thus, the seeming paradox of increasing emphasis on organization-maintenance coupled with more revolutionary goals is understood as an essential counterpart of rationalization if viewed in terms of the interaction between *internal* and *external* exigencies.

The succession of external goals is of primary importance in this study. As outlined on pages 169-170 of this chapter, this process shows the rationalizing protest system moving from essentially reform goals to revolutionary goals.[107] Though they may be phrased in "respectable" terms, in the context of Stage I Traditional Control, Stage IV goals of universalistic rationality *are* revolutionary. The movement of goals toward this stage can be summarized by analyzing the progression of sociocultural organization levels attacked by the protest system. Essentially the movement is:

| I. | II. | III. | IV. |
|---|---|---|---|
| local, situational | local, situational | economic | political |

The ongoing challenges to the total system are articulated at the level of everyday grievances and inconveniences suffered by a minority member. In Stages I and II, the challenge to the system is directed at essentially the same targets, but in Stage II, publicity, numbers and increasing successes prepare the system for movement to more general goals.

The protest enters an essentially economic phase in Stage III, consonant with the growth of adaptive exigencies at this stage. Thus the system takes its first big step toward attacking more general (and therefore more important) grievances than simply those at a situational level. The boycott becomes important, the economic goals of the total system come in for increasing questioning, the unequal distribution of goods and access is examined—all of which functions to get the protest system asking more and more general questions about the ultimate sources of control over allocative processes in the host system.

By Stage IV, the goals have expanded to encompass no less than an all-out challenge to the traditional system of political control. If "artifically maintained formal authority"[108] is to be deposed (and most politically under-represented minority groups could be said to be artificially and illegitimately "kept in their place"), protest leaders must accumulate enough political sophistication and power to drive a permanent bargaining wedge into the heart of the formal control mechanisms of the host system. Indeed, Killian and Turner cite this "power shift" or "period of consolidation of power" as the essential feature of the mature revolutionary movement.[109]

An accumulation of succession problems (both leadership and goal) at boundaries, then, produces stress points. Four logical types of inter-stage stress points may be distinguished in the rationalization paradigm, with their conditions representing a macro model of the numerous sub-stress points existing at various levels throughout the system. The types are: (1) the I/II interchange, (2) the II/III interchange, (3) the III/IV interchange, and (4) the $IV_1/I_2$ interchange.

### *The I/II Interchange: Relative Deprivation and the 'Take-Off'*

Sociologists endlessly ask "Why?" about the emergence of protest and collective behavior from the stage of Traditional Control. But for the present study this is a "When?" question—one having to do with social change instead of social development. Our "Why?" queries focus on those structural conditions which occur in the natural course of social system life and predispose latent protest systems to "take-off."

The take-off of a protest system (i.e., the Charismatic Breakthrough into Stage II) occurs *when a sense of relative deprivation has become widespread enough in a minority population to cause a breakdown in effectiveness of the traditionally successful mechanisms of social control.* This explanation, centering on the two broad concepts of relative deprivation and social control, synthesizes most powerfully, I believe, the many approaches found in the literature.

Relative deprivation[110] is *that feeling of dissatisfaction with one's own conditions of living which arises as a result of meaningful exposure to other conditions*. More specifically, its sequential elements include:

(1) A previous unquestioning acceptance of Traditional Control, which exists in its purest form in primitive societies exposed to a minimum of cultural contact.

(2) Introduction of comparative standards of judgment of this condition—*any* standards—through such mechanisms as education,

travel, religion, communication with travelers or members of other cultures or subcultures.[111]

(3) The subsequent broadening or raising of expectations to a dimension or a level unattainable under the present conditions of existence.

(4) Realization of the gap between current conditions and the new expectations, and therefore subjectively feeling relatively deprived.

The crucial structural condition for the development of a sense of relative deprivation is *mobility*—intellectual, geographical, spiritual, economic—which puts individuals into contact with comparative standards (2). It should be emphasized that the new conditions need not be objectively "better" than the traditional state; it is the *feeling* of deprivation (and not the actual condition of deprivation as measured on some absolute scale) which leads to realization of the gap and subsequent translation of attitudes into action to bridge the gap.

Relative deprivation thus leads to a new ideology: a new vision of the world, the actor's place in it and his responsibility to act *on* it. The importance of this context of rising expectations has been emphasized frequently in the literature, and called variously "master symptoms,"[112] "incubation,"[113] "the stage of popular excitement,"[114] "the pre-conditions for take-off,"[115] "appropriate symptoms of disturbance" and "[heightened] structural conduciveness,"[116] and "interest group incubation."[117] Recently James C. Davies has added an important dynamic dimension to this phase, demonstrating that ". . . revolutions are most likely to occur when a prolonged period of objective economic and social development is followed by a short period of sharp reversal. People then subjectively feel that ground gained with great effort will be quite lost."[118] Applying this principle to rationalization theory, one can expect the take-off or Charismatic Breakthrough to occur when expectations and achievements of a minority group both have been rising at a fairly rapid rate, and *perceived* achievements suddenly fall off or level off.

The link between the condition of relative deprivation and the breakdown in social control is the concept of *strain*—structures and interchanges which tend to disrupt systemic and intersystemic equilibrium. When relative deprivation becomes widespread in the latent protest system, traditional mechanisms of control no longer can enforce conformity with the norms. Brinton, Moore, Parsons, Smelser and A. F. C. Wallace speak of several sources of strain which lead to the breakdown in social control and, thus, the Charismatic Breakthrough.[119] Systematically ordered, they are:

| *Source of Strain* | *Examples* |
|---|---|
| Demographic Imbalances | fluctuations in fertility and mortality rates (Moore), epidemics (Wallace). |
| Universal Scarcities | deprivation (Smelser), changes in physical environment, socio-economic distress, political subordination (Wallace). |
| Normative Imbalances | class antagonisms, governmental inefficiency, economic expansion (Brinton), social system instability (Parsons), ambiguity (Smelser). |
| Value Imbalances | alienative motivation (Parsons), acculturational pressures (Wallace). |

In summary, all social systems provide "safety valve"[120] mechanisms through which strain-bred personal stresses (hostility, frustration, aggression) are drained off in the day-to-day life of the system. If rigidity of the system prevents drain-off, personal stress accumulates, the effectiveness of traditional social control mechanisms decreases, and latent protest emerges into full-scale conflict in the Charismatic Breakthrough.

### *The II/III Interchange: Charismatic Innovators and Succession Problems*

The break of radical innovators from adherence to traditionally controlled norms is the most significant action component of Stage II. Adherents of the recently emerged charismatic ideal find their identity by differentiating themselves *from* the total system rather than assimilating *to* the system and its demands. The force of the protest depends on their innovation and willingness to "be different" in Stage II.[121] But the innovators must become, in White's terms, "lost objects," if the protest is to move past the honeymoon stage. Rationalization can take place only when innovation no longer is dependent on the elites. Whether the latent dissatisfaction *becomes* a public protest system is the problem of the I/II stress point. Now we see that the second crucial stress point at the II/III interchange (the initial transfer of charisma and its embodiment in institutional forms) determines whether the newly emerged system will *maintain itself* and grow—that is, whether it will rationalize, or fall to disorganization and ineffectiveness as the charisma wanes. The system's successful negotiation of this potential crisis point largely depends on its ability to incorporate the techniques of goal and leadership succession discussed earlier. The development of a succession crisis at this juncture may be fatal to the protest system for, as Killian and Turner note, "Such crises essentially force on the adherent an irrevocable choice between the movement and the outside world."[122]

### *The III/IV Interchange: From Social Reform to Subtle Revolution*

The protest system which endures well into Stage III, begins to turn to political goals and means for reasons outlined above. The III/IV stress point thus revolves about (a) the willingness to put aside formerly effective local-economic strategies and (b) the technical ability to devise new cosmopolitan-political strategies to implement the broader goals.

Appeals to the now-diminished Stage II charisma are of no avail—idealism has waned and the opposition is smarter. Idealistic recruiting appeals no longer work—the form of protest activity is not that attractive anymore, and the commitment demanded is much more intense. Here, then, the protest system has arrived at the basic generating process of bureaucratic structures: recruitment on the basis of technical competence. Only *deeply committed adherents with a high level of technical skill* can bring the protest through this stress point.

It is this need for efficiency that tends to turn the rationalizing protest system against its own stated goals in connection with the III/IV stress point. Although universalistic democracy in human relations is the emerging ideal toward which the system consciously strives, leaders soon learn that democracy is far from the most efficient mode of group organization. The system enters a phase of authoritarian administrative leadership which is designed to draw together structural and motivational "loose ends" and speed the group toward rationality.[123]

There are several sources of crisis inherent in this stress point, among them: (a) the group may idealistically attempt to block the ascendancy of authoritarian or oligarchical administrative tendencies, (b) the straightforward and impersonal mode of operation of a highly efficient authoritarian administration may not be able to elicit a sense of legitimacy and cooperation from rank-and-file idealists, and (c) the display of authoritarian leadership may tend to elicit authoritarian tendencies from lower levels and thus have a disintegrating effect on the group. If crisis-forestalling integrative mechanisms are not developed continuously and creatively, the III/IV stress point could prove fatal for the protest system.

### *The $IV_1/I_2$ Interchange: Toward a More General Value Consensus*

Perfect rationality is never achieved in any social system. But a major theme of this study is that with each rationalization cycle, systems move closer to rationality in their structure as well as in their ideologies. In a real sense, opposing systems which have resolved an issue through conflict have "gotten above" that particular issue when the mutually acceptable solution has been rationalized. The new stage of Traditional Control which emerges, then, represents a higher level value consensus than that which existed before introduction and rationalization of the innovation. Each succeeding Charismatic Breakthrough usually deals with a problem closer to the pure rationality pole of a *charisma—rationality* continuum.

Perhaps Stage $I_2$, then, is no more than a later version of Stage $IV_1$. In the ongoing reality of society, certainly this is true. But for analytical purposes there is a point where the highly rationalized system becomes so rigid in certain areas that it bends toward traditionalism and thus invites another Charismatic Breakthrough.[124]

The $IV_1/I_2$ stress point may not be stressful for the protest system, but for the total system it involves several potentially disruptive transactions. The *cycling* of which we spoke earlier (page 163) is a constant threat to the host system's equilibrium. A further product of cycling is *telescoping*—the more rapid rationalization of individual innovations with each successive cycle. These situational processes, which contribute to potential disequilibrium, are introduced and kept dynamic by the ongoing process of relative deprivation. Only if a social system can absorb relativization can it hope to maintain its various subsystems at a sufficiently rationalized (i.e., stable) Stage IV level to prevent the tipover to a new (and inherently unstable) rigid traditionalism.

### *The Paradox of Rationalization*[125]

Despite the formality with which the theory of rationalization is presented, protest is ultimately non-rationalizable.[126] Herein lies a basic paradox: rationality is both desired and avoided by the protest system. The emergent end-goal for intergroup relations protests is the treatment of all persons as whole individuals, without the interpersonal protection of stereotypes and rigid role specifications. Yet the essence of rationality is specialization and the judging of persons in terms of their functional utility to the system. The rationalized system must view the individual only in terms of his technical qualifications—the Card-filer, the Fund-raiser, the Idea-man.

The *need for structural rationality* and the *desire for I-Thou relationships* never can be perfectly reconciled. The bureaucratic specification of institutionalized impersonality cannot be achieved in a social system dedicated to the ideal of interpersonal relations unbound by rigid stratification. That the system continuously strives for the realization of both goals at the same time prevents the full attainment of either one.

Inherent in the structure vs. spontaneity paradox are four further dilemmas:

(1) The specific goal of protest systems is institutionalized innovation—the development of innovative mechanisms which can be rationalized and diffused, yet still maintain their effectiveness. The whole argument of this chapter is directed toward showing the difficulties inherent in such an endeavor.

(2) The goals (and in some cases, the strategies) of rationalizing protest become revolutionary at the same time as they are becoming institutionalized. The rationalization process combines revolution and respectability in a way that extinguishes Stage I Traditional Control as a viable alternative for even the most conservative members of the host system.

(3) The negotiation and compromise phases of the rationalization of protest involve equal-status contact between antagonists in a way that promotes a universalistic achievement-orientation—often in violation of the deepest ethnocentrism of the host system members involved.

(4) While rationalization leads to greater interdependence of units within a system, it also promotes greater estrangement of the individuals involved—specifically because they are viewed as *units*.

These dilemmas are taken up again in the final chapter as predictions are formulated. But first the rationalization paradigm is applied to the data of direct action in chapter 8.

EIGHT

# A Sociological Paradox: The Rationalization of Direct Action Protest

That is the destiny of every new idea. It is crystallized in formulas so that it may be propagated. It is intrusted to a body of interpreters so that it may be preserved. That body is prudently recruited, sometimes specifically paid . . . Thus every new idea invariably ends by becoming fixed, inflexible, parasitical, and reactionary.

— Silone[1]

We don't like to refer to our group as an "organization." I didn't come out of school to become an Organization Man.

— Charles Sherrod, SNCC[2]

Data from the direct action protest movement from 1960 to 1962 now are viewed in the light of the explanatory framework presented in the last chapter. The purposes of this juxtaposition of theory and data are:

(1) to explain an empirical case in terms which permit generalization to similar cases—and thus help to build theory;

(2) to test the viability of the theory of rationalization of protest outlined in chapter 7, particularly as it applies to the *internal* development of protest structures; and

(3) to demonstrate the inherent paradox involved in the attempt to rationalize protest, and show how this condition affects the level of rationality at various stages of development.

Following is a brief elaboration on each of these purposes.

(1) The framework developed in chapter 7 is intended as a general theory applicable to protest systems involved in "movements" or "collective behavior" at an intrasocietal level in highly differentiated societies.[2] A major goal of the project is to show the usefulness of the theory in explaining and predicting the rationalization of other cases of protest occurring within the above conditions.

In chapter 7, the dimensions of the theory are outlined in terms of *priority problems* instead of stages; i.e., ideal-type solutions to problem *L.I.* (ideological content) are traced through each of the four stages, and the same is done for each of the other 17 problems. The rationalization chart (see fold-out at the end of the book) was explained in this way for purposes of conceptual continuity and clarity. In the present chapter, however, data from the movement are analyzed in terms of *temporal stages* for sociohistorical continuity and because the movement does not even enter the final stage of rationalization during the time period covered. Thus, the total structure of Stage I (Traditional Control) is examined in the light of all the problem-solutions before the analysis moves on and through each of the other three stages.

(2) A preliminary test of the theory is made by applying it step-by-step to the *internal* rationalization of the direct action protest movement. The protest system itself must be the focal point for any analysis of the effects of a developing movement; it may even be regarded as the independent variable *vis-a-vis* other relevant systems, since they only come into the scope of this theory because of their reactions to protest. Soon affected systems initiate action (often taking the form of counter-movements) which feeds back to the protest system and becomes an important causal variable. Before undertaking any extensive analysis of other relevant systems, then, it is necessary to examine in detail the dimensions of rationalization of the protest system itself.

Thus the application of theory to data in this chapter focuses on internal rationalization of the movement as a whole, with brief comment on three subsystems. The subsystems are the three organizations most deeply involved in direct action—the Congress of Racial Equality, the Southern Christian Leadership Conference and the Student Nonviolent Coordinating Committee.[3]

(3) Underlying the analysis in this chapter—and made explicit in the final chapter—is a sense of the paradox involved in the attempted rationalization of protest. There are several levels of the paradox as specified at the end of the last chapter, all having to do with the juxtaposition of freedom and structure, of spontaneity and institutionalization. One is desired, the other is necessary. The very nature of protest makes it successful only if it is relatively free and unbound; if it is domesticated and becomes predictable, its effectiveness is lost. Yet some degree of structure, rationality and predictability is required if the goals of the innovators are to be achieved with optimum efficiency. The halting progress toward rationality observed throughout the analysis of the movement, then, is to be understood as partially a result of this insoluble paradox. That the system *wants* to strive for spontaneity and *needs* to strive for structure simultaneously prevents the full attainment of either goal.

### *A Foreword on Conflict and Revolt*

Protest involves, by definition, *conflict* and a *revolt against authority*. *Conflict* is analyzed specifically as a major adaptive mechanism to external systems in Stage II, but it should be pointed out that the process operates at all levels and in all stages. It will be recalled that the theory assumes that conflict is a frequent component of social interaction—an intensified and publicized extension of ever-present social competition. Conflict is viewed, then, as a major mechanism through which desegregation takes place: it publicizes grievances, refines value positions, elicits personal commitment and, most important of all in the long run, it resocializes individuals in society-at-large. The latter function is accomplished largely through mass media reports of conflict which lay the cognitive groundwork for re-education and attitude change.

Although the thrust of this study is not essentially psychological, the personality variable of *authority-rejection* must be considered briefly before an adequate sociological analysis is possible. There is good evidence that the revolt against authority manifested in the direct action movement has been highly functional for the personalities involved—mainly by giving long-frustrated individuals a sense of being able to *do* something to remove the causes of the frustration.[4] We shall see also that the *object of rejection* changes as the protest rationalizes.

In Stage II, for instance, latent hostility emerges against adults, members of The Establishment, the white segregationist in general, law enforcement officers, state and local laws, discriminatory customs, the Negro middle class in general, Uncle Toms, Nervous Nellies, Negro college administrators, pie-in-the-sky religion, the NAACP, parents and less militant peers, to name a few. In short, the objects of open rejection are every perceived perpetrator and supporter of the segregated system.

Much of the energy for protest at every stage is generated through this process of personal revolt. I have been in pre-demonstration mass meetings in which every object mentioned above has been derided with growing enthusiasm as the participants soared to a peak of high motivation for protest. The archetypal example is a joke told before a mass meeting in Atlanta in 1960. Student leader Bernard Lee told of the Montgomery Negro who thought he was a Big Man and informed the police about protest plans in advance. One day, the story goes, the Big Man was hailed by two policemen (who did not know he was a Big Man). "Hey, boy, come over to this here car." The Negro obeyed, to the point of sticking his head in the window when the policeman asked him to lean in so they could hear him more clearly. Then, continued the story-teller, the policemen rolled up the window, choking the Big Man and leaving his feet dangling off the ground. The response to this story was a 15-second laugh and cheer which said, in effect, *this is what happens to a sell-out.*[5]

The revolt against religion was evident in the same meeting. "We've been praying, writing spirituals and saying 'Lord, please lead us to the Promised Land,' for a hundred years," said Atlanta student leader Lonnie King. "It's now time for us to lead ourselves . . . You and I are the salvation of the Negroes—and America."

In Stage III of the direct action movement, the objects of repudiation for student protestors changed—the revolt now was largely against "white liberals" and Negro civil rights leaders, especially Martin Luther King. As situations (an accumulation of jail sentences and prolonged absence from college, for instance) forced protestors into an even further separation from middle class standards, they needed more elaborate justifications for their militancy. Even discussion and analysis became signs of the non-militant, the do-nothing.[6] The anti-King sentiment, probably prompted by King's greater prestige and access to the media, is recorded in this chapter's section on the development of SNCC. General anti-adult feeling (against whites, Negroes, organizational leaders and anyone who disagrees on strategy) comes through in all phases of the analysis. It is summed up by the student who told me in August of 1960, when the movement was just six months old, "Let this go down in your record: I hate the bourgeoisie. Anybody who doesn't support the movement, I call him an Uncle Tom."[7]

The pure rationality of Stage IV by definition excludes any strong and sustained authority-rejection, at least on the surface. Rather, rationality requires a cool and objective calculation of ends and means, and a complex division of labor enlisting all possible resources—including, in this case, the established and prestigious "adult" organizations. The movement has not reached this stage; interpretations of post-1962 developments and predictions are made in chapter 9.

There is no better way to convey the tone of *identity-affirmation through authority-rejection* than through the songs of the direct action movement. Many of the tunes and some of the words were appropriated—often unknowingly—from the labor movement of the 1930s. Others came from old spirituals. "We Shall Overcome" caught on immediately as the hymn of the movement. Its words are a simple affirmation:

We shall overcome,
We shall overcome,
We shall overcome someday.
Deep in my heart I do believe,
We shall overcome someday.

We'll walk hand in hand . . .

We are not afraid . . .

The truth shall make us free . . .

Revolt and protest themes at various stages come through in the following verses, which are representative of the pathos-tempered-with-humor of movement songs:

### *They Go Wild, Simply Wild Over Me*—Nashville, 1960[8]

They go wild, simply wild, over me,
And I've never done no wrong that I could see.
There's no freedom in this land, they would throw you in the can,
They go wild, simply wild, over me.

Oh the manager, he went wild over me,
When I went to town one day and sat for tea.
He was breathin' mighty hard, when his cares I'd disregard,
He went wild, simply wild over me.

Oh the judge, he went wild over me,
And I plainly saw we never could agree.
So I let His Nibs obey what his conscience had to say,
And he went wild, simply wild, over me.

Will my children go wild or go free
When it's their turn to go and sit for tea?
Will those bed sheet-wearin' whites still yell, "Down with civil rights,"
Or will justice have come to Tennessee?

### *The Freedom Trilogy*—1961[9]

Oh Freedom,
Oh Freedom,
Oh Freedom over me,
And before I'd be a slave, I'd be buried in my grave,
And go home to my Lord and be free.

No more moanin' . . .

No more Jim Crow . . .

No segregation . . .

---

Take this hammer, carry it to the cap'n . . .
Take this hammer, carry it to the cap'n . . .
Take this hammer, carry it to the cap'n . . .
Tell him I'm gone, boys, tell him I'm gone.

If he asks you, was I laughin' . . .
. . . Tell him I was cryin', boys, tell him I was cryin.'

If he asks you, was I runnin' . . .
. . . Tell him I was flyin', boys, tell him I was flyin.'

---

I'm on my way to freedomland . . .
I'm on my way to freedomland . . .
I'm on my way to freedomland . . .
I'm on my way, great God, I'm on my way.

Gonna ask my cap'n, come go with me . . .

If he won't let me, I'm goin' anyhow . . .
. . . I'm on my way, great God, I'm on my way.

### *I'll Be Waitin' Down There*—Albany, 1962[10]

If you come down to the pool room
And you can't find me no where,
Just come on down to the Albany Movement,
I'll be waitin' down there.

If you come down to the Albany Movement
And you can't find me no where,
Just come on down to the drug store,
I'll be sittin'-in there.

If you come down to the drug store,
And you can't find me no where,
Just come on down to the jail house,
I'll be waitin' down there.

If you come down to the jail house,
And you can't find me no where,
Just come on up to the court room,
I'll be waitin' up there.

If you come down to the court room
And you can't find me no where,
Just come up to the Supreme Court,
I'll be winnin' up there.

*Which Side Are You On?*—Mississippi, 1962[11]

Don't listen to Mr. Charlie,
Don't listen to his lies.
Us black folks ain't got a chance
Unless we organize.

Which side are you on, boy,
Which side are you on?

Down in Mississippi
There are no moderates;
You either are a Freedom Fighter
Or a stooge for Ross Barnett.

Which side are you on, boy,
Which side are you on?

## *a. I. TRADITIONAL CONTROL: SEEDS OF THE REVOLT AGAINST AUTHORITY*

The goals, structure and strategies of the desegregation effort before 1960 provide the data on which the analysis of Stage I focuses. "Traditional Control" refers to the state of social organization in society-at-large at the time the analytical framework enters, and our concern is how desegregation activities were carried on within this framework of control. The data show that the direct action movement of 1960 arose not only as a protest against societal enforcement of segregation—but also against civil rights leaders and organizations perceived as accomodationists. The goal of this section, then, is to understand the external and especially the internal context in which this revolt developed.

It should be remembered that the movement began and flourished in the Border and Middle South where, as several informants put it, segregation barriers were crumbling and ready to be pushed.[13] Traditional control was loosening for demographic and economic reasons, and the protestors unknowingly capitalized on this state of readiness. But the symbols of segregation were still intact, and the power behind them entrenched. Government by the nepotistic white "regime of 'favourites'" (as Weber labels traditional authority[14]) was the order of the day in the particularistic South, and popular political participation was low.

Pre-1960 desegregation efforts—the latent components of the direct action movement—are now interpreted in terms of the theory of the rationalization of protest. This section is, of necessity, short and speculative, since my research was not focused on this period.

### Stage I
### L: IDEOLOGY

1. *Content: particularistic, exclusive* — Seeds of conflict between civil rights organizations existed within groups like the NAACP and CORE, who carried on the protest against segregation with limited budget and professional staff. Groups like this were viewed with suspicion as "radicals" by society-at-large—and even by some "white liberals." Their small numbers in the face of an enormous task tended to produce a strong sense of rightness of the cause and limited goals. Example: ever since its founding for the "talented tenth,"[15] the NAACP has been a middle-class organization striving for goals (school desegregation, for example) which benefit the Negro middle class almost exclusively.[16] The inclusive notion of an all-out attack on poverty, unemployment and housing had not been developed.

2a. *Range of Appeal: narrow (specific subgroups)* — Civil rights groups prior to 1960 were able to appeal to only a small range of subgroups within American society. Only several hundred actively participated in CORE—the only national group specifically committed to bringing desegregation through nonviolent direct action; the test of commitment was too intense and the necessary devotion of time too great for a wide appeal. Most of the sustaining contributions for organizations like the NAACP, CORE, and SCEF came from small memberships, long-time white liberals, labor unions and Negro religious and fraternal groups. Limited staff and resources prevented any broad-based mail appeals. CORE in 1958-59, for instance, had only 5,000 names on its national appeals mailing list.[17]

2b. *Range of Intensity: latent* — Before 1960, the ideology of desegregation attracted only small numbers who were willing to work full time for the cause, as societal mechanisms of social control prevented the desegregation drive from gaining wider respectability and support. As yet only limited channels of expression were available—through the courts, conferences and, in a very few cases, direct action.

3. *Dominant Maintenance Mechanism: ideal-centrism* — Appeal to the ideals of the organization was sufficient to *maintain* commitment in individuals who had made the leap to this form of deviant identification. Once the identification was made, there were few questions about the rightness of the cause. In surveying the pre-1960 literature of the major civil rights organizations, I have found virtually no debate about goals—only the assumption that anyone who commits himself to *this* group at *this* point in history understands and accepts the essential correctness of the ideology.[18]

## Stage I
## I: INTEGRATION

1. *Internal Organizational Structure: fragmented, undifferentiated* — The small staffs of civil rights organizations in Stage I lent themselves to a personalistic and informal internal structure. (a) There was a primitive *division of labor* in the total movement for desegregation: the NAACP leaned more to legalistic and educational approaches, the Urban League and the Southern Regional Council concentrated almost wholly on education, and CORE emphasized direct action.[19] There was little coordination of overall purposes or strategy. And there was little specialization *within* the individual civil rights groups.[20] (b) There was no formal *hierarchy of authority* in pre-1960 desegregation efforts, for the number of participants was small and there were few organizational interconnections. The NAACP was informally recognized as the most important group working for Negro rights; its Executive Secretary Roy Wilkins and Legal Director Thurgood Marshall were regarded as titular heads of the drive for desegregation. (c) I find no evidence of a *precise system of rules* governing desegregation activities; there was no formal coordination of organizational goals or strategies. Again, administrative rules existed only *within* specific organizations—and these, especially in the case of CORE, were informal, vaguely defined and not often in written form.[21] (d) There was an obvious *emphasis on efficiency* in the pre-1960 civil rights groups, but financial and personnel limitations prevented this from becoming a major concern . . . they were simply too busy responding to situational exigencies *as separate groups* to place a formal emphasis on inter-organizational efficiency *per se*.[22] (e) No rational means existed for *selection and promotion* of staff members of desegregation groups . . . new personnel often were recruited after satisfactory performance in local situations,[23] or on the basis of particularistic ties with present staff.[24] (f) *Institutionalized impersonality* is one requirement of rationality which never has been met in the civil rights movement. In Stage I, as in later stages, there is little differentiation of personal and professional roles. The publicity afforded protestors prevents it. Too, the intensity of commitment, the small numbers involved and the unity bred by deviant identification help make protesting a 24-hour role.

2a. *Bases of Recruitment of Members and Leaders: narrow* — Although membership at this stage largely consisted of nominal supporters (prime examples are financial contributors to the Urban League, CORE, NAACP and SCEF), the appeal was not wide; most support came from individual donations and those of labor unions and Negro churches. Active members (in CORE, for instance) were recruited from an even smaller base due to limited access to the media and the lack of common prestige awards available to participants. Recruitment of leaders was discussed in 1(e) above.

2b. *Dominant Leadership Role: all-purpose professional* — Roy Wilkins of the NAACP, while one of the major civil rights leaders in America during the 1940s and 1950s, filled nearly every kind of latent role available: ideologue, symbol, strategist, bureaucrat, propagandist, agitator and fund-raiser.[25] The same is true of the CORE staff during the 1940s and 1950s.[26] It is important to note that the role of the all-purpose professional was developing througn local protest efforts in the 1950s, too, as militant Negro leaders replaced the old intercessory leadership. Protests in Montgomery, Orangeburg, South Carolina, Shreveport and Tallahassee, as documented in chapter 3, were recruiting and training new militant leadership in all of the roles necessary to carry on a desegregation campaign—and thus laying the groundwork for emergence of leadership in the Southwide and nationwide movement that was to come.[27]

2c. *Dominant Membership Role: nominal supporter* — Americans who were "with you in spirit" were the dominant type of member of the existing civil rights organizations before the 1960s. CORE had a mailing list of 5,000 persons who were called "members" by virtue of their occasional response to thrice-yearly appeals. But the professional staff numbered seven, the annual budget about $60,000 and members of local chapters in the low hundreds. The NAACP, while having almost 300,000 members in local chapters, got (and gets) only minimal support from them; local executive secretaries and sometimes local chapter presidents (often ministers) carried on the program, while members paid dues without necessary commitment to action.[28]

3. *Dominant Integrative Mechanism: tradition-centrism* — Integration of individual groups was maintained through informal and traditional (in the Weberian sense, i.e., particularistic) forms of social control—leisure-time activities shared by the work group, sharing tasks in a poorly rationalized work group, etc. I have experienced these forms of social control in working with several organizations in the early stages of the movement in 1960, including CORE, the NAACP and a local protest group in Boston. The sense of inherent rightness of the ideology supports the commitment to organizational unity in a way analogous to the localistic traditional society.

## Stage I
## G: GOAL-ATTAINMENT

1a. *Nature and Structure of Internal Goals: ideal-centered* — There were few internal goals for the protest effort as a whole, for there was little sense of "movement." Energy which in later stages will be consumed by internal rationalization was directed toward fulfillment of the ideal in society. There was a major exception in subsystems—especially the NAACP, which was old enough as a separate organization (50 years in 1959) to be highly concerned with members, budget and chapter growth.[29]

1b. *Nature and Structure of External Goals: ideal-centered* — There was little debate about long-range external goals in pre-movement civil rights organizations—the goals were bound by the ideology and so rarely even approached that there was little chance to modify them against the test of reality. The NAACP's goal of ". . . [ending] racial discrimination and segregation in all public aspects of American life"[30] is a representative example: it is so general that it is not open to question. And since there was so much work to be done to even approach the general goal, nearly any ideal-based short-range goal (and/or technique) was acceptable.

2. *Range of Goals: situational* — For most of its existence, CORE was involved in essentially fire-fighting activities, working in local situations (like Washington, St. Louis and Baltimore[31]) which happened to come to the attention of the national office and where sufficient local interest in protest could be aroused. The NAACP—again, because of its longevity—was more involved in long-range planning. But in both groups, the range of goals was restricted by the narrow range of ideological appeal, small memberships, lack of access to the media and to prestige, and thus limited funds and staff.

3. *Dominant Achievement Mechanism: localized protests* (responding) — The major strategy for the latent protest system was to capitalize on local readiness or initiative and help create situations which require negotiation and, hopefully, compromise of some form by segregationists in power. Prior to 1960, the protests were essentially legal (led and sustained largely by the NAACP, many on a federal court level) and education (groups like the Urban League, Southern Regional Council, Anti-Defamation League, SCEF, church groups, etc.). CORE—the one group intensely involved in direct action before 1960—was more successful in developing short-range challenges to specific grievances. Dramatic presentation of demands through sit-ins, wade-ins and stand-ins brought quicker desegregation than the tedious legal or educational process, and laid the groundwork for the emergence of a direct action movement.

## Stage I
## A: RELATION TO OTHER SYSTEMS

1. *External Organizational Structure: latent, fragmented, situation* — In the latent protest system as-a-whole, adaptive mechanisms were not yet rationalized . . . they were tied to specific crisis situations developed in relation to specific protest groups. But again, on the level of the protest groups themselves, various adaptive mechanisms were highly developed; this is true without question for the NAACP repertoire of legal techniques.

2a. *Range of Relevant Systems: narrow, specific* — By definition, the range of effectiveness of protest *before* take-off is small. With few exceptions, desegregation efforts in America before 1960 affected small numbers of persons in society at-large. Records of CORE and individual direct action attempts (see chapter 3) in the 1940s and 1950s show that success was sporadic at best. Those protests which succeeded brought the issue before the public for at least a short time *in the area itself*. But there was no nationwide sense of *movement* or involvement, and most of the country could go on feeling unaffected. The major exception is the school desegregation drive through the courts, engineered by the NAACP. School systems on every level from graduate to elementary were affected, and cases were fought in several sections of the nation leading up to the 1954 U.S. Supreme Court decision banning segregation in the public schools. This decision had a wide-ranging effect . . . it brought more defiance than compliance, and the frustrating delay caused by organized evasion emerged as a strong motivating factor for protestors in the 1960s.[32]

2b. *Rate of Desired Change: slow* — Limited resources, small staffs and lack of a nationwide sense of the urgency of protest kept the pace of desegregation very slow until 1960. The NAACP's legal attack on school segregation, for instance, had been in progress for 20 tedious years before the 1954 decision was handed down—and by 1960 only six percent of the Negro students in the 17-state area affected by the decision were attending classes with whites. There was no school desegregation at all in the five Deep South states of Alabama, Georgia, Louisiana, Mississippi and South Carolina.[33] On other fronts, CORE had experienced sporadic success with public accommodations in northern and border cities (see chapter 3).

3a. *Dominant Adaptive Mechanisms to Subsystems: latent* — Before 1960, there was no "movement" for desegregation and there was no all-inclusive organizational structure concerned with the relations of subsystems to it and to one another. Desegregation professionals knew one another personally, and there was some intermingling of staffs. For example, James Farmer (National Director of CORE since 1961) had served alternately as a CORE Field Director and Director of NAACP Youth Work during the 1940s and 1950s. Each group had its own projects and areas of concern, and the field was so big that they rarely bumped into one another—thus there was rarely need for any degree of rationality in subsystem relations.

3b. *Dominant Adaptive Mechanisms to External Systems: competition; challenge* — The history of race relations in America is a story of continuous *competition* between minority groups and dominant groups for limited rewards. Prior to 1960, the enforcers of Traditional Control succeeded in keeping the competition at a relatively unpublicized level; rarely was there widespread public recognition of racial problems. Even as late as the summer of 1964—four years *after* the direct action movement had begun—one could still hear the City Manager of riot-wracked Rochester, New York, say incredulously that "We have never had any race problems in our city. Race relations have been good—even exemplary, I would say."[34] The goal of civil rights groups has been to present *challenges* to the segregated status quo in hopes of heightening competition so it breaks through into overt conflict which must be dealt with by the system. Court suits, lobbying for legislation, direct action demonstrations—all are examples of challenges which have taken place during the recent history of American race relations. Until 1960, traditional mechanisms of control were able to contain these challenges within sub-movement limits.

In summary, limited financial resources and personnel, lack of access to the media, a limited base of popular support, low general prestige of minorities and their cause, and a wavering policy of federal commitment to desegregation prevented desegregation efforts from emerging into a full-scale social movement before 1960.

## *b. THE CHARISMATIC BREAKTHROUGH: EMERGENCE OF A REFORM MOVEMENT*

The charismatic breakthrough of nonviolent direct action in American race relations took place in at least two stages, only one of which is treated in detail here.

The first stage of the breakthrough was culminated in Montgomery in 1955 and 1956 when Dr. Martin Luther King, Jr., symbolized for the nation's Negroes and sympathetic whites the power of nonviolence in the bus boycott. As documented in chapter 3, Montgomery laid the ideological groundwork for the emergence of a full-scale social movement against segregation. The notion that nonviolence was a viable strategy for desegregation efforts began to break through into the American consciousness as words and pictures of the boycott's dignified leaders and successes were diffused from Montgomery. A well-developed ideology thus was "waiting" to help spread the sit-ins when they began on February 1 of 1960.

Application of the theory in this section deals with the second stage—approximately the first six months of the sit-in movement, from February to August, 1960.[35] Perhaps the charismatic stage of this or any movement should be analyzed in two time phases rather than one, for solutions to the L and G functional imperatives logically must precede I and A solutions in the concrete situation. This sequence is represented on the master chart in chapter 7 by the arrows reaching from cells L and G in Stage II through cells I and A in Stage I—literally pulling them to "catch up" with the new ideology and achievement mechanisms which have developed. Application of the categories in this section may be viewed in two-cell temporal sets, L I and G A, to put the relationship in proper perspective.

Revolutions never spring from the system full-blown. A crucial contention of this study is that, contingent on the fulfillment of certain structural conditions, a rationalizing revolutionary movement may develop from a spontaneous reform movement. The ideological justification for racial revolution in America was present in nonviolent philosophy from the beginning, but the goals of participants in the charismatic phase were essentially reformist—changing such institutional inconveniences as lunch counter and restaurant segregation, without questioning the value-bases of the society itself. The intense sense of commitment to reform goals generated in Stage II is perhaps the major prerequisite for the development of a revolutionary perspective at later stages; it must be sufficiently intense to carry the protest through the paralyzing effects of routinization, and to generate a sense of dissatisfaction with *any* goals achieved.

The charismatic phase in all movements is short; it is the *kairos* of which theologians speak—those unique periods in history in which chronological time, situation and human actors come together to accomplish something qualitatively different. It is supremely important as the time in which a new moral demand is perceived, a new authority responded to. The charismatic ideal evokes "a devotion born of stress and enthusiasm."[36] I hope its *kairotic* importance does not get submerged in the ensuing analytical chronology.

## Stage II
## L: IDEOLOGY

1. *Content: divergent modification* — The first formal clarification of ideology in connection with the sit-ins took place at the Raleigh Conference on Easter Weekend of 1960, two months after the movement began. The call to the meeting contained the seeds of the new vocabulary: Freedom, Human Dignity, potential for social change, Freedom Fighters. Martin Luther King's statement to the press further specified the components of the emerging ideology: "selective buying," jail over bail, reconciliation and the beloved community.[37] SNCC's first Statement of Purpose from the Raleigh Conference affirmed the new identity with appeals for the beloved community through nonviolent love, which ". . . matches the capacity for evil to inflict suffering with an even more enduring capacity to absorb evil, all the while persisting in love."[38]

   Existing organizations caught up in the sit-ins soon assimilated the most appealing aspects of the movement's ideology. The NAACP, for instance, has been making statements reaffirming its belief in direct action "as one of *many* methods" since the sit-ins began.[39]

   The ideological diverging process operates between individual groups within the movement, as well as between the movement and the outside world, predisposing the system for organizational conflicts preceding and during rationalization. Representative of SNCC's diverging (and of course, morally superior) conception of itself is Chairman Charles McDew's statement: "Sure, the adults [including established civil rights groups] have helped us a lot in this movement. But that knitty-gritty work of getting whipped in the head and thrown in jail is always done by the students."

2a. *Range of Appeal: focused* — The sit-ins had an immediate appeal to types of groups which had never been involved in this kind of activism before. Most of the groups responding to the appeal of the nonviolent ideal in the spring of 1960 were predisposed to do so by their structural position, which enabled them to identify with sit-inners and their goals. Examples, as documented in chapter 4, included voluntary associations serving interests of youth, religion, high school and college students, labor and persons professionally interested in human relations.

2b. *Range of Intensity: high* — High intensity of commitment to the new ideology is perhaps *the* distinguishing feature of the charismatic stage. Nine of the 13 students said that participation in the movement had given them a "new commitment, a renewed sense of identity and personal efficacy."[40] There was everywhere the sense of duty, the feeling that it was a moral obligation to respond to the charismatic ideal. "We saw that students were the only ones economically free enough to do anything," said Lester McKinnie of Nashville, "*so we were obligated to launch this movement*."[41] Nashville students jailed in the first wave of the sit-ins (in March 1960) manifested their sense of moral rightness and intense commitment to an atypical ideology in their statement to the press:

> While we graciously thank the people who have made money for fines available to us, we cannot find it in our hearts to go against the moral principles that we hold dear. We feel that if we pay these fines we would be contributing to and supporting the injustices and immoral practices that have been performed in the arrests and convictions.[42]

James Gibson of Atlanta put it most succinctly in discussing the differences of the movement in 1962 from the movement in 1960: "We used to burn up with the kind of intensity it's impossible to sustain."

3. *Dominant Maintenance Mechanism: existential-centrism* — Maintenance of ideological commitment in adherents during the charismatic stage of any movement is no problem; by definition this is the stage in which commitment is "naturally" the highest. The sit-in movement is no exception. That most sit-inners in the early days found a new sense of meaning and purpose in their activity is evidence that their very participation reinforced their ideological commitment. The research of others as well as my own interviews indicate that most sit-in participants in 1960 felt that for the first time they were actually *doing something* to help bring social reality in line with their ideals. Hear the students:

Patricia Stephens, Tallahassee — "We are all so very happy that we are able to do this for our city, state and nation."[43]

Mae King, Marshall, Texas — ". . . through the sit-ins we are playing a significant role . . . in seeking the perfection and survival of democracy in this country."[44]

A young white student — "I have never felt so intense, alive, such a sense of well-being."[45]

Charles McDew, second Chairman of SNCC — "I feel very good consistently . . . I have the feeling within myself that I can do something myself . . . I have a real feeling of manhood."

Diane Nash Bevel, Nashville — "The feeling of right, the moral rejuvenation is the only thing that carries you over . . . With the mayor [Ben West] in 1960 I had a moment of divine inspiration."

In short, as former SCLC staff member James Wood said in October of 1960, "Never have so many little people been so happy to belong to something good."[46]

## Stage II
## I: INTEGRATION

1. *Internal Organizational Structure: small, undifferentiated; surface cohesion, but latent instability* — Development of internal organizational structure lags behind development of the ideology, but high intensity of the charismatic ideal makes up for the structural primitiveness. Sense of movement unifies participating subsystems, even though personal and organizational conflicts soon come to the surface. The sense of defensiveness and conflict was apparent in the memorandum of "The Meaning of the Sit-Ins" issued by one of two meetings of the National Council of Churches, SNCC, SCLC, CORE and the NAACP in the summer of 1960:

> Nonviolent direct action is not the only method which is feasible, and traditional methods, such as legal action, education, etc., must not be neglected when nonviolent direct action is employed . . . There has been an unfortunate tendency in the press to emphasize nonviolent direct action in terms of an attack on other methods previously used in the struggle for human dignity. It is recognized that nonviolent direct action is important in this struggle and does not necessarily conflict with other methods. It is further recognized that nonviolent direct action, by itself, would not be sufficient.[47]

(a) In some senses there was less specialization of role responsibilities than pre-take-off; all organizations were caught up in the sweep of direct action, and bent their approaches to it.[48] Some *division of labor* developed between protestors (usually students and/or CORE members) and non-protesting supporters (usually adults and organizations like local churches or NAACP chapters who provided bail money and legal advice). (b) *Authority hierarchy* was based on ability to fulfill charismatic ideal; the major symbolic leader for a short time was Dr. King. Local (and soon movement-wide) leadership came to be based on militancy, with demonstrating, arrest and jail as necessary parts of the credentials.[49] (c) *System of rules* began to grow almost immediately, first locally, then on a movement-wide level through SNCC and the established civil rights organizations. The main rules emerging at this point had to do with legal procedure and dos and don'ts of nonviolence.[50] (d) No need for formal *emphasis on efficiency* during charismatic stage . . . the protests were self-validating for participants and inherently "efficient" in their confrontation and shaking up of the white community. (e) *Selection and promotion* based on demonstrated commitment and militancy, both at local and movement-wide level. All of the 13 students elected as the first SNCC representatives at the Raleigh Conference, for instance, had been jailed at least once.[51] (f) Little *differentiation of personal and professional roles*; as data in L.2.b. and L.3 indicate, early participants *lived* the movement 24 hours a day—in many cases to the exclusion of studies and social life.[52]

2a. *Bases of Recruitment of Members and Leaders: situationally broad* — If a charismatic outburst is to become a full-scale social movement, recruitment of personnel must take place at every level of the social structure during this phase. In intense protest situations, persons from all classes in the Negro community (and some from the white community) joined after the initial wave of recruitment among students. Functionally speaking, students were the leaders because of their greater degree of freedom from traditional modes of social control—especially their *economic* independence from the enforcers of Traditional Control.

2b. *Dominant Leadership Role: charismatic* — For the thousands of sit-inners early in 1960, it was literally love at first sight. "You can't explain it . . . the movement is like a love affair" . . . "When I said these things in 1960, people just listened" . . . "It was spooky and beautiful, the way those kids just walked down the street and poof! there went segregation."[53] These were some of the ways informants described their "devotion born of stress and enthusiasm" to the charismatic ideal in the first days of the movement. Martin Luther King is unquestionably *the* charismatic symbol in the early stages (77 percent of the Students and 88 percent of the Adults listed him as one of the "most important leaders in the movement").[54] Local leaders emerged on the basis of the "gift" — Ezell Blair in Greensboro, Diane Nash in Nashville, Charles McDew and Tom Gaither in Orangeburg, South Carolina, Lonnie King and Julian Bond in Atlanta, the Stephens girls in Tallahassee, Henry Thomas in Washington. They had had no professional training in protest. The "intensity with which we used to burn up" carried new charismatic leaders through in situation after situation, and rational administrative skills were simply irrelevant to them for this brief *kairotic* period. Rational professionals like CORE's Gordon Carey and the NAACP's Herbert Wright were only catalytic at this point, but they were to become major movers later when the charisma wore off.

2c. *Dominant Membership Role: unspecialized functionary* — Correlative with the limited division of labor described in I.1, most early participants performed every task as the need arose. Even the student *leadership* performed all available membership roles. Of eleven leaders from all over the South interviewed in the summer of 1960, all eleven had planned and directed demonstrations, attended mass meetings, sat-in, done clerical work for the movement, served on a local coordinating committee and cooperated with a boycott. Nine had been arrested and gone to jail, eight had picketed, five had served on SNCC and all had participated in various other activities such as fund-raising and voter registration.[55]

3. *Dominant Integrative Mechanism: ideal-centrism* — Solutions to all other problems in L and I imperatives combine to form integrative content. Devotion to the ideal as described especially in L.2b, L.3, I.1 and I.2b was sufficient to

briefly maintain integration; latent energy for internal conflict was drained off through (a) high intensity of ideological commitment and (b) conflict with external systems.

## Stage II
## G: GOAL-ATTAINMENT

1a. *Nature and Structure of Internal Goals: latent* — Expenditure of energy as outlined in Stage II L and I imperatives made internal goals temporarily unimportant. But, as described in I.1, latent instability soon came to the surface and had to be dealt with in the form of "unity meetings" and other integrative mechanisms.

1b. *Nature and Structure of External Goals: norm-oriented* (reform) — The first goal of the sit-ins was the desegregation of lunch counters and other public accommodations. For at least the first year, the goals were essentially of this reformist nature—the desire to change certain norms which prevented minorities from realizing cultural values. All of my participant observation contacts during that time validate this point. A North Carolina survey in April of 1961 found that of 827 sit-inners at three Negro colleges, about half listed "resentment against everyday injustices" as their motivation for protest, and no other category (many of which were related) got more than 20 percent of the first ranks. The authors concluded that sit-in activity came largely from "identification with/and desire for white middle class standards."[56] And of the eight leaders I interviewed in 1960 who responded to a question about the "ultimate effect" of the sit-ins, seven answered in reformist terms: "ending discrimination," "bring democracy which is written in the Constitution," "complete integration in all areas of public accommodations," "equality for minorities," etc.[57]

2. *Range of Goals: focused, specific* — Situations which brought instant recruits, high participation intensity and fairly rapid successes characterized the early days of the sit-ins; thus, for a short time, goals essentially remained tied to the excitement of the local situation. Early attempts at movement-wide communication were aimed at stimulating and sustaining local movements—not prescribing cosmopolitan goals (see chapter 4 and II.G.1b above).

3. *Dominant Achievement Mechanism: spontaneous mass appeal demonstrations* (communication) — Within one month in the spring of 1960, mass demonstrations against lunch counter segregation had spread from Greensboro to 30 cities in seven southern states; by two months, demonstrations had occurred in 78 cities in all 13 southern states; by the end of the school year in June—four months later—nearly 100 cities had been affected. There were more than 50,000 participants, more than 2,000 were arrested, students were expelled, faculty members fired (details in chapter 4). Boycotts developed in

Nashville, Atlanta, Savannah, Birmingham, Knoxville and other cities almost immediately. Volume in four S.H. Kress southern stores dropped 15-18 percent in February. Woolworth's national business was down 8.9 percent in March. Other stores reported losses as high as 65 percent in the height of the sit-ins.[58] For several months, the protest movement was not controlled by any civil rights organizations—rather, the movement carried them along in its wake. The sociological dynamics of this period are elaborated in A.3a. (internal mechanisms) and A.3b. (external mechanisms) below.

## Stage II
## A: RELATION TO OTHER SYSTEMS

1. *External Organizational Structure: diffuse, undifferentiated, unsophisticated* — The institutionalization of adaptive structures theoretically lags behind goal-attainment methods in the immediate situation, but my limited evidence (inter-organizational memos, communiques with store managers, etc.) indicates that development proceeded rapidly in the direct action movement. See II.A.3a. and b below.

2a. *Range of Relevant Systems: situationally broad* — In nearly every sit-in in the spring of 1960, all levels of the Negro community were involved: students sat-in and picketed, some of their professors and ministers went with them, parents and businessmen raised money and joined in "selective buying" campaigns. In Petersburg, Virginia, for instance, the most economically vulnerable group of all—the domestics—joined by threatening mass resignation when one of their number faced firing because of her son's activities in the protest.[59]

2b. *Rate of Desired Change: growing* — Change took place rapidly in modes of Negro-white relationships, for white elites now were forced to bargain with Negroes who spoke from a position of power . . . their power was the potential to disrupt the surface tranquility of the community, and therefore its economic life and industry-attracting image. In the long run, sociologists probably will see this speeding up of the Negro-white power confrontation as the most important kind of change. But a more direct and immediate measure of the increasing rate of change is the number of cities desegregating lunch counters during the first six months of the movement:[60]

| | |
|---|---|
| March 16 — | first desegregation of lunch counters resulting from the movement in San Antonio, Texas.[61] |
| May 1 — | eight cities have desegregated lunch counters (opening of counters in Nashville on May 7 was an important symbolic breakthrough). |
| June 1 — | 18 cities. |

August 1 — 27 cities.

By October 1, 94 cities had desegregated facilities; see this section (A.2b) in Stage III for details and interpretation.

3a. *Dominant Adaptive Mechanism to Subsystems: communication* — Formation of the Student Nonviolent Coordinating Committee at the Raleigh Conference was, above all, an attempt to establish lines of communication among protests groups and communities scattered throughout the South. Leaders at this stage—James Lawson, Martin Luther King, Jr., and Ella Baker among the Adults, and Henry Thomas, Jane Stembridge and Marian Wright among the Students—saw the danger of killing the movement by trying to take over its direction. But they saw the need to develop formal mechanisms of communication between protest groups and that nebulous, almost spiritual force they called *the movement*. SNCC was never, in itself, the movement, but for a time it served as an adaptive vehicle *for* the movement, both internally and externally. Committees on Coordination, Communication and Finance were set up at Raleigh, but my analysis of the Coordination Committee indicates that it, too, was essentially concerned with internal communication. See section c of this chapter for an analysis of SNCC's communication function. The organizational "unity meetings" of summer 1960 were another response to the perceived need to harness and diffuse the movement's charisma.

3b. *Dominant Adaptive Mechanisms to External Systems: conflict, crisis* — Challenge transformed long-smoldering racial competition into *conflict* in almost 100 southern cities in the spring of 1960. The levels and dimensions of the conflict were analyzed in chapter 4 and summarized at the beginning of this chapter: young innovators vs. The System in all of its manifestations. Others were drawn into the conflict: white "moderates" vs. die-hard segregationists, the commercial interests of southern cities vs. "Southern Tradition," white policemen's sense of duty vs. their personal prejudices. Opinion polarized . . . everyone asked, "Which side are you on, boy, which side are you on?" Conflict was to remain an essential element of the rationalizing protests system, but it belongs in Stage II in the formal theoretical framework because of its newness and unusual effectiveness at this point. Definition of the situation by the enforcers of Traditional Control as serious enough to demand rapid resolution (*crisis*) is the state toward which all protest efforts are consciously or unconsciously directed, and the position from which serious negotiation for change begins. It is present in some form at most levels in all stages of protest, but it is injected into the framework here because its effect is foremost at this stage. San Antonio desegregated lunch counters on March 16 because white community leaders defined *potential demonstrations* as a crisis situation. Nashville desegregated on May 7 because white leaders defined *continued demonstrations, jailings and the threat of a Negro boycott* as a crisis. Many other southern cities desegregated during the summer to avoid the potential crisis of

> more demonstrations in the fall when colleges opened up again. Margaret Long of the Southern Regional Council summed it up: "every trouble spot was a great turning point."[62]

The charismatic breakthrough of this or any movement, then, is intense and short-lived. Commitment is high, internal conflict is low, and crisis in relation to external systems begins to bring about desired changes in the social order. The charismatic period is especially short in the movement under study here, for (a) 24-hour-a-day intense commitment to a non-profit movement is impossible to sustain for personal economic reasons, (b) movements born into a highly rationalized culture find a ready-made organizational structure eager to absorb and rationalize then, and (c) with much at stake, the opposition soon develops sophisticated anti-movement techniques—thus forcing the movement to rationalize its techniques.

### *c. III. ROUTINIZATION: THE REFORM MOVEMENT BECOMES A REVOLUTIONARY PROGRAM*

The II/III interchange involves several crucial stress points which the emerging protest must successfully negotiate if it is to become an enduring and effective system. Among these are the succession of goals (L and G), leadership (I) and techniques (A), which began to rationalize almost immediately after the sit-ins began, on both local and movement-wide levels. If the paralyzing effects of routinization are to be avoided, rational solutions must be found to replace the charismatic solutions to priority problems which worked so well, temporarily, in Stage II. For purposes of analysis, the ideal-typical third stage of the theory—Routinization—will be applied to the period beginning September 1960. The principles of this stage can be applied to direct action protests up to the present, since the pure rationality of Stage IV never is fully achieved. But the formal data here only take us up to February 1, 1962. The ongoing interaction in the desegregation movement between charisma (II) and routinization (III) leading to rationality (IV) is treated in the final chapter, with postdictions and predictions from 1962 on.

This study contends that a spontaneously-generated social reform movement may take on a revolutionary character while simultaneously undergoing institutionalization. While it will be pointed out that the sit-in *movement* largely was absorbed as a *program* of various existing and *ad hoc organizations*,[63] I will attempt to show that the long-range program developing from this stage is essentially revolutionary, i.e., designed to reshape certain economic and political *values* as well as their institutional expression. And the revolutionary program only came about because of rigorous and highly rational planning and research.

It should be remembered that rationalization of a social movement is essentially a speeded-up and public version of the natural institutionalization process operating in all social systems at all times. The movement's L-G innovation is explicitly stated and exposed to public scrutiny and debate, thus prompting a more open and immediate resolution of nonrational elements.

## Stage III
## L: IDEOLOGY

1. *Content: democratic modification* — As a movement, broader and broader ideological perspectives were tolerated and incorporated—from labor, Judaism, Social Gospel Christianity, the radical left, etc. But although the ideology of the movement calls for inclusiveness as its ultimate goal, subsystems were, at this stage, manifesting growing exclusiveness (see the comments on organizational conflict in I.1 below). Democratic modification was promoted on a purely cognitive level in all subsystems, however, and this fact prompted more rapid rationalization. "We are aware of more complications now," said Diane Nash Bevel, "so we try to figure them into a logical structure."

2a. *Range of Appeal: expanding* — Consonant with democratic modification, media publicity and success in the charismatic stage, the ideology began appealing to a wider range of issues and, thus, a wider range of social groups. Through the stimulation of organizations like SCEF, NSA and SDS as well as various human relations professionals and academicians, student protestors were soon introduced to issues ranging from civil liberties to international peace and academic freedom. The Atlanta SNCC Conference in October of 1960, for instance, attracted almost as many observers as protestors, and dealt with such topics as "After the Sit-Ins, What?", "Political Activity," "Employment," "Education," and "Relationship with National and non-southern Groups."[64] The expansion to broader economic and political issues of the Nashville seminar of summer 1961 was interpreted in chapter 6. And SNCC's spring conference of 1962 treated voter registration, the filing of omnibus suits, community organizations, civil liberties and academic freedom. Again at this conference, there were a large number of observers, representing groups ranging from the NSA to the Committee for Nonviolent Action (a peace group) and the Young Socialists' Alliance.[65]

2b. *Range of Intensity: waning* — "The larger the movement became," said informant Charles Whittenstein, "the more diluted became the commitment to nonviolence." "It doesn't warm the cockles any more like it did," said Harold Fleming in 1962. Student leader Diane Nash Bevel added, "In 1960 I was able to say things people *responded* to." And in response to the question, "In what ways does the movement seem different to you now than it was in the beginning in 1960?" posed in 1962, 64 percent of the Students and 55 percent of the Adults said "loss of spontaneity."[66] The ideology had become worldly—and had paid the price of lowered intensity.

3. *Dominant Maintenance Mechanism: movement-centrism* — "Back in 1960 . . ." was a phrase heard often during the second year of the movement. Ideological commitment was now maintained largely through an appeal to the clear power of the movement itself, as remembered in the charismatic phase. But You Can't Go Home Again, so an ideological lag developed; I heard students in 1962 parroting the same unsophisticated interpretations of nonviolence which they had memorized from Gandhi, King and Lawson during the high intensity days of 1960. The concern now, as demonstrated in the IGA solutions in this stage, was with structure and "what works" (see especially I.3, G.3 and A.3b below).

## Stage III
## I: INTEGRATION

1. *Internal Organizational Structure: expanding, differentiating, unstable* — The phenomenon which had been the sit-in movement was at a crucial organizational juncture when the bulk of the formal interviews for this study were conducted in early spring 1962—and it had been at this point for over a year. The problem was the "tragedy which befalls every revolution" and the central focus of this study: the internal structural transition during routinization of charisma. Internal difficulties combined with growing challenges from counter-movements (see below) to make the I-A imperatives focal points in stage III. The prestige-value of participation was considerably lower than during the charismatic stage. The direct action movement had great difficulty establishing secular authority after the ideal no longer elicited a consensual sense of sacred authority from adherents. Interpersonal and interorganizational conflict were heightened while the movement's authority structure rationalized: "The problem," commented Harold Fleming, "is that there was too much institutionalized competition when the movement started."[67] The dilemma eventually was resolved in SNCC through a transitional period of authoritarian leadership as described later in this chapter, and this forthright action clarified the situation for other subsystems and the movement at large.

(a) The *division of labor* continued to get more elaborate, with role responsibilities for organizations as well as individuals becoming more specific. By late 1960, the NAACP legal wing was involved in thousands of sit-in cases provided them largely by local protests and CORE, SCLC and SNCC efforts. Southern Regional Council and the National Urban League were called on often by the press for "objective" research information on the movement and its goals and successes.[68] See I.2b and 2c below for a discussion of individual role differentiation.

(b) The theory does not call for an unusual degree of conflict at this point, but in the case of direct action, the development of a *hierarchy of authority* within the movement and within the movement's product, SNCC, was a halting, conflictful and disequilibrating process. This was largely due, I propose, to one of the paradoxes of the rationalization of protest—the impossibility of separating personal and professional roles (see [f] below). No clear criteria for leadership had developed, and leaders no longer "naturally" arose out of the charisma of the situation. Thus, competition in militancy came to be a major criterion; appropriately, Charles McDew, second SNCC Chairman, had 26 arrests to his "credit" as of March 1962. Competition for credit prevented cohesion between subsystems.[69] CORE officials pointed out for some time that *they* called the nationwide boycott in February of 1960—and the NAACP did not "come along" until March 17. A CORE field report from South Carolina in March was representative of the mood: "Leaders are speaking out openly about CORE and are willing to give us credit for being the leading organization in the sit-in movement."[70] And the NAACP rushed into print a booklet called "The Day They Changed Their Minds" to point out that NAACP-led sit-ins in Oklahoma City in 1958 were the real beginning of ". . . what we now call the 'sit-in movement.'" "What was *started* in Oklahoma City and renewed in Greensboro . . .", we read.[71] Within SNCC, one might point to the fact that most Negro college students had not been prepared by their paternalistic high school and college training to develop and lead a democratic organization.[72] The problem eventually was resolved for SNCC through the leadership takeover analyzed in chapter 6 and interpreted further in the section on SNCC below.

(c) The established subsystems of the movement (NAACP, CORE, etc.) already had *systems of rules* rationalized to some degree, but formal rules designating the responsibilities of subsystems and intersystemic adaptive mechanisms were never enacted. The lull in demonstrations during the summer of 1960 gave SNCC the opportunity to formulate six pages of recommendations and three pages of rules for the Atlanta conference in October. A formal constitution was adopted there, and revised in the fall of 1961.[73]

(d) I found little formal *emphasis on efficiency* in SNCC literature of this period or in my extensive participant observation in the organization. In fact, this lack of emphasis seems to be part of the total pattern of rebellion; there were no regular office hours for most staff members (even though they generally worked late into each evening), SNCC members rarely were punctual for appointments with the press, other organizations and "adults" in general, and rational efficiency was mocked ("pretty soon we'll be writing memos about memos in quadruplicate."[74]).

(e) There was a growing emphasis on *selection and promotion* based on technical qualifications, instead of only a high degree of militance. SCLC could hire never-jailed Rev. Andrew Young late in 1961, and he was quickly accepted by others in the movement because of his competence. And some SNCC staffers (Julian Bond and Norma Collins, for instance) purposely stayed away from potential arrest situations to assure continuity of organization. One Adult informant most accurately described the rationalizing effect in this area: "Leaders now tend to be appointed or elected rather than rising out of the demands of the immediate situation."[75]

(f) Contrary to the theory, a very *small* degree of *differentiation of personal and professional roles* developed during the first two years of the movement (and up to the present). The goals of this social system do not lend themselves to easy categorization; persons so long denied personal autonomy and dignity had here made a *total* commitment to achieving it. On occasions too numerous to document, tacit pacts "not to talk about the movement at lunch" or "at the party" were broken. It is not an exaggeration to say that the great majority of persons I know who now hold full-time positions in the movement have very weak or nonexistent boundaries between their personal and professional roles. This intense personalism of one's commitment and the heady gratification of long-denied prestige combined to retard normal development of rational internal structure. "Personal rivalries," said Fleming, "were translated into internal difficulties in SNCC because there was no firm authority structure." And another insider, first SNCC secretary Jane Stembridge, commented that much of the conflict within the movement ". . . came from students who *needed* the movement because they didn't want to go back to school."

2a. *Bases of Recruitment of Members and Leaders: expanding* — If a movement is to maintain itself as the charisma of its ideology wanes, the bases of its recruitment must expand. By 1961, the direct action movement was recruiting solid support from many quarters—the churches, labor, education, etc. The Freedom Rides gave many persons from these backgrounds their first experience in dangerous direct action. And as the movement went consistently into more dangerous and more rural Deep South areas, a bifurcation[76] took place between a small band of militants and a growing number of persons who resembled Stage I nominal supporters at a more sophisticated level.

2b. *Dominant Leadership Roles: (a) administrator, (b) adaptor* — The charismatic leadership of King and others was dormant during much of this period—and often forthrightly rejected. Growing external challenges (everyday financial needs, communications problems, tougher opposition necessitating better planning, etc.) prompted a big turnover in leadership between 1960 and 1962.

All five major civil rights organizations within the movement got new executive directors—the archetype of our administrator role: CORE (James Farmer, 1961); SCLC (Wyatt T. Walker, 1960); SNCC (James Forman, the first executive director in September of 1961, replacing a relatively powerless "secretary" role); National Urban League (Whitney M. Young, Jr., 1961, who brought a much more activist and militant stance to the group); and SRC (Leslie W. Dunbar in 1961, replacing Harold Fleming, who responded to the "new receptiveness of the Kennedy administration to civil rights" by becoming first director of the Potomac Institute).[77] These changes brought a higher degree of experience and rational skills to the position in every organization with the possible exception of SRC, where both Fleming and Dunbar were experienced professionals.

In this context of changing leadership, one can see the two roles differentiating out of the Stage I all-purpose professional. In the movement's product, SNCC, the position of *administrator* was created for Forman in 1961, and he began a period of authoritarian leadership (see I.3 below). Need for finances was the major exigency calling forth the development of the *adaptor* role in the direct action movement. The established organizations involved in the movement already had channels of financial support rationalized to some degree, and by 1963 they were to combine in the Council for United Civil Rights Leadership to more fully exploit the potential of the civil rights charity dollar. But the adaptor role started to formally differentiate in SNCC in 1961. Paul Brooks came to "work the Auburn Avenue beat" in Atlanta; James Monsonis explored New York contacts; the Northern Student Movement was formed in the fall of 1961 specifically, in Forman's words, "to man the supply lines—that means *money*, man."[78] Too, there was growing contact with hostile external systems in the form of negotiation and bargaining, but I observed as of March 1962 that SNCC had not yet designated a formal role of negotiator.

2c. *Dominant Membership Role: multi-specialty functionary* — In the direct action movement, the multi-specialty functionary role emerges as a more sophisticated version of the unspecialized functionary of Stage II. A division of labor is needed at this level in the transition to rationality, but it was accomplished largely through specialization *within individuals* instead of *between roles*. It was not always accomplished well, however. "We need more fund-raisers," said Diane Nash Bevel. "Our field secretaries are far better integrators than they are fund-raisers." At this point one sees some jumping ahead to the member role-types of Stage IV, especially in relation to the bifurcation which differentiated out the militant cadre of leadership—thus leaving a large group of nominal supporters raising money, South and North.

3. *Dominant Integrative Mechanism: success-centrism* — "Back in 1960 . . ." was heard often in SNCC during this period as a testimony to the passing of the good old days. Development of effective integrative mechanisms was hampered by the difficulty of replicating Stage II charismatic methods (see discussion of "technique lag" in G.3 and A.3b below) in addition to the growing pains of

rationalization (I.1 above). The ideological bases of day-to-day integration were appeals to perceived successes of Stage II and early Stage III. But movements cannot live by charisma alone, and in the case of SNCC, a complementary condition—authoritarian leadership—became the dominant integrative mechanism. Leadership based only on commitment and demonstrated militancy was not sufficient. "There are certain periods in all revolutions," said James Forman, the administrator of SNCC since 1961, "when functions have to be taken over . . . There comes a time when certain transitory powers have to be exercised to carry a movement over." SNCC Field Secretary Paul Brooks put it more bluntly early in 1962: "SNCC needs a dictator to organize and pull strings and tell us what to do—and I've been trying to get Forman to do this."

## Stage III
## G: GOAL-ATTAINMENT

1a. *Nature and Structure of Internal Goals: movement-centered* — The external and internal exigencies discussed above helped re-channel expenditure of energy to movement-centered goals, at least for SNCC. Discussion of external goals and strategies *between* and *within* movement subsystems was more possible than during the days of self-validating charismatic action. Much of the evidence for this development in SNCC was presented in I.1 above, and it should be added that at the crucial routinization meeting (the Atlanta SNCC conference of October 1960) approximately 70 percent of the time was devoted to discussion of problems of internal structure.[79]

1b. *Nature and Structure of External Goals: situation-oriented* — The summer 1961 debate over "direct action vs. voter registration" is symbolic of the limbo of external goals during this period. Direct action had worked well in the early charismatic stage of the movement; it was aimed at essentially reformist goals (". . . to have equal opportunity to own a large car and TV, get fat, and engage in all the other evils of the white man," as one informant put it[80]). Voter registration, on the other hand, was directed toward revolutionary goals—nothing less than changing the whole political structure (and thus, the values) of the South and the nation. Both were attempts to replicate reinforcing situations of Stage II and thus recapture their mass appeal and success-potential. Ella Baker best described the ambiguity of this "technique lag": ". . . We're working for the ideal of the *fully integrated society*, but still using the *token desegregation* techniques." See G.3 and A.3b below.

2. *Range of Goals: expanding* — Expanding bases of recruitment (I.2a) and expanding goals necessarily complement one another if the movement is to maintain itself as ideological intensity (L.2b) wanes. More than 30 percent of both samples (Student—36%, Adult—31%) freely mentioned "broadening of goals" when asked to comment on the differences in the movement in March 1962 from that in 1960.[81] Only four months after the movement began, a

leading southern integrationist journal said ". . . it was evident that the movement . . . had now reached the stage of digging in, organizing and building a firm base." The article cited SNCC's calls for nonviolent workshops and college students' initiating action in their home towns during the summer, then noted that protest objectives were "broadening to include jobs" and other important goals.[82] And NSA Southern Project Director Constance Curry, who has been a close advisor and analyst of the movement, wrote in February of 1962:

> In the beginning, the majority of the students in the Movement were thinking only in terms of freeing Negroes from the segregated system, but in increasing numbers, they are beginning to think of their freedom and rights as students in a university, and as citizens in a democratic society.[83]

3. *Dominant Achievement Mechanism: planned mass-appeal demonstrations* (coordination) — Students and Adults named "mass demonstrations or '-ins'" as the major form of protest "being used most frequently" early in 1962.[84] And the majority of informants recognized the amount of planning going into the aging protest. In response to the question, "Are there 'spontaneous' demonstrations in various cities today like those which took place in the first few months of the sit-ins? Or is everything organized?", 46 percent of the Students and 61 percent of the Adults said "no, 'everything is organized,'" or "not in the same sense."[85] Most of the informants agreed that further intensive planning was needed. When asked, "What are some of the things that could be done to make the movement more effective?", most responses assumed the need for more training and coordination within the movement:

Figure 8

. . . TO MAKE THE MOVEMENT MORE EFFECTIVE (VI.4, both forms)

| | *Students* (n = 9) | *Adults* (n = 23) |
|---|---|---|
| more cooperation (less conflict) among civil rights groups | 7 (77%) | 5 (22%) |
| new leadership training | 4 (44%) | 14 (61%) |
| better financial support | 4 (44%) | 2 ( 9%) |
| develop master plan (better structuring, etc.) | 3 (33%) | 5 (22%) |
| political emphasis | 3 (33%) | 6 (26%) |
| new values of participants | 3 (33%) | 5 (22%) |
| more participation | 2 (22%) | 10 (43%) |
| education emphasis | 0 ( 0%) | 2 ( 9%) |

Planning now was necessary to generate mass protests because of the increasing sophistication of counter-movements (especially as represented by the much-heralded "nonviolent police methods" of Albany police chief Laurie Pritchett) and the ever more dangerous areas into which the protest was moving. SNCC leader Robert Moses summed it up best: "You can't realistically expect action from folks down there [in the rural Deep South] without outside help."[86]

Attempts at internal coordination were increasing, reaching their peak in 1963 (see Stage IV). With SNCC—which was still trying to recreate the movement of 1960 and guide it—the role of coordinator was replacing that of communicator. A September 1960 SNCC release boldly announced in its lead sentence: "The Southwide student movement against segregation is now being coordinated by the Student Nonviolent Coordinating Committee, with offices at . . ." A *Southern Patriot* article in October 1960 analyzed SNCC's emerging role:

> This is the group that has taken on the herculean task of coordinating student integration activities in . . .147 southern [protest] areas . . .
>
> They know the value of local initiative, and do not want to lose it . . . They do not see their job as laying down a

> Southwide blueprint for action. Instead, they view the Committee's role as a clearinghouse, coordinator, and—where needed—a spokesman for the movement.
>
> It was partly because of SNCC's activities that student protests continued and in some cases expanded during the summer instead of dying, as some had predicted they would.[87]

But, as elaborated in A.3b below, a "technique lag" developed, and for a time the movement had serious difficulty launching effective protests. Goals were becoming more complex, and means failed to keep up with them. "There is a real lack of understanding of what is a real *revolution* compared to a sporadic program," said Ella Baker. "The students' problems are mainly due to their not taking time to sit down and think about the movement. They are so involved in action they don't have time to sit down and develop a program for a mass movement with varying levels of effective leadership." Harold Fleming felt the "strained and contrived tone it didn't have in the beginning," and Herman Long pointed out that ". . . a good part of the movement's effort is an attempt to replicate a formula for action rather than attempting to discover new strategies—and this limits inventiveness and imagination."

## Stage III
## A: RELATION TO OTHER SYSTEMS

1. *External Organizational Structure: expanding, differentiating* — The movement was forced to organize adaptive facilities by intersystemic challenges which had been accumulating for some time; day-to-day monetary needs, waning intensity of the charismatic ideal and the growing sophistication of counter-movements, as pointed out above. What was left of the movement at this point was being held together by SNCC as the more established groups went out about executing their newly militant programs. But all subsystems were, of necessity, expanding mechanisms for external adaptation. SNCC Executive Director James Forman offered an excellent analysis of the major factor prompting external differentiation in SNCC—economic exigencies. Early in 1962 he said:

> Once SNCC solves its financial problems, it can get into more creative plans . . . Creative plans go down the drain as we struggle to keep the organization going from day to day . . .
>
> This lack of money and lack of organization is responsible for the decline of the so-called spontaneity . . . There is no social revolution in this country or in the world which can survive without organization. It may *arise* spontaneously, but it cannot survive unless it is encouraged . . . And until October of 1961, the image of SNCC as an organization *needing* funds did not exist.

The external organizational structure which developed from Forman's analysis of the movement's needs in the fall of 1961 was built around the theme of financial appeals based on suffering. SNCC releases and the role of the Northern Student Movement and the Southern Student Freedom Fund in raising suffering-money are analyzed in 3b. below.

2a. *Range of Relevant Systems: expanding* — That the word "sit-in" made its way into American dictionaries in 1962 is evidence enough of the impact the movement had made on all levels of society. Expansion of movement goals (to jobs, voting, etc.) affected many social systems concerned with maintaining segregation. And expansion of newsletter lists and appeals lists promoted further diffusion of the movement and its ideal. CORE, as noted earlier, had only 5,000 on its nationwide appeals lists before the movement began, but had well over 100,000 regular contributors by 1963.

2b. *Rate of Desired Change: rapid* — Desegregation now was taking place as a result of the many protests launched in the spring of 1960. We noted in A.2b under Stage II that by August 1, 1960, 27 cities had desegregated lunch counters and other facilities as a result of the sit-ins. In the fall of 1960, the figures went up dramatically:

> October 1, 1960 — 94 cities; this large increase over August partially reflected a meeting of Attorney General William Rogers with national chain managers in June at which he reportedly urged announcement of desegregated facilities in as many cities as possible.
>
> November 1, 1960 — more than 115 cities.
>
> December 1, 1960 — 126 cities.
>
> March 1, 1961 — 139 cities.
>
> September 1, 1961 — 175 cities.[88]

The above figures represent conservative reports of desegregation. After mid-1961 the rate of *announcement* of success-cities tapered off, largely because most large southern and border cities had experienced some lunch counter-type desegregation by this time. Too, "success" became harder to measure as the movement turned to less public tasks like equal job opportunities and voter registration; one now is faced with an almost impossible task of counting individual *units* of desegregation within communities.

3a. *Dominant Adaptive Mechanisms to Subsystems: coordination* — As indicated throughout the analysis of this stage, it is hard to determine analytically whether, in fact, a *movement* existed after the first spontaneous months of mass demonstrations in the spring of 1960. I conclude from the data available that a movement did, indeed, exist, but that no one organization or confederation of organizations was successful in coordinating it. Early attempts at coordination led to conflict, as indicated all through this section. SNCC comes closest to representing the movement-at-large of any formal group, and Director James Forman admitted that it had ". . . failed as a communication center in 1960 and 1961 because of a lack of personnel and funds." But he added in 1962, "We're closer to this function now." An important reason SNCC was closer to being able to serve as a communicator (and, eventually, as a coordinator) was the leadership take-over described in chapter 6 and I.3 above. "Certain non-democratic powers are often necessary in a period of rapid transition," said Forman, "to build a structure which can eventually achieve democratic ends—like the war powers of Congress." So, within SNCC, Forman's authoritarian leadership helped produce a firm organizational base which could take the movement into the rural Deep South.

There are other important levels of coordination during this period, among them the protest community and submovements. A major adaptive technique for the protest community was to unite local Negro organizations under a general name like the Albany Movement, the Jackson Nonviolent Movement or the Nashville Nonviolent Movement. And in May of 1961, CORE, SCLC, SNCC and the NAACP joined in the short-lived Freedom Ride Coordinating Committee to try to integrate protest, fund-raising and legal activities in connection with the Rides.

3b. *Dominant Adaptive Mechanisms to External Systems: confrontation, communication* — In virtually every city which experienced direct action demonstrations from 1960 to 1962, white leaders eventually defined the situation as a crisis, which then led to realistic *confrontation* of legitimate demands of the minority community. Once a crisis-definition produces a confrontation, *communication* (face-to-face bargaining, each side from a position of some power) usually follows rapidly as the major means by which the situation is re-equilibrated. In Nashville, threat of more Negro demonstrations and a boycott brought post-crisis communication. The same was true in Atlanta and other cities. In San Antonio, Texas, Asheville, North Carolina and other cities, merely the possibility of demonstrations moved white leaders to a bargaining position. Later in Birmingham, it took 3,500 arrests and nationally circulated wire pictures of police dogs and fire hoses before white segregationist decision-makers defined the situation as a crisis. The confrontation in this Stage also came through court cases growing out of Stage II demonstrations.[89] The only city which did not move almost immediately to this confrontation-communication stage after direct action was Albany. But a potentially more severe crisis did move the city—passage of the Civil Rights Act of 1964. The lesson was learned; public facilities were desegregated immediately, and one city leader explained, "We're not going to give Martin Luther King any reason to come back" (see chapter 6).

The importance of communication at this Stage reaches beyond its technical meaning in the conflict resolution process. Two other interrelated functions were of growing importance: reaching members of already sympathetic subsystems (the Negro community, white liberals, labor, etc.) and appealing to potential outside support through the mass media. There was a growing proliferation of communications techniques used to reach both audiences, among them:

— The Southern Student Freedom Fund, which existed for several months late in 1962 with the aid of the National Student Association. The purpose was to raise bail and scholarship money for southern demonstrators.

— The Northern Student Movement, which was founded in the fall of 1961 as a fund-raising group for the southern movement, and since has grown into a broad-based movement attacking urban slum problems in the North.

— Songbooks, records and books, proceeds of which usually go to the movement. Especially prominent are records, some sample titles of which are (in order of release): "We Shall Overcome: Songs of the 'Freedom Riders' and the 'Sit-ins'" (Nashville: Folkways); "Freedom in the Air: A Documentary on Albany, Georgia, 1961-1962" (SNCC); "Sit-In Songs, Songs of the Freedom Riders" (CORE); "My Brother's Keeper" (Dick Gregory); "A Jazz Salute to Freedom" (CORE); "March on Washington, The Official Album" (produced by WRVR, the non-profit FM station of the Riverside Church in New York, for the participating organizations); "We Shall Overcome!" ("Authorized Recording Produced by the Council for United Civil Rights Leadership"); and "We Shall Overcome" (Peter Seeger and the Albany Freedom Singers at Carnegie Hall).

— New publications prompted at least in part by the emergence of the movement. Examples are *Freedomways: A Quarterly Review of the Negro Freedom Movement* (begun in the spring of 1961); *New University Thought* (begun at the University of Chicago in 1961); *SDS Newsletter* (begun in 1961 by newly formed Students for a Democratic Society); *Student Voice* (SNCC newspaper); *New Freedom* (begun by graduate students at Cornell University in 1962); *Commitment* (begun in 1963 by the National Catholic Conference for Interracial Justice); *NSM News-Observer* (begun by the Northern Student Movement in 1963); and many other religious and local campus political publications.

— "Suffering releases," especially of SNCC and CORE, telling of jailings, arrests and brutality as a basis for financial appeals. SNCC's heavy reliance on this method of appeal is shown in the

> fact that, of 69 appeals sent to its general mailing list between March 1, 1961, and March 1, 1963, 58 (84 percent) dealt with the militance and suffering of SNCC workers and others in the movement. Examples: "Students Face Mississippi Violence for YOU!"; ". . . they were chained hand and foot, beaten, illegally transported across state lines, and forced to return to Albany and stay in jail without being tried"; ". . . who charges that two policemen forced her to remove her clothing and then beat sensitive areas of her naked body with their belts"; ". . . [a SNCC worker who is] now five months pregnant . . . is in the Hinds County Jail facing two years behind bars"; ". . . the 'brutal beatings' of the Cairo, Illinois, police who sprayed tear gas on civil rights demonstrators"; and ". . . the wave of terror and violence sweeping Mississippi and Southwest Georgia."[90]

Finally, there has been a special problem of communication with and through the mass media. "With the novelty of the movement wearing off, news services paid less attention to it." "The mass media now consider student demonstrations as routine, no matter what their basic significance. This hampers efforts to widen the struggle,"[91] said the *Southern Patriot*. SNCC's Forman complained that ". . . we have had to fight to get a national identity, and it's been hard since the press ignores us unless we stage a spectacular."

These are some of the ways, then, in which the direct action movement experienced the beginnings of rationalization between August 1960 and February 1962. Two events were important turning points during this period—the Freedom Rides (May-July 1961) and the reorganization of SNCC (summer 1961). Both Student and Adult informants judged the Freedom Rides to be an important juncture, but only the Students named the SNCC restructuring in significant numbers. Either the Adults simply did not know about this change (as of March 1962 when the interviews were conducted), or did not foresee its far-reaching significance:

(See Figure 9 on the following page.)

Figure 9

THE BIGGEST 'TURNING POINTS' SINCE 1960 (I.9, both forms)[92]

| | *Students* (n = 13) | *Adults* (n = 29) |
|---|---|---|
| Freedom Rides | 7 (54%) | 12 (40%) |
| Summer 1961 (the move to voting) | 6 (46%) | 3 (10%) |
| mass participation and/or arrests | 1 ( 8%) | 4 (14%) |
| Albany | 1 ( 8%) | 2 ( 7%) |
| federal government involvement | 1 ( 8%) | 1 ( 3%) |
| economic pressure - adults | 0 ( 0%) | 5 (17%) |
| publicity and press coverage | 0 ( 0%) | 3 (10%) |
| parent and college pressure | 0 ( 0%) | 2 ( 7%) |
| quick successes | 0 ( 0%) | 3 (10%) |
| world crisis influence | 0 ( 0%) | 1 ( 3%) |
| other | 1 ( 8%) | 9 (31%) |

As described in chapters 5 and 6 and elaborated here, the Freedom Rides and the 1961 SNCC reorganization manifested the movement's increasing needs for rational structure—indeed, they now raised the question of whether a "movement" continued to exist at all. We may conclude that what once was a reform movement was becoming a revolutionary program, as measured by the various indices of the theory of rationalization. In March of 1962 Ella Baker best interpreted where direct action had come to that point:

> In 1960 the movement was a spontaneous reaction with little thought of form or direction, and little awareness of the *need* for organization. The established groups were responding to a phenomenon they had had little to do with creating and for which their experiences had ill-prepared them. But now the movement has become fragmented and has taken on many characteristics of

> the organizations. It is now being used as a technique by these organizations . . . There is not the spontaneity of 1960, but now there is great potential for a well-organized revolutionary approach to the broad spectrum of problems in American race relations.

### *d. A COMMENT ON SUBSYSTEM RATIONALIZATION: THE DIRECT ACTION ORGANIZATIONS*

Applying the extensive analytical system to more than the movement itself is beyond the scope of this study. Instead, brief comment is offered on the role of the three major direct action groups in the light of the theory of rationalization.

Here, as throughout this study, the movement is seen as the independent variable, for its emergence has brought two of the organizations into existence (SCLC and SNCC) and radically expanded the role of the other (CORE) in the desegregation process. This section analyzes the adaptation of these subsystems to the growth and rationalization of the movement, dealing only with certain crucial problems of intersystemic relations. Analytical categories I.1 (Internal Organizational Structure), G.1a (Nature of Internal Goals) and A.3a (Dominant Adaptive Mechanisms to Subsystems) are the theoretical grounding for this discussion.

Informant Lester Carr's whimsical prediction that "Pretty soon they'll be running bus races on Route 40" sets the theme for this brief discussion of the organizations' roles from 1960 to 1962. One of the most persistent problems almost from the beginning had been the *conflict among organizations* participating in the movement. We have already noted that both Student and Adult informants named "organizational conflict" often in describing what they thought was "the biggest problem" in the movement early in 1962.[93] Most informants further confirmed their concern for this problem by calling for more cooperation and less conflict among the groups when asked what ways they would ". . . like to see the movement changed."[94]

### *In the Beginning: the National Association for the Advancement of Colored People*

The role of the NAACP has been great, both in preparing the way for emergence of the movement and in actual participation and support. Founded in 1909 ". . . to end racial discrimination and segregation in all public aspects of American life,"[95] the NAACP worked through educational, legal and legislative channels to build the foundation of equal opportunity which was ultimately institutionalized in the legal structure with passage of the strong federal Civil Rights Law of 1964.

Roy Wilkins, Executive Secretary since 1955, has been a major confidant of the Kennedy and Johnson administrations. He agreed (at first reluctantly) to endorse the 1960 chain stores boycott and the activities of COFO in Mississippi beginning in 1963 (but withdrew his support in 1965), he has supported the expenditure of hundreds of thousands of dollars of NAACP money for legal defense of demonstrators, and has been arrested for picketing in Jackson, Mississippi. NAACP Youth Councils in various cities have been active in demonstrations.

But the Association's defensiveness in responding to the movement has been great, too. Several key informants including Dunbar and Fleming commented on it, and NAACP leaders confirmed it by their actions. In responding to my first interview question about how she initially became involved in the movement, Southeastern Regional Secretary Ruby Hurley felt moved to tell me at length that there were "only about three" of the 100 sit-ins cities of 1960 where the NAACP was not "intimately involved" in initiating and supporting the movement.[96] And the long-brewing conflict became more public than ever in January of 1962 when Wilkins told *Time* magazine that he "deplores" SNCC's tactics. "They don't take orders from anybody," he continued. "They don't consult anybody. They operate in a kind of vacuum; parade, protest, sit-in. How far up the road does that get you? When the headlines are gone, the issues still have to be settled in Court."[97]

Thus the oldest, most powerful and best established civil rights group in America was shaken by the growth and success of a spontaneous and initially uncoordinated protest movement. The three major direct action organizations now are viewed in this context of competition and rationalization.

### *The Congress of Racial Equality: That Lonesome Road South*[98]

CORE was founded in Chicago in 1942, and until the sit-in movement, had concentrated its activity largely in the North. During that time, it was the only national group devoting full time to direct action against segregation. Its extensive campaigns brought desegregation at lunch counters, theatres, amusement parks and other accommodations in a number of cities, including St. Louis, Baltimore and Washington, as documented in chapter 3.

CORE's formal goals are "to abolish racial discrimination through application of the Gandhian philosophy and techniques of nonviolent direct action."[99] Goal-achievement mechanisms center around the "-ins"; CORE pioneered sit-ins, stand-ins and wade-ins in the 1940s and 1950s, and led the Journey of Reconciliation through the Middle South in 1947. Until 1960, CORE had less than 20 local chapters throughout the nation, but by 1961 that number had doubled. Local chapters tend to be small, since a high degree of activism is required of members. CORE's financial support (the budget jumped from $60,000 annually to more than $600,000 annually in the first two years after the sit-ins began) comes largely from individuals, labor and religious groups on an appeals list which numbered more than 50,000 names in 1962, compared to about 5,000 in pre-movement days.[100]

CORE had done things in the North in the 1940s and 1950s which were not feasible in the South until the 1960s. When the sit-in movement swept the South in the spring of 1960, CORE faced the most difficult problems of rationalization of any of the established organizations. It had always been a small, well-disciplined group with relatively narrow appeal and scope of programs. But it was imperative for the life of the organization to keep up with the exploding direct action movement, to lead it and to train participants where possible.

A CORE pamphlet issued in the summer of 1960 said that the sit-ins had ". . . used the methods and techniques CORE . . . began developing eighteen years ago . . . If these sit-ins are to continue successfully, we must develop additional leadership."[101] From February 1960 to September 1960, CORE hired 10 new field staff members to help cope with the growing needs for training and extension of nonviolent direct action in the South. Most of them were expelled sit-inners with little rational bureaucratic experience—and most of them lasted less than six months.

This experience was typical of the kinds of difficulties CORE has had in extending its sphere of operation into the South—an extension which *had* to be made if the group were to maintain its position as the leading American advocate of direct action against racial segregation. Some of the most significant CORE attempts to deal with the challenge of direct action-become-movement now are interpreted chronologically in light of the theory of rationalization.

*The 1960 Annual Convention, St. Louis, June 29—July 3.* I attended all sessions of the Convention, and found it marked by excitement at CORE's new prestige, heavy program emphasis on the history of nonviolent protest and Gandhian philosophy (compared to a more secular-practical emphasis in later national meetings), and problems of organizational rationality. As an example, two of the hastily-signed field secretaries submitted their resignations at this meeting. One (Attorney Len Holt of Norfolk) had resigned or had been released earlier, and there was an undercurrent of rumors about the reasons. Others in the movement had told me that Holt had been let go because of "leftist tendencies" (L problems), but CORE Executive Secretary James Robinson explained to the Convention that he "failed to keep schedules set by the National Office and did not follow CORE organizational procedures with local chapters" (I and A problems). The opening two paragraphs of Robinson's report to the Convention tell in most succinct form the Stage III-type difficulties already encountered by his organization:

> The year just ended . . . will go down as the year in CORE history when we ceased to hide our light under a bushel . . . For the first time we have great publicity in the general press . . . We can claim to have gone forward very significantly during the year just ended. Public information, program, and staff development have seen far greater advances than in any previous year. For the second straight year, income has more than doubled. Membership also increased more than last year . . .
>
> This was a year of our greatest opportunity, and also of our greatest disorganization. From the time that the sit-ins began in February, the growth and demands made upon us were so great that we sometimes felt that everything was falling apart. When I get far enough away from the office to get a chance to think about it, I am astounded that anyone on the staff is still speaking to anyone else . . .

*The 1960 CORE Interracial Training Institute, Miami, August 14—September 5.* The Institute was a microcosm of the problems of rationalization experienced by local movements and national organizations during the "digging-in" period when charisma was waning. The program was designed to give the 30 participants experience in all phases of nonviolence—philosophy, planning demonstrations, protesting, negotiating, educating, etc. A basic teaching tool was the sociodrama, with racial roles often reversed. Eighteen of us were arrested "accidentally" on a project on the fourth day of the Institute, so activity revolved around the jail and trial process for the rest of the meeting.

There is room to relate only three of the many problems at Miami which were characteristic of the movement at all levels during that phase: (1) local-national conflict, (2) the role of relevant external systems and (3) the student revolt against authority.

(1) Problems of integration within the movement (or adaptation of the movement to its subsystems) were dominant after the arrests. Miami CORE President John Brown told me, in discussing his displeasure at the arrests, "Well, the national leaders need to get publicity." Local member Blanche Calloway said in an evaluation session, "We had had sit-ins weeks before you came and many counters opened up. We didn't want to have sit-ins while negotiations were taking place . . . but we're behind you 100 percent." Anti-rationality in social movements feeds on just this kind of ambivalence.

(2) I saw firsthand how organized labor could swing into action behind the desegregation movement; James Carey, head of the International Union of Electrotypographers, wired Miami Mayor Robert King High shortly after the arrest that the IUE's convention set for Miami the following month would be withdrawn if charges against the protestors were not dropped. He intimated that he would tell all of his labor friends planning on Miami conventions about the arrests, too. In addition, CORE leaders were asked by national AFL-CIO to find out whether the arresting store was unionized, to see what forms of persuasion could be applied. A third external system which contributed mightily to the Institute was the Jewish Cultural Center of Miami Beach, which sponsored a Sunday beach picnic that turned into a wade-in, honored the demonstrators with an evening party and generally offered their support.

(3) Most striking of all problems of rationalization at the Institute was the student revolt against authority. The revolt often was manifested in militancy vs. non-militancy terms, with younger participants implicitly (and sometimes not so implicitly) accusing older participants of "going slow." Following are representative bits of dialogue from my notes:[102]

*Blanche Calloway* (local Negro adult) — "You youngsters came to learn."

*Tom Rowland* (California white student) — "Don't think we're 'youngsters' . . . we've been through all kinds of rough action before."

*James McCain* (Negro CORE Field Secretary) — "We shouldn't demonstrate at Shell's [scene of the arrests] until we see whether he'll negotiate with us as he said he would."

*Bernard Lafayette* (Nashville Negro Student) — "No! We shouldn't wait for a negotiation. Let's demonstrate now and get Miami CORE to go with us."

———

And the most revealing and representative piece of personal dialogue in all of my data on the movement is contained in notes two students passed back and forth in an Institute session with Martin Luther King:

*Dorothy Miller* (New York white student) — "My rough impression of him is that he's not too willing to do the leg work. I may be wrong. What do you think? *I don't think he is too likely to do anything but talk.*"

*Ruth DeSpenza* (New Orleans Negro student) — "Jackie Robinson lives in the North and he is twice as active as Dr. King."

*Miller* — "I bet he'll also be twice as friendly—I haven't seen him [King] crack a smile yet."

*DeSpenza* — ". . . I think he is a little arrogant . . . what do you think?"

*Miller* — "I agree . . . there's something wrong . . . don't know exactly. He's very aloof and cold . . . doesn't seem to communicate a spirit of working together. He must have been different in Montgomery because I can't see him inspiring anyone, much less thousands of people. Perhaps he's tired of it all by now. I'm coming to realize more and more that if it weren't for you kids, The Movement would at best be sporadic and not very well organized or publicized."

*DeSpenza* — ". . . I told you all he is is talk because *he says stay in jail but he never does.*"

———

*The 1961 CORE Council Meeting, Lexington, Kentucky, February 11-12, 1961*. CORE took a step further south—from St. Louis to Miami to Kentucky in six months.[103] Already there was a difference in tone from the

St. Louis meetings, as most of the program was devoted to discussing goal-achievement mechanisms instead of Gandhian philosophy (the Freedom Rides were planned here) and hearing reports of action from the 30-odd local chapters who sent representatives. Sample items on the official agenda were "Introduction of James Farmer, National Director," "The sit-in movement and the Northern Supporting Boycott," "Summer Program: Interracial Action Institute, Housing Workshop and Deep South Project [Freedom Rides]," "Membership cards and CORE pins," "Membership Director's Report," "National Theatre Project," "Branch Office" [eventually established in New Orleans], and "Legal problems in relation to direct action." The Executive Secretary's Report continued the emphasis on expansion noted at St. Louis, with the first section subtitled, *Explosive Growth and the CORE Future*.

*The Freedom Rides and their Aftermath, 1961* (more fully documented in chapter 5). Alabama's violent reception of the Freedom Rides brought CORE more national publicity than ever before, thus giving the group more income and recruiting potential. Mississippi's legalistic reception strained the group's finances as never before. The combination of these events spurred CORE's drive toward internal rationality as never before—in fund-raising, in recruitment and in long-range strategy. An example: soon after the first Rides, CORE was distributing mimeographed application blanks for "new Freedom Rides . . . in the *immediate* future," including a space for signature of "parent or guardian if applicant is under 21 years of age."

As noted in chapter 5, the Rides also were an important turning point as the movement headed for concentrated work in the rural Deep South. The Jackson (Mississippi) Nonviolent Movement grew from the Freedom Rides, and CORE was instrumental in staffing and supporting it during the difficult early days in the summer of 1961.[104] Soon Jackson became a microcosm of conflict in the movement, with three variant factions: local militant students and organizational representatives, local less-militant adults, and the national organization. Former student sit-inner Tom Gaither, who was a CORE Field Secretary in Jackson in 1961-62, said that ". . . most of the friction has been passed on from the top to local levels. In Jackson, for instance, there is a split between the state conference of the NAACP, the local president and Wilkins himself. And we always have trouble with the adult community not realizing that many of these students are just as mature and capable of being adults as they are—then these adults want to 'straighten out the students!'"

Since the Freedom Rides, CORE has continuously diversified and expanded its financial adaptive mechanisms, to the point of hiring professional fund-raisers at times. "Suffering appeals" have been a constant format, and low-key rational appeals have been frequent. On September 28, 1961, CORE issued a straight factual account of the money already spent on the Rides ($256,900) and the money yet needed ($300,000 for legal costs alone). A combination of these types of appeals was sent to potential contributors in 1963. It was headlined simply, "A Few of the Ways in Which Your Gifts Help . . .", and listed such items as:

$2 will buy 500 sample voter registration applications in South Carolina or 100 *I Am Registered* buttons

$5 . . . provides food and lodging for one participant in a weekend workshop on nonviolence in Louisiana or Mississippi

$10 will pay the bondsmen's fee on a $100 bail bond

$20 pays the rent on the CORE office in Plaquemine, Louisiana, for one month

$120 provides transportation for voter registrants in Canton, Mississippi for one month

CORE's development since February of 1962 has been one of progressive growth, differentiation and subsequent rationalization. The budget as of January, 1965, was almost $1,000,000 annually. There were 124 affiliated chapters, a professional staff of 137, and a "membership list" (contributors) of some 80,000.[105] The program is solidly diversified: housing and other urban problems in northern ghettos, the establishment of a southern regional office in New Orleans in 1963, leadership in voter registration and development of community centers in the Deep South. In short, CORE has survived the heady disorientation of the charismatic breakthrough and is now settled down into the initiation and coordination of long-range programs characteristic of Stage IV in the theory.

The road south for CORE has been a lonesome one from the beginning. "They'll have a hard time being effective in the South," said Wyatt Walker in 1962, "because they are not church-oriented." And the road is still lonesome; it was CORE Field Secretary Michael Schwerner who had established a community center in Meridian, Mississippi, so successfully that he was a target for the Neshoba County triple lynching in 1964. This kind of grass-roots organizing over the years has given CORE an unquestioned place among the leading civil rights groups in the nation. Despite its small budget and staff in 1962, 85 percent of the Student informants and 82 percent of the Adults freely named CORE as one of the "civil rights organizations [which have] played the most important parts in the movement."[106]

### *Southern Christian Leadership Conference: The Shaman Principle*

SCLC is the organizational extension of the charismatic symbol of direct action, its president, Dr. Martin Luther King, Jr.[107] Basic organizational difficulties of SCLC have centered around the classic Weberian problem—the diffusion and routinization of charisma. We have already affirmed the necessity for the *structural routinization* of the charismatic ideal (in this case, nonviolence) if it is to have any long-range effectiveness; SCLC's problems of rationalization have been compounded because it is structured around the original *bearer* of the charismatic ideal, who undergoes *personal routinization*.

Founded in 1957 after the Montgomery bus boycott brought success in 1956, SCLC's stated goals are: "To achieve full citizenship rights, and total integration of the Negro in American life . . . to disseminate the creative philosophy and technique of nonviolence . . . to secure the right and unhampered use of the ballot for every citizen . . . to reduce the cultural lag."[108] SCLC has steadily grown and differentiated its structure and program since then. In 1960, when the national office moved from Montgomery to Atlanta, there were a dozen affiliates throughout the South, most of them in cities where bus or other protests had occurred—Tallahassee, Shreveport and Nashville, for instance. There was a full-time staff of five and an annual budget of about $50,000. By 1965, there were more than 100 affiliates (mostly Negro church and civic groups like the Dallas County Voters League in Selma, Alabama) in some 30 states. Staffed offices were operating in New York, Los Angeles and Chicago. The budget had grown, with the aid of foundation funds for voter education, to $500,000 in 1963 and to almost $1,000,000 today. In 1965 there are more than 300 full-time staff members. A further index of rationalization is the *SCLC Newsletter*, which grew from a four page fold with several thousand circulation in 1961 to a 12-to-16 page two-color magazine with 100,000 circulation by 1964.[109]

SCLC is an almost pure-type case of the bureaucratic structure organized to diffuse charisma and embody it in permanent organizational form. I refer to SCLC's major technique for extension of its influence as the "shaman principle" because it involves the transfer of charisma from King through local leaders to their followers. In virtually every city in which an affiliate is established, King leads a Freedom Rally to officially mark its formation, and there is a veritable laying-on of hands as he (or aides like the Revs. Ralph Abernathy and Andrew Young) charge the newly-designated local representative to carry on his work.[110] Many times I have heard Walker say, "Dr. King is my boss," "Dr. King would say that . . .", and the like. And informant Tom Hayden reported that a newly-emerged Negro leader of an SCLC affiliate in Edentown, North Carolina, prefaced nearly every conversation or mass meeting remark by reminding would-be followers that "I am proud to be Dr. Martin Luther King's representative here in . . ."

Two difficulties inhere in the perennially charismatic organization: maintaining the high level of personal and structural charisma, and domesticating potentially threatening virtuosi who would use the charisma outside the aegis of the organization. First, King literally *has* to go to jail at least once a year and SCLC *must* engage in publically militant activities regularly to keep the person and the organization in the consciousness of potential contributors. SCLC personnel have told me that upsurges in the group's income from personal contributions follow closely behind crises. Informally charting important crisis points, we see:[111]

Figure 10

RELATION BETWEEN CRISES AND CONTRIBUTIONS TO SCLC

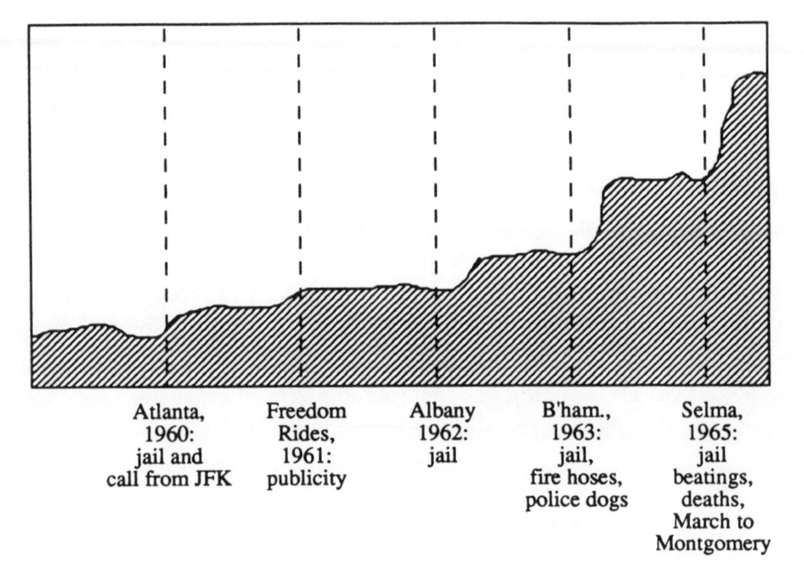


Second, several virtuosi have challenged King (purposely or not) for the symbolic leadership of the desegregation movement within the scope of SCLC, among them Revs. Wyatt Walker, Ralph Abernathy and James M. Lawson, Jr. In each case, their potential charisma has been absorbed by SCLC—Walker as Executive Director from 1960 to 1964, Abernathy (who barely lost to King for leadership of the Montgomery Improvement Association in 1956) as SCLC Vice President, Treasurer and King's personal confidant, and Lawson as (part-time) director of training in nonviolence. While leaders like CORE's James Farmer and the NAACP's Roy Wilkins have gained prestige through post-1960 militancy, neither approaches the position King holds in the minds of most Negro Americans.[112]

Problems of balancing charismatic power with rational structure are seen in a brief analytical chronology of important events for SCLC.

*The Raleigh Conference, April 15-17, 1960.* Planned and carried out largely by King's executive director, Ella Baker, the Raleigh Conference was instrumental in setting up initial lines of communication between sit-inners in the early days. King gave the major address and was well-received by most of the students in attendance; the sit-ins as a movement were only two months old, and for most of the conferees this was the first time they had met King personally. King provided for the students a ready-made theology and ideology for their movement, and was widely known for his success in Montgomery. SCLC was still small, occupying a two-room office (later to be shared with SNCC) in Atlanta, arranging speaking engagements for King and laying plans to gain grass-roots support throughout the South.

*Summer 1960.* Walker joined the staff in August as Director, and quickly rose to the top past older employees to become King's number one strategist and speech-writer. The hiring of Walker started SCLC's rapid drive toward a differentiated and rationalized program. He talked often with me about the need for a "new image" for SCLC, and shortly after he came on the staff he prepared a confidential "General Program" for 1960 and 1961 for distribution to Board Members.[113] The brochure included an elaborate organizational chart and the outline of a sophisticated many-faceted attack on segregation—including some approaches which only now are gaining wide use in the civil rights movement. A formal presentation was made of the wide range of methods to be used to "redeem the soul of America by creating the 'Beloved Community:'"

> Coordinated mass attack on segregation from national posture through creative protest.
>
> Continuous pressure by use of protest device.
>
> Construction of boycott for national application but on local base.
>
> Coordinated negotiation program at national and local levels where feasible.
>
> Conduct intensive educational programs aimed at building political awareness to promote voting.
>
> Implement voter registration by intensive program under recent Civil Rights Law.
>
> Program to educate the citizen to regard money as buying power and how to use it in investment and group development of business enterprises for community influence, profit and to provide jobs and training where not available.
>
> To develop a youth program by concentrating a major part of the total program effort.

The program was divided into three phases—Action, Education and Fund-Raising. Again, Walker had conceived of most of the kinds of protest techniques which were to be used in the next five years:

> Coordinated, simultaneous, Southwide, nonviolent mass action . . . On a given day, at a given hour, with time adjustment, 15, 20, 30, 40 communities will feel the onslaught of nonviolent mass action.
>
> Southwide Institute on Nonviolence (annual).
>
> Retreat of key personnel—representing every facet of American life.
>
> Summer Youth Seminar, Summer Adult Seminar.
>
> Fund-Raising: Crusades via SCLC leaders
> Affiliate program, state and local
> Individual subscriptions
> Foundation and grants
> Proceeds from books, magazines, etc.

There were sections on Administrative Function, Organization of Affiliates and a sample "Launching of National Program," but of greater interest for us was the section on Public Relations Program, which represented the ultimate in packaged charisma:

> *SCLC Leadership Symbol*
> In the person of Martin Luther King, Jr. Devout, reverent but not pious. Humble, determined, modest, but not retiring. Dedicated but not fanatic. Courageous, aggressive but not intimidating.
>
> *National Image of the Movement*
> Must reflect the qualities of the leadership symbol in operation, selection of personnel and their conduct, the make-up of written publicity, choice of operational devices (media, etc.), character of radio and television productions and programming in all other ways basic to public reaction and formation of opinion.
>
> *Value*
> The effectiveness of defeating the Negro stereotype by this national image of the movement will serve with positive value in every phase of

> operation . . . Public relations accent [should be] on success and progress . . .

Walker and his program were already well into Stage III in most phases of the operation of the SCLC subsystem.

*Fall 1960*. Disenchantment with King and SCLC's easy prestige was evident among student participants at SNCC's Atlanta Conference, October 16-18, 1960. I carefully noted the students' disinterest during his standard speech on "The Philosophy of Nonviolence," and their too-automatic standing applause afterwards. But, as Will Campbell commented, King soon "beat 'em at their own game:" he went to jail with demonstrating Atlanta students on October 19, was transferred to a south Georgia jail, received the famous telephone call from presidential candidate John F. Kennedy and added to the aura of his own and SCLC's image.

*The Freedom Rides and their Aftermath, 1961*. The crisis in the movement's organizational subsystems surrounding the Freedom Rides was discussed in chapter 5. While external factors (violence, exorbitant legal fees, etc.) were chiefly to blame for internal conflict, the unique position of King and SCLC added to the disequilibrating situation. It is all explained in one picture which accompanied a *New York Times* story of May 24, 1961. In the picture were King, Abernathy, CORE leader Farmer and SNCC leader John Lewis. The caption begins, "The Rev. Dr. Martin Luther King, Jr., right, announced in Montgomery, Alabama, the 'Freedom Riders' will resume their bus journey through the South." In truth, King, who had cancelled a northern speaking engagement to fly to Montgomery after CORE- and Nashville-sent Riders were beaten, was *against* resuming the Rides after Attorney General Robert Kennedy asked for a "cooling-off period." Farmer, Lewis, Walker and others talked him into supporting their resumption. But when the press covered the news conference, King, as always, drew the prestige, to the chagrin of student militants like Lewis—who appeared in the picture with a bandaged head from a Montgomery beating.

The crisis in subsystem relations worsened when King returned to Atlanta, was not helpful in giving strategic advice to the short-lived Freedom Ride Coordinating Committee and declined the invitation to join a later Ride and go to jail—and an SCLC release announced that "In response to a directive from Martin Luther King, Jr.," an "intensive, large-scale assault on segregation in the hard-core states of the South" was being initiated.

*Albany and Beyond, December 1961*. But King "beat 'em at their own game" again by responding to the jail call in Albany beginning in December of 1961 (see chapter 6). SCLC prestige wavered as a result of the Albany situation, for the city resisted pressure to desegregate (doing so only when the Civil Rights Law was passed in 1964) and civil righters talked of Albany as the only real "failure" in the direct action campaign.

At the same time, however, SCLC was differentiating its program to include the first professional center (at Dorchester, Georgia) for intensive training in citizenship education and voter registration. Rev. Andrew Young and Mrs. Dorothy Cotton have, since that time, directed monthly training sessions for persons from throughout the South in techniques of economic and political change. I attended a session in March of 1962 and found a training ground for a cadre of professional revolutionaries envisioned by Walker two years earlier, in which leadership was (a) recruited locally, (b) trained by the movement and (c) sent back to the grass-roots areas to organize communities.

The basic community organization techniques which were to be used with increasing frequency by all the organizations are so well represented in the following material from Dorchester, that it is reproduced in full here:

SUGGESTIONS FOR BLOCK LEADERS

Because of your nearness to members in your block, you are in a good position to help your neighbors become better informed citizens. You are also in a position to encourage them to become *active* voters and *regular* participants in *all* civic affairs. In view of such an important job before you, the following suggestions are offered to guide you in your work.

1. Contact the people in your block.
   a. Visit each home in your block
   b. Explain the following:
      (1) Purpose of visit.
      (2) Group you represent.
      (3) Objectives of group's program.
      (4) Relationship between block leader, citizenship committee, and people residing in your block.

2. Solicit their cooperation in carrying out the program's objectives.
   a. Explain benefits that they will derive from voting, such as
      (1) Just consideration from elected representatives.
      (2) Better housing facilities.
      (3) Better schools.

(4) Better job opportunities.
(5) Adequate recreational facilities.
(6) Others.

b. Encourage them to support the work of the citizenship committee by
(1) Attending and taking part in its meetings.
(2) Helping to accomplish objectives.

3. Leave your hosts with the feeling that you have sincere concern for their welfare, and remind them that
   a. You are the block's representative for the citizenship committee.
   b. You may be contacted for any of their community problems.
   c. You will keep in contact with them about further developments.

The following are some suggested Do's and Don't's for your consideration:

| DO | DON'T |
|---|---|
| 1. Be friendly and sincere | 1. Be impatient |
| 2. Explain your committee's program | 2. Antagonize |
| 3. Let the hosts talk | 3. Do all the talking |
| 4. Keep in contact with block members | 4. Talk over the heads of your hosts |
| 5. See that they become qualified voters | 5. Put off making visit |
| 6. See that they vote | |
| 7. Schedule a timely follow-up visit | |

---

Technically, the scope of this study stops with February 1962, but it is only reasonable to trace the charisma—structure tension in SCLC from that time to the present. In our March 1962 interview, King spoke of future rational needs of the movement, calling for a "more effective division of labor" between the organizations. He saw the NAACP specializing in litigation ("for which they are superbly equipped"), CORE as "our direct action organization in the North," SNCC as the "storm troopers" who can do more adventurous things because "they do not have to think of their families, their positions and who's going to preach next Sunday like we do," and SCLC as a predominantly grass-roots southern organization with wide connections in the Negro community, especially in the churches. King was keenly aware, during that particular lull in the movement, that his fund-raising responsibilities were great—not only for SCLC ("I must raise at least $100,000 a year for our programs speaking in the North") but also for Ebenezer Baptist Church in

Atlanta, where he is Assistant Minister ("I have to help raise $40,000 by May for the church's 75th anniversary").

Programs and strategies within SCLC have continued to differentiate and rationalize, largely on the sporadic charismatic appeal of King. SCLC prepared an appeal to the President on May 17, 1962, "On Behalf of The Negro Citizenry of the United States of America, in Commemoration of the Centennial of the Proclamation of Emancipation" (most of it came from an earlier document of the Southern Regional Council, "The Federal Executive and Civil Rights"). A "National Committee for the Albany Defendants" was formed, and circulated thousands of petitions to be signed and sent to the President. The boycott was employed more frequently and systematically; SCLC reported that St. Augustine (Florida) tourism was off "as much as 50 percent in some instances" in the summer of 1964 during direct action confrontations. A 1964 mailing reviewed the wide range of projects "Your Contribution to SCLC Supports":

— Voter Registration (Southwide)
— Citizenship Clinics and Workshops on Nonviolence
— Direct Action Projects to end segregation
— Merit Employment Programs to end job discrimination
— Special Educational Scholarships
— Legal Defense and bail for victims of racial injustice
— Citizenship and literacy schools

King remains the leading personal symbol of the movement. Birmingham, 1963, stimulated pressure for the federal Civil Rights Law of 1964. Birmingham hoses and dogs helped restore the charisma, and King's nationwide prestige soared along with contributions to SCLC. The NBC Television Network broadcast an unprecedented three hour special on civil rights on September 2, 1963, and King and SCLC were at the forefront of the program. King was named *Time Magazine*'s Man-of-the-Year for 1963 and the winner of the Nobel Peace Prize for 1964. But even these representatives of The Establishment were unable to routinize him to any great degree. The month after he received the Nobel Prize, he was back in jail in Selma, Alabama, for leading voter registration attempts—and he had taken thousands to jail with him. He took thousands more on a 50-mile march to Montgomery in the process of eliciting the Voting Rights Law of 1965 from the federal administration and Congress.

*The Student Nonviolent Coordinating Committee: From Sit-ins to Live-ins*

Much about the formation and growth of SNCC is chronicled in chapters 4-6.[114] Now SNCC is analyzed in the light of rationalization theory. The essential point of this section is that SNCC began as a clearing house for communication among local student protests in the sit-in movement in 1960, and by 1962 it had become a cadre of professional revolutionaries trained in community organization techniques—sending "teams of professional sit-inners into the bush," as informant Jane Stembridge said, to initiate, coordinate and sustain local protests.

To the Weberian sociologist, SNCC represents the ultimately unrationalizable association. The history of SNCC is the history of various forms of revolt against authority—against segregation, against "adults" and other civil rights groups with the movement, against the notions of structure and rationality *within* SNCC. The revolt has become a vital part of SNCC's style, and it impedes the development of rational organization at the same time that it motivates SNCC workers to ". . . take the message of freedom into areas where the bigger civil rights organizations fear to tread."[115]

SNCC's goal when it was formed at the Raleigh Conference in April 1960 was to build ". . . a social order of justice, permeated by love." By early 1962, SNCC had incorporated this statement into its constitution, but only as a philosophical gesture. The bulk of the constitution talked about SNCC's serving as ". . . a coordinator and administrative body for the student movement in the South."[116] Ideal goals (Stage II) seemed to have been translated into organizational goals (Stage III). And by mid-1963, the long-range goal was to build ". . . an interracial democracy [that] can be made to work in this country,"[117] with everyday emphasis on voter registration and the use of economic pressure.

Thus was manifested the classical secularization of the charismatic ideal. At the April 1962 SNCC conference in Atlanta, there was not one item on the program concerning violent philosophy; rather civil liberties and techniques of economic and political organization were emphasized. Too, the revolt against the too-prestigious Martin Luther King had come full circle: King (for whom I had been asked by SNCC to write inspirational quotes in a kneel-in release less than two years earlier) was not even invited to the meeting.

SNCC's structural history shows a halting growth from a one-person staff issuing newsletters from a spare desk in the corner of the SCLC office in

1960, to an executive staff and field secretaries numbering more than 200 in 1965:[118]

<u>April to December 1960</u>
Staff: One Secretary
Budget: $2,500
Support: Contributions from individuals and religious, civil rights and labor groups.
Activities: Communication, correspondence, newsletters, etc., to local protest groups represented in SNCC.

<u>January to September 1961</u>
Staff: One secretary
Budget: $15,000
Support: Same
Activities: Same, with attempts to initiate local protests.

<u>September 1961 to January 1963</u>
Staff: Differentiated staff of 16, with Atlanta office staff and field workers
Budget: About $75,000 annually
Support: Same, but expanding to foundations for some programs, and help from NSM and SSFF.
Activities: Community organization through direct action and voter registration in rural Deep South.

<u>1963</u>
Staff: Between 41 and 108 staff members, including 12 office staff
Budget: About $160,000 annually.
Support: Above, plus growing connections with local movements.
Activities: Same, including expansion of voting work in Mississippi through COFO.[119]

<u>1964-1965</u>
Staff: Office staff of about 20, more than 200 full-time field workers, fund-raisers in the North, additional hundreds of volunteers.
Budget: More than $200,000 annually.
Support: Northern friends of SNCC, National Council of Churches and other Sources added to above.
Activities: Predominantly voter registration and community organization in all Deep South states; Mississippi Summer Project.

Important events in SNCC's halting drive toward rationality are summarized below.

*The Raleigh Conference, April 15-17, 1960.* As analyzed in chapter 4, the Raleigh Conference was the first attempt to structure the sit-in movement which had been developing Southwide since February. SNCC was voted into existence, and monthly executive committee meetings in May and June established a primitive separation of functions into Communication, Coordination and Finance. "Their great virtue during this period," said Leslie Dunbar two years later, "was the grandly disorganized way in which they proceeded. Nobody, including SNCC, knew what they were going to do next. Their whole genius was spontaneity and an antipathy to organization."

*Summer 1960.* First SNCC Secretary Jane Stembridge summarized the organizational difficulties of SNCC during the first "let-down" period when colleges recessed for the summer: "These kids who came right out of the front lines sat down and tried to form a committee." They had little experience in democratic decision-making in their often-paternalistic Negro colleges, there were no universally recognized criteria for structure and leadership selection, and they possessed few sophisticated bargaining skills when swept into "unity meetings" with the now threatened established civil rights organizations.

Much of Jane Stembridge's summer was spent compiling address lists in an attempt to get widespread protestors in touch with one another, financing and planning the coming fall conference, and getting several SNCC representatives (including Chairman Marion Barry and Alabama representative Bernard Lee) off to Los Angeles and Chicago to make presentations at the national political conventions. The Executive Committee met each month in Atlanta, and tried to spark a Southwide kneel-in movement by attending "white" churches during the August meeting. But the idea did not catch on, and the movement remained in a "holding" position, still under the influence of the euphoric spring of 1960.

*The Atlanta Conference, October 14-16, 1960.* The October conference was an attempt to (a) recapture the charisma and sense of movement of the first months of the sit-ins and (b) take steps toward effective rationalization of SNCC's structure. SNCC's proposal for the conference showed the yearning for the good old days:

> The program of the conference . . . is designed to refine the thinking of those who have been deeply involved in nonviolent action, and initiate them more fully into the basic philosophy behind it. Lectures, discussions, and workshops

> have been planned to clarify the many problems which confront the South in the area of human relations, to make students aware of the nature of nonviolent solutions, and to foster cooperation among the many elements in all areas of the country that are committed to the achievement of desegregation.
>
> . . . The conference will bring together two student-leaders from each southern community which has participated in nonviolent action, leaders from each of the statewide coordinating committees, and potential participants from areas of the South in which this type of activity has not as yet been a factor in intergroup relations.
>
> . . . Understanding and cooperation can only come when there is genuine communication. The potential of a free America can be conceived and realized only when we, as students, understand all of the implications and ramifications of our struggle . . . We need to come together to *begin anew* our effort to cleanse this great nation. The conference must find us all *again standing behind our commitment* . . . (emphasis added).

Many speakers stressed local initiative and autonomy of protest groups in a Stage III-type attempt to recreate the charismatic phase. But the representatives elected in Raleigh had made a covert pact, and succeeded in maintaining control when a "permanent coordinating committee" was established. One participant lied about his scholastic status, claiming he was still a student, to get elected to the committee; he was, in fact, a former student who had dropped out of school to work for the Fellowship of Reconciliation.

The constitution drawn up and accepted at Atlanta called for state SNCC organizations to coordinate protest activity, but they did not materialize; one full-time staff person could not administer such a broad and differentiated structure. Thus the lethargic period which began in the summer was extended and crystallized in organizational forms.

*The Jail-ins, February 1961*. The jail-ins are an important point in SNCC's history because of their ineffectiveness. As noted in chapter 4, they were an example of a studied attempt to apply Stage II charismatic methods in an essentially Stage III external situation—that is, in a social system no longer predisposed to be moved by primitive charismatic techniques. Several hundred students were arrested in several locations, but there was no sense of mass movement as there was a year earlier. SNCC was learning that spontaneous social protest is not easily planned and initiated. The "grandly disorganized way of proceeding" of early Stage II no longer is a virtue in Stage III.

Lack of competent *local* leadership compounded the organizational difficulties. Many outstanding student leaders of 1960 had either (a) gone to work for civil rights organizations (particularly CORE and the NAACP) or (b) rededicated themselves to a college education, and thus were spending more time studying and less time protesting. It was not as "easy" as it was in 1960 when excitement and participation were high nationwide.

The difficulties of SNCC during these early stages of rationalization were reflected in the budget for 1961. The original division of labor had called for "Coordination" as well as "Communication" in addition to "Finances," but the 1961 budget encompassed only "Administration," "Interpretation" and "Communication." In this sense, the G and A solutions had not rationalized beyond Stage II levels.

Problems of achieving even a minimal degree of rationality also were reflected in a "proposal for a Southern Project" prepared by SNCC staff member James Monsonis in January 1961. He wrote:

> The Negro civil rights student movement needs a center—a focal point. At present it has an office and a wandering staff for the region, and some well organized centers of local activity. SNCC is the center of the movement mostly in a symbolic fashion.
>
> Somewhere there needs to be established a locus for long range study and thought as to the goals, purposes, direction of the student movement. Those who think and those who act are not now in significant conversation.

*The Freedom Rides, the Reorganization, Albany and Beyond, 1961*. In chapter 6 it was argued that the major effect of the Freedom Rides on the movement (and SNCC in particular) was to force the realization that, without a carefully planned, concentrated, sustained attack, the movement would not come in force to the rural Deep South for many years. SNCC was reorganized for this attack ("taken over," said many of the informants who were part of it) with a staff of 16 dedicated to organizing communities and initiating local protests. This was the first major differentiation of function between policy-making and implementation levels in SNCC; it did not take place "naturally" over a long period of time, as is the case in most organizations, but rather was rationally planned and executed by Tim Jenkins and others, as noted in chapter 6.

A SNCC memo in the fall of 1961 indicated the group's awareness of its precarious new position: ". . . SNCC is at a critical juncture in its own development, and, indeed, in the development of the entire desegregation movement." Planning had been centralized, voting workers were being beaten and jailed and attracting large local followings in McComb, Mississippi, and

Albany, Georgia,—and SNCC needed money. The Northern Student Movement, founded at Harvard and Yale in October, 1961, helped answer this need. "McDew [newly-elected SNCC chairman] is getting pretty good at drinking tea and begging in the North," said Jenkins. And the various forms of "suffering appeals" were used often by SNCC.[120]

A summary list of the important characteristics of SNCC's developing structure (I) and strategies (GA) at this juncture gives some indication of the degree of differentiation and rationality—and the difficulties of domesticating protest:

(1) SNCC's internal structure had been what some informants called "horizontal"—that is, it had no well-defined system of vertical stratification. It had remained this way partly because of SNCC's anti-structural attitudes. There were no rational status criteria; this meant that, almost literally, whoever had been in jail most recently had the highest prestige. The takeover and the appointment of James Forman as Executive Director late in 1961 provided a period of authoritarian leadership which brought SNCC's internal structure a higher degree of rationality.

(2) A real sense of the folk movement was developing within the SNCC staff, who were gaining the ability to combine intensely personal commitment with highly rational methods. SNCC's work in Albany was the beginning of the movement's turn to "the common people," as Cordell Reagon expressed it—a pattern which now is familiar to anyone aware that Mississippi exists. Reagon said in 1962:

> You have to act like, dress like, speak like and associate yourself with the common people. This is what we've done in Albany. We're just like neighborhood boys. We're part of the people . . . we go to dances and everything else. The maids and laborers have to realize that they're going to have to work to get up. You don't achieve anything with the preachers, teachers and businessmen until you work with the common people first.

The degree of identification of SNCC workers "living-in" the local community is shown in this "Message from SNCC" in a roughly mimeographed issue of *The Student Voice*, Albany, Georgia, March 26, 1962:

> The members of the SNCC who have for the past few months been working in Albany would again like to express our very deep gratitude for the very warm way which you and the Albany citizens have taken us into your homes, hearts and lives.

> Those of us who have been away for several weeks have very greatly missed you here at home. We come back to Albany with renewed spirits and determination to see that the noble cause of the Albany Movement is achieved. We again give our full time energy, minds, souls and bodies to you the citizens of Albany and if need be our meager lives . . .

(3) SNCC now clearly saw itself as ". . . coordinator and administrative body for the student movement in the South," as expressed in the revised constitution adopted at the Atlanta Conference, April 27-29, 1962. Voter Registration Director Robert Moses put it in even stronger terms: "SNCC has taken over the function of keeping the student movement going." The relation to subsystems now was clearly specified in the constitution:

> . . . Local groups are autonomous and shall be considered the primary unit of the student protest movement in a given area. SNCC Field Secretaries at work in any place shall work through or with the cooperation of the local group.
>
> Local groups shall expect visits and assistance from SNCC as a regular occurrence and part of the task of coordination given to the Student Nonviolent Coordinating Committee . . . [121]

(4) The cadre pattern mentioned earlier now was firmly established: James Bevel and Bernard Lafayette went into Jackson after the Freedom Rides to organize the Jackson Nonviolent Movement; Moses, John Hardy and Reggie Robinson went to McComb, Mississippi, in August; and Sherrod and Reagon went to Albany in October. Civil rights observers in 1965 know that this living-in pattern has *become* the movement, from Selma to Chicago.

One might ask, finally, who were these SNCC people in 1962, who were doing the footwork for the Deep South revolution that was to come?[122] When the bulk of the interviews for this study were done early in 1962, SNCC consisted of 16 young persons (ages 20 to 32) who had left schooling or jobs to devote full time to bringing the movement to the rural Deep South. I was able to interview 13.

First they might be defined by what others thought of them—and they inspired strong opinions from everyone connected with the movement, then and now. Most Adult informants had respect for what the SNCCers were doing, but felt that they were not very well versed in nonviolent philosophy,[123] and that the organization would be short-lived. A comparison of Student and Adult responses on this last point is illuminating:

Figure 11

PREDICTIONS FOR SNCC'S FUTURE (Form 1, IV.5b; Form 2, IV.4b)

| | *Students* (n = 13) | *Adults* (n = 32) |
|---|---|---|
| will broaden base, become more representative | 5 (38%) | 1 ( 3%) |
| will gain in size, power, reputation and/or effectiveness | 5 (38%) | 3 (9%) |
| will disintegrate within five years | 0 ( 0%) | 10 (31%) |
| will be absorbed by other civil rights organizations | 0 ( 0%) | 6 (8%) |
| various other answers | 6 (46%) | 11 (34%) |

---

As this study is submitted three years later, SNCC is stronger and more militant than ever.

Five of the 13 in the sample came from Nashville—a testimony to the nonviolent training of Rev. James M. Lawson, Jr., and the Nashville Christian Leadership Conference. Five of them said they considered nonviolence a way of life (Form 1, II.3), but eight said that "most of the students in SNCC" use it only as a technique (Form 1, II.8). As a group, they had very poor knowledge of the history of nonviolent direct action against segregation in the United States described in chapter 3: five said there had been "very little" and six said "virtually none" of this kind of protest before the sit-ins (*Form 1*, II.6).

They were oft-jailed (see chapter 2) and optimistic. Only two offered pessimistic responses when asked about "changes in the patterns of segregation . . . within the next five years" and none were pessimistic about "the next 25 years" (*Form 1*, Ix.1a and 1b).

But they are more easily defined by their style-of-life—their posture toward the world and its authorities—than by their actions or others' impressions of them. They are the archtypical rebels, the perennial radicals, the professional non-professionals. Sometimes the rebellion is expressed in constructive channels of protest, in the search for new techniques or in the cynical humor of a dig at pompous institutions. But under the pressure of the movement to constantly re-establish and reaffirm deviant identity, the revolt often takes on bitter forms.[124]

There have been no more convenient objects of derogation for SNCC workers during Stage III than Martin Luther King and the Justice Department. After civil rights had become "in" in America, disparagement of the standard "segregationists and the evil system" no longer was sufficient for SNCC super-militants, for everyone was doing it. I have many pages of data demonstrating the negative feeling about King among SNCCers—data ranging from "De Lawd" scribbled under a *Jet* cover of King on the SNCC office wall to the eagerness with which Student informants talked of King's lack of militance in the interviews. Only six of the 13 Students (46 percent) could bring themselves to label King as "THE symbol" or even "the articulator of the movement."[125] Hear a sampling of Student opinion (most of it elicited *before* any formal question about King's role was asked):

> We were all sort of inspired by him, I guess (white male).
>
> I think that Martin's values have become somewhat distorted by allowing himself to look at the movement from plush hotels and across the table from Bobby and Jack Kennedy (black male).
>
> He provided spiritual images at a time when the students were feeling very spiritual . . . Dammit! Let's start some redemption of the soul of the nation . . . Martin says, 'We're fighting down there,' and I think the peasants actually see Martin there sitting at the lunch counters with us (black male).
>
> If there were a union of organizations, I'm sure Doc would be one of the heads (black male).

There seems little question that a source of much of the anti-King hostility is his great prestige and easy access to the press, which tends to sweep up others in its wake. "We had to tell a couple of the cats at UPI that we're *not* part of SCLC!" bemoaned James Forman. "SCLC is bleeding off a lot of the money that could have been used in the movement," McDew told me. Forman was convinced early in 1962 that "Martin's engagement book [for fund-raising speeches in the North] has doubled since the sit-ins." And phrases like ". . . by the man who is heading sit-in demonstrations in the South today" on the cover of Ballentine's Fall, 1960, reissue of King's *Stride Toward Freedom* anger the students who feel that King is rarely with them to "put his body on the line."[126]

The U.S. government and the Justice Department in particular are favorite objects of repudiation for SNCC militants, who claim that federal support of their constitutionally-guaranteed activities has been lacking most of the time. SNCC hesitated in joining the foundation-supported voter registration efforts in 1961 because the drive had the blessing of the Justice Department and the Kennedy Administration, and the students were afraid they would be bought-off from future direct action demonstrations.[127]

What of SNCC since 1962? The numerical dimensions of its expansion were noted at the beginning of this section. In predictable fashion, its program continues to differentiate and, to at least a necessary extent, rationalize. Representative of the broad revolutionary goals being assumed by SNCC are the following program excerpts:

> (1) Freedom Walk in memory of William Moore, a Baltimore postman who was shot to death on an Alabama highway on April 23, 1963. A SNCC Urgent Release asked supporters to
> — organize protest groups and sympathy demonstrations when the walkers are arrested
> — write letters to your congressmen, to the Governor of the State of Alabama, to the Justice Department
> — continue your fund efforts
> — inform your organizations' membership of this effort.
>
> (2) In an August 1963 brochure: ". . . *someone* [will] *have to TAKE the freedom movement to the millions of exploited, disfranchised and degraded Negroes of the Black Belt* . . . SNCC workers have organized and guided local protest movements which are never identified as SNCC projects. This is part of its program of developing, building, and strengthening indigenous leadership."
>
> (3) A November 1963 SNCC conference in Washington had as its theme, simply "FOOD AND JOBS," with resource persons from the Manpower Development and Training Agency, the Migrant Health Section of HEW, the AFL-CIO, the National Sharecroppers Fund, etc.
>
> (4) The Mississippi Summer Project of 1964, which has focused unprecedented national attention and effort for civil rights on a particular area.

The relationship of SNCC to the movement, then, is ever-changing. For one brief period, the history of SNCC was the history of the movement. Later it *spoke for* the movement. Then it was simply *symbolic of* the movement. Still later it was *expanding* and *sustaining* the movement. Whatever may be predicted about the rationalization of this particular movement, we may be sure that SNCC will try hardest—consciously or not—to stay at least one step ahead of the predictors.[128]

NINE

# Reintegration and Predictions: The Relationship Between Rationalization and Social Change

> Most of us work simply for concessions from the system, not for transforming the system . . . But if after 300 years, segregation is still a basic pattern rather than a peripheral custom, should we not question the "American way of life" which allows segregation so much structural support?
>
> —Rev. James M. Lawson, Jr.[1]

While the formal research for this study ended in February, 1962, there is little point pretending that the final form of the argument is uninformed by what has happened in the desegregation process in America since. The most general prediction that I had made in 1962 became social reality: the movement turned essentially political, and helped present the nation with such unprecedented phenomena as the 1964 Civil Rights Law and the Voting Rights Law of 1965.[2] Rarely are social changes which were initiated through conflict, institutionalized so rapidly at the political-legal level.

The purpose of this final chapter is to apply the theory's Stage IV categories in an attempt to (a) formulate higher level questions about the rationalization of protest in general and (b) generate predictions about the direct action movement against segregation in America. Thus the major part of the argument consists of a mixture of interpretations and predictions phrased in terms of the theory of rationalization—all informally informed by developments in American racial patterns since 1962.

First one might ask what kinds of changes in the movement were *desired* by participants and sympathetic observers in 1962. *Desired* changes may be taken as the ***basis for predictions*** when actors who want the changes are in a position to implement them. Such is the case with the Student and Adult informants in this study. Of the 45 interviewed, 43 still (mid-1965) are in positions which keep them closely connected with desegregation efforts, whether as activist, adviser or observer.[3] Such a remarkably high degree of sustained commitment in the three years since the interviews makes this group uniquely qualified to speak as potential agents of social change for that period.

Students and Adults in 1962 agreed that there was a need for more cooperation among civil rights groups. Beyond that, their emphasis on desired changes diverged; Students wanted more emphasis on political action and better financial support, and Adults were concerned about new leadership training and more sophisticated values for participants, and the development of some kind of master plan to attack segregation.[4]

Figure 12

WAYS THE MOVEMENT SHOULD BE CHANGED (both forms, I.8)

| | *Students* (n = 13) | *Adults* (n = 30) |
|---|---|---|
| more cooperation (less conflict) among civil rights groups | 9 (69%) | 10 (33%) |
| political emphasis | 5 (38%) | 4 (12%) |
| better financial support | 5 (38%) | 2 ( 6%) |
| develop master plan (better structuring, etc.) | 4 (31%) | 11 (37%) |
| more participation | 3 (23%) | 7 (23%) |
| new leadership training | 3 (23%) | 13 (43%) |
| new values of participants | 3 (23%) | 11 (37%) |

| | | |
|---|---|---|
| education emphasis | 1 ( 8%) | 2 ( 6%) |
| merger of civil rights groups | 1 ( 8%) | 1 ( 3%) |

---

The application of Stage IV categories which follows indicates that all of the high priority desires have been realized to some degree. And the predictions made from the paradigm generally point to increasing emphasis on these kinds of changes in the future.

### *a. IV. RATIONAL-LEGAL ORGANIZATION: THE UNATTAINABLE GOAL*

Pure rational-legal organization (i.e. pure rationality) is, by definition, unattainable in this kind of ideal-typical analysis. But the elements of the system approach rationality in varying degrees and at varying times in its life history. So the application of Stage IV categories can show, at best, how and why certain components of the direct action movement tend to become more rationalized than others.

While pure rationality is unattainable, social systems seem to reach a progressively higher level of rational organization with each new charismatic challenge to the system. That is, certain kinds of inconsistencies are resolved each time the system incorporates a charismatic innovation, and often the system does not have to go through that problem again in future similar situations. For example, the direct action movement has rationalized fund-raising techniques at all levels—local, regional and national. So when a new local protest breaks out, it does not have to struggle through trial-and-error methods for appeals and budgetary arrangements; rather, it picks up these mechanisms well rationalized from other subsystems or the movement at-large. This phenomenon may be called *cumulative rationalization*.[5] It is basic to the analysis which follows, and is explored more explicitly in the final section.

Certain paradoxes inherent in the rationalization of protest were presented in chapter 7, and they are discussed again at the end of this chapter. But two such conditions should be noted here as background for understanding the uneven rationalization observed in the direct action protests. Stanley H. Udy writes that the development of rationality requires, minimally, (1) "orientation to limited objectives" and (2) "some modicum of organizational independence" from the social setting.[6] Protest against segregation can fulfill neither of these criteria for (1) the objectives encompass no less than the totality of social interaction, and (2) the character of the internal organizational structure is dependent on the condition of the social setting to a very high degree.

Stage IV categories now are applied to the desegregation movement. Note that "direct action movement" has become "desegregation movement," for the sit-ins brought a feeling and vocabulary of *movement* to one phase of the desegregation protests (public accommodations) which soon transferred to the total effort.

## Stage IV
## L: IDEOLOGY

1. *Content: universalistic, democratic rationality* — The "secularization" process already is noted (recall, as one example, the April, 1962, SNCC conference which included nothing on philosophy or religion in its program). I predict even greater democratic modification of the desegregation ideology, both internally (for support from every possible segment of society is needed as the struggle intensifies) and externally (prolonged crisis forces opponents into dialogue and, often, to a more realistic consideration of grievances—and thus, of common bonds and needs).

2a. *Range of Appeal: wide, differentiated* — Civil rights activity in America is becoming more "respectable" all the time. I predict an ongoing broadening of the bases of ideological appeal as the movement becomes more deeply involved in community organization and, in Boulding's terms, "cultivates ambitions for political dominance."

2b. *Range of Intensity: low* — Intensity does not remain regularly low in the desegregation movement, for intersystemic challenges (of the order of Sheriff Jim Clark's actions in Selma, Alabama) continue to refuel the charismatic ideal. Because of the intense personalism of the ideology, desegregation protests seem destined always to be more than "just a job"—regardless of how professional and rational the approach may become.

3. *Dominant Maintenance Mechanism: rationality-centrism* — The concern with "what works" continues to sustain the ideology, but it is consciously rooted in a radical affirmation of essentially non-rational ideals—"freedom" and the "dignity of man" rather than, say, the profit-motive or the law of supply and demand. I never expect the desegregation movement to become highly rational;

while appeals for ideological orthodoxy may be phrased in terms of rationality and practicality, they are ineffective unless a prior personal commitment to the goals has been made.

## Stage IV
## I: INTEGRATION

1. *Internal Organizational Structure: differentiated* — Internal organizational structure of the movement gets progressively more differentiated, but does not approach the type of pure bureaucratic rationality.

   (a) Centrifugal and centripetal forces conflict as the movement tries to establish a functionally specialized *division of labor*. The drive for subsystem autonomy coexists with the drive for movement-wide coordination and interdependence, and they mutually prevent satisfaction of either one. Whitney Young, Executive Director of the National Urban League, and Martin Luther King of SCLC both spoke of a division of labor which they would like to see develop out of the potential inherent in the various subsystems in 1962:

| Young | King |
|---|---|
| NAACP—legal aid and defense, civil rights lobby and information group | litigation and legislation |
| CORE—direct action in North | "our direct action group in the North"—especially in difficult areas like housing |
| SCLC—direct action in South | direct action and Negro community action in South because of our roots in grass roots groups like the Negro church |
| SNCC—"do in South what CORE does in North" | "nonviolent storm troopers" in South; they can do things we can't; for own survival should become more and more related to SCLC |
| Urban League—work on policy level with government and private power groups; implementing in urban areas | (no comment) |

(b) The *hierarchy of authority* never will be stable in the desegregation movement, because authority continues to be based at least partially on recent militancy—and not all leaders can be militant all the time. Further, specific situations often "accidentally" call leaders into militant action where it was not anticipated. The major civil rights organizations will continue to hold two or three unity meetings each year, and the United Council on Civil Rights Leadership may become more active, as it was in the period surrounding the March on Washington in 1963. National vs. local problems will continue to be a major cause of an unstable movement-wide authority hierarchy. Thomas Gaither, James Forman and others cited examples of this problem in 1962 (a preacher-led, unsophisticated NAACP chapter in Albany was one of them), and there have been many since. The unwillingness of the more conservative national office of the NAACP to fully support COFO at first alienated many local chapters in Mississippi in 1963—and further alienated them in 1965 when support was withdrawn from the Mississippi Freedom Democratic Party. The perennial rebellion of SNCC against being "taken-in" by the other organizations or the friendly federal government adds to the tension.[7]

(c) Movement-wide recognition of the need for local autonomy and initiative has prevented promulgation of a universal *system of precise rules*. While norms may be highly specific for a particular groups (such as CORE's "Rules for Action") or a local movement (the Albany Movement's two pages of instructions for block-work), there never will be more than informal standards set for the movement as a whole.

(d) *Emphasis on efficiency* is a major organizational goal for most subsystems within the movement,[8] and will become more important as the tasks get more difficult and complex. But at many points efficiency may continue to take a back seat to purposeful disorganization as participants recall the effectiveness of relatively unplanned Stage II action for certain types of situations.

(e) Consonant with the wide and differentiated range of ideological appeal (L.2a) is the *selection* and *promotion of personnel* based on technical competence. We can expect to see more lawyers, teachers, ministers and M.D.s, for instance, giving volunteer time to the movement in the Deep South or responding to calls to go full-time with various civil rights groups.[9] Recruitment of personnel, it should be added, seems to be the crucial element distinguishing between "spontaneous" (Stage II) protest and rational-legal protest (Stage IV): in Stage II, the mechanism of recruitment is identification with a role-model in a specific charismatic situation, while in Stage IV, recruitment is more often accomplished through organizations matching available skills with perceived needs.

(f) Inability of movement members to maintain a sharp *separation of personal and professional roles* is the ultimate barrier to a high degree of internal rationalization. A bureaucratic structure necessarily demands ". . . a sharp segregation of the sphere of office from . . . private affairs."[10] But because of the all-encompassing nature of the goals of the desegregation movement, there is and always will be a constant fusion of "office" (professional) statuses with "private" (personal) statuses. The significance of "I thought we said we were not going to talk about the movement tonight!" already has been explained. A prototypical example of the eternally weak boundaries between the movement and one's whole identity is the Christmas card my wife and I received in 1963 from a friend whom we met through a desegregation conference. The personal note on the bottom was in stark contrast to the Christian message:

> HASTEN, MORTALS TO ADORE HIM;
> LEARN HIS NAME TO MAGNIFY
> TILL IN HEAVEN WE SING BEFORE HIM
> GLORY BE TO GOD MOST HIGH

> Phoenix Hotel now willing to negotiate because of renewed CORE picketing!!

2a. *Bases of Recruitment of Members and Leaders: wide, differentiated* — A complex division of labor (I.1 [a] above) necessarily requires participants with a wide variety of skills. Thus recruiting must move beyond a small group of the chosen to many groups with many technical skills in society at-large. The lawyers, teachers, ministers and M.D.s helping in Mississippi and Alabama are the best current example. The role of organized religion in passing the Civil Rights and Voting Rights Laws was crucial.[11] We can predict that bases of recruitment will continue to expand as the conflict over segregation itself rationalizes. We may expect to see the emergence of more top leaders like SCLC's Andrew Young and the Urban League's national director, Whitney Young, both of whom are highly respected for their technical competence, even though neither is a professional jail-goer.[12]

2b. *Dominant Leadership Roles: (II.) ideologue, symbol* — The roles of *ideologue* and *symbol* are differentiated out of the Stage II charismatic role. In the case of direct action, differentiation of leadership roles often has proceeded more rapidly than other Stage IV developments. Martin Luther King clearly has maintained the role of symbol, but not that of ideologue. He always has had behind him men more at home in the ways of ideology, press relations and strategy. In Montgomery, there was Bayard Rustin, then Wyatt Walker and Andrew Young with SCLC. Other examples in direct action subsystems:

| Organization | Symbol | Ideologue |
|---|---|---|
| CORE | James Farmer | Gordon Carey, Marvin Rich, Richard Haley |
| SNCC | John Lewis (or the current chairman, usually elected for his publicly militant image) | James Forman (executive director), Robert Moses (director of voter registration), Tim Jenkins (who never had a formal position, but has been a major shaper of SNCC's policy) |

In the case of the March on Washington, A. Philip Randolph was clearly the symbol during pre-March days, and King became the major symbol after his "I have a dream . . ." speech. But Bayard Rustin was ideologue and coordinator.[13]

(III.a) *strategist, bureaucrat* — Although the roles of *strategist* and *bureaucrat* formally differentiate from the Stage III administrator role, I find them often combined with the ideologue role as the movement presses toward Stage IV rationality. Walker and Rustin, for instance, have served as both ideologue and strategist for King. The role of *leader-bureaucrat* is filled by bureau heads hired as the various subsystems expand. All of the major direct action groups, for instance, have structural provisions for such varied tasks as voter registration, public relations and research-information.

(III.b) *propagandist, agitator, fund-raiser* — The division of labor in CORE, SCLC and SNCC seems to be moving toward the establishment of at least three types of adaptor roles. Since 1960, all have developed a specific role or bureau concerned with press and public relations (*propagandist*). All have field secretaries (*agitator*). And while the charismatic leaders of each group (Farmer, King and Lewis) do their share of *fund-raising*, each organization has role-specifications for this task. The outstanding example is SNCC, which receives support from various northern Friends of SNCC groups, the Northern Student Movement, and Washington and New York offices maintained to "work the foundations and other liberals." In perhaps no other system may one see so much of what Weber calls "regularized begging"—which is an apt name for what we have been calling "suffering appeals."

2c. *Dominant Membership Roles: bureaucrat, agitator, active supporter, nominal supporter* — I have had little opportunity to observe the day-to-day internal operations of most of the civil rights organizations since 1962, so I am unable to comment on all of the membership roles specified in the theory. It is clear, however, that the role of *active supporter* is becoming increasingly important since SNCC's 1964 Mississippi Summer Project and SCLC's SCOPE in 1965, in which hundreds of volunteers took part.[14] The expanded appeals lists of groups like CORE (see chapter 8) testify to the growing functionality of the *nominal supporter*—the provider of funds.

3. *Dominant Integrative Mechanism: rationality-centrism* — The empirical case seems to deviate from the theory at this point, for I have found appeal to bureaucratic practicality an integrative mechanism of *low* priority. Again the anti-structural ideology seems to mitigate against rationality: the system's internal structure never will be stable for a long enough period to become an object of practical reverence.

## Stage IV
## G: GOAL-ATTAINMENT

1a. *Nature and Structure of Internal Goals: subsystem-centered* — Again it is impossible to predict from the theory that the movement will progressively turn in on itself as subsystems rationalize—for when each charismatic breakthrough comes, the subsystems "forget themselves" and return to more primitive (i.e., Stage II) internal mechanisms. Too, from the beginning, there has been a specific and conscious effort among movement leaders to avoid just such organization-centrism (Ella Baker's feelings about the 1960 Raleigh and Atlanta SNCC conferences, for instance).

1b. *Nature and the Structure of External Goals: value-oriented (revolutionary)* — The major goal of the desegregation movement as this is written is no less than the overthrow of the politically and economically-supported racism which continues to exist in America. This goal has been developing on a broad scale for several years, largely as a result of the movement's movement into the hard-core areas of the rural Deep South, where structurally-supported racism is most blatant. At this point, there can be no other prediction than that the goals will become more revolutionary as the resistance becomes predictably more reactionary. Laue writes, ". . . The emerging goal of all the civil rights organizations seems to be social and economic self-help within a framework of equal opportunity . . . But . . . self-help . . . [is] only possible within representative political institutions."[15] And making the Deep South politically representative—for whites as well as Negroes—*is* revolutionary. (See G.3 and A.3b for a discussion of the achievement mechanisms involved).

Two leading informants made especially perceptive comments on the revolutionizing of the movement's goals. Thomas Gaither put it in straightforward personal terms: "I want *more* than the white man wants—more than education, a job, a home, a car and social stagnation!" And James Forman foresaw in our 1962 interview the importance of Negro nationalism as a political force in America. There are many other indications of the radicalization of the movement. The most notable example of this study is the recent (1964) emergence of the Southern Student Organizing Committee, a group of southern college students dedicated to building ". . . a democratic South free from racism, fear, and poverty."[16] My observations[17] indicate that SSOC is attracting the same kinds of students who joined SNCC efforts in 1960—but SNCC now has become too radical, too professional, too full-time revolutionary to recruit large numbers of idealistic college students. So, SSOC—with similarly radical goals but a more "respectable" image—is filling the void left by the radicalization of SNCC.

2. *Range of Goals: wide and diffuse* — Revolutionary goals are, by definition, aimed at a wide and diffuse series of societal targets. Since 1962 direct action has been applied with increasing frequency and intensity to problems of discrimination in the North (the construction demonstrations in New York, Philadelphia and Cleveland are good examples). There is developing a more and more conscious link between civil rights protest and the peace movement.[18] The relationship between civil rights and civil liberties has been a concern of SCEF for some time, and will become of increasing importance for all the organizations, I predict, as Deep South segregationists continue to use the communist smear technique against desegregation workers.[19] In short, the verbalized goal of "Freedom Now" is a deceptively simple way of saying that every segment of the segregated "American Way of Life" now is under attack.

3. *Dominant Achievement Mechanism: disciplined long-range programs (initiation-coordination)* — If even a moderate degree of Stage IV rationality is achieved, one may expect a sharp differentiation between *achievement mechanisms* (the topic under consideration here) and *adaptive mechanisms* to external systems (A.3b below). We are seeing more and more that initiation and coordination of long-range programs are the major techniques used to *develop* change-producing crises in Stage IV, but the resolution of crises (and, therefore, the change itself) comes about through processes of compromise outlined in A.3b below. The community organization programs of all the major civil rights groups are representative of the kinds of disciplined long-range programs of which we can expect to see more in the near future. They attack the root problems: poverty, poor education, low job skills, voter discrimination, etc.[20] Thus, more planning is required than in previous stages, and mass demonstrations (so prominent in Stages II and III) now are only one part of a total program.

   I predict the progressive radicalization of the long-range programs of the organizations. Some indication of this trend is found in Tim Jenkins' proposal for SNCC's long-range program, formulated in 1962 and undertaken with fervor since:

> The ultimate objectives of the Project . . . [are to] radically challenge on the national level . . . the evils of one party domination [in the South]; the fraudulent amassing of seniority; the minority domination of major committees; the disproportionate weight given geography instead of people; the

> unrepresentative offer of political candidates; the unseemly coalition between racists and reactionaries to thwart progressive programs.[21]

Former SDS President Todd Gitlin sounded the same theme in his discussion of the radicalization of SNCC. He wrote in 1963 after the Birmingham church bombing, that integrationists must use ". . . every possible means to exert pressure on the corporation executives who control much of Birmingham's economic and racial policies. These industrialists, by their silence and inaction, are supporting the killing of innocent children."[22]

And Jenkins is even more explicit about what we may expect to see in the way of achievement mechanisms. In our 1962 interview, he said,

> People are moved by *power*; they only do what they have to do. When they recognize that you can throw them out of office, tie up their traffic, close their stores—*they'll move*! Our problem is to get enough hell going in Mississippi to equal the government's concern for Berlin.[23]

## Stage IV
## A: RELATION TO OTHER SYSTEMS

1. *External Organizational Structure: differentiated, sophisticated* — External as well as internal organizational structure in the protest movement is largely determined by the system's current relations with *external* systems. Because these relations are very unstable, one is not able to predict a consistently high degree of differentiation and sophistication for either structure. Intensification of counter-movements (unexpected arrests, brutality or other forms of resistance, for instance) may, within a very short time, cause great fluctuations in such adaptive activities as press relations, negotiation and fund-raising. I suspect that the unique characteristic of the desegregation movement will be the continued unpredictability of its intersystemic relations.

2a. *Range of Relevant Systems: broad, differentiated* — By definition, a social system with revolutionary goals and a high degree of internal and external structural differentiation participates in a wide variety of other social systems. In this sense, the movement reached Stage IV proportions some time ago, for participation and support has come from all class, racial, religious and geographical categories—and the effects of the movement are progressively extending to all facets of all societal institutions.[24]

2b. *Rate of Desired Change: waning to moderate* — While the actual amount of desegregation is harder than ever to measure today, it appears that the rate will level off at a moderate level—lower than Stage III, but higher than precharismatic days. The obvious indices of desegregation (numbers of specific facilities) no longer are available. But we may predict that the integration of Negroes into American economic life, for instance, will progress steadily as equal opportunity provisions in federal contracts are enforced, even though social scientists may not be able to measure such progress as easily as that in public accommodations.

3a. *Dominant Adaptive Mechanisms to Subsystems: initiation-coordination* — "SNCC was established to *coordinate* far-flung activities," said Harold Fleming in 1962, "but this didn't work. So, the hard-core of SNCC went out to generate action." With countermovements getting stronger, the movement itself turned to the initiation of long-range programs discussed in G.3 above . . . otherwise there would have been nothing to coordinate. We may expect to see a growing number of intra-and inter-organizational conferences like those reported at various points during the analysis. Efforts now must be coordinated if programs initiated are to be successful.

The need for diverse initiatory roles (and thus coordination) within the movement has been recognized by all of the organizations. James Monsonis' minutes of the March 24, 1962, SNCC Regional Meeting in Atlanta show this awareness in SNCC.[25]

> *Charles Black* — What are the unique differences of SNCC?
>
> *Charles Jones* — Let us take Albany as a clear example. The other groups of necessity are institutions, with an institution to maintain, and cannot take too many risks. Before starting a project they must see fairly clearly where it will lead. SNCC is not tied down in this way, and takes more risks. It can simply go to jail at crucial points. Its willingness to sacrifice in this way is a vitally important tactic. [Secondly], since we do not have the responsibility of building chapters at local levels, we can work to form community *movements*, not organizations.
>
> [later] *Julian Bond* — And when we leave, we leave behind a community movement with local leadership, not a new branch of SNCC.
>
> [later] *Charles Sherrod* — At first our role was information from one place to another. We then developed a great structure, but it failed because we didn't have an office and people to handle it. Now we have stumbled into our present structure and program. We do not need to throw out the past and start something new, but to put new life into the old structure.

3b. *Dominant Adaptive Mechanisms to External Systems: compromise, change* — Crises initiated by G.3 mechanisms are resolved at this level. If the desegregation movement were fully institutionalized in society-at-large, communities would often skip the agony of prolonged conflict and crisis when challenges develop, and short-circuit the resolution process directly to compromise and change. But even though American society probably never will approach that degree of rationality, we can predict that this type of conflict-resolution will be utilized more and more. Although we have seen numerous examples of the Crisis → Compromise → Change sequence throughout this study, the following example from Macon, Georgia, in 1962 is prototypical of the type of reasoning I expect to see in many white segregationists in coming years:

> We've been watching these freedom rides and boycotts in other cities, and we're getting the picture. Even Robert E. Lee finally had to surrender, didn't he?
>
> Thus Edgar Wilson, crew-cut Mayor of this Deep South city, assesses the impact of the spreading Negro campaign to speed up integration through public demonstrations . . .
>
> 'Most of us didn't want any part of the trouble that cities around us have been experiencing,' says a white member of a secret Macon businessmen's committee which spearheaded the integration drive . . . 'In Savannah we learned a Negro boycott cut retail sales as much as 50% in some places. Stores weren't the only ones hurt, either. Bankers, insurance men, small loan companies—all of them felt it.'[26]

Finally, one of the elements of compromise is conciliation. With the Civil Rights Law providing a permanent crisis situation for recalcitrant segregationists, one can expect to see the role of the conciliator grow more important. Already the role is beginning to be institutionalized in private human relations consulting services (such as that headed by George Schermer in Washington) and in government agencies (the best example is the Community Relations Service, created specifically for this purpose by Title X of the Law).

---

This brief application of the theory indicates that many of the changes in the movement hoped for by our informants in 1962 have begun to take place—more cooperation (but still a good deal of antagonism) among civil rights groups, a growing political emphasis, extensive training for leaders and participants, etc. The best information I can bring to bear on the problem at this point leads to the prediction that we will see progressive radicalization of the movement, paradoxically combined with the respectabilization that comes from world recruiting. James Forman read the situation precisely in 1962:

> These minor concessions aren't significant to the masses, man. Having a cup of coffee downtown doesn't mean very much to the cat who's unemployed.

## *b. RATIONALIZATION AND SOCIAL CHANGE: THE UNRESOLVABLE TENSION*

The major theme emerging from this study is the constant tension between charisma and structure which exists in all phases of the life of every social system—and the especially crucial nature of this tension during the expansive phase of social movements. We have followed the emergence of a charismatic movement, its difficulties during diffusion and routinization, and its changed character as it strives for rational-legal organization.

In concluding, it is appropriate to underscore some of the most important theoretical comments and predictions which have developed in the course of the analysis. They all flow from the assumption of structural differentiation—that social systems progressively develop more specialized parts and functions and, therefore, an ever greater degree of interdependence.

One aim of this summary is to formulate these comments and predictions in a way that will make them useful for future researchers and theoreticians. Thus they are presented in terms as succinct as possible. They are intended both as contributions to theory and general predictions—both of which hopefully may facilitate the asking of more intelligent research questions than was possible here.

(1) *Direct Action as a Safety Valve*. Direct action against segregation in America has served as an effective safety valve mechanism, in Coser's terms. That is, disciplined direct action protests provide a vehicle for the release of frustration and tension for the victims of discrimination—phenomena which otherwise may surface as such seriously disruptive forms of deviance as rioting, crime, family disorganization or alcoholism. Safety valve mechanisms in the form of social movements, we may add, almost always begin at the level of everyday social or economic grievances (instead of political grievances), for spontaneous recruiting flourishes best with an accumulation of day-to-day indignities on which to feed. Such movements move to sustained political activity only after a high degree of rationalization or protest efforts has occurred.

(2) *Cumulative Rationalization*. In pure terms, each successive subsystem outburst within a rationalizing charismatic movement routinizes more rapidly than the previous one. The total sweep of the innovative movement is

charted as an elongated S with the upsweep representing the charismatic period. The course of innovation within particular communities may be charted as smaller S's on this general curve in the order of their occurrence. In other words, each new subsystem S is shorter than previous ones because the rapid diffusion of rational protest information through organizations and the media to *both* protestors and countermovements shortens the charismatic stage and speeds up rationalization.

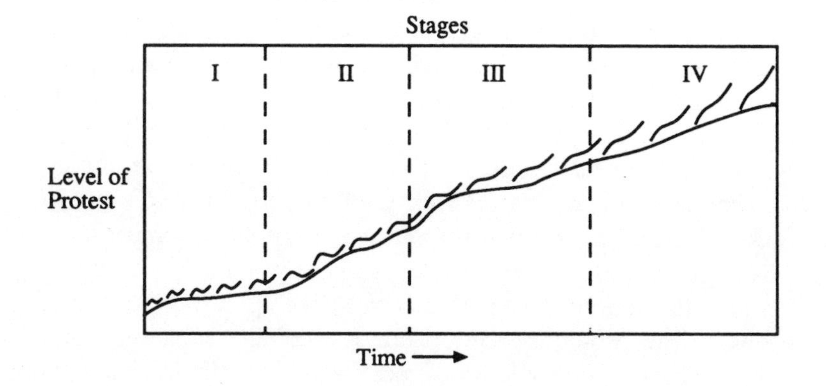


This "telescoping" effect may be expected to become increasingly common in social movements occurring in highly differentiated societies, for (a) the highly rationalized structure of voluntary associations offers pre-cut channels for absorption of the initial charisma, (b) mass communications technology aids the rapid geographical spread of an innovating mechanism, and (c) ready-made ideologies exist on a wider level, and are more readily disseminated by the highly rationalized media system.[27]

(3) *The Paradoxes of Rationalization*. Of the many paradoxes inherent in the general process of structural differentiation is the fact that social system units (including role-playing persons) become increasingly estranged personally as they become increasingly interdependent functionally. Rationalization partakes of this and other paradoxes. In the direct action movement, the paradoxes preventing extensive rationalization arise from the following sequence of facts: (a) the movement desires optimum efficiency in reaching its internal and external goals; (b) optimum efficiency requires development toward pure rationality; (c) pure rationality requires a depersonalization of relationships within the social system; but (d) one of the

major goals of the movement is the universal extension, internally and externally, of deeply personal, I-Thou relationships. Rational bureaucracy, says Max Weber, ". . . develops the more perfectly the more [it] is 'dehumanized,' the more completely it succeeds in eliminating from official business love, hatred, and all purely personal, irrational, and emotional elements which escape calculation."[28] It is more than a truism to say that this is simply impossible to achieve—especially when one is engaged full time in *putting his body on the line*.

(4) *Crisis and Social Change*. In reviewing the development of my own thinking during this project, I find that the "8 C's" which make up the theory's Dominant Adaptive Mechanisms to External Systems (A.3b) seem to have the greatest range of applicability to various kinds of change situations. Thus, they are worth underscoring here in summary form. Social systems exist in a constant state of *competition* between actors for limited rewards. Latent protest systems in society offer a series of *challenges* to the status quo, which often heighten the officially suppressed competition so it breaks through to a more intense and public level—*conflict*. *Crisis* occurs when important decision makers (usually those in a position to grant concessions to the protest system) define the conflict situation as serious enough to demand rapid resolution. From this point, the dominant groups rapidly move to a more realistic *confrontation* with the grievances of the protestors, and the realization that they will have to enter into *communication* (face-to-face bargaining) with them. Each side gives and takes (*compromise*) until a new, more inclusive state of competitive equilibrium is reached (*change*). This sequence has been followed in literally every community where direct action against segregation has taken place—modified only by the power structure's implicit realization of the sequence, and their subsequent short-circuiting from challenge directly to communication to avoid the agony of prolonged conflict.[29]

(5) *Severe Racial Crises to Come*. In the light of the above theoretical speculations and predictions, we may expect a number of severe racial crises in America in the next several decades. I predict more Birminghams, more ghetto outbreaks like those of summer, 1964 and 1965, despite efforts of various conciliatory agencies and mechanisms to prevent them.[30] Chicago will be the major crisis of summer, 1966.[31] In terms of the theory, severe crises may be avoided only if segregationist state and local leaders learn the lesson of the "8 C's" and move early to crisis-definitions to avoid the community-

disintegrating effects of prolonged conflict. I predict they will not learn very fast.

(6) *Reintegration of the Movement.*[32] Close cooperation of the civil rights groups which now sustain the desegregation movement has been taking place with greater frequency in the last few years, largely because of (a) the growing sophistication of countermovements in hard-core segregationist areas and (b) the more complicated and long-range programs being initiated by the movement. Such "de-differentiation" will increasingly become a practical necessity as rationalization of goals (L), structure (I), strategies (G), and the opposition's effectiveness (A) progresses. We may predict, then, more phenomena like the March on Washington, the secret "summit meetings" and unity meetings of organizational leaders, the United Council on Civil Rights Leadership and the Council of Federated Organizations in Mississippi.

(7) *The Emergence of the Moderate.* We may predict that the role of the moderate will become increasingly important in the American desegregation process in the coming years. For years, the moderate (especially the "white liberal") has been much maligned by militants—and perhaps rightly so, for what was needed for change was *crisis*, not compromise or moderation. But with 1960 and the direct action movement, desegregationists found a mechanism with which to create bargaining crises. And now the implementation of the federal Civil Rights Law of 1964 and the Voting Rights Law of 1965 presents segregationists with a permanent crisis. Therefore, what is needed now is *institutionalization of the bargaining process*—in short, the emergence of dedicated, shrewd, and sophisticated moderates who can hasten the process of desegregation by working out its terms with the sure knowledge of the eventual outcome.[33] Already this is taking place, as noted earlier, with the work of the federal Community Relations Service and private, state and local intergroup relations consultants.

Speculation on the growing importance of militant moderates is reinforced by the comments of two of the most respected informants in this study. Rev. Will Campbell noted in 1962 that the movement already had forced segregationists into dialogue with persons who only shortly before, were considered too "radical" to deal with. "Two years ago I was a real radical," said Campbell, "but today I am getting calls from political leaders and restaurant owners who wouldn't have touched me then. *My* position hasn't changed, but *their* perception of the enemy has." And National Urban League Director Whitney M. Young, Jr., predicted that ". . . the role and importance of Urban League-type supplementing agencies" would become more crucial and better understood in the desegregation process. "We'll have to go through the same period of slugging it out and getting to the sophisticated bargaining level the labor union movement did."

(8) *The Politicizing of the Protest Movement*. With social and economic self-help within a framework of representative political institutions as the emergent long-range goal of all the movement's subsystems, it is not surprising that the protests already are well into the essentially political phase of Stage IV. Success in this area has been little short of phenomenal. *The 1964 Civil Rights Law and the 1965 Voting Rights Law are unprecedented examples of the rapidity with which the goals of a charismatic protest movement have been achieved and institutionalized in law*. The direct action movement was barely four years old when the Civil Rights Act was signed into law on July 2, 1964. It had been only a year since the Birmingham dogs and fire hoses had prompted President Kennedy to propose the legislation. And the beatings at the Selma bridge in March, 1965, were the catalyst which moved President Johnson to say "We Shall Overcome" on prime-time television and introduce the Voting Rights Act—which became law only four months later.

Such rapid legislation took place in a context of the movement's increased emphasis on citizenship education and voter registration since 1962. The Voter Education Project alone registered more than 550,000 new Negro voters in the South from March, 1962, to July, 1964.[34] The Mississippi Summer Project and the Mississippi Freedom Democratic Party's challenge at the Democratic National Convention drew wide attention in 1964. So did the MFDP's challenge to the Mississippi Congressional Delegation in 1965. Only united protest efforts can effectively challenge such entrenched blocs of political power; we may expect politicization and internal reintegration of protest to continue to complement each other as important characteristics of the rationalizing desegregation movement in America.

---

The movement never ends, the process of rationalization never ends, but dissertations must. It is only fair to the data and to myself to end this study with a reminder of the ongoing and ultimately nonrationalizable character of its subject. Perhaps this can be accomplished by presenting three bits of data from sources widely separated in space and time, but joined by their common bond to the movement.

First, I recall from field notes made in August 1960, the comments of white onlookers as members of our CORE institute silently and peacefully picketed the store which had arrested 18 of us:

> *A 30-year-old man in a sport shirt* — "You communistic bastards."
>
> *A fat, well-dressed, middle-aged man* (in response to my observer's question to him about what was happening here) — "I just wanted to razz that white son-of-a-bitch."
>
> *A teen-age boy* — "I hope it rains . . . it'll drown the bastards."
>
> *A matronly lady* (to the store's bag-boys) — "Take a shotgun to 'em."

Four years and much desegregation later, we read the record of violence in Mississippi during a part of 1964:

> . . . [during the summer] 3 murders, at least 80 persons beaten, 35 churches burned, more than 1,000 persons arrested, 30 homes and other buildings bombed, and 35 shooting incidents.
>
> In connection with the Freedom Democratic Party's mock election campaign, COFO reported between October 18 and November 2, 119 arrests and 63 other harassments, including tear-gassing of a home and several shootings.[35]

And 1965 (not yet completed as this is submitted) has seen its share of beatings, home and church bombings, arrests, tear-gassings, cattle-proddings, economic harassments and other subtler forms of social control, North and South. At least 13 persons are dead because they put their bodies on the line for the movement in 1965—shot by state troopers, clubbed by a white mob, shot from a speeding car on a U.S. highway late at night, shotgunned point-blank on the courthouse square in the middle of the day, etc.[36]

One can only remind himself and Max Weber that, when these kinds of phenomena become the "official business" of a rationalizing social system, it is at best futile to hope for the "complete elimination" of ". . . love, hatred, and all purely personal, irrational, and emotional elements which escape calculation."

# Appendices

## APPENDIX A

# Informants Who Participated in an Interview, February 21 to April 8, 1962

1. *Members of the Student Nonviolent Coordinating Committee**

The Reverend Mr. Bernard Lafayette, Field Secretary. February 24; 3 hours (now on the staff of the American Friends Service Committee, Chicago).

Julian Bond, Field Secretary. March 6; 2 hours, 15 minutes (now SNCC Director of Information and Representative from Atlanta to the Georgia State Legislature).

Charles McDew, Chairman of SNCC from November 1961 to July 1963. March 5-6; 2 hours, 45 minutes (now on the staff of the United Planning Organization, Washington, D.C.).

J. Robert Zellner, Field Secretary. March 7, 16; 3 hours (now a graduate student at Brandeis University and movement organizer in Boston area).

James Monsonis, Field Secretary and Program Assistant. March 18; 3 hours (now a representative for SNCC and Students for a Democratic Society, New York).

The Reverend Mr. Charles Sherrod, Field Secretary. March 22; 2 hours (now a student at Union Theological Seminary in New York and a summer SNCC Field Secretary in southwest Georgia).

Lester McKinnie, Field Secretary and Coordinator of the Jackson Nonviolent Movement. March 24; 3 hours.

Cordell Reagon, Field Secretary. March 27; 2 hours (now SNCC Field Secretary in Alabama and Mississippi).

Charles Jones, Director of Voter Registration. March 27; 2 hours, 45 minutes.

Diane Nash Bevel, Field Secretary. March 28; 3 hours (now on staff of Southern Christian Leadership Conference in Chicago).

The Reverend Mr. Paul Brooks, Field Secretary. March 29-30; 3 hours.

James Forman, Executive Secretary. March 30-31; 4 hours, 15 minutes (still in same position).

Robert Moses, Field Secretary and Director, Mississippi Voting Project. April 7-8; 3 hours, 15 minutes (now Robert Parris, informally connected with SNCC and the peace movement).

*And their position at the time of the interview. Exact present position indicated in parentheses where known.

2. *Adults*

Carroll Barber, Staff Associate, Race Relations Department, Fisk University, Nashville, Tennessee. February 21; 3 hours (in same position today).

The Reverend Mr. Will Campbell, Southern Representative, National Council of Churches of Christ in America, Nashville. February 21; 3 hours (now Director of the Fellowship of Southern Churches).

The Reverend Mr. Kelly Miller Smith, President, Nashville Christian Leadership Conference. February 23; 1 hour, 45 minutes (still pastor of First Baptist Church, Nashville, and active in NCLC).

Lester Carr, Instructor in Psychology, Fisk University. February 25; 3 hours, 30 minutes.

Dr. Herman Long, Director, Race Relations Department, Fisk University. February 26; 2 hours (now President, Talladega College, Talladega, Alabama).

The Reverend Mr. J. Metz Rollins, Office of Church and Society of the Board of Christian Education of the United Presbyterian Church in the U.S.A., Special Field Representative in Nashville. February 25-27; 4 hours, 45 minutes (now with the national office in New York).

Dr. Vivian Henderson, Professor of Economics, Fisk University. February 26; 3 hours, 15 minutes (now President, Clark College, Atlanta).

Dr. Lewis W. Jones, Race Relations Department, Fisk University—for many years Professor of Sociology at Tuskegee Institute. March 1; 5 hours, 30 minutes (now in Race Relations Department at Fisk).

The Reverend Mr. James M. Lawson, Jr., Special Projects Director, SCLC. March 1; 1 hour, 15 minutes, incomplete (now minister of Centenary Methodist Church in Memphis and consultant on nonviolence to SCLC).

Jane Stembridge, SNCC Secretary from June to October 1960. March 4; 1 hour, 30 minutes, incomplete (now free-lance writer and activist).

Claude Sitton, Southern Correspondent, *New York Times*. March 6; 3 hours (now Associate Editor, *New York Times*, New York).

Dr. Leslie W. Dunbar, Executive Director, Southern Regional Council. March 9; 3 hours, 30 minutes (now Executive Director, Field Foundation).

The Reverend Mr. John B. Morris, Executive Director, The Episcopal Society for Cultural and Racial Unity. March 10; 3 hours (in same position today).

Constance Curry, Director, Southern Student Human Relations Project of the National Student Association. March 2; 11; 3 hours, 30 minutes (now on the staff of the American Friends Service Committee in Atlanta).

James Gibson, Executive Secretary, Atlanta Branch of the National Association for the Advancement of Colored People. March 12; 1 hour, 45 minutes.

Arthur Levin, Director of the Southern Office of the Anti-Defamation League, Atlanta. March 7, 13; 2 hours, 45 minutes (now Assistant Director of the Potomac Institute, Washington, D.C.).

Dorothy Miller, Research Assistant, Southern Regional Council. March 5, 13; 3 hours, 30 minutes (later with SNCC and now Dorothy Miller Zellner, raising a family and organizing for SNCC in the Boston area).

Dr. Howard Zinn, Professor of History and Chairman of the Department of Social Sciences, Spelman College, Atlanta. March 14; 2 hours (now Associate Professor of Government, Boston University).

Mrs. Ruby Harley, Southeastern Regional Secretary of the NAACP, Atlanta. March 16; 1 hour, 45 minutes (in same position today).

The Reverend Mr. Wyatt T. Walker, Executive Director of the Southern Christian Leadership Conference. March 14, 16-17; 2 hours (now President, Educational Heritage, publishers).

Ella Baker, Special Project Staff, National Student Young Women's Christian Association. March 15, 17, 19; 4 hours, 15 minutes (now free-lance activist and advisor to SNCC, the Council of Federated Organizations, Mississippi Freedom Democratic Party, etc.).

Charles Whittenstein, Southeast Region Area Director, American Jewish Committee, Atlanta. March 15, 19; 3 hours (in same position today).

Margaret Long, Director of Information and Editor of *New South* for the Southern Regional Council. March 20; 1 hour, 15 minutes (in same position today).

Bruce Galphin, Race Relations Reporter, *Atlanta Constitution*. March 20; 2 hours, 30 minutes (now in Editorial Department of the *Constitution*).

Bernard Lee, Student Liaison for SCLC. March 21; 45 minutes, incomplete (now Special Assistant to Dr. Martin Luther King, Jr., of SCLC).

Dr. Charles Gomillion, Chairman of the Department of Social Science and Dean, Tuskegee Institute, Alabama. March 23; 1 hour, 45 minutes (in same position today).

Thomas Gaither, Field Secretary for the Congress of Racial Equality and Acting Chairman, Adult Advisory Board of the Jackson Nonviolent Movement. March 24; 3 hours (now in armed services).

Thomas Hayden, free-lance writer and Field Representative for Students for a Democratic Society. March 21, April 1; 4 hours, 15 minutes (now an organizer for SDS with the Newark Community Union Project).

The Reverend Dr. Martin Luther King, Jr., President of SCLC. April 4; 1 hour, 30 minutes (in same position today).

Harold Fleming, Executive Director, The Potomac Institute, Washington, D.C. April 5; 3 hours, 45 minutes (in same position today).

Timothy Jenkins, free-lance activist and former National Student Association National Affairs Vice President. April 8; 2 hours, 45 minutes (graduate of Yale Law School, now in a Philadelphia law firm).

Whitney Young, Jr., Executive Director, National Urban League. April 8; 2 hours, incomplete (in same position today).

APPENDIX B

# The Interview Schedule, 1962

There were two forms of the interview schedule, Form 1 for Students and Form 2 for Adults (as defined in chapter 2). The cover page on both forms was the same; it is reproduced below.

INTERVIEW SCHEDULE FOR

PROTEST LEADERS AND OBSERVERS

form [1 or 2]

James H. Laue
Dept. of Social Relations
Harvard University
Cambridge 38, Mass.
Spring, 1962

This is a guide sheet for questions to be asked of leaders and observers of the direct action protest movement against segregation. Many of the questions do not call for specific answers, but rather are to be used as guides to more general discussion topics. The purpose is to determine the important characteristics of the movement's organization and leadership. This material will be used for a doctoral dissertation at Harvard University. I will appreciate permission to quote interpretative statements in the dissertation.

Name__________________

Position______________

Address_______________

Date______Interview Number______

## FORM 1—STUDENTS

### I. GENERAL IMPRESSIONS

1. How did you first become involved in the movement? (When and how did you first hear of the movement?).

2. What do you think were the most important factors in the start and rapid spread of the sit-ins at this time?

3. Approximately how many persons do you think have participated in the movement all over the country, including sympathy demonstrations in the North?

4. In what ways does the movement seem different to you now than it was in the beginning in 1960? Please explain. Have these changes helped or hindered the movement?

5. What are the ultimate goals of the movement? How successful has the movement been in reaching these goals? How long have you felt this way?

6. What is the biggest problem you see in the movement? How long have you seen this as the biggest problem?

7. In your opinion, what has been the biggest change in the movement since it began?

8. In what ways would you like to see the movement changed?

9. Have there been any big "turning points" in the course of the movement? Do you remember if you thought of them as "turning points" at the time?

### II. ON NONVIOLENCE

1. How did you first hear of nonviolent direct action?

2. Do you remember any of your first impressions about this?

3. Does nonviolence seem feasible to you as a total philosophy, as a way of life? When did you begin to feel this way about it?

4. Before the movement started, had you read:

| | yes | no | title(s) |
|---|---|---|---|
| Gandhi | | | |
| Thoreau | | | |
| Muste | | | |
| Gregg | | | |
| M.L. King, Jr. | | | |

5. Have you ever attended a workshop or clinic in nonviolent philosophy and methods? If yes, when and where? Were you a leader or a participant?

6. Was there much nonviolent direct action against segregation before the sit-ins began?

7. Had you ever participated in a direct action *project* before the sit-ins began?

8. How do most of the students in SNCC feel about nonviolence? Other participants in the movement? Have there been any changes in this since the sit-ins began?

---

## III. LEADERSHIP

1. Who are the most important leaders in the movement today?

2. How has the leadership of the movement changed in the last two years?

3. How have these changes affected the movement?

4. What part has adult leadership played in the movement?

5. How do the student leaders of the movement today differ from the leaders at the beginning of the sit-ins?

---

## IV. ON THE STUDENT NONVIOLENT COORDINATING COMMITTEE

1. Tell me briefly about your part in SNCC.

2. Does SNCC "speak for the movement"? Has this been true from the beginning?

3. Has SNCC's function changed very much since it was formed? If yes, when and why did these changes take place?

4. Do current SNCC staff members differ from the very first student representatives to SNCC in any important ways?

5. Do you see SNCC as a permanent organization? Will there be any big changes in SNCC's role in the movement?

---

## V. ON NON-STUDENT PARTICIPATION

1. What area or national civil rights organizations have played the most important parts in the movement? At what points in the movement has their influence been the greatest?

2. In what ways have organizations helped the movement most? Be specific.

3. Have there been times when organizations have actually held back progress in the movement? Be specific.

4. From what individuals and/or groups in the white community have you received the greatest opposition to the movement? What do you think are the main reasons for this opposition? Has this been true during the whole movement?

5. Can you tell me about any opposition in the Negro communities?

6. How important is white participation in the movement? In what ways have they been most helpful? Has their participation hurt the movement in any way?

7. Tell me briefly about the role of the Northern Student Movement.

8. Does the work of the various civil rights organizations play a bigger part in the movement today than it did in the beginning?

9. Can you tell me anything more about the place of Martin Luther King, Jr., in the protest movement?

10. Would you say that this has been mostly a *student* movement, or have adults helped a lot? When and how?

11. For each of the following groups, rate whether you think they are mostly in favor of, neutral towards, or opposed to the goals and methods of the protest movement:

a. your parents
b. Negro adults you know
c. Negro college students in your area
d. white college students in your area
e. college students in general throughout the country
f. Negro college administrators
g. Negro community leaders around here
h. Negro community leaders in most southern cities
i. the press in the South
j. the press nationally
k. southern law enforcement officials
l. the local white businessmen
m. national offices of the chain stores
n. the federal government

## VI: THE FORMS OF PROTEST

1. What forms or kinds of protests (demonstrations) are being used most frequently now? How does this compare with the first few months of the movement?

2. What kinds of protest have been most effective (have brought about the most progress)?

3. Are there "spontaneous" demonstrations in various cities today like those which took place in the first few months of the sit-ins? Or is everything organized?

4. What are some of the things that could be done to make the movement more effective?

## VII. YOUR OWN PARTICIPATION

1. Has your participation in the movement changed your outlook on life?

2. Is your part in the movement now different from what it was at the beginning?

3. What was the most important event in the movement for you?

4. How long do you expect to stay actively involved in the movement? Did you feel this way at the beginning of the movement?

---

## VIII. PERSONAL INFORMATION

1. College or university and city.
2. College major.
3. Last grade completed.
4. Current status (in school, leave of absence, expelled, etc.).
5. Hometown.
6. Place of birth.
7. Age.
8. Sex.
9. Race or nationality background.
10. Religious preference or affiliation.
11. Political preference or affiliation.

Family Information

Father

12. Age.
13. Occupation.
14. Place of birth.
15. Education (last grade)
16. Religious pref. or aff.
17. Political pref or aff.
18. Organizations.

Mother

12a. Age.
13a. Occupation.
14a. Place of birth.
15a. Education (last grade).
16a. Religious pref. or aff.
17a. Political pref. or aff.
18a. Organizations.

High School Information

19. Public or private?

20. Approximate standing in class.

21. High school activities . . . both in and out of school.

22. Do you remember if you discussed the 1954 Supreme Court desegregation decision in school? To what extent? Do your feelings about the decision differ now from what they were in 1954?

College Information

23. How did you decide to attend your college? Are you happy with your choice?

24. Approximate percentage standing in class.

25. College activities . . . both in and out of school.

26. Would you say your views on segregation and discrimination are alike or unlike those of most students at your college?

27. Tell me about your travel experiences. Have you ever been in the North?

28. Had you seen any marked changes in prejudice and discrimination against Negroes in your lifetime before the sit-ins began?

29. In what ways have you participated in the protest movement?

a. planning and directing demonstrations
b. attending mass meetings
c. picketing
d. sitting-in
e. Freedom Ride
f. working on posters, office work, etc.
g. serving on a local committee
h. serving on SNCC (when?)
i. cooperation with boycott
j. fund-raising
k. other (specify)

30. How many times have you been arrested for your participation in the movement?

31. How many times jailed?

32. How much time spent in jail?

33. Where?

---

## IX. FUTURE OF THE MOVEMENT

1. What changes in the patterns of segregation do you expect to see within the next five years? In the next 25 years?

2. What changes within the movement do you expect to see in the next five years?

## FORM 2—ADULTS

## I. GENERAL IMPRESSIONS

1. How did you first become involved in the movement? (When and how did you first hear of the movement?).

2. What do you think were the most important factors in the start and rapid spread of the sit-ins at this time?

3. Approximately how many persons do you think have participated in the movement all over the country, including sympathy demonstrations in the North?

4. In what ways does the movement seem different to you now than it was in the beginning in 1960? Please explain. Have these changes helped or hindered the movement?

5. What are the ultimate goals of the movement? How successful has the movement been in reaching these goals? How long have you felt this way?

6. What is the biggest problem you see in the movement? How long have you seen this as the biggest problem?

7. In your opinion, what has been the biggest change in the movement since it began?

8. In what ways would you like to see the movement changed?

9. Have there been any big "turning points" in the course of the movement? Do you remember if you thought of them as "turning points" at the time?

## II. ON NONVIOLENCE

1. How did you first hear of nonviolent direct action?

2. Do you remember any of your first impressions about this?

3. Does nonviolence seem feasible to you as a total philosophy, as a way of life?

4. How well versed in nonviolent philosophy are the student leaders? What do they know about the Montgomery bus boycott?

5. Do most of the student protestors accept nonviolence as a way of life or as a technique? Was this true at the beginning of the movement?

## III. LEADERSHIP

1. Who are the most important leaders in the movement today?

2. How has the leadership structure of the movement changed in the last two years?

3. Have these changes generally helped or hurt the movement?

4. Has the movement been led and coordinated predominantly by adults or students?

5. At what points has adult leadership played its greatest part in the movement?

6. How do the student leaders today differ from the leaders at the beginning of the movement? When and how do you think these changes began to take place?

## IV. ON THE STUDENT NONVIOLENT COORDINATING COMMITTEE

1. Does SNCC "speak for the student movement?" Has this been true from the beginning?

2. Have SNCC's functions changed appreciably since it was formed? If yes, when and why did these changes take place?

3. In what ways, if any, do current SNCC staff members differ from the first student representatives chosen to SNCC in the spring of 1960?

4. What changes in SNCC's structure and approaches do you foresee? Is it a permanent organization?

---

## V. ON NON-STUDENT PARTICIPATION

1. Have there been any changes in the attitudes of the students toward participation by *non*-students since the movement began?

2. What area or national civil rights organizations have played the most important parts in the movement? At what points in the movement has their influence been the greatest?

3. Are the students generally receptive to assistance from adults and organizations? Has it been like this all during the movement?

4. What do you think have been the main sources of antagonism between the students and these organizations and adult leaders?

5. What groups and/or individuals in the Negro community have been least willing to cooperate with the movement?

6. How important is white participation in the movement? In what ways have whites been most helpful? Have they actually hindered the movement in any way? Has this been true during most of the movement?

7. Can you tell me anything more about the place of Martin Luther King, Jr., in the protest movement?

8. For each of the following groups, rate whether you think they are mostly in favor of, neutral or ambivalent toward, or opposed to the goals and methods of the protest movement:

a. Negro college students in your area
b. white college students in your area
c. college students in general throughout the country
d. Negro college administrators

e. Negro community leaders
f. most Negro adults
g. the press in the South
h. the press nationally
i. southern law enforcement officials
j. the local white businessmen
k. national offices of chain stores
l. the federal government

---

## VI. THE FORMS OF PROTEST

1. What forms or kinds of protests (demonstrations) are being used most frequently now? How does this compare with the first few months of the movement?

2. What kinds of protests have proved most effective?

3. Are there "spontaneous" demonstrations in various cities today in the same sense as those which took place in the first few months of the sit-ins? Or is everything organized?

4. What are some of the things that could be done to make the movement more effective?

---

## VII. FUTURE OF THE MOVEMENT

1. What changes in the patterns of segregation do you expect to see within the next five years? In the next 25 years?

2. What changes within the movement do you expect to see in the next five years?

APPENDIX C

# Tabulation of Results

The development of coding techniques and categories for the spring 1962 interview data was described in chapter 2. Each of the 13 Student and 32 Adult interviews was coded on a 3 x 5 card, and marginals and cross-tabulations were calculated by hand. [Sample cards in the dissertation are not included here.]

Included below are the responses to the interviews, as coded and tabulated for analysis of the direct action movement in this study. *Form 1* (Student) responses are presented first, with results from corresponding items in *Form 2* (Adult) combined into one chart. Tabulations included in the text are not repeated in the Appendix; rather, page numbers where they may be found in the text are cited for quick referral.

---

## FORM 1 (STUDENT)

### I. GENERAL IMPRESSIONS

1. How did you first become involved in the movement? (When and how did you first hear of the movement?).

(n = 13)

| | |
|---|---|
| through Negro campus in February, 1960 | 7 (54%) |
| through Negro campus and mass media in February, 1960 | 2 (16%) |
| in February, 1960 | 1 ( 8%) |
| through Negro campus after February, 1960 | 1 ( 8%) |
| mass media after February, 1960 | 1 ( 8%) |
| after February, 1960 | 1 ( 8%) |

2. What do you think were the most important factors in the start and rapid spread of the sit-in movement at this time?

(reported with corresponding results from *Form 2* in chapter 3, pp. 62-63).

3. Approximately how many persons do you think have participated in the movement all over the country, including sympathy demonstrations in the North?

| | *Students* (n = 12) | *Adults* (n = 17) |
|---|---|---|
| 10,000 or less | 0 ( 0%) | 0 ( 0%) |
| 10 - 24,000 | 3 (25%) | 1 ( 6%) |
| 25 - 49,000 | 4 (33%) | 3 (18%) |
| 50 - 74,000 | 0 ( 0%) | 2 (12%) |
| 75 - 99,000 | 0 ( 0%) | 6 (35%) |
| 100 - 199,000 | 3 (25%) | 2 (12%) |
| more than 200,000 | 2 (17%) | 3 (18%) |

(One Student and 14 Adults refused to estimate.)

## II. ON NONVIOLENCE

1. How did you first hear of nonviolent direct action?

| | *Students* (n = 13) | *Adults* (n = 32) |
|---|---|---|
| the movement | 3 (23%) | 2 ( 6%) |
| Gandhi | 3 (23%) | 16 (50%) |
| Montgomery and/or M.L. King, Jr. | 2 (16%) | 7 (22%) |

| | | |
|---|---|---|
| in college | 2 (16%) | 2 ( 6%) |
| Greensboro | 2 (16%) | 0 ( 0%) |
| CORE | 0 ( 0%) | 2 ( 6%) |
| Thoreau | 0 ( 0%) | 2 ( 6%) |
| Christianity | 0 ( 0%) | 1 ( 3%) |
| other | 1 ( 8%) | 2 ( 6%) |

2. Do you remember any of your first impressions about this?

| | *Students* (n = 12) | *Adults* (n = 29) |
|---|---|---|
| strongly favorable | 7 (58%) | 10 (34%) |
| favorable | 1 ( 8%) | 12 (41%) |
| indifferent or neutral | 1 ( 8%) | 2 ( 7%) |
| unfavorable | 1 ( 8%) | 5 (17%) |
| strongly unfavorable | 1 ( 8%) | 0 ( 0%) |
| strongly unfavorable changed to strongly favorable | 1 ( 8%) | 0 ( 0%) |

3. Does nonviolence seem feasible to you as a total philosophy, as a way of life? When did you begin to feel this way about it?

| | *Students* (n = 13) | *Adults* (n = 29) |
|---|---|---|
| yes, I live by it | 5 (38%)* | 5 (17%) |
| yes | 1 ( 8%) | 6 (21%) |
| don't know or don't understand it | 0 ( 0%) | 2 ( 7%) |

| | | |
|---|---|---|
| probably not | 2 (16%) | 6 (21%) |
| definitely not | 2 (16%) | 7 (24%) |
| other | 3 (23%) | 3 (10%) |

*(Four of the five said they began to feel this way after the movement started.)

4. Before the movement started, had you read:

(n = 13)

| | |
|---|---|
| Thoreau | 7 (54%) |
| Gandhi | 5 (38%) |
| M.L. King, Jr. | 5 (38%) |
| A.J. Muste | 1 ( 8%) |
| others | 1 ( 8%) |

5a. Have you ever attended a workshop or clinic in nonviolent philosophy and methods?

| | |
|---|---|
| yes | 11 (84%) |
| no | 2 (16%) |

5b. If yes, when and where? (omitted because responses uncodable)

5c. Were you a leader or a participant?

| | |
|---|---|
| leader | 9 (53%) |
| participant | 8 (47%) |

6. Was there much nonviolent direct action against segregation before the sit-ins began?

(n = 13)

| | |
|---|---|
| yes [good understanding of history] | 1 ( 8%) |
| qualified yes [a guess . . . some understanding] | 1 ( 8%) |
| don't know | 0 ( 0%) |
| very little | 5 (38%) |
| virtually none | 6 (46%) |

7. Had you ever participated in a direct action *project* before the sit-ins began?

| | |
|---|---|
| yes | 5 (38%) |
| no | 8 (62%) |

8a. How do most of the students in SNCC feel about nonviolence?

(n = 13)

| | |
|---|---|
| technique | 8 (62%) |
| way of life | 3 (23%) |
| other | 1 ( 8%) |
| don't know | 0 ( 0%) |
| uncodable | 1 ( 8%) |

8b. How do other participants in the movement feel about nonviolence?

| | (n = 11) |
|---|---|
| technique | 8 (73%) |
| way of life | 2 (18%) |
| other | 1 ( 9%) |
| don't know | 0 ( 0%) |

8c. Have there been any changes in this since the sit-ins began?

| | (n = 9) |
|---|---|
| more take it as a way of life now | 4 (44%) |
| more take it as a technique now | 3 (33%) |
| no changes | 1 (11%) |
| don't know | 1 (11%) |

---

## III. LEADERSHIP

1. Who are the most important leaders in the movement today?

| | *Students* (n = 13) | *Adults* (n = 32) |
|---|---|---|
| Martin Luther King, Jr. (SCLC) | 10 (77%) | 28 (88%) |
| James Farmer (CORE) | 6 (46%) | 14 (44%) |
| SNCC leaders other than James Forman | 6 (46%) | 6 (20%) |
| SCLC leaders other than King or Wyatt Walker | 4 (31%) | 10 (31%) |

| | | |
|---|---|---|
| local leaders | 3 (23%) | 2 ( 6%) |
| NAACP leaders | 3 (23%) | 7 (22%) |
| James Forman (SNCC) | 2 (16%) | 5 (16%) |
| James Lawson (SCLC) | 2 (16%) | 8 (25%) |
| Wyatt Walker (SCLC) | 2 (16%) | 2 ( 6%) |
| CORE leaders other than Farmer | 1 ( 8%) | 2 ( 6%) |
| other | 1 ( 8%) | 0 ( 0%) |

2. How has the leadership changed in the last two years?

| | *Students* (n = 9) | *Adults* (n = 26) |
|---|---|---|
| more leaders, more spontaneous local action | 3 (33%) | 4 (16%) |
| emergence of institutionalized leadership | 3 (33%) | 7 (27%) |
| SNCC playing bigger role | 2 (22%) | 2 ( 8%) |
| fewer adults | 2 (22%) | 2 ( 8%) |
| SCLC playing bigger role | 1 (11%) | 3 (12%) |
| NAACP playing bigger role | 1 (11%) | 3 (12%) |
| more adults | 1 (11%) | 0 ( 0%) |
| CORE playing bigger role | 0 ( 0%) | 4 (16%) |
| loss of grass roots leadership | 0 ( 0%) | 8 (31%) |

3. How have these changes affected the movement?

| | (n = 6) |
|---|---|
| helped | 4 (67%) |
| hurt | 0 ( 0%) |
| both | 2 (33%) |

4. What part has adult leadership played in the movement?

| | *Students* (n = 11) | *Adults* (n = 28) |
|---|---|---|
| financial help | 4 (36%) | 17 (61%) |
| has hindered movement | 4 (36%) | 0 ( 0%) |
| advice and support | 2 (18%) | 14 (50%) |
| legal aid | 2 (18%) | 10 (36%) |
| active leadership and direction | 1 ( 9%) | 10 (36%) |
| support boycott | 1 ( 9%) | 6 (21%) |
| has done very little | 1 ( 9%) | 0 ( 0%) |
| negotiation | 0 ( 0%) | 11 (39%) |
| cannot separate adult-student | 0 ( 0%) | 1 ( 4%) |

5. How do the student leaders of the movement today differ from the leaders at the beginning of the sit-ins?

| | *Students* (n = 7) | *Adults* (n = 18) |
|---|---|---|
| more professional ("calculating," "less idealistic," etc.) | 6 (83%) | 13 (72%) |
| greater political awareness | 2 (29%) | 0 ( 0%) |
| more leaders | 1 (14%) | 0 ( 0%) |

| | | |
|---|---|---|
| larger turnover in leadership | 1 (14%) | 2 (11%) |
| little difference | 1 (14%) | 1 ( 6%) |
| poorer quality | 0 ( 0%) | 4 (22%) |
| fewer leaders | 0 ( 0%) | 2 (11%) |

---

## IV. ON THE STUDENT NONVIOLENT COORDINATING COMMITTEE

1. Tell me briefly about your part in SNCC.

| | (n = 13) |
|---|---|
| a. purposeful professional | 9 (69%) |
| Raleigh SNCC representative | 3 (23%) |
| early participation, quit school or expelled, joined SNCC | 2 (16%) |
| b. field representative | 8 (67%) |
| leader | 2 (17%) |
| bureaucrat | 2 (17%) |

2a. (1a. on *Form 2*). Does SNCC "speak for the student movement?"

| | *Students* (n = 13) | *Adults* (n = 29) |
|---|---|---|
| yes | 8 (62%) | 2 ( 7%) |
| as much as any organization | 2 (16%) | 6 (21%) |
| no | 2 (16%) | 6 (21%) |
| partially | 1 ( 8%) | 3 (10%) |
| no, never did | 1 ( 8%) | 6 (21%) |
| once did; does not now | 0 ( 0%) | 6 (21%) |

2b. (1b. on *Form 2*). Has this been true from the beginning?

| | *Students* (n = 10) | *Adults* (n = 18) |
|---|---|---|
| yes | 7 (70%) | 13 (72%) |
| no | 3 (30%) | 5 (28%) |

3a. (2a. on *Form 2*). Has SNCC's function changed very much since it was formed?

| | *Students* (n = 13) | *Adults* (n = 25) |
|---|---|---|
| yes | 12 (92%) | 24 (96%) |
| no | 1 ( 8%) | 1 ( 4%) |

3b. (2b. on *Form 2*). If yes, when did these changes take place?

| | *Students* (n = 11) | *Adults* (n = 11) |
|---|---|---|
| summer, 1961 (Nashville seminar, voter registration) | 6 (55%) | 4 (36%) |
| Atlanta Conference, October, 1960 | 3 (27%) | 6 (55%) |
| Freedom Rides | 1 ( 9%) | 1 ( 9%) |
| impetus from successes | 1 ( 9%) | 0 ( 0%) |
| other | 1 ( 9%) | 0 ( 0%) |
| summer, 1960 | 0 ( 0%) | 3 (27%) |
| Raleigh Conference, April, 1960 | 0 ( 0%) | 1 ( 9%) |

3c. (2c. on *Form 2*). If yes, why did these changes take place?

| | *Students* (n = 11) | *Adults* (n = 11) |
|---|---|---|
| to sustain the movement | 5 (45%) | 4 (36%) |
| need to initiate action | 10 ( 9%) | 9 (82%) |

4. (3 on *Form 2*). Do current SNCC staff members differ from the first student representatives to SNCC in any important ways?

| | *Students* (n = 10) | *Adults* (n = 20) |
|---|---|---|
| no important ways | 5 (50%) | 0 ( 0%) |
| more professional (emphasis on strategy, not students, more calculating, etc.) | 5 (50%) | 14 (70%) |
| in movements by deliberate choice now | 1 (10%) | 11 (55%) |

5a. (4a. on *Form 2*). Do you see SNCC as a permanent organization?

| | *Students* (n = 11) | *Adults* (n = 20) |
|---|---|---|
| yes | 7 (64%) | 3 (15%) |
| no | 4 (36%) | 17 (85%) |

5b. (4b. on *Form 2*). Will there be any big changes in SNCC's role in the movement?

(reported with corresponding results from *Form 2* in chapter 8, p. 250)

## V. ON NON-STUDENT PARTICIPATION

1a. (2a. on *Form 2*). What area or national civil rights organizations have played the most important parts in the movement?

| | *Students* (n = 13) | *Adults* (n = 28) |
|---|---|---|
| CORE | 11 (84%) | 23 (82%) |
| NAACP | 9 (69%) | 19 (68%) |
| SCLC | 7 (54%) | 24 (86%) |
| all others named (including SCEF, NSA, ESCRU, NSCF, SRC, ACLU and national church organizations | 6 (46%) | 19 (68%) |

1b. (2b. on *Form 2*). At what points in the movement has their influence been the greatest?

| | *Students* (n = 13) | *Adults* (n = 22) |
|---|---|---|
| direct leadership | 9 (69%) | 14 (64%) |
| financial-legal assistance | 8 (62%) | 17 (73%) |
| publicity | 7 (54%) | 7 (32%) |
| in specific situations in the movement | 4 (31%) | 4 (18%) |

2. In what ways have organizations helped the movement most? Be specific.

| | (n = 11) |
|---|---|
| legal help | 7 (64%) |
| access to media | 6 (55%) |

| | |
|---|---|
| leadership | 5 (45%) |
| bail money | 5 (45%) |
| advice and support | 4 (36%) |

3. Have there been times when organizations actually have held back progress in the movement? Be specific.

(n = 13)

| | |
|---|---|
| NAACP specifically | 8 (62%) |
| SCLC specifically | 6 (46%) |
| too slow | 6 (46%) |
| CORE specifically | 4 (31%) |
| competition between groups has hurt | 3 (23%) |
| no | 1 ( 8%) |

4a. From what individuals and/or groups in the white community have you received the greatest opposition to the movement?

(n = 9)

| | |
|---|---|
| political leaders | 8 (88%) |
| racist organizations and individuals | 5 (55%) |
| economic leaders | 4 (44%) |
| police - courts | 4 (44%) |
| moderates | 4 (44%) |
| church - ministers | 2 (22%) |
| media | 1 (11%) |
| everybody | 1 (11%) |

4b. What do you think are the main reasons for this opposition?

| | (n = 8) |
|---|---|
| ignorance | 4 (50%) |
| the power structure | 4 (50%) |
| prejudice | 2 (25%) |
| financial vested interests | 2 (25%) |
| political vested interests | 1 (13%) |
| pathological | 1 (13%) |

4c. Has this been true during the whole movement?

| | |
|---|---|
| yes | 6 (100%) |
| no | 0 ( 0%) |

5. Can you tell me about any opposition in the Negro community? (on *Form 2*, 5: What groups and/or individuals in the Negro community have been least willing to cooperate with the movement?)

| | *Students* (n = 12) | *Adults* (n = 20) |
|---|---|---|
| older ministers | 9 (75%) | 4 (20%) |
| business leaders | 8 (67%) | 14 (70%) |
| the social elite | 6 (50%) | 12 (60%) |
| those dependent on white community (teachers, etc.) | 4 (33%) | 6 (30%) |
| college faculty and administration | 3 (25%) | 5 (25%) |
| established civil rights leadership | 3 (25%) | 6 (30%) |

| | | |
|---|---|---|
| Negro nationalists | 2 (17%) | 1 ( 5%) |
| parents | 1 ( 9%) | 1 ( 5%) |
| lower socioeconomic strata | 1 ( 9%) | 2 (10%) |

6a. How important is white participation in the movement?

| | *Students* (n = 13) | *Adults* (n = 13) |
|---|---|---|
| very important | 3 (23%) | 16 (55%) |
| moderately important | 10 (77%) | 9 (33%) |
| of little importance | 0 ( 0%) | 4 (14%) |

6b. In what ways have they been most helpful?

| | *Students* (n = 11) | *Adults* (n = 24) |
|---|---|---|
| more efficient and/or help interracial communication | 7 (64%) | 15 (62%) |
| moral support for Negroes | 4 (36%) | 11 (46%) |
| keep the focus on the issue as one of justice rather than race | 3 (27%) | 11 (46%) |
| financial aid | 2 (18%) | 1 (4%) |
| legal aid | 0 ( 0%) | 0 ( 0%) |

6c. Has their participation hurt the movement in any way?

| | *Students* (n = 6) | *Adults* (n = 16) |
|---|---|---|
| unstable personality types | 3 (50%) | 8 (50%) |
| antagonizes segregationists and/or community leaders | 2 (33%) | 8 (50%) |
| ideological liabilities | 1 (17%) | 3 (19%) |

7. Tell me briefly about the role of the Northern Student Movement.

| | (n = 9) |
|---|---|
| fund-raising | 8 (88%) |
| naive, but helpful | 2 (22%) |
| need to strengthen NSM–SNCC relationship | 1 (11%) |
| not helpful | 1 (11%) |

8. Does the work of the various civil rights organizations play a bigger part in the movement now than it did in the beginning?

| | |
|---|---|
| yes | 13 (100%) |
| no | 0 ( 0%) |

9. (7 on *Form 2*). Can you tell me anything (more) about the place of Martin Luther King, Jr., in the protest movement?

| | *Students* (n = 8) | *Adults* (n = 26) |
|---|---|---|
| failure in providing grass roots leadership | 6 (75%) | 1 ( 4%) |
| objective importance dwindling | 5 (63%) | 4 (15%) |
| THE symbol, most important leader, etc. | 5 (63%) | 14 (54%) |
| correct beliefs and articulation, but weak commitment to action | 4 (50%) | 4 (15%) |
| the articulator | 4 (50%) | 12 (46%) |
| growing disaffection of students | 1 (50%) | 3 (12%) |

10a. Would you say that this has been mostly a *student* movement, or have adults helped a lot?

(n = 11)

| | |
|---|---|
| mostly student *and* adults have helped a lot | 6 (55%) |
| mostly student | 3 (27%) |
| cannot call it a student movement–all levels involved | 2 (18%) |

10b. When and how have adults helped a lot?

(n = 7)

| | |
|---|---|
| advice and support | 2 (29%) |
| supply money for bail | 2 (29%) |
| cannot separate adult-student | 2 (29%) |
| active leadership and direction | 1 (14%) |
| negotiations | 1 (14%) |

11. For each of the following groups, rate whether you think they are mostly in favor of, neutral toward, or opposed to the goals and methods of the protest movement.

[Respondents were given a card with the following categories:

7. strongly in favor
6. in favor
5. mildly in favor
4. neutral or undecided
3. mildly opposed
2. opposed
1. strongly opposed

On their own request, respondents were allowed to split responses for goals and methods. Only five of the 182 responses from the Students were split, as indicated to the right of the chart (B = goals response, C = methods response).]

| | 1 | 2 | 3 | 4 | 5 | 6 | 7 | NA | | |
|---|---|---|---|---|---|---|---|---|---|---|
| your parents | 0 | 0 | 0 | 0 | 1 | 5 | 6 | 0 | B7 | C6 |
| Negro adults you know | 0 | 0 | 0 | 1 | 1 | 7 | 4 | 0 | B7 | C7 |
| Negro college students in your area | 0 | 0 | 0 | 1 | 3 | 4 | 3 | 0 | B7 | C6 |
| white college students in your area | 0 | 0 | 2 | 8 | 2 | 0 | 0 | 1 | | |
| college students in general throughout the country | 0 | 0 | 0 | 7 | 3 | 1 | 2 | 0 | B5 | C2 |
| Negro college administrators | 0 | 1 | 2 | 4 | 1 | 4 | 0 | 0 | | |
| Negro community leaders around here | 0 | 1 | 1 | 1 | 1 | 4 | 5 | 0 | | |
| Negro community leaders in most southern cities | 0 | 0 | 1 | 3 | 4 | 1 | 3 | 0 | B6 | C3 |
| the press in the south | 3 | 6 | 2 | 2 | 0 | 0 | 0 | 0 | | |
| the press nationally | 0 | 0 | 3 | 3 | 2 | 5 | 0 | 0 | | |
| southern law enforcement officials | 9 | 1 | 0 | 1 | 1 | 0 | 1 | 0 | | |
| local white businessmen | 4 | 4 | 2 | 1 | 0 | 1 | 0 | 1 | | |

| | | | | | | | | |
|---|---|---|---|---|---|---|---|---|
| national offices of the chain stores | 1 | 1 | 1 | 7 | 0 | 2 | 0 | 1 |
| the federal government | 0 | 1 | 2 | 0 | 5 | 3 | 2 | 0 |

[8. on *Form 2*: the question and instructions were the same, but some of the categories were different, as indicated below. Several respondents split for goals/methods on some items, but did not on others. Thus, three charts are needed to present the data: A (Goals and Methods), B (goals only), and C (methods only).]

A. GOALS AND METHODS

| | 1 | 2 | 3 | 4 | 5 | 6 | 7 | NA |
|---|---|---|---|---|---|---|---|---|
| a. Negro college students in your area | 0 | 0 | 0 | 1 | 3 | 5 | 13 | 0 |
| b. white college students in your area | 0 | 3 | 6 | 8 | 3 | 1 | 0 | 2 |
| c. college students in general throughout the country | 1 | 1 | 0 | 4 | 9 | 9 | 2 | 0 |
| d. Negro college administrators | 0 | 0 | 2 | 4 | 4 | 9 | 0 | 0 |
| e. Negro community leaders | 0 | 0 | 2 | 5 | 6 | 7 | 1 | 3 |
| f. most Negro adults | 0 | 0 | 0 | 0 | 5 | 9 | 8 | 0 |
| g. the press in the South | 1 | 11 | 2 | 7 | 0 | 2 | 0 | 1 |

| | | | | | | | | |
|---|---|---|---|---|---|---|---|---|
| h. the press nationally | 0 | 0 | 2 | 5 | 7 | 7 | 1 | 2 |
| i. southern law enforcement officials | 10 | 6 | 2 | 2 | 1 | 0 | 0 | 1 |
| j. local white businessmen | 4 | 12 | 1 | 4 | 1 | 0 | 0 | 0 |
| k. national offices of the chain stores | 1 | 6 | 2 | 7 | 1 | 2 | 1 | 2 |
| l. the federal government | 0 | 3 | 0 | 2 | 8 | 8 | 1 | 0 |

B. GOALS

| | 1 | 2 | 3 | 4 | 5 | 6 | 7 |
|---|---|---|---|---|---|---|---|
| a. | 0 | 0 | 0 | 0 | 0 | 0 | 6 |
| b. | 0 | 1 | 0 | 2 | 1 | 1 | 0 |
| c. | 0 | 0 | 0 | 1 | 0 | 2 | 1 |
| d. | 0 | 0 | 0 | 0 | 0 | 4 | 3 |
| e. | 0 | 0 | 0 | 0 | 0 | 4 | 2 |
| f. | 0 | 0 | 0 | 0 | 0 | 2 | 3 |
| g. | 1 | 1 | 0 | 1 | 2 | 0 | 0 |
| h. | 0 | 0 | 0 | 0 | 1 | 3 | 0 |
| i. | 0 | 3 | 0 | 0 | 1 | 0 | 0 |
| j. | 0 | 1 | 2 | 1 | 0 | 0 | 0 |
| k. | 0 | 0 | 0 | 3 | 2 | 1 | 0 |
| l. | 0 | 0 | 0 | 0 | 2 | 3 | 1 |

## C. METHODS*

| | 1 | 2 | 3 | 4 | 5 | 6 | 7 |
|---|---|---|---|---|---|---|---|
| a. | 0 | 0 | 0 | 1 | 3 | 0 | 1 |
| b. | 0 | 2 | 3 | 1 | 0 | 0 | 0 |
| c. | 0 | 0 | 1 | 0 | 1 | 2 | 0 |
| d. | 1 | 1 | 1 | 3 | 0 | 0 | 0 |
| e. | 0 | 2 | 2 | 2 | 0 | 0 | 0 |
| f. | 0 | 0 | 0 | 1 | 1 | 3 | 0 |
| g. | 2 | 2 | 0 | 0 | 0 | 0 | 1 |
| h. | 0 | 1 | 1 | 0 | 1 | 0 | 1 |
| i. | 3 | 1 | 0 | 0 | 0 | 0 | 0 |
| j. | 3 | 2 | 0 | 0 | 0 | 0 | 0 |
| k. | 2 | 3 | 0 | 1 | 0 | 0 | 0 |
| l. | 0 | 1 | 2 | 2 | 1 | 0 | 0 |

*one no answer response

---

## VI. THE FORMS OF PROTEST

1a. What forms or kinds of protests (demonstrations) are being used most frequently now?

| | *Students* (n = 11) | *Adults* (n = 23) |
|---|---|---|
| mass demonstrations ("-ins") | 3 (27%) | 12 (52%) |
| community mobilization approach | 2 (18%) | 0 ( 0%) |

| | | |
|---|---|---|
| direct action with fewer participants | 2 (18%) | 5 (22%) |
| economic boycott | 2 (18%) | 8 (35%) |
| voter registration drives | 1 ( 9%) | 2 ( 9%) |
| legal approach | 1 ( 9%) | 2 ( 9%) |

1b. How does this compare with the first few months of the movement?

| | *Students* (n = 10) | *Adults* (n = 18) |
|---|---|---|
| different | 8 (80%) | 13 (72%) |
| about the same | 2 (20%) | 5 (28%) |

2. What kinds of protest have been most effective (have brought the most progress)?

| | *Students* (n = 13) | *Adults* (n = 26) |
|---|---|---|
| economic boycott | 5 (38%) | 16 (62%) |
| mass demonstrations | 4 (31%) | 11 (42%) |
| negotiation | 2 (16%) | 3 (12%) |
| community mobilization approach | 1 ( 8%) | 1 (4%) |
| education of white community | 1 ( 8%) | 3 (12%) |
| voter registration drives | 0 ( 0%) | 4 (16%) |
| legal approach | 0 ( 0%) | 3 (12%) |

3. Are there "spontaneous" demonstrations in various cities today like those which took place in the first few months of the sit-ins? Or is everything organized?

(reported with corresponding results from *Form 2* in Preface to Section C, p. 141)

4. What are some of the things that could be done to make the movement more effective?

(reported with corresponding results from *Form 2* in chapter 8, p. 219)

---

## VII. YOUR OWN PARTICIPATION

1. How has your participation in the movement changed your outlook on life?

(n = 13)

| | |
|---|---|
| new commitment, sense of identity, efficacy | 9 (69%) |
| great change | 3 (23%) |
| changed career plans | 2 (16%) |
| nonviolence now seen as a way of life | 2 (16%) |
| no effect at all | 2 (16%) |
| have faced death | 1 ( 8%) |
| other ideological changes | 1 ( 8%) |

2. Is your part in the movement now different from what it was at the beginning?

(n = 11)

| | |
|---|---|
| more organizational (restricted, defined, professional) | 9 (82%) |
| more power over other persons now | 2 (18%) |
| feel better able to lead | 1 ( 9%) |

3. What was the most important event in the movement for you?

| | (n = 13) |
|---|---|
| specific situation (Freedom Ride, McComb, Rock Hill, Monroe, etc.) | 9 (69%) |
| first demonstration | 4 (31%) |
| ideological conversion | 2 (16%) |
| first arrest | 1 ( 8%) |

4a. How long do you expect to stay actively involved in the movement?

| | (n = 13) |
|---|---|
| as long as possible (financial problems, school, etc., may interfere) | 6 (46%) |
| the rest of my life | 5 (38%) |
| less than a few years | 2 (16%) |
| a few years | 1 ( 8%) |

4b. Did you feel this way at the beginning?

| | |
|---|---|
| yes | 4 (40%) |
| no | 6 (60%) |

## VIII. PERSONAL INFORMATION

Biographical data obtained in the interviews which are relevant to this study are summarized in chapter 2, pp. 38-40. The role of student protestors is analyzed in light of the theory of rationalization in chapter 8.

## IX. FUTURE OF THE MOVEMENT

1a. (1a. in VII in *Form 2*). What changes in the patterns of segregation do you expect to see within the next five years?

| | *Students* (n = 12) | *Adults* (n = 24) |
|---|---|---|
| special progress in education | 4 (33%) | 5 (21%) |
| total desegregation in *all* areas | 2 (17%) | 0 ( 0%) |
| total desegregation of public facilities | 2 (17%) | 1 ( 4%) |
| partial desegregation of *all* areas | 2 (17%) | 3 (13%) |
| special progress in public facilities | 2 (17%) | 9 (38%) |
| special progress in employment | 2 (17%) | 12 (50%) |
| special progress in political rights | 2 (17%) | 3 (13%) |
| pessimistic | 2 (17%) | 1 ( 4%) |
| special progress in housing | 1 ( 9%) | 1 ( 4%) |
| generally high optimism | 0 ( 0%) | 3 (13%) |
| more "private club" businesses | 0 ( 0%) | 2 ( 9%) |

1b. In the next 25 years? [response categories in same order as 1a].

| | *Students* (n = 10) | *Adults* (n = 23) |
|---|---|---|
| special progress in education | 0 ( 0%) | 1 ( 4%) |
| total desegregation in all areas | 2 (20%) | 0 ( 0%) |

| | | |
|---|---|---|
| total desegregation of public facilities | 0 ( 0%) | 2 ( 9%) |
| partial desegregation of all areas | 0 ( 0%) | 5 (22%) |
| special progress in public facilities | 0 ( 0%) | 1 ( 4%) |
| special progress in employment | 1 (10%) | 5 (22%) |
| special progress in political rights | 1 (10%) | 2 ( 9%) |
| special progress in housing | 1 (10%) | 3 (13%) |
| generally high optimism | 6 (60%) | 8 (35%) |
| more "private club" businesses | 0 ( 0%) | 0 ( 0%) |
| more desegregation in North than South | 0 ( 0%) | 4 (17%) |

2. What changes within the movement do you expect to see in the next five years?

| | *Students* (n = 13) | *Adults* (n = 26) |
|---|---|---|
| greater tie with grass roots areas, more participation | 7 (54%) | 1 ( 4%) |
| not predictable | 4 (31%) | 3 (12%) |
| broadening of goals, influence, and membership ties | 3 (23%) | 5 (19%) |
| more emphasis on political | 3 (23%) | 7 (27%) |
| organizational reintegration | 2 (16%) | 6 (23%) |
| move toward more strategic, less dramatic activities | 1 ( 8%) | 6 (23%) |
| tie with labor movement | 1 ( 8%) | 2 ( 8%) |

| | | |
|---|---|---|
| dependent on government action | 0 ( 0%) | 6 (23%) |
| direct relation to civil rights progress | 0 ( 0%) | 5 (19%) |

---

## FORM 2 (ADULT)

Reported here are only the Adult responses which were not included with the corresponding Student results in the text or in the preceding pages in the Appendix.

### I. GENERAL IMPRESSIONS

1. How did you first become involved in the movement? (When and how did you first hear of the movement?)

(n = 32)

| | |
|---|---|
| mass media in February, 1960 | 13 (41%) |
| mass media after February, 1962 | 2 ( 6%) |
| job involvement in February, 1960 | 16 (50%) |
| job involvement after February, 1960 | 1 ( 3%) |

4. How well versed in nonviolent philosophy are the student leaders? What do they know about the Montgomery bus boycott?

(n = 30)

| nonviolent philosophy | much | some | little | no response |
|---|---|---|---|---|
| very well-versed | 1 | 0 | 0 | 0 |
| moderately well-versed | 0 | 3 | 0 | 1 |

| | | | | |
|---|---|---|---|---|
| satisfactory | 0 | 0 | 0 | 0 |
| not too well-versed | 0 | 9 | 4 | 3 |
| very poorly-versed | 0 | 3 | 6 | 0 |

5. Do most of the student protestors accept nonviolence as a way of life or as a technique? Was this true at the beginning of the movement?

(n = 28)

| | true at beginning | not true at beginning | no change |
|---|---|---|---|
| way of life | 0 | 0 | 0 |
| technique | 16 | 2 | 8 |
| don't know | 0 | 1 | 1 |

[three informants said the students' commitment had moved from technique to way of life since the beginning]

---

## III. LEADERSHIP

3. Have [changes in the leadership structure] generally helped or hurt the movement?

(n = 20)

| | |
|---|---|
| helped | 5 (25%) |
| hurt | 10 (50%) |
| both | 5 (25%) |

4. Has the movement been led and coordinated predominantly by adults or students?

(n = 28)

| | |
|---|---|
| adults | 4 (14%) |
| students | 12 (43%) |
| both | 12 (43%) |

6b. When and how do you think [changes in student leadership in the movement] began to take place?

(n = 10)

| | |
|---|---|
| summer, 1961 (voter registration, the Nashville seminar) | 4 (40%) |
| summer of 1960 | 2 (20%) |
| Atlanta Conference, October, 1960 | 2 (20%) |
| Freedom Rides | 1 (10%) |
| other | 3 (30%) |

---

## V. ON NON-STUDENT PARTICIPATION

1. Have there been any changes in the attitudes of the students toward participation by *non*-students since the movement began?

(n = 21)

| | |
|---|---|
| more receptive to "outside" help | 11 (52%) |
| no change | 4 (19%) |
| less receptive to "outside" help | 3 (14%) |
| other | 3 (14%) |

2. Are the students generally receptive to assistance from adults and organizations? Has it been like this all during the movement?

(n = 25)

| | yes | no |
|---|---|---|
| Receptive | 13 | 8 |
| Like this all during the movement? | 3 | 1 |

4. What do you think have been the main sources of antagonism between the students and these organizations and adult leaders?

(n = 27)

| | |
|---|---|
| students' revolt, lack of personal and organizational maturity | 15 (55%) |
| students' impatience at *perceived* accommodationist leadership | 8 (30%) |
| perceived threat by organizations | 7 (26%) |
| accommodationist Negro leadership | 3 (11%) |
| competition for funds | 3 (11%) |
| lack of communication | 3 (11%) |

## APPENDIX D

# The 1960 Interviews

In July and August of 1960, I interviewed 11 of the first sit-inners—many of them founding members of the Student Nonviolent Coordinating Committee. These exploratory interviews served many functions, some of which were alluded to in chapter 2:

(a) discovery of chronological specifics and important personality dimensions of protestors in the first months of the sit-in movement.

(b) a method of determining relevant variables for more systematic study later.

(c) a kind of pre-test for many questions on the interview schedule administered in 1962.

(d) solidification of my relationship with early leaders—and thus a reference point for relationships with movement and leaders later.

Data from these interviews form the basis for interpretation in much of chapters 3 and 4 in this study, and are specifically footnoted in several places.

## 1. Informants (with position at time of interview).

Ezell Blair (freshman at North Carolina A & T; informal leader of the four students who first sat-in in Greensboro on February 1, 1960).

Thomas Gaither (1960 graduate and student body president of Claflin College in Orangeburg, South Carolina; sit-in leader and CORE worker).

Frank James (student council president at Philander Smith College; Arkansas representative to SNCC).

Edward King, Jr. (expelled from Kentucky State College for participation in sit-ins; became secretary of SNCC in October, 1960).

Lonnie King (Atlanta University student; major leader in Atlanta Committee on Appeal for Human Rights; Georgia representative to SNCC).

Bernard Lee (expelled from Alabama State College for leadership in movement; later became an aide to Dr. Martin Luther King, Jr.).

David Richmond (freshman at North Carolina A & T; one of four students in first 1960 sit-in).

Marvin Robinson (student body president at Southern University; expelled for leadership in the movement and hired by CORE).

Patricia Stephens (Florida A & M sophomore; spent 49 days in jail in spring of 1960; recognized as leader by CORE and others).

Priscilla Stephens (sister of Patricia; Florida A & M sophomore, spent 49 days in jail; recognized as leader).

Henry Thomas (Howard University freshman; Washington, D.C., representative to SNCC; later worked for CORE).

## 2. The 1960 Interview Schedule

Following is a general description of the 1960 interview schedule. The cover page read as follows:

INTERVIEW SCHEDULE FOR SIT-IN LEADERS

* * * *

> This is a guide sheet for questions to be asked of some of the leaders of the student lunch counter protest. Many of the questions do not call for specific answers, but rather are to be used as guides to more general discussion topics. The purpose is to find out if there are some common factors in the personalities and backgrounds of the students who have been leading the sit-ins. While I record your name for future communication, the results of individual interviews remain completely anonymous. This information will be transferred to electronic data processing cards and tabulated, and will be published only in professional sociological journals or in a doctoral dissertation. I appreciate your help and cooperation.

James H. Laue
Harvard University
Department of Social Relations
Summer, 1960

Interview Number________

Name____________________

Leadership Position________
School Address____________

Home Address_____________

General categories covered were:

I. *Biographical information* — on college, hometown, religious and political affiliation, etc.

II. *Family Information* — age, occupation, hometown, educational, religious and political attributes of parents, and some data on siblings and grandparents.

III. *High School Information* — data on location, public or private, scholastic performance, extracurricular activities, leadership positions, perception of 1954 Supreme Court decision on public school segregation.

IV. *College Information* — on reasons for attending informant's school, scholastic performance, extracurricular activities, leadership positions, campus organizational structure and student views on segregation and discrimination.

V. *On Nonviolent Philosophy* — previous reading on nonviolence, attendance at workshops, participation, strategy vs. way of life, relationship of nonviolence to religious convictions.

VI. *The Sit-In Protest Movement* — forms of participation, estimates of national participation in the sit-ins, peer group influences on informant's activities, parental attitudes toward informant's participation, the role of local and national organizations, opposition and help from groups in the white and Negro communities, effectiveness and duration of the movement, arrest and jail record, travel experiences, etiology of the movement, personal motivations for participation.

VII. *Interest Groups and the Movement* — rating of groups like "Negro college students in your area," "Negro adults you know," "the press in the South," and "national offices of the chain stores" or their orientation toward the movement.

VIII. *Prejudice and Discrimination* — informants' experience with prejudice and discrimination, their views on the development of these phenomena and their effect on society and individuals.

## APPENDIX E

# Other Key Informants

Many persons in addition to those formally interviewed have contributed to this study through informal conversations, correspondence, co-participation in the movement, as my teachers, colleagues and students. While often it has been difficult for me to trace a particular interpretation or piece of data, it is sure that the source is to be found in my relationship with one of the following—whose help made this project possible.

1. *Civil Rights Organizational Leadership*

*Congress of Racial Equality*
Gordon Carey, Field Director
The Reverend Mr. James Farmer, National Director
Richard Haley, Southern Director
James McCain, Field Staff
Marvin Rich, Community Relations Director
James Robinson, former Director

*National Association for the Advancement of Colored People*
The Reverend Mr. R.R. Wilkinson, President, Roanoke (Virginia) Branch

*Northern Student Movement*
William Strickland, Executive Director

*Southern Christian Leadership Conference*
The Reverend Mr. Ralph D. Abernathy, Vice-President and Secretary-Treasurer
The Reverend Mr. James Bevel, Head of Direct Action
Randolph Blackwell, Program Director
Mrs. Septima Clark, Voter Registration
Mrs. Dorothy Cotton, Director of Citizenship Education
Ann and Eric Kindberg, Research Department
The Reverend Mr. Frederick D. Reese, President, Dallas County (Alabama) Voters League
Mrs. Edwina Smith, Secretary to Mr. Young
The Reverend Mr. C.T. Vivian, Director of Affiliates
James Wood, former Director of Public Relations and now Program Director for WAOK radio in Atlanta
The Reverend Mr. Andrew J. Young, Executive Director

*Southern Conference Educational Fund*
Mrs. Anne Braden, editor of *The Southern Patriot* and author of *The Wall Between*
Carl Braden, Field Secretary

*Student Nonviolent Coordinating Committee*
John Lewis, Chairman
Cleveland Sellers, Field Secretary

*Southern Regional Council*
Paul Anthony, Executive Director since November 1, 1965
John Constable, former staff member
Vernon Jordan, Assistant to the Executive Director
Pat Watters, Information Department

2. *The Press*

*Atlanta Constitution*
Harold Martin, editorial staff
Ralph McGill, Publisher
Reg Murphy, Political Editor
Eugene Patterson, Editor and a member of the U.S. Commission on Civil Rights
Marvin Wall, editorial staff

*Chicago Daily News*
Nicholas Von Hoffman

*Greenville (South Carolina) News and Piedmont*
Gil Rowland, Religious Editor

*Los Angeles Times*
Jack Nelson, Southern Correspondent and former investigative reporter for the *Atlanta Constitution*

*New York Times*
John Herbers, Washington Correspondent (former Southern Correspondent)
Roy Reed, Southern Correspondent
Gene Roberts, Southern Correspondent

3. *Teachers, Colleagues and Students*

*Teachers*

Dr. Gordon W. Allport, Professor of Psychology, Harvard University
Dr. Robert B. Bailey, III, Professor of Sociology, Wisconsin State University at River Falls
Dr. Herbert Kelman, Professor of Psychology, University of Michigan
Dr. Florence R. Kluckhohn, Lecturer in Sociology, Harvard University
Dr. Richard D. Mann, Associate Professor of Psychology, University of Michigan
Dr. Talcott Parsons, Professor of Sociology, Harvard University
Dr. Thomas F. Pettigrew, Associate Professor of Social Psychology, Harvard University
Dr. William Taylor, Associate Professor of History, University of Wisconsin

*Colleagues*

Mrs. Gloria Bishop, Instructor in English, Howard University
Dr. John Burma, Professor of Sociology, Grinnell College
Dr. M. Richard Cramer, Assistant Professor of Sociology, University of North Carolina
Dr. John Doby, Professor of Sociology and Anthropology, Emory University
Dr. Kai T. Erikson, Associate Professor of Sociology, Emory University
Mrs. Zelda Gamson, graduate student, Harvard University, 1959-62
Dr. Robert Johnson, Professor of Sociology, Wilberforce University
Dr. Lewis M. Killian, Professor of Sociology, The Florida State University
Mr. Arnold Levine, Assistant Professor of Sociology and Anthropology, Emory University
Dr. Staughton Lynd, Assistant Professor of History, Yale University
Dr. Meyer Nimkoff, Professor of Sociology, The Florida State University (deceased)
Dr. Murray Wax, Associate Professor of Sociology, University of Kansas

*Students*

Mrs. Jane Schlesinger Brummett, Hollins College, 1960-64; presently at Indiana University School of Social Work
Eugene Guerrero, Emory University, 1962-present
Susan Hall, Hollins College, 1960-64; Princeton Seminary, 1964-present
Sandra Ludlum, Hollins College, 1961-65; University of Chicago School of Social Work, 1965-present
Lansing Rowan, Hollins College, 1961-65; University of Chicago School of Social Work, 1965-present
Henry Stembridge, Emory University, 1961-65

4. *Others*

James Bishop, Special Assistant to the Governor of Massachusetts for Race Relations
The Reverend Mr. Malcolm Boyd, Field Secretary, The Episcopal Society for Cultural and Racial Unity
W. Haywood Burn, Yale Law School student and author of *The Voices of Negro Protest in America*
The Reverend Mr. James S. Hall, Pastor, Springfield Baptist Church, Greenville, South Carolina
Dorothy Hampton, United Church of Christ, Department of Race and Cultural Relations
George Lawrence, former President, Roanoke Valley Council on Human Relations
Louis Lomax, author of *The Negro Revolt* and other books
Burke Marshall, former Assistant U.S. Attorney General for Civil Rights [interviewed in April, 1962]
Dr. Benjamin Mays, President, Morehouse College
Donna McGinty, former secretary, National Student Association Southern Student Human Relations Project
George McMillan, free-lance writer, Aiken, South Carolina
Hayes Mizell, Director, NSA Southern Project
Rosa Parks, Detroit, Michigan
Mrs. Eliza Paschal, Director, Greater Atlanta Council on Human Relations
Mrs. Frances Pauley, Director, Georgia Council on Human Relations
Merrill Proudfoot, former Professor of Religion at Knoxville College and author of *Diary of a Sit-In*
Richard Shapiro, Federal Programs Specialist, U.S. Commission on Civil Rights
A. Byron Smith, civil rights leader, Roanoke, Virginia
Lillian Smith, author of *Killers of the Dream* and other books
Richard Stephens, Assistant Director, NSA Southern Project
William Stringfellow, New York attorney and author
Minister Malcolm X (deceased)

APPENDIX F

# Spread of the Southern Sit-Ins and Related Demonstrations: The First Wave, February – May, 1960

Following is a chronological listing of the southern cities where sit-ins and related protests occurred as the movement began in February — May, 1960. This chart accompanies the map on p. 80 in chapter 4. The data are condensed and arranged for these purposes from "The Student Protest Movement, Winter, 1960" (Atlanta: Southern Regional Council, 1960), especially pp. xix-xxv, and materials in my clippings file.

| First Date | City and Population | Form of Protest | Comments |
|---|---|---|---|
| Feb. 1 | Greensboro, N.C., 85,000 | sit-in | "Cooling off" period called at end of first week, but sit-ins resumed. |
| Feb. 8 | Durham, N.C., 80,000 | sit-in, picketing | 55 miles from Greensboro; arrests in early May. |
| | Winston-Salem, N.C., 100,000 | sit-in, march | 30 miles from Greensboro; stools removed at one lunch counter and desegregated. |
| Feb. 9 | Charlotte, N.C., 150,000 | sit-in, picketing | 80 miles from Winston-Salem |
| | Fayetteville, N.C., 40,000 | sit-in, picketing | 80 miles from Durham |

| | | | |
|---|---|---|---|
| Feb. 10 | Raleigh, N.C., 75,000 | sit-in, picketing, prayer meeting on state capitol steps | 15 miles from Durham |
| Feb. 11 | Elizabeth City, N.C., 14,000 | sit-in | 150 miles from Durham |
| | High Point, N.C., 42,000 | sit-in | 15 miles from Greensboro |
| | Hampton, Va., 7,000 | sit-in, picketing, march | 200 miles from Durham (60 miles from Elizabeth City) |
| Feb. 12 | Concord, N.C., 18,000 | sit-in, march, religious service on courthouse lawn | 20 miles from Charlotte |
| | Norfolk, Va., 250,000 | sit-ins | 10 miles from Hampton |
| | Portsmouth, Va., 90,000 | sit-ins, march, attempted boycott | 20 miles from Hampton; first violence of movement involving high school students |
| | Rock Hill, S.C., 28,000 | sit-in, picketing | 30 miles from Charlotte |
| | Deland, Fla., 12,000 | sit-in | 400 miles from Rock Hill |
| Feb. 13 | Nashville, Tenn., 200,000 | sit-in, picketing | 500 miles from Winston-Salem; Negro leader expelled from Vanderbilt Divinity School |
| | Tallahassee, Fla., 35,000 | sit-in, march | |
| Feb. 16 | Salisbury, N.C., 22,000 | sit-in | |

(Feb. 17, Dr. King arrested for alleged tax-evasion; formation of Committee to Defend Martin Luther King)

| | | | |
|---|---|---|---|
| Feb. 18 | Shelby, N.C., 17,000 | sit-in, picketing | Negro picket attacked |
| | Suffolk, Va., 15,000 | sit-in | |

| | | | |
|---|---|---|---|
| Feb. 19 | Chattanooga, Tenn., 150,000 | sit-in | Riots Feb 23-25 |
| Feb. 20 | Richmond, Va., 260,000 | sit-in, picketing | |
| | Baltimore, Md., 1,100,000 | sit-in, picketing | Picketing directed at theater |
| Feb. 22 | Newport News, Va., 50,000 | sit-in, picketing, march | |
| Feb. 25 | Montgomery, Ala., 135,000 | sit-in (at public building), march, mass rally on campus | Violent attacks on Negroes Feb. 28; riot March 6 |
| | Orangeburg, S.C., 18,000 | sit-in, march | 388 arrested; fire hoses, tear gas March 12 |
| | Henderson, N.C., 14,000 | sit-in | Negro student assaulted white man |
| | Charleston, S.C., 80,000 | march | |
| Feb. 27 | Lexington, Ky., 75,000 | sit-in | |
| | Tuskegee, Ala., 7,500 | march, attempted boycott | Tuskegee students also marched in Montgomery |
| | Petersburg, Va., 40,000 | sit-in, negotiating teams visited stores asking for desegregated service and rest rooms | Sit-in took place in public library |
| Feb. 28 | Chapel Hill, N.C., 15,000 | sit-in | |
| Feb. 29 | Denmark, S.C., 3,500 | sit-in | |
| | Tampa, Fla., 165,000 | sit-in | |
| Mar. 1 | Monroe, N.C., 12,000 | sit-in | |
| Mar. 2 | St. Petersburg, Fla., 125,000 | sit-in | |
| | Sarasota, Fla., 25,000 | sit-in | |

| | | | |
|---|---|---|---|
| | Daytona Beach, Fla., 50,000 | sit-in, attempted boycott | |
| | Columbia, S.C., 95,000 | sit-in, march | Negroes attacked several cars at white drive-in restaurant on March 5 |
| Mar. 3 | Atlanta, Ga., 400,000 | sit-in, picketing, newspaper ad | |
| Mar. 4 | Sumter, S.C., 23,000 | sit-in | |
| | Florence, S.C., 25,000 | sit-in | |
| | Orlando, Fla., 75,000 | sit-in | |
| | Miami, Fla., 350,000 | sit-in | Adult ministers led protest |
| Mar. 5 | Houston, Tex., 700,000 | sit-in, picketing | KKK carved in Negro youth's chest March 7 |
| | Xenia, Ohio, 15,000 | sit-in | Restaurant desegregated after three-day closing |
| Mar. 7 | Sanford, Fla., 17,000 | unsuccessful meeting with manager | |
| | Bluefield, W. Va., 25,000 | sit-in, picketing | Theater included in demonstrations |
| | Knoxville, Tenn., 150,000 | sit-in | |
| Mar. 8 | New Orleans, La., 650,000 | parade on campus | |
| Mar. 10 | Little Rock, Ark., 125,000 | sit-in | |
| | Huntsville, Ala., 18,000 | march | |
| Mar. 11 | Austin, Tex., 160,000 | march, picketing | Demonstrations directed against segregationist housing, athletic, drama policies of University of Texas |

| | | | |
|---|---|---|---|
| | Galveston, Tex., 80,000 | sit-in | Eventual desegregation |
| Mar. 12 | Jacksonville, Fla., 280,000 | sit-in | |
| Mar. 13 | San Antonio, Tex., 525,000 | ultimatum conference | Desegregated service begun without demonstration, March 16 |
| Mar. 15 | St. Augustine, Fla., 20,000 | sit-in | Fights suppressed by police |
| Mar. 16 | Savannah, Ga., 150,000 | sit-in, picketing, attempted boycott | Police dispersed white and Negro mobs, March 17; Negro student punched, April 16 |
| Mar. 17 | New Bern, N.C., 18,000 | sit-in | |
| Mar. 18 | Memphis, Tenn., 475,000 | sit-in, meeting with city commission | Concentration on libraries and art galleries |
| Mar. 19 | Wilmington, N.C., 55,000 | sit-in | |
| | Arlington, Va., 40,000 | sit-in | sit-in led to fight between store owner and Negroes |
| | Lenoir, N.C., 9,500 | sit-in | Protest at library successful |
| Mar. 21 | Statesville, N.C., 19,000 | sit-in | |
| Mar. 22 | Oak Ridge, Tenn., 40,000 | newspaper ad | |
| Mar. 25 | Pine Bluff, Ark., 45,000 | attempted boycott | |
| Mar. 26 | Lynchburg, Va., 60,000 | sit-in | |
| | Charleston, W. Va., 85,000 | sit-in | |
| | Marshall, Tex., 28,000 | sit-in, mass gathering on courthouse square | Fire hoses and dogs, March 30 |

| | | | |
|---|---|---|---|
| Mar. 28 | Baton Rouge, La., 160,000 | sit-in, march | Leaders expelled from Southern University, other students threatened to withdraw in protest |
| Mar. 29 | Shreveport, La., 160,000 | sit-ins | |
| Mar. 31 | Birmingham, Ala., 400,000 | sit-in | |
| Apr. 1 | Charleston, S.C., 85,000 | sit-ins | Protests renewed after unsuccessful negotiation |
| Apr. 2 | Columbus, Ga., 100,000 | sit-in | White servicemen sitting in at Negro lunch counter |
| | Frankfort, Ky., 16,000 | sit-in | |
| | Danville, Va., 45,000 | sit-in at library | |
| Apr. 5 | Pensacola, Fla., 65,000 | sit-in | |
| Apr. 9 | Augusta, Ga., 90,000 | sit-in | Negro soldier arrested |
| Apr. 11 | Jackson, Miss., 50,000 | boycott | Students planned boycott; no demonstration |
| Apr. 17 | Biloxi, Miss., 50,000 | "wade-in" | Negro attempted to swim at white public beach, arrested; riot April 24 as 100 Negroes attempted to swim at white beach |
| Apr. 28 | Dallas, Tex., 525,000 | sit-in | Sit-in by Negro minister showed apparent integration |

# Notes

## CHAPTER ONE

1. Ignazio Silone, *Bread and Wine* (New York: Signet, 1961–original, 1937), p. 142.
2. This information is compiled from a variety of sources, including 45 personal interviews and a number of releases and statements from the Southern Regional Council and the Congress of Racial Equality. These figures are at best conservative approximations, since demonstrations, arrests and desegregation of facilities are often under-reported. They are explained more fully in the summary at the end of chapter 6.
3. Bruce Galphin, Race Relations Reporter, *Atlanta Constitution*, interview, March 20, 1962. (For the first quotation from an interview, the informant's name, title and the date of the interview will be given. Each subsequent quotation from the same interview will be identified only by the informant's name in the text. See chapter 2 and the Appendix for data on the sample, the instrument and techniques of interviewing in this study).
4. Merriman-Webster Unabridged Dictionary, 1962.
5. This series, written by Nan Robertson, began on May 14, 1962, as the culmination of a four weeks' cross-country campus tour.
6. NBC's Nashville White Paper has been used as a recruiting device in many protest communities, and was subpoenaed in 1962 by a Mississippi court.
7. I at first questioned the influence of the direct action protests on this record when I heard it on a Brooklyn juke box in April, 1962. But I listened closely to the "lyrics" and found that they concerned the singer's *right* to sit on the young lady's front porch until she gave into his sit-in and gave him "alla" her love:

   The only right you can't ignore
   Is my right to sit at your front door . . .

8. The majority of the informants, both student and adult, talked of the impact of the sit-ins on the American college community and the possible new political role of American students.
9. See especially Harvey Wish, "American Slave Insurrections Before 1861," *Journal of Negro History* 22, 3 (July, 1937), pp. 299-320, and Herbert Aptheker, *American Negro Slave Revolts* (New York: Columbia University Press, 1943), and *Essays in the History of the American Negro* (New York: International Publishers, 1945).
10. See especially the writings of Frederick Law Olmstead and Hinton Rowan Helper, now collected in two volumes by Putnam (New York: Capricorn

Books), *Slave States* (1959) and *Ante-Bellum* (1960). See also Stanley Elkins, *Slavery: A Problem in American Institutional and Intellectual Life* (Chicago: University of Chicago Press, 1959).

11. Charles Jones, Director of Voter Registration, Student Nonviolent Coordinating Committee, interview, March 27, 1962.
12. Wirth continues, "The existence of a minority in a society implies the existence of a corresponding dominant group with higher social status and greater privileges" (Quoted in George Simpson and J. Milton Yinger, *Racial and Cultural Minorities* [New York: Harper and Brothers, 1953], p. 21). Thus, a minority is defined in terms of *power* rather than numbers, for the status of, say, the Negroes in Macon County, Alabama, carries with it exclusion from full participation in the life of the society—even though they number over 80 percent of the county's population.
13. Gordon W. Allport, *The Nature of Prejudice* (Garden City, N.Y.: Doubleday Anchor, 1958—original in 1954), pp. 6-10.
14. Robin Williams, quoted in Simpson and Yinger, *Racial and Cultural Minorities*, p. 18.
15. Allport, *The Nature of Prejudice*, p. 15.
16. "The Strategy of Protest: Problems of Negro Civic Action," *Journal of Conflict Resolution* 5, 3 (September, 1961), p. 292.
17. For the most complete discussion of these campaigns, see Mohandas K. Gandhi, *An Autobiography* (Boston: Beacon, 1957) and Louis Fischer, *Gandhi: His Life and Message for the World* (New York: Signet, 1954).
18. New Haven: Yale University Press, 1957, pp. 72-94.
19. "The Sit-Ins: Passive Resistance or Civil Disobedience?" *Social Action* 27, 5 (January, 1961), p. 15.
20. "CORE Rules for Action," published by the Congress of Racial Equality, New York.
21. Written by Rev. James M. Lawson, Jr., for the Raleigh Conference of sit-in leaders, April 15-17, 1960. See chapter 8 for a discussion of the secularization of SNCC.
22. James Q. Wilson, "The Strategy of Protest," p. 293 (some of the examples are my own). This typology does not represent a logically tight or exhaustive system of classification, for *types* of verbal and physical protest are employed in carrying out *specific economic and political protests*.
23. "Reflections on the Latest Reform of the South" (Atlanta: SRC, 1960), p. 1. Dunbar was, until October 1965, Executive Director of the Southern Regional Council, an Atlanta-based research group whose aim is ". . . to attain the ideals and practices of equal opportunity for all peoples in the South." He now heads the Field Foundation.
24. From a series of reports issued by the Southern Regional Council and CORE in 1960.
25. Based on a compilation of press reports by the Southern Regional Council and informal quantification by major informants and the author.

26. On this point I find the smallest degree of consensus among social movements theorists; it is, however, essential in our developing theory of the rationalization of spontaneous social protest, and it is dealt with at length in later chapters.
27. The "leadership" here refers to that on a movement-wide level, for a division of labor rapidly develops among the various local and organizational subsystems. This problem is treated in chapters 7-9.
28. See especially Herbert Blumer, "Social Movements," pp. 199-220 in Alfred McClung Lee (ed.), *Principles of Sociology* (New York: College Outline Series, 1961); C. Wendell King, *Social Movements in the United States* (New York: Random House, 1956); and Paul Meadows, "Theses on Social Movements," *Social Forces* 24, 4 (May, 1946), pp. 408-12. Hereafter the three major journals are cited as abbreviated: *SF* (*Social Forces*), *ASR* (*American Sociological Review*) and AJS (*American Journal of Sociology*).
29. This list is in no sense intended to be exhaustive, but rather is to serve as a representative sampling of the kinds of work that social movements theorists have been doing in recent decades. These works themselves represent syntheses of the earlier writings in the field—LeBon and y Gassett, for instance. Contributions from the broader area of general theory and social change theory are considered in chapter 7. For the most up-to-date bibliography on all facets of social movements, see Neil J. Smelser, *Theory of Collective Behavior* (New York: The Free Press of Glencoe, 1963).
30. *Introduction to Sociology*, revised edition (New York: The Ronald Press Company, 1935), chapter 19.
31. Paul Meadows, "Sequence in Revolution," *ASR* 6, 5 (October, 1941), pp. 702-709.
32. *Ibid.*, p. 709 (adapted from H.D. Lasswell, *Politics*, New York: McGraw Hill, 1936).
33. Meadows, "Theses on Social Movements," pp. 408-12.
34. *ASR* 14, 3 (June, 1949), pp. 346-57.
35. New York: Random House.
36. P. 44, emphasis added.
37. As an example, leaders of several civil rights organizations had conceived of this possibility individually, and at least one group (CORE) had been involved in active efforts to initiate this kind of movement for several years. At least one informant (SNCC's James Forman) had independently written a book about just such a movement four years before the sit-ins–a novel which was rejected by two publishers as too provocative.
38. Evanston, Illinois: Row and Peterson, 1958 (second edition).
39. Englewood Cliffs, N.J.: Prentice-Hall, Inc., 1957.
40. In Hans Gerth and C. Wright Mills, *From Max Weber* (New York: Oxford University Press, 1958), p. 293.
41. *Ibid.*, p. 293.
42. Pareto seems to be discussing the same phenomenon in his distinction between "logical" and "non-logical" types of social action.
43. Robert N. Bellah, seminar, Harvard University, September 28, 1961.

44. Max Weber, *The Theory of Social and Economic Organization*, second edition (translated by A.M. Henderson and Talcott Parsons, Glencoe, Ill.: The Free Press, 1947), p. 123.
45. Gerth and Mills, *From Max Weber*, p. 51.
46. *Ibid.*, p. 51.
47. Quoted in Edgar Thompson and Everett Hughes (ed.), *Race: Individual and Collective Behavior* (Glencoe, Ill.: The Free Press, 1958), pp. 424-25.
48. The understanding of the paradigm utilized here rests on interpretations of Winston White (May 8, 1962) and Talcott Parsons (November 16, 1960, and May 25, 1962), in addition to *The Structure of Social Action* (Glencoe, Ill.: The Free Press, 1949), *The Social System* (Glencoe, Ill.: The Free Press, 1951), *Toward a General Theory of Action* (Cambridge, Mass.: Harvard University Press, 1959, edited by Parsons in conjunction with Edward Shils), "An Outline of the Social System" in Parsons, *et al* (ed.), *Theories of Society* (New York: The Free Press of Glencoe, 1961), and Neil J. Smelser, *Social Change in the Industrial Revolution* (Chicago: University of Chicago Press, 1959). See chapter 7 for elaboration.
49. This definition, derived from general theory, is based on Norman Storer, "Federal Science Policy and the Sociology of Science" (unpublished paper, Harvard University, January, 1962), p. 1.
50. Parsons and Henderson, p. 18 in *The Theory of Social and Economic Organization*.

## CHAPTER TWO

1. *Street Corner Society* (Chicago: University of Chicago, 1955), p. 303. Readers are asked to accept the use of the personal pronoun in this chapter as the most direct and honest way of presenting the life history of a research project.
2. Peter A. Munch, "Empirical Science and Max Weber's *Verstehende Soziologie*," *ASR* 22, 1 (February, 1957), p. 31.
3. Florence R. Kluckhohn, "The Participant Observer Technique in Small Communities," *AJS* 45, 3 (November, 1940), p. 331.
4. The concept of sociological research as dialogue is more fully explored in James H. Laue, "Meaning and Marginality" (unpublished paper, Harvard University, 1961).
5. Howard Becker and Blance Geer, "Problems of Inference and Proof in Participant Observation," *ASR* 23, 5 (October, 1958), pp. 652-53. Morris Zelditch, Jr.'s "Some Methodological Problems of Field Studies" (*AJS* LXVII, 5 [March, 1962], pp. 566-76) contains a complementary discussion and typology of the validity of participant observation for obtaining various kinds of data.
6. Munch, "Empirical Science . . .", p.32.
7. This example is from Selltiz, *et al*, *Research Methods in Social Relations* (revised edition, New York: Holt-Dryden, 1960), p. 437.

8. David Riesman, "Interviewers, Elites and Academic Freedom," *Social Problems* VI, 2 (Fall, 1958), p. 124.
9. Norbert Elias, "Problems of Involvement and Detachment," *British Journal of Sociology* 7, 3 (September, 1956), p. 240. Emphasis added.
10. *Cf.* Munch, "Empirical Science . . .", pp. 28-29.
11. *Ibid.*, p. 31.
12. John Dollard, *Caste and Class in a Southern Town* (Garden City, N.Y.: Doubleday Anchor Books, 1949), p. 17, tense corrected.
13. *Cf.* Whyte, *Street Corner Society*, p. 300. Negro sociologist Lewis Jones stresses the importance of *local sponsorship of research* (interview, March 1, 1962), and tells of how his studies of race relations in Deep South rural counties were only possible because of a letter from the local sheriff–usually a diehard segregationist.
14. Such friendship has taken many different forms in the course of this project. For the most part, it has meant either specifically ignoring racial designations, or making light of them in the most irreverent ways. After several less-than-comfortable encounters with James Forman, the highly militant executive director of SNCC, I felt quite rejected and "outside" due to what I perceived as a strong anti-white feeling on his part. But after we got beyond the more formal attempts at rapport and understood each other's position, we reached a unique symbiosis in which I call him "James $X_1$" and he calls me "James $X_2$." In another case, a Negro student informant whose first name is Charles, calls me "Boss," and I retaliate with "Mister Charlie." In a third indication of how bonds of militancy mean more than color ties, many Negro informants were quite liberal in their use of a "cotton field accent" in describing their more moderate or acquiescent brothers. The friendships extended to the intricacies of sociological theory, too. After completing an interview schedule with a major white confidant and friend of long-standing, I was questioned about the theoretical bases of the dissertation. It took her only a second to suggest an appropriate title for a novel she might write on the movement—"I Lost my Charisma in the Struggle!"
15. Several human relations agency executives and social scientists commented on the easy entrance and acceptance I had established with all of the movement's competing factions.
16. Much of this material is contained in James H. Laue, "The Sit-Ins: A New Decade and a New Generation?" (unpublished paper, Harvard University, 1960).
17. I am grateful to Gordon W. Allport and Thomas F. Pettigrew, who secured for me the first of two grants from the Taconic Foundation to carry out this research.
18. Since February 1965, I have devoted full time to analysis of the desegregation process and conciliation of racial disputes as Assistant Community Analysis Officer for the Federal Community Relations Service (created by the Civil Rights Law of 1964). This work has further expanded my perspective in the field and aided, I believe, the interpretations I have been able to derive from the data of this project.

19. Selltiz, *et al*, *Research Methods in Social Relations*, p. 521. Matilda W. Riley, (*Sociological Research: A Case Approach*, New York: Wiley, 1962, pp. 296-300) calls this the "focused sample" and sees it as appropriate for intensive consideration of a small number of cases.
20. Time, jail and geographical limitations prevented me from interviewing four persons who–on these bases–should have been in the sample. These are two SNCC field secretaries, Roy Wilkins of the NAACP and James Farmer of CORE. The SNCC "sample" is still nearly complete: 13 of the population of 15 are included. Two NAACP leaders who have been much closer to the direct action by virtue of their position in the southeast region replace Wilkins, and my personal friendship and correspondence with Farmer over the years (plus an interview with his Mississippi representative) cover this viewpoint satisfactorily, I believe.
21. See Appendix for complete list of respondents and their positions.
22. Very few informants questioned the use of the term "movement"–and those who did usually were interested in clarification, agreeing on the criteria of self-consciousness, broad-based support, broadening focus and common ideology as used in this study.
23. With pre-coded questions, the same problem is encountered *before* the interview.
24. While this item may have yielded some useful data, it should be noted that many informants (including the more social scientifically sophisticated) were uneasy at being forced to structure their judgments in rigidly pre-categorized responses.
25. This kind of interview relationship is predicated on informants' perception of the researcher's *knowledge* of the situation and *trustworthiness*. Specific techniques included explaining in a straightforward manner some of the difficulties involved in this kind of research, letting the informant know that *I* knew certain kinds of information, and posing an interpretation of a particular element of the movement to demonstrate the thinking and synthesis I had done in the area.
26. Charles Whittenstein, Southeast Area Director, American Jewish Committee, interview, March 15, 19, 1962.
27. Charles Sherrod, SNCC Field Secretary, March 22, 1962.
28. Interview, March 30-31, 1962.
29. My wife, Mariann R. Laue, helped considerably in parts of this operation.
30. Sidney Siegal, *Nonparametric Statistics for the Behavioral Sciences* (New York: Wiley, 1956), p. 19.
31. John G. Peatman, *Introduction to Applied Statistics* (New York: Harper, 1963), p. 363, emphasis in original.
32. Letter from Thomas Gaither, CORE Field Secretary, Rock Hill, S.C., Prison Camp, February 5, 1961.
33. Especially helpful have been conversations with Gordon W. Allport, Zelda Gamson, Talcott Parsons, Thomas F. Pettigrew and Winston White at Harvard University, John H. Burma of Grinnell College, John T. Doby and Arnold Levine of Emory University, Meyer Nimkoff and Lewis M. Killian of The

Florida State University and M. Richard Cramer of the University of North Carolina.

34. "Action Research and Minority Problems," in Gertrud Weiss Lewin, ed., *Resolving Social Conflicts* (New York: Harper and Brothers, 1948), pp. 202-203, 204.
35. I even encountered problems of rapport with some southern social scientists I interviewed, who viewed me as a naive outsider from an Ivy League school trying to pre-empt their private research province. As with participant-informants, I had to establish my credentials by convincing them of my trustworthiness, inside knowledge of the situation–and that I did not conform to their stereotype of the Ivy League scholar-snob.
36. Exploratory action research does not require the intrusion of an independent or manipulative variable as is true in much action research. In fact, the social conditions of the research situation at this stage may be upset and the chances for further research damaged by the too-early introduction of such a formal methodological procedure.
37. The concept of "dialogue" developed in this research is based on the work of Martin Buber. See especially his *I and Thou*, reprinted in Will Herberg, *The Writings of Martin Buber* (New York: Meridian Books, 1956). For a cogent discussion of the place of action research in intergoup relations, see Lewis M. Killian, "Leadership in the Desegregation Crisis," in Muzafer Sherif (ed.), *Intergroup Relations and Leadership* (New York: Wiley, 1962), pp. 142-46, 162-65.
38. Consider how these conditions differ from those surroundings the more standard interview situation–notably, at least *transience of the relationship* and *protection for anonymity*. See David Riesman and Mark Benney, "The Sociology of the Interview," an address delivered to the Midwest Sociological Society, Des Moines, April 22, 1955, and reprinted in *The Midwest Sociologist* (full citation not given on reprint).
39. Rev. Wyatt T. Walker, Executive Director, Southern Christian Leadership Conference, March 14, 16, and 17, 1962.
40. David Riesman, "Some Observations on the Interviewing in Teacher Apprehension Study," in Paul Lazarsfeld and Wagner Thielens, Jr., *The Academic Mind* (Glencoe, Ill.: The Free Press, 1958), p. 370. Riesman also reports the uncomfortable responses to "the cultivated attitude of neutrality" (of interviewers) experienced by a group of elites who should know better–social scientists. And Harold Fleming echoed my experience that "the quasi-detached mood of interviewing is not appreciated by these students, who are anything but detached."
41. David Riesman and Mark Benney make this distinction between sharing and surrendering data in "Asking and Answering," *The Journal of Business of the University of Chicago* 29, 4 (October, 1956), p. 227.

# CHAPTER THREE

1. Quoted in Martin Luther King, Jr., *Stride Toward Freedom* (New York: Ballantine, 1958), pp. 14-15.
2. "Montgomery and/or M.L. King, Jr.," was a distant second with 22 percent (*Form 2*, Item II.1). Only three of 13 students mentioned Gandhi (*Form 1*, II.1).
3. From "Civil Disobedience," in *The Writings of Thoreau* (New York: Random House, 1950), p. 640. There is evidence that persecuted Quakers utilized passive resistance in eighteenth-century New England (see Kai T. Erikson, *Wayward Puritans*, to be published by Wiley in 1966).
4. Thoreau, *Ibid*., p. 646.
5. Louis Fischer, *Gandhi* (New York: New American Library, 1954), p. 37.
6. Gandhi's campaigns are adequately documented in many sources. See especially Fischer, *Gandhi*; Mohandas Gandhi, *An Autobiography* (Boston: Beacon Press, 1957); Jawaharlal Nehru, *Toward Freedom* (Boston: Beacon Press, 1958); and Arne Naess, "A Systematization of Gandhian Ethics of Conflict Resolution," *Journal of Conflict Resolution* 2, 2 (July, 1958), pp. 140-55.
7. Fischer, *Gandhi*, p. 38.
8. From mailings and newsletters of CORE, FOR and SCLC, 1960-65.
9. In contrast, a 1963 *Newsweek*-sponsored national poll found that only 10 percent of 100 top Negro leaders believed the U.S. Supreme Court had "done most for Negroes" among a series of possible forces and agencies (William Brink and Lou Harris, *The Negro Revolution in America*, New York: Simon and Schuster, Inc., 1963, p. 116).
10. Reported to me by Dr. Benjamim Mays, President of Morehouse College, January 16, 1963. This was only one of a number of such meetings which have come to my attention.
11. Herbert Garfinkel, *When Negroes March* (Glencoe, Ill.: The Free Press, 1959), p. 187.
12. *Ibid*. Garfinkel gives a well-documented analysis of the events surrounding the March on Washington Movement.
13. *Ibid*., p. 191.
14. From 1962 War Resisters League calendar (New York).
15. *Ibid*.
16. *Ibid*., and Garfinkel, *When Negroes March*, p. 192.
17. *Southern Patriot* 16, 1 (January, 1962), p. 1.
18. See especially Garfinkel, *When Negroes March*, and records of CORE, FOR and WRL.
19. Reported from court records by Thomas F. Pettigrew, lecture, Harvard University, September 27, 1961.
20. Alan Westin, "Ride-In," *American Heritage* 13 (August, 1962), p. 59.
21. Reported to me by Constance Baker Motley of the NAACP legal staff, September 4, 1962.

22. Westin, "Ride-In," and C. Vann Woodward, *The Strange Career of Jim Crow* (New York: Oxford University Press, 1957).
23. See Roscoe E. Lewis, "The Role of Pressure Groups in Maintaining Morale Among Negroes," *Journal of Negro Education* 12, 3 (Summer, 1943), pp. 472-73.
24. Garfinkel, *When Negroes March*, p. 190.
25. *Ibid.*, p. 189.
26. *Ibid.*, pp. 101-102.
27. CORE, *Cracking the Color Line* (New York, 1959).
28. James Peck, *Freedom Ride* (New York: Simon and Schuster, Inc., 1962), chapter 1, "First 'Freedom Ride'–1947," pp. 14-27.
29. From 1962 WRL calendar.
30. Garfinkel, *When Negroes March*, p. 192.
31. From 1962 WRL Calendar.
32. *Ibid.*
33. *Ibid.*
34. CORE, *Cracking the Color Line*.
35. *Ibid.*
36. The following description of the Montgomery bus boycott is adapted with permission from the succinct summary by W. Haywood Burns in *The Voices of Negro Protest* (London: Oxford University Press, 1963), pp. 37-41. The interpretative passages, however, are mine. For a detailed account, see Martin Luther King, Jr., *Stride Toward Freedom*, and L.D. Reddick, *Crusader Without Violence* (New York: Harper and Row, 1959).
37. King, *Stride Toward Freedom*, p. 40.
38. *Ibid.*, p. 51.
39. *Ibid.*, pp. 96-97.
40. *Ibid.*, p. 63.
41. Ella Baker, personal conversation, October 17, 1960.
42. These kinds of charges were to be matched a hundred times over in the sit-ins with such accusations as "criminal anarchy," "parading without a permit" and "ejection of undesirable guests."
43. James W. Vander Zanden has suggested that nonviolent direct action has a special appeal for Negro Americans because of its ethic of (a) loving protest and (b) willingness to suffer for just actions. Aggression legitimated by love makes protest possible, he argues, for a people trying to overcome socialized submission. And the suffering (jail, beatings, loss of jobs, etc.) which follows provides built-in expiation for the aggression-caused guilt. See Vander Zanden's "The Non-Violent [sic] Resistance Movement Against Segregation," *AJS* 68, 5 (March, 1963), pp. 544-50. This point is considered more in detail in Section C.
44. Lawson, March 1, 1962.
45. Charles McDew, Chairman of SNCC (November, 1961–Summer, 1963), interview, March 5-6, 1962.
46. NAACP, "The Day They Changed Their Minds" (New York, 1960), p. 3.

47. Howard Zinn, former Professor of History and Chairman, Department of History and Social Science, Spelman College, Atlanta, Ga., interview, March 14, 1962. Dr. Zinn is now Associate Professor of Government at Boston University.
48. CORE, *Cracking the Color Line*.
49. NAACP, "The Day They Changed Their Minds."
50. CORE, *Cracking the Color Line*.
51. Reported to me by Sandra Cason Hayden, March 21, 1962.
52. Reported to me by John Brown, Chairman of Miami CORE, August 17, 1960.
53. Lawson, March 1, 1962. Bernard Lafayette (former SNCC Field Secretary, interview, February 24, 1962), notes that many students who were to become movement-wide leaders took part in these workshops. Among them were Marion Barry (first Chairman of SNCC), John Lewis (Freedom Ride leader and Chairman of SNCC from summer, 1963–present) and Diane Nash Bevel (Freedom Ride leader and Mississippi voting organizer).
54. Reported in *The CORElator*, No. 80 (January-February, 1960).
55. From 1962 WRL Calendar.
56. This institute was a local forerunner of the CORE National Action Institute I attended in Miami in 1960.
57. James Monsonis, former SNCC Field Secretary, interview, March 18, 1962.
58. Garry Fullerton, "New Factories Thing of Past in Little Rock," *Nashville Tennessean*, May 31, 1959. A Report of the Executive Director to Members and Friends of the Southern Regional Council, October 19, 1959, describes the same awareness and move to moderation in many southern communities.
59. Rev. J. Metz Rollins, Special Field Representative, United Presbyterian Church in the U.S.A., interview, February 27, 1962.
60. Arnold Rose, *The Negro in America* (Boston: Beacon, 1948), p. 234, emphasis in original.
61. *Negro Politics* (Glencoe, Ill.: The Free Press, 1960), chapter 9.
62. Tilman Cothran, Atlanta University, March 13, 1962.
63. Tilman Cothran, "Negro Leadership in a Crisis Situation," *Phylon* 22, 2 (Summer, 1961), p. 118.
64. Race Relations Department, American Missionary Association, Fisk University, interview, February 28, 1962.
65. Lewis M. Killian and C.U. Smith, "Negro Protest Leaders in a Southern Community," *SF* 38, 3 (March, 1960), p. 256.
66. Thomas F. Pettigrew and Ernest Q. Campbell, *Christians in Racial Crisis* (Washington: Public Affairs Press, 1959), p. 80.
67. T.P. Monahan and E.H. Monahan, "Some Characteristics of American Negro Leaders," *ASR* 21, 4 (August, 1956), p. 595.
68. I saw this in travels and contacts in a number of cities, among them Nashville, Atlanta, Miami, Greenville, S.C., and Albany, Ga.
69. Burns adds the sound interpretation that "Montgomery was an important sign of a great restiveness among American Negroes and their growing willingness to turn to unfamiliar and untried ways to express their grievances and to gain redress" (*The Voices of Negro Protest*, p. 41).

70. The legitimation of ideological bases at this stage in social protest is covered more fully in Section C of this paper.

## CHAPTER FOUR

1. Related by Dr. Charles Gomillion, Dean and Head of the Division of Social Sciences, Tuskegee Institute, Alabama, interview, March 23, 1962.
2. Lonnie King, first co-chairman of the Atlanta Committee on Appeal for Human Rights, interview, August 10, 1960.
3. *Economic and Social Status of the Negro in the United States* (New York: National Urban League, 1961), p. 17.
4. See *Ibid.* and Vivian W. Henderson, *The Economic Status of Negroes: In the Nation and in the South* (Atlanta: Southern Regional Council, 1963).
5. Further implications of this approach are explored in the light of theories of relative deprivation in Section C of this study.
6. Data on Greensboro come largely from my research trip there in August, 1960. Included were interviews of several hours each with Ezell Blair and David Richmond, two of the four students who participated in the February 1st sit-ins.
7. While this study does not focus directly on personality dynamics, it should be noted here that Blair's account is typical of the hundreds of sit-inners with whom I have talked.
8. See *c. A Diffusion of Political Awareness* at the end of this chapter.
9. From CORE, SNCC and Southern Regional Council reports, and from personal observations, calculations and conversations.
10. Source: Constance Curry, Director, Southern Project of the United States National Student Association. See chapters 8 and 9 for a more comprehensive discussion of this issue.
11. From Southern Regional Council reports. Students threatened demonstrations, but a biracial committee settled the issue without sit-ins, capping the transition with an appropriate *rite de passage*: Jackie Robinson speaking to an interracial banquet on March 19. A similar challenge-negotiation-desegregation pattern occurred early at Asheville, N.C.
12. Wallace Westfeldt, "Settling a Sit-In" (a report prepared for the Nashville Community Relations Conference, 2001 Division Street, Nashville 4, Tennessee), p. 1.
13. The movement was so powerful a force for social change that former President Harry Truman had labeled it "Communist-inspired" within a month. Rarely does a social movement gain such status in so short a time. Truman later partially retracted his charge. There is some evidence that Communist organizers have tried to infiltrate the sit-ins, but in every known case it has been a weak and immediately rejected attempt (observations from Ruby Hurley, T.F. Pettigrew and James H. Laue).
14. *Form 1* and *Form 2*, I.2.
15. Miller, March 5, 1962.

16. Cordell Reagon, SNCC Field Secretary, interview, March 27, 1962.
17. The theme of frustration, *anomie* and readiness is dealt with more fully in Section C.
18. See Thomas F. Pettigrew and M. Richard Cramer, "The Demography of Desegregation," *The Journal of Social Issues* 14, 4 (1959), pp. 61-71.
19. Martin Oppenheimer analyzes these factors in an essentially demographic approach to the sit-in movement, "The Genesis of the Southern Negro Student Movement (Sit-In Movement): A Study in Contemporary Negro Protest," Ph.D. Dissertation, University of Pennsylvania, 1963 (University Microfilms order no. 63-7075).
20. These and similar data in this section are distilled from a series of SRC reports.
21. Pettigrew and Cramer, "The Demography of Desegregation," especially pp. 66-70.
22. *Form 1*, I.2.
23. Researched and written largely by Leslie W. Dunbar, then SRC Research Director. Harold Fleming, SRC Executive Director at that time, said later that his group was ". . . the movement's best press agent . . . They could not get this hearing in the press without SRC, and we could only do it for them if we weren't a party to the movement" (April 5, 1962).
24. Dunbar considers this a vital step in differentiating the image of these protests from the labor "sit-down," thereby enhancing the chances of ready acceptability of the movement and incorporation of the term into everyday parlance. Needless to say, he was right. And it is easy to see the convenience of the "-in" suffix for other action . . . whoever heard of a "wade-down"?
25. SRC, "The Student Protest Movement, Winter, 1960," p. 5.
26. Miss Ella Baker, Special Project Staff, National Student YWCA, interview, March 15, 1962.
27. Leslie Dunbar, "Reflections on the Latest Reform of the South" (Atlanta: Southern Regional Council, mimeographed paper, July, 1960), p. 3.
28. Gomillion, interview, March 23, 1962. Representative of this were 1960 leaders Lonnie King and Julian Bond in Atlanta, and Marion Barry and Diane Nash in Nashville—two pivotal locations. All told of their initial action as responses of students to a student challenge (research notes, summer, 1960).
29. Michael Walzer, "A Cup of Coffee and a Seat," *Dissent* 7, 2 (Spring, 1960), p. 114.
30. These and other data in this section were reported to me by Gorden Carey, research notes, July 1, 1960.
31. Louis Lomax, *The Negro Revolt* (New York: Harper Brothers, 1962), pp. 123-24.
32. LaFayette, interview, February 24, 1962.
33. Nashville student leaders later told me (research notes, summer, 1960) they were disappointed and even angered that Greensboro students had "beaten us to the punch."
34. James Gibson, Executive Director, Atlanta Branch of the NAACP, interview, March 12, 1962.

35. Emphasis added. I am grateful to Marvin E. Robinson, an early participant from Southern University and a former CORE Field Secretary, for giving me access to this and other important material from the Raleigh Conference.
36. *The Student Voice*, 1, 1 (June, 1960), p. 1. For a discussion of SNCC's ideological "Statement of Purpose," see chapter 9 of this paper.
37. Reported by my special research assistant in the Midwest–my mother.
38. Research notes, June, 1960.
39. Here as in other parts of this section, these calculations are made from organizational releases, newspaper clippings and the estimates of reliable informants.
40. A Raleigh Conference resolution gave SNCC the mandate for a fall conference.
41. *New York Times*, October 18, 1960.
42. Conference theme as stated in a SNCC letter to prospective delegates, September 2, 1960.
43. Reported to me by Jane Stembridge, then SNCC Staff Secretary, October 13, 1960. The leader in question was Bayard Rustin who was accepted by labor and other supporting groups in his role as organizer of the March on Washington in 1963. This broadening of ideological tolerance is discussed as a general function of rationalization in chapter 8.
44. Research notes, October 14, 1960.
45. Research notes, October 13, 1960. SNCC's internal rationalization problems associated with the conference are covered more fully in Section C.
46. Miss Stembridge resigned as Staff Secretary, and the new position of Executive Secretary was filled until late summer of 1961 by Edward King, Jr., a Negro student expelled for his sit-in leadership at Kentucky State College.
47. The first death directly associated with the movement occurred during this period (in August, 1960) when Charles Davis, a Negro, was fatally shot during the aftermath of demonstrations in Jacksonville, Florida (Mary Chapnick, "Civil Rights Casualties, 1954-65," Washington, D.C.: Community Relations Service, 1964, unpublished). See chapter 5, footnote 53, for an account of other deaths during the period under study and beyond.
48. SNCC brochure obtained at the October, 1960, Atlanta Conference. Among other things, it called for a change in Senate Rule 22 to outlaw the filibuster.
49. Letter from Thomas Gaither, York, S.C., February 7, 1961. Later the League for Industrial Democracy published a pamphlet by Gaither, "Jailed-In," available through CORE.
50. The summary in the following three paragraphs is condensed from James H. Laue, "Race Relations Revolution: The Sit-In Movement," Harvard University, 1961 (mimeographed).
51. Information on the Atlanta boycott from research notes, February, 1961; Savannah information from Field Report of James T. McCain, supplied through the courtesy of CORE's national office.
52. There had been ride-ins before, of course. But, significantly, this type of action now has a ready-made name.
53. Orangeburg had 388 arrests on February 25, 1960. The Columbia convictions–on breach of the peace charges–were overturned 8-1 by the U.S.

Supreme Court (February 25, 1963) in one of the most important judicial rulings on direct action.

54. Conversation, April 29, 1962.
55. Baker, interview, March 15, 1962; Galphin, interview, March 20, 1962; L.W. Jones, interview, February 28, 1962; Miller, interview, March 5, 1962; Rev. John Morris, Executive Director, Episcopal Society for Cultural and Racial Unity, interview, March 10, 1962; Jane Stembridge, SNCC Staff Secretary from April 1960–October 1960, interview, March 4, 1962.
56. This material is condensed from a case study analysis of EPIC in James H. Laue, "The Sit-Ins: A New Decade and a New Generation?", Harvard University, 1960 (mimeographed), pp. 23-49.
57. See James H. Laue and Leon M. McCorkle, Jr., "The Association of Southern Women for the Prevention of Lynching: A Commentary on the Role of the 'Moderate,'" *Sociological Inquiry* 35, 1 (Winter, 1965), pp. 80-93.
58. Clippings from Southern Regional Council "Sit-Ins" file.
59. Today only small private and denominational colleges in the South have remained untouched by the student activism generated by the sit-ins.
60. Clippings from SRC "Sit-Ins" file.
61. *Ibid.*
62. For a listing of these statements, see Pettigrew and Campbell, *Christians in Racial Crisis*, Appendix.
63. See, for example, the feature by Associated Press Religion Editor George W. Cornell, "In Civil Rights the Church is Truly Militant," May 30, 1965.
64. This information is compiled from my files of organizational mailings, SNCC files of communiques from supporting organizations, and a SNCC press release dated March 2, 1961.
65. Interview, March 19, 1962. "Only the Association of Southern Women for the Prevention of Lynching of the 1930s and the March on Washington Movement in the 1940s came at all close to generating this kind of revolution in the past," she says.

## CHAPTER FIVE

1. Quoted in "The Freedom Ride, May, 1961," (Atlanta: Southern Regional Council, 1961), pp. 9-10.
2. Frank Randall, "The Freedom Riders: A Historian's View" (reprinted by CORE from the *Amherst College Alumni News*, no date given).
3. This theme is treated more extensively in Section C.
4. Research notes at CORE Council Meeting, February 10-12, 1961, Lexington, Kentucky.
5. The growing role of organizational initiation at this stage of the movement is underscored by the fact that SNCC was planning a project similar to the Freedom Rides at almost the same time. SNCC hoped to "rally student action with a '*DRIVE AGAINST TRAVEL BIAS*'" to be carried out by college students on their way home from school in late May and early June. An April

release calling this the "School Closing Project" asks for the action on the same judicial and Interstate Commerce Commission grounds used by CORE. Many students who would have participated in the SNCC project were thus primed to play an important role in carrying on the Freedom Rides after the initial CORE Ride was over.

6. This account is necessarily limited. To get the full impact of the Freedom Rides–their intensity, the violence, the hate and fear–see the following more complete descriptions: Burns, *The Voices of Negro Protest in America*; SRC, "The Freedom Ride, May, 1961"; "Freedom Rides" (July-August, 1961 issue of *New South* 17, 7-8); Lomax, *The Negro Revolt*; Peck, *Freedom Ride*; and Robert Williams, *Negroes With Guns* (New York: Munsell and Marzani, 1962).
7. Peck, *Freedom Ride*, p. 114. Mississippi Senator James Eastland, predictably and with a minimum of information and good judgment, opined before the U.S. Senate later that the Rides had started in Moscow.
8. "Agenda–National Council," 1961 CORE Council Meeting, February 10-12, 1961, Lexington, Kentucky.
9. CORE release, "*FREEDOM RIDE, 1961*" (no date; *circa* March-April, 1961).
10. Southern Regional Council, "The Freedom Ride, May, 1961," p. 3.
11. Adapted largely from the SRC report (*ibid.*) and research notes from informants, with exceptions noted. The SRC report, it should be noted, conforms in important details to my clipping files from the Associated Press, United Press International, *Christian Science Monitor*, *New York Times*, and the various civil rights organizations.
12. On May 16 a member of the mob gave a sworn statement to the FBI that he was called by the Ku Klux Klan to come to the Birmingham terminal (*New York Times*, May 17, 1961).
13. Peck, *Freedom Ride*, p. 124.
14. Farmer, speech for Harvard-Radcliffe Liberal Union, Cambridge, Mass., October 5, 1961.
15. Peck, *Freedom Ride*, p. 138.
16. *Ibid.*, p. 138.
17. George Lincoln Rockwell and about a dozen followers chartered a bus, attached signs bearing anti-Negro and anti-integration slogans, and tried to follow the original Freedom Ride route to speak and distribute racist literature (see May 22-24 description).
18. It is significant that these white men—as well as those in most of the other mobs encountered by the Freedom Riders—were young and apparently lower class. This conforms to the South's traditional patterns of mob violence described by Arthur Raper, W.J. Cash, Lillian Smith and others, in which the proletariat's n'er-do-wells do the violent bidding of segregationist officials and businessmen.
19. The SRC chronology ends here. The account from this point is compiled wholly from other sources as noted.
20. Peck, *Freedom Ride*, p. 141.
21. Many sources document this brutality. In addition to information I have received from a number of informants, accounts may be found in 1961 and

1962 publications of SCLC, SNCC and CORE, especially the *SCLC Newsletter* and the *CORElator*.

22. "Memorandum to Affiliated Groups and Friends," CORE, August 5, 1961.
23. Burns, *The Voices of Negro Protest in America*, p. 56.
24. CORE "Memorandum," *cf.* footnote 22.
25. Associated Press, September 23, 1961.
26. Peck, *Freedom Ride*, p. 159.
27. *Forms 1* and *2*, I.9. See Appendix for complete marginals on this question.
28. Thomas Kahn, "The Political Significance of the Freedom Rides," prepared for the Liberal Study Group of the National Students Association Congress, August 19-30, 1962, and distributed by Students for a Democratic Society.
29. SCLC official Rev. Andrew Young stated the principle cogently in referring later to the aims of the Mississippi Summer Project of 1964: "We're just trying to get some of those northern white folks to *use* some of that power they've had all along" (conversation, July 11, 1964).
30. *St. Paul Pioneer Press*, August 3, 1961.
31. *Chicago Sun-Times*, July 31, 1961.
32. Public Opinion News Service (American Institute of Public Opinion), June 21, 1961. Of the 63 percent of a sample of 1,502 who indicated they had some knowledge of the Freedom Rides, 24 percent said they approved, 64 percent disapproved and 12 percent had no opinion. A week later, 27 percent of a nationwide sample told Gallup pollsters they thought "sit-ins and Freedom Buses" would "help the Negro's chances of being integrated in the South," and 57 percent thought it would hurt. A southern sample split 20 percent-70 percent on the same question.
33. See chapters 8 and 9 for an analysis of the expanding bases of fund-raising at this stage in the rationalizing direct action movement.
34. Several SNCCers proposed, for example, that the Fall, 1960 conference be held in Jackson, Miss. (research notes, August 7, 1960).
35. Leslie W. Dunbar, "The Freedom Ride," *New South* 17, 7-8 (July-August, 1961), p. 10.
36. SRC, "The Freedom Ride, May, 1961" p. 6.
37. Reprinted in the *Christian Science Monitor*, May 23, 1961.
38. SRC, "The Freedom Ride, May, 1961" p. 7. And the politicians learned fast: Jackson and Mississippi white leaders watched Alabama mobs attack the Riders, and simply saw to it that *not a single incident of public violence* occurred in Mississippi during the arrest of more than 300 protestors. Note that this exercise of civilized power did not extend to the jails and prisons where brutality was common (see June-July description on p. 105 above).
39. Robert McAfee Brown, "The Freedom Riders: A Clergyman's View" (reprinted by CORE from the *Amherst College Alumni News*, no date given).
40. Mrs. Bevel is a field secretary for SNCC. Interview, March 28, 1962.
41. Interview, March 24, 1962.
42. James H. Laue, "The Movement: Negro Challenge to the Myth," *New South* 18, 7-8 (July-August, 1963), p. 12.

43. Rev. Paul Brooks, SNCC Field Secretary, interview, March 29, 1962. Further analysis of these problems is contained in Section C.
44. See chapter 9.
45. Hedrick Smith in the *Christian Science Monitor*, May 25, 1961.
46. This interpretation has been impressed upon me in several different contexts by Leslie Dunbar and Harold Fleming, to whom I am indebted for much more than this.
47. Culmination of the Rides' aim to activating latent federal power is seen, of course, in the federal Civil Rights Law passed July 2, 1964, and the Voting Rights Law of 1965, discussed in chapter 9.
48. See "Executive Support of Civil Rights" (Southern Regional Council, March 13, 1962) for a detailed account of executive actions of the Kennedy Administration's first year.
49. Important from an organizational standpoint were the formation in the fall of 1961 of the Northern Student Movement and the Southern Student Freedom Fund, in response to fund-raising needs of the movement. See chapters 8 and 9 for further discussion of the role of these organizations.
50. Late in the summer of 1961, for instance, a long-brewing conflict came to the surface in Monroe, North Carolina (on the South Carolina border), when several experienced direct actionists came to help local Negroes organize and sustain their protest. Local officials added to the production of a crisis by labeling the civil rights workers "freedom riders." The bitterness, bearing of arms and threat of retaliation from Monroe Negroes dramatically confronted the civil rights organizations with another dimension of the difficulties of an all-out effort in the Deep South. See Williams, *Negroes With Guns*.
51. CORE release "To Local Chapters and Advisory Committee," July, 1961.
52. As of September 28, 1961, for instance, CORE had spent more than $250,000 ". . . on the direct action and immediate costs of the Freedom Rides"—a "staggering amount," as the groups says, "for an organization that raised less than $240,000 in all of [the previous] year" (Memo to CORE groups and friends on "Freedom Ride Costs," September 28, 1961). The organizational growth of CORE and other civil rights groups is covered more fully in chapter 8.
53. From the perspective of 1965, one can see the truth of this premonition by examining the number of deaths attributable to civil rights activities. From February 1, 1960 to February 1, 1962, three persons were killed–one in Jacksonville, Fla., in August of 1960 (*cf.* chapter 4, footnote 47), and two in connection with the SNCC voter campaign in McComb, Miss., in the fall of 1961 (see "A Detour: McComb," in chapter 6). All were Negroes. In the three and one-half years since February, 1962, 47 persons have died either directly or indirectly related to civil rights activities, including four Negro girls killed in a Birmingham church bombing; Mississippi NAACP Field Secretary Medgar Evers (sniper); William Moore during a freedom walk in Alabama (sniper); James Chaney, Andrew Goodman and Michael Schwerner (Mississippi Summer Project workers kidnapped, shot and buried by a mob); and Jimmy Lee Jackson, Rev. James Reeb, Mrs. Viola Liuzzo and Jonathan Daniels (in

connection with 1965 voting drives near Selma, Alabama—respectively shot by Alabama highway patrolmen, clubbed by three men on a Selma street, shot from a speeding car at night, and killed by daylight shotgun blast by Thomas Coleman in a Hayneville store). In addition to the 47, current Mississippi NAACP Field Secretary Charles Evers lists at least six deaths in Mississippi alone which went unrecorded (Mary Chapnick, "Civil Rights Casualties, 1954-65").

It is interesting that civil rights deaths during 1960 and 1961 did not have the catalytic effect on the movement that killings have had since then–especially the 13 listed in the last paragraph. Perhaps this has been true because the more recent deaths are seen as more direct reprisals for specific civil rights activities, and the movement has insisted on answering violence with renewed commitment ever since rejecting the federal government's plea for a "cooling off" period during the Freedom Rides. Many movement leaders have said, "We must show the racists and the world that violence cannot stop the movement. Therefore we *must* respond with greater commitment and nonviolent activity whenever we are attacked."

## CHAPTER SIX

1. Interview, March 22, 1962, and p. 6 of an untitled, unpublished paper on Albany. I am grateful to Mr. Sherrod for permission to keep the only copy of this paper in circulation.
2. "Albany," (Atlanta: Southern Regional Council, January 8, 1962), p. 20.
3. Recent efforts in the urban ghettoes of the North are building toward SCLC's full-scale campaign in Chicago, which will launch massive direct action projects beginning in the spring of 1966.
4. Sherrod, March 22, 1962.
5. Forman, March 31, 1962.
6. Moses, Curry and other insiders freely talk of the change in these terms, referring not to its rightness of wrongness, but to the way in which it was accomplished.
7. Jenkins, April 8, 1962.
8. *Ibid.* Until otherwise noted, most of the information on the Nashville seminar comes from this interview with Jenkins, verified and expanded in interviews with Baker, Curry, Forman, C. Jones, Monsonis, Moses and Reagon.
9. From seminar agenda furnished me by Jenkins.
10. James Forman was leading demonstrations in Monroe, North Carolina, Robert Moses was working rural Mississippi in an effort to stir voting interest, and Robert Zellner was attending the NSA Southern Human Relations Seminar in Madison, Wisconsin.
11. Ella Baker, March 19, 1962.
12. Diane Nash Bevel, March 28, 1962. Ella Baker and Charles Sherrod have given similar interpretations of this situation.
13. Ella Baker, March 19, 1962.

14. Conversation, October 14, 1960.
15. Personal observations plus reports from Ella Baker, Constance Curry, Leslie Dunbar, Tim Jenkins and others.
16. Dr. Martin Luther King, Jr., told me that Attorney General Kennedy had called him before the Freedom Rides about a drive to register voters. King suggested that the various groups pool their efforts, and they were called together for initial planning sessions under the auspices and finances of the Taconic Foundation. It is significant that long before this—in the summer of 1960—Robert Moses toured Mississippi supported by SCLC and SNCC to establish liaison points for future voting work. Moses was to become in 1963 the major figure in coordinating the Mississippi voter drive, and the director of the Mississippi Summer Project of 1964.
17. This information is synthesized from several sources, including Jenkins, C. Jones, Harold Fleming, Ella Baker and Constance Curry.
18. It is significant that Mrs. Bevel and Berry are both products of Nashville and the in-depth training for nonviolent direct action of James Lawson.
19. Jenkins, April 8, 1962.
20. Concomitant changes in other organizations and the movement at-large are considered briefly at the end of this chapter, and extensively in chapter 8.
21. Jenkins, April 8, 1962.
22. This discussion of Albany is set against the background of two research trips there, in March and August-September, 1962. In addition to interviewing civil rights leaders and observing all phases of the protest, I examined newspaper files, talked with local newsmen, and had several long sessions with local white ministers and officials of the Retail Merchants Association.
23. Zinn, "Albany," p.8.
24. Killed were Herbert Lee, a Negro farmer who had registered to vote, and Eli Brumfield. Neither had worked actively in the voter campaign.

    It should be obvious by now that it is painful to have to condense the barbarism displayed by segregationists in McComb and other areas into cold objective description and theory-building. Innocent blood has been spilled at dozens of points already recorded in this paper. For a more comprehensive account of the McComb violence, see Tom Hayden, "Revolution in Mississippi" (New York: Students for a Democratic Society, 1962).
25. Sherrod paper, p. 1.
26. In 1961 Albany had a population of approximately 58,000, of whom 23,000 were Negroes.
27. Sherrod paper, pp. 2-3.
28. Reagon, March 27, 1962.
29. Zinn, "Albany," p. 10.

    Albany Negroes had been stirring for some time. Despite the efforts of a relatively substantial group of middle class Negroes to erase at least the most humiliating practices of discrimination, the town was almost totally segregated in 1961 . . . even tax forms for Negroes had a special color. And the black community told the story of a $400 fine for a traffic offense levied against a Negro businessman whose independence "irritated" the city fathers.

The "We have always had good race relations here" and "Our colored folks are happy" cliches were heard everywhere in the white community in 1961. This meant, of course, that communication with Negroes was so bad that whites actually may have believed that the large proportion of local Negroes were satisfied with their "place" because they had not protested overtly, and that "good race relations" could only break down if outside agitators interfered.

Some progress had been made: white lawyers had handled cases for indigent Negroes, streets were paved in some Negro areas and the Negro football field lighted in the 1950s, and there was the recently built Negro school [I heard many times in two short visits, "Why, they have the only air-conditioned school in all southwest Georgia!"–JHL.] There was even a mayor's liaison committee to keep contact with the Negro community; ironically, it fell into disuse when it began talking about hiring Negro policemen. But any gains that did take place were to the Negro community ". . . like improving the food inside a prison," writes Zinn, for they were made within the context of a completely segregated system (condensed from Zinn, "Albany," pp. 4-6).

30. *Ibid.*, pp. 8-9.
31. Sherrod paper, pp. 9-10.
32. *Ibid.*, p. 10.
33. Quoted in Zinn, "Albany," p. 11.
34. SNCC Chairman James Forman writes about the significance of the Albany mobilization: "In Jackson . . . most of the civil rights organizations wanted to see the jails filled. Yet it took more than three months to get 300 arrested... In Albany . . . it took less than a week to mobilize more than 800 people to go to jail" ("Nonviolence Leader Tells Organization of 'Fill the Jails' Movement in Albany," *New University News* 1, 1 [January, 1962], p. 7).
35. This chronology is synthesized from the papers of Zinn and Sherrod, interviews with C. Jones, Reagon and Sherrod, and my own research notes from Albany files and field trips.
36. Quoted in Zinn, "Albany," p. 13.
37. *Ibid.*, p. 14.
38. The city commissioners had refused to negotiate with "troublemakers and law-breakers"–which included virtually the entire leadership of the Albany Movement, all of whom had been arrested at one time or another. (Research notes, March 28, 1962, and conversation with Mrs. Edwina Smith, secretary to Rev. Andrew J. Young of SCLC, July 3, 1964.)
39. Zinn, "Albany," p. 26. It is also curious that the federal government did not intervene in Albany the way it did in other Deep South areas to protect ICC-guaranteed rights. Best opinion in Atlanta civil rights circles is that Georgia Governor Vandiver's obedience to federal law in the desegregation of the University of Georgia was being rewarded by a hands-off Albany policy.
40. Quoted in Sherrod paper, p. 37.
41. Conversation, March 27, 1962. See Chapter 9 for extended voting registration figures.
42. AP dispatch, Albany, Ga., July 3, 1964.

43. Civil rights visitors to Albany in the early days of the movement exemplified each of the three types of entre: (a) Dr. King, SCLC, CORE, and the NAACP by invitation; (b) the 10 "Freedom Riders" as a response to news of a local protest; and (c) SNCC's Sherrod and Reagon on the basis of prior research.
44. This problem is so crucial that the Southern Regional Council is considering my recommendation (included in a recent self-study) that professionally trained Negroes be supported to live in protest communities for several years to help develop and sustain local leadership.
45. Forman, March 30, 1962.
46. Louis E. Lomax, "The Kennedys Move in on Dixie," *Harper's Magazine* 224, 1344 (May, 1962), p. 28.
47. *Ibid.*, p. 28.
48. "A Statement of the Research Aims and Methods of the Voter Education Project" (Atlanta: Southern Regional Council, February, 1963), pp. 1-2.
49. The major part of the grant came from the Taconic and Field Foundations and the Stern Family Fund ("First Status Report, Voter Education Project, September 20, 1962," Southern Regional Council). I am grateful to Jack Minnis, VEP Research Director, for allowing me access to this confidential report. Director of the Project during the initial two-year grant period was Wiley Branton, a Little Rock lawyer who is now Special Assistant for Civil Rights to U.S. Attorney General Nicholas Katzenbach.
50. Southern Regional Council, "A Statement of Research Aims . . .," pp. 5-6.
51. This is how the SRC-VEP report labels SNCC, and I am happy to accept their judgment as a further indication of the importance of this movement-produced organizational structure.
52. Even before the VEP was formalized, grass roots civil rights organizations were moving further into the Deep South. The NAACP for many years had conducted nominally successful voting drives in the Border and Middle South which provided organizational formats for the coming Deep South activities. More extensive analysis of these campaigns, plus those of CORE, SNCC, and SCLC, is found in Section C.
53. Southern Regional Council, "A Statement of Research Aims . . .," pp. 9-10.
54. Summer Community Organization and Political Education project.
55. Appalachian Economic and Political Activities Committee.
56. "Nonviolence Leader Tells Organization of 'Fill the Jails' Movement in Albany," p. 7.
57. Sherrod paper, p. 39. Emphasis added (except for "at last").

## PREFACE TO SECTION C

1. The reporting of much of the tabulated interview data has been reserved for this summary of the movement's first two years, since the interviews were conducted at the end of that time.
2. It is impossible to document this statement precisely because few records were kept on this kind of desegregation before a conscious sense of movement

developed in 1960. I have talked with a number of social scientists and intergroup agency personnel who are in a position to know, and all have agreed that this generalization is correct.

3. This term, as used in the socio-legal context of the desegregation process in America, includes privately-owned facilities vested with the public interest or operated to make a profit by serving the public.
4. Several sources agree on this estimate of cities affected by direct action in this period, including CORE Community Relations Director Marvin Rich, *Los Angeles Times* southern correspondent Jack Nelson (formerly of the *Atlanta Constitution*), and former Southern Regional Council Executive Director Leslie W. Dunbar. Many of the cities desegregated facilities without demonstrations at the request of federal agencies (including the Justice Department) or on the recommendation of a local biracial committee—in most cases to avoid the possibility of demonstrations. Since February 1, 1962, the number of cities desegregating facilities as a direct or latent result of the movement grew sporadically until the federal Civil Rights Law of July 2, 1964, outlawed (and, in most areas even of the Deep South, actually removed) discrimination in the accommodations challenged by direct action.
5. This is a conservative estimate based on a Southern Regional Council report, "The Student Protest Movement: A Recapitulation, September, 1961" and later clippings. The figure had passed 35,000 by fall, 1965, including the movement "record" of 2,947 in a single city (Birmingham, May, 1963). In a *Newsweek*-sponsored survey in the fall of 1963, pollster Louis Harris found that four percent of a nationwide random sample of "rank and file Negroes" (extrapolated to total population: 800,000) said they had gone to jail (Brink and Harris, *The Negro Revolution in America*, p. 203).

   In addition, at least 141 students and 58 faculty members were dismissed for sit-in activity, and one group of 236 students withdrew from Southern University to protest the dismissal of sit-in leaders (SRC, "The Student Protest Movement . . .", p. 3).
6. SRC's report (*Ibid.*) conservatively estimates that "at least 70,000 Negroes and whites . . . actively participated in some way" from February, 1960, to September, 1961, exclusive of the thousands taking part in the Freedom Rides. Estimates of my 45 informants (interviewed in February, March and April of 1962) range from 10,000 to 200,000 or more—including one Student leader who set the figure at 10 million. The median and the mode for Student estimates (N = 12) fall in the 25,000-49,000 range, and both the median and mode for Adult estimates (N = 17 – many refused to guess) are in the 75,000-99,000 range (*Forms 1* and *2*, I.3). Despite these consciously conservative estimates, there is little doubt that 100,000 or more persons actively participated during the period under study.

   The figure as of fall, 1965, easily approaches several hundred thousand participants as the Birminghams, Selmas and Mississippis continue. Brink and Harris (*The Negro Revolution in America*, p. 203) found late in 1963, for instance, that 1/3 of a nationwide sample of Negroes alone said they either had "marched in a demonstration," "picketed a store," "taken part in a sit-in," or "gone to jail." One-third (many of them overlapping, to be sure) said they had "stopped buying at a store" to support the movement. While this extrapolated figure of more than 6,000,000 is, of course, much too high, the extensive impact of direct action is shown simply in the fact that so many Negroes should want to *claim* such participation. Brink and Harris also report on a "widespread conviction [among Negroes] that the struggle will be won by their own direct action." (*Ibid*., p. 130).

7. This support is more fully documented for the early days of the movement in chapter 5. It should be sufficient here to point to the formation of two national groups, the Student Nonviolent Coordinating Committee and Students for a Democratic Society, and the conservative reports of support from "40 religious groups representing every major faith" and "at least 70 colleges outside the South" offered by the Southern Regional Council's 1961 report (pp. 15-16). *Time* reported in 1962 that a survey of 353 college campuses showed the formation of 315 "new political groups" in 1961, 169 of them conservative and 146 liberal–and that the pace in 1962 was even faster ("The Need to Speak Out," *Time*, 79, 8 [February 23, 1962], p. 74). This activation and polarization of sentiment—both integrationist and segregationist— continues to this writing with each new crisis.
8. Documentation of this point for the last decade—and the high proportion of these monies expended as a direct result of direct action—is found in "The Price We Pay," compiled by Margaret Price for the Anti-Defamation League and the Southern Regional Council (New York and Atlanta: 1964).
9. These figures represent conservative estimates from SRC and the U.S. Conference of Mayors, who report that in 1950 there were only 17 such local commissions in the nation–primarily in the large industrial centers of the North. The growth curve of such committees evidently reached a take-off point in 1964 with the impending passage of the Civil Rights Law. Late in 1963 the U.S. Conference of Mayors said that 179 American cities over 30,000 (more than half of them in the South) had established "committees to improve race relations," noting that *2/3 of these were formed since 1960*. By mid-August, 1964, the Conference said that "there is now a trend among cities to establish local community relations commissions to deal with racial matters before they get into the streets . . . At least 225 of the 589 U.S. cities with more than 30,000 population now have such agencies, and 75 percent of all cities with more than 100,000 population have local commissions" ("Cities Turning to Committees in Race Issues," Atlanta *Journal-Constitution*, August 23, 1964).
10. Florida, under Governor LeRoy Collins, who later directed the Community Relations Service established under the Civil Rights Law from July, 1964, to July, 1965.
11. The ongoing impact of direct action is further demonstrated by reports that between 930 (Southern Regional Council) and 1,412 (U.S. Justice Department) individual public protest demonstrations took place in the summer of 1963. SRC reports (release, November, 1963) that at least 115 cities in 11 southern states were affected, that measurable desegregation of facilities took place in 186 localities, that the number of southern cities with biracial

committees had grown to 102 and that there were more than 20,000 known arrests—all during the summer of 1963 (Justice Department figures quoted in Brink and Harris, *The Negro Revolution in America*, p. 46).

12. Of the 11 different Adults giving this response, only two are activists—the rest are observers outside the civil rights organizations.
13. *Forms 1* and *2*, III.2 and 3.
14. *Form 1*, III.5; *Form 2*, III.6: "How do the student leaders today differ from the leaders at the beginning of the movement?" The response was coded "more professional" if such themes as an increase in rationality and calculation and a decrease in idealism appeared. These changes as they relate to SNCC are dealt with in chapter 8.
15. *Form 2*, V.1. The theme of student revolt is covered more fully in chapter 8.
16. *Form 1*, V.1b. In a similar question (*Form 2*, V.2b), 77 percent of the Adults mentioned "financial-legal assistance," 64 percent "direct leadership" and 32 percent "publicity."
17. *Form 1*, V.1a. It is probably safe to conclude, despite the unavailability of comparative data, that student judgment of the role of the established civil rights organizations of necessity grew more favorable from 1960 to 1962. Speculation on why CORE and even the NAACP ranked higher with the Students than Martin Luther King's SCLC is reserved for chapter 8. In a similar question (*Form 2*, V.2a) the Adults ranked SCLC (86 percent), CORE (83 percent) and NAACP (68 percent) at the top.
18. *Forms 1* and *2*, VI.1b.
19. *Forms 1* and *2*, VI.1a.

## CHAPTER SEVEN

1. *The Theory of Social and Economic Organization*, p. 123.
2. *Bread and Wine*, p. 142.
3. This definition is phrased in the most general terms possible. The dimensions of the process of rationalization are more precisely specified as the theory unfolds. See chapter 1 for background on the development of this concept.
4. Stanley H. Udy, Jr., "Administrative Rationality, Social Setting, and Organizational Development," *AJS* 68, 3 (November, 1962), p. 299. For purposes of this study, we are laying aside Weber's distinction between formal and substantive rationality, which applies more to economic analysis than to the more general sociological approach being developed here. Parsons, drawing on both Pareto and Weber, offers a similar definition in *The Structure of Social Action*, p. 58.
5. *Responsible deviance* refers to violation of norms (and in some cases, values) which is (a) conscious, (b) deliberate, and (c) undertaken with an awareness of the possible consequences and a willingness to endure them (i.e., to be "responsible" for one's action).

6. This concept of *system* has developed largely as a result of attempts to order and clarify sociological phenomena with colleagues and students during the past several years. The greatest debt is to Talcott Parsons of Harvard University and to several philosophers and natural scientists with whom I have discussed the problem of order.
7. This well-known set of distinctions is most recently summarized in Parsons' interpretative essays in Parsons, *et. al.* (ed.), *Theories of Society* (New York: The Free Press, 1961).
8. Sociologists have referred to "process" and "cycle" as contrasted with "change." See, for example, Robert M. MacIver, *Social Causation* (Boston: Ginn and Co., 1942); Florian Znaniecki, *Cultural Sciences* (Urbana, Ill.: University of Illinois Press, 1952); Alvin Boskoff, "Social Change: Major Problems in the Emergence of Theoretical and Research Foci," in Howard Becker and Alvin Boskoff (ed.), *Modern Sociological Theory* (New York: Dryden Press, 1957); and Alvin Boskoff, "Functional Theory as a Source of a Theoretical Repertory and Research Tasks in the Study of Social Change," in George K. Zollschan and Walter Hirsch (ed.), *Explorations in Social Change* (New York: Macmillan, 1964).
9. Pitirim Sorokin refers to this process as "immanent change," whose nature he states in a logico-empirically derived proposition:

   > Any system which is, during its existence, a going concern, which works and acts and does not remain in a state of rest, in the literary sense of the word, cannot help changing just because it performs some activity, some work, as long as it exists (*Social and Cultural Dynamics*, revised edition [Boston: Porter Sargent, Publishers, 1957], p. 235).

   Kenneth Bock extends the point with his well-documented contention that both functionalists and evolutionists assume change to be inherent property of all social systems. ". . . In the most general philosophical terms," he concludes, "the secret of Becoming is to be found in Being." ("Evolution, Function and Change," *ASR* 28, 2 [April, 1963], p. 235).
10. Parsons first explores this process in *The Social System* (Glencoe, Ill.: The Free Press, 1951) in a brief discussion of the "trend to rationality" (p. 350). Then, in a more extended treatment, he says that ". . . there seems to be no doubt that there is an inherent factor of directionality of change in social systems, a directionality which was classically formulated by Max Weber in what he called the 'process of rationalization'" (p. 499). "Process," he writes, in referring to what we are defining as "development," ". . . cannot be simply random change from one state of the system to another. It must, through time, have direction . . ." (*Ibid.*, p. 502).

    Wilbert Moore, under the general heading of "modernization," speaks of "a number of processes associated with advanced societies which never seem to reverse direction." The major one is *specialization*, which, he agrees, should be regarded as "a kind of natural law." Such processes make up what he calls "continuous change," which represents some phases of *social development* as used here. See *Social Change* (Englewood Cliffs, N.J.: Prentice-Hall, 1963), chapter 5, especially p. 108. Moore also draws attention to the cultural level, suggesting that ". . . a rational, technical orientation to the natural or social order is an essentially irreversible intellectual revolution" ("A Reconsideration of Theories of Social Change," *ASR* 25, 6 [December, 1960], p. 813).

11. Parsonians usually refer to this "natural course" as *structural differentiation*, which may be represented as follows at the level of the total system or whole society:

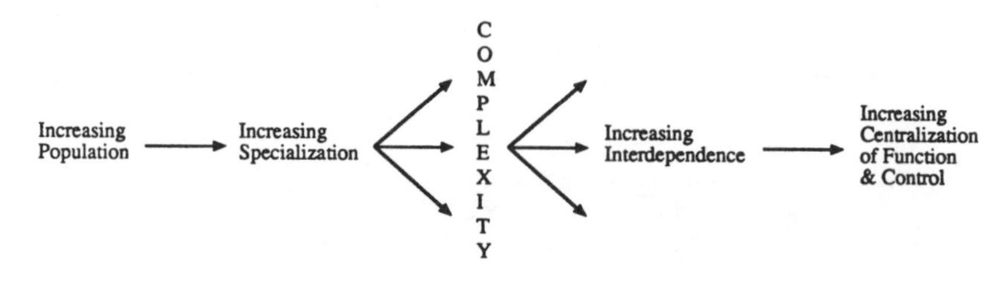


As a society grows larger, sheer size necessitates greater specialization to adequately solve the functional problems of the system's expanding population. Specialization usually takes the form of "individual role differentiation and the organization of collectivities around highly particularized functions" (Moore, *Social Change*, p. 108. See also Parsons, *The Social System*, pp. 506-508, and Parsons and Neil J. Smelser, *Economy and Society*, Glencoe, Ill.: The Free Press, 1956). Specialization creates a greater complexity of structures and functions and their interrelations. The smaller proportion of self-sufficient social units resulting from specialization of role and function necessitates a growing interdependence of existing units with the now system-wide organization of production and allocation of value, goods and services. The move to greater centralization of function and control to preserve system equilibrium is prompted by the need for formal, rational and impersonal ways of governing relations of individuals (and social units) who do not share a joint socialization in all aspects of life and therefore do not share common orientations to one another. Moore cites the "institutionalization of rationality"—especially in administrative roles—as a basic condition which must be achieved if large societies are to function effectively (*Social Change*, p. 94).

12. But the initial take-off toward rationality *in the total system* is largely a function of population increases. Emile Durkheim made the point more emphatically than any other early sociologist. His thinking about rationality (contained in his well-known conception of the universal trend from mechanical solidarity to organic solidarity) begins with growth in population and the subsequent increase in "moral destiny" of society. His position is as firmly developmental and directional as that of Weber. The division of labor, he writes, is ". . . directly proportional to the volume and density of societies, and if it progresses

in a continuous manner in the course of social development, it is because societies become regularly more dense and very generally voluminous" (Quoted from *Division of Labor* . . . in Harry Alpert, *Emile Durkheim and His Sociology* [New York: Columbia University Press, 1939], p. 91).

13. Note, for instance, that the direct action movement as explained in chapters 3-6 was not even a possibility 50 years ago—before racism had been tempered somewhat by the legal-rational processes of the courts and the detraditionalizing effects of travel and the mass media, and before quick transportation and communication were available for the spread and coordination of such a geographically widespread movement.

    The foregoing discussion of social development makes explicit a teleological orientation which I believe appears in the writings of most sociological theorists. The strong implication is that social systems evolve toward an ever more complex structure and toward democratic rationality in the interpersonal relationships of system members. My position might be called that of a "spiraling evolutionist," in which the system halts and stutters, to be sure, but continues to drive toward differentiation, rationality and universalistic-achievement orientations.

    This interpretation attempts to take into account the varied emphases of the classical typologies of societal development, especially Durkheim's mechanical-organic, Weber's traditional-charismatic-rational-legal, Redfield's folk-urban, Parsons and Sorokin's undifferentiated-differentiated, Toennies' *Gemeinschaft-Gesellschaft*, Maine's status-contract, MacIver's communal-associational, Becker's sacred-secular and others focusing on ascription-achievement variations in social organization. All of these men are basically evolutionists, for their typologies always imply movement through time, however haltingly, to the latter term in the dichotomy.

    Evolutionary thinking among sociologists (especially structural-functionalists) may be on the verge of becoming more explicit and self-conscious. Parsons' most recent discussion of social change ("Evolutionary Universals in Society," *ASR* 29, 3 [June, 1964], pp. 339-57) in effect specifies the major variables of societal evolution and discusses their development as social systems mature (i.e., increase their adaptive capacity). Chief among them is the breakdown in ascription, which is the most important developmental variable in the present study.

14. This definition is modified from Boskoff, "Functional Theory as a Source of a Theoretical Repertory and Research Tasks in the Study of Social Change," p. 216.

15. Moore deals with change in *rate* and *direction* in "The MacIver Lecture: Predicting Discontinuities in Social Change," *ASR* 29, 3 (June, 1964), pp. 331-38. Changes in *intensity* and *scope* are important variables in the theory developed later in this chapter.

16. These *modes* of change should not be confused with *sources* of change (and/or development) such as diffusion, relative deprivation, etc., which are treated later in this chapter.

17. The contribution of this theory may be viewed as analogous to the development of a personalized actuarial table—one which not only predicts the probability of *group* deaths but is able to specify the particulars of the death of *individuals within the group*, as well. The process of rationalization is the "actuarial" dimension of theory; there is no question that the Stage II "take-off" of the system *will* take place, as analyzed in this chapter. The rationalization of goals and means *will* proceed. These phenomena have their place in a theory of social development. But *when* the take-off will come, *how fast* it will proceed, *which particular substantive direction* it will take, with *what intensity* it will develop and *with what scope*—these are questions of social change. The theory is intended to throw light on both the development and change dimensions of social variation.
18. This formulation emphasizes the "antagonistic" element of William Graham Sumner's concept of "antagonistic cooperation": individuals can only gratify their own self-centered needs through combination with/and use of other persons, but the smooth facade of cooperation must be maintained for the well-being of the social system. See Sumner's *Folkways* (New York: Dover, 1959, originally published in 1906), pp. 16-18.

    There are several sources of the social competition which is always present in all social systems. The most important sources for this study are:

    (a) the nature of man, which behavioral scientists agree is basically self-centered (i.e., gratification-oriented);
    (b) a hierarchy of limited rewards available for gratification;
    (c) imperfect socialization—not every actor can be made to *want* to do what he *has* to do to perfectly fulfill his position in the stratification system; and
    (d) the virtual impossibility of absolute role specification, even in tightly integrated social systems—a phenomenon which interacts with source (c) to produce and sustain role-conflict.

    The above listing is developed from four sources: Moore, "A Reconsideration of Theories of Social Change"; Jessie Bernard, *American Community Behavior* (New York: Holt, Rinehart and Winston, 1962), especially chapters 5 and 6; Alvin L. Bertrand, "The Stress-Strain Element of Social Systems: A Micro Theory of Conflict and Change," *SF* 42, 1 (October, 1963), pp. 1-9; and observations from my intergroup relations research since 1960.
19. Some of the mechanisms which are most prominent in the systems under study in this paper are controlled stratification, goal-substitution, opportunity limitation and myths of inferiority.
20. James S. Coleman cites numerous examples of the phenomenon of "surfacing" in *Community Conflict* (Glencoe, Ill.: The Free Press, 1957).
21. Lewis A. Coser, interpreting the theories of Georg Simmel, has offered an extensive discussion of the positive functions of conflict. He would call the structures through which clarification and catharsis take place "safety-valve

institutions." See *The Functions of Social Conflict* (Glencoe, Ill.: The Free Press, 1956), especially pp. 41-48.

22. Quoted from "The Methodology of the Social Sciences" in Coser, *The Functions of Social Conflict*, p. 21. Simmel's conception of the precarious equilibrium of social systems is much like Weber's. In writing of the relationship between peace and conflict, he contends that "both in the succession and simultaneity of social life, the two are so interwoven that in every state of peace the conditions of future conflict, and in every conflict, the conditions of future peace, are formed" ("On Conflict," p. 1,324 in Parsons, *et. al.*, eds., *Theories of Society*, from Georg Simmel, *Conflict and The Web of Group Affiliations* [Glencoe, Ill.: The Free Press, 1955], pp. 107-110).
23. Further implications of the inherently conflictual and instable nature of social systems are discussed in *The Paradox of Rationalization* at the end of this chapter.
24. Discussion of the more specific dimensions of this process is reserved for the exposition of the theory, but we may note here Robin Williams' summary of the *minimum conditions* for intergroup conflict: visibility, contact and competition (*The Reduction of Intergroup Tensions*, Social Science Research Council, Bulletin 57 [New York: 1947], pp. 54-56).
25. While the theory is limited in its literal application to systems with specifically defined properties, I believe it is general enough to provide fruitful analogies with the processes of change *in* and *of* total systems. The theory as limited and specified seems to speak to a need expressed by many contemporary theorists, including Parsons:

> . . . A general theory of the processes of change of social systems is not possible in the present stage of *knowledge*. The reason is very simply that such a theory would imply complete knowledge of the laws of process of the system and this knowledge we do not possess. The theory of change in the structure of social systems must, therefore, be a theory of particular sub-processes of change *within* such systems, not of the over-all processes of change *of* systems as systems (*The Social System*, p. 486, emphasis in original).

The theory of rationalization of protest tries to explain various processes within and between subsystems in relation to the developmental processes of the total system. Parsons' 1964 essay on evolutionary universals in society (*cf.* footnote 13, this chapter) attempts to lay the groundwork for a general theory of change while fully recognizing that many of the gaps in knowledge he pointed to in 1951 still exist. Others agree that such gaps exist. See, for instance, Charles P. Loomis, *Social Systems: Essays on Their Persistence and Change* (New York: Van Nostrand, 1960), pp. 8-10; Don Martindale, *Social Life and Cultural Change* (Princeton, N.J.: Van Nostrand, 1962), p. 30; and Alvin Bertrand, "The Stress-Strain Element in Social Systems . . .", pp. 1-3.

26. Robert E. Park and Ernest W. Burgess, in their *Introduction to the Science of Sociology* ". . . identified 'social unrest' as the most elementary form of collective behavior and the condition out of which other forms develop" (Killian and Turner, *Collective Behavior*, p. 7).
27. Killian and Turner cite this distinction as *one* part of their extended definition of collective behavior (*Ibid*., p. 12), but in the light of further research, I am considering it the crucial defining attribute.
28. Killian and Turner (*Ibid*., p. 3), use these categories. They appear to be a somewhat refined version of Blumer's listing, which also includes the more specific phenomena of mobs, panics and stampedes [crowds], fashion, fads, public opinion and dancing crazes [mass behavior and the behavior of publics], and revolution and reform [social movements] ("Collective Behavior" in *Principles of Sociology*, p. 167).
29. I believe that, as with the extrapolation of intrasocietal conflict principles to intersocietal situations (condition 2), many of the general principles developed here also apply with some accuracy to pre-rational societies.
30. It should be emphasized again that the theory of rationalization was developed from a juxtaposition of field research on direct action with existing possible sociological theories and explanations. It was constructed in an attempt to place the movement in a comparative general framework for explanation and prediction.
31. By "theory" I mean a logically interrelated set of conceptions about the relationships between variables whose predictive ability can be verified through scientific testing.
32. The essence of Weber's description of this typology is found in *The Theory of Social and Economic Organization*, pp. 324-92.
33. Parsons' most recent formal discussion of this classification is found in *Theories of Society*, pp. 36-41 and 60-70.
34. Moore ("A Reconsideration of Theories of Social Change") and S.N. Eisenstadt ("Institutionalization and Change," *ASR* 29, 2 [April, 1964], pp. 235-47), take as a basic principle ". . . the argument that every . . . social system is inherently predisposed to change because of basic problems to which there is no overall continuous solution" (Eisenstadt, p. 235).
35. The chart is arranged in X/Y axis form instead of the more customary four-fold tables to facilitate readable comparisons of stages and solutions. It is hoped that, through the use of arrows and lines within this format, boundary interchanges may be clearly and conveniently articulated.
36. See *The Theory of Social and Economic Organization*, pp. 346-58.
37. That is, social control never *allows* the questioning to reach an overt level.
38. *The Theory of Social and Economic Organization*, p. 347.
39. The implications for social control are considered more fully at the end of this chapter, where the process is discussed as a whole.
40. Parsons, *The Structure of Social Action*, p. 664.
41. See "The Sociology of Charismatic Authority," pp. 245-52, in *From Max Weber*.
42. *The Theory of Social and Economic Organization*, p. 75.

43. White, conversation, May 8, 1962.
44. *The Social System*, p. 502.
45. *From Max Weber*, p. 248.
46. *The Structure of Social Action*, p. 663.
47. The essentials of Weber's discussion of the routinization of charisma are contained in *The Theory of Social and Economic Organization* (pp. 363-92) and Gerth and Mills, *From Max Weber* (pp. 262-64). The relationship between charisma and routinization is seen clearly in a contemporary American political example. President Kennedy was, without question, one of the most charismatic leaders of our day. Yet during his three years in office, he was able to implement only a few of his ideas through legislation. President Johnson, on the other hand, is one of the most effective "routinizers" in American political history, having secured legislative passage of virtually every program proposed by his predecessor, and many more of his own.
48. *From Max Weber*, p. 253.
49. Parsons discusses these processes as they relate to revolutionary movements in *The Social System*, pp. 525-29.
50. Weber discusses the distinction between substantive and formal rationality in his essay on "The Social Psychology of the World Religions" (pp. 267-301 in Gerth and Mills, *From Max Weber*, especially pp. 298-99), and shows how the "transformation of charisma in an anti-authoritarian direction" is virtually synonymous with the drive toward formal rationality (*The Theory of Social and Economic Organization*, pp. 386-90).
51. Parsons makes essentially this argument in "Evolutionary Universals in Society." See especially pp. 342-45, and p. 356, where he discusses the crucial nature of "differentiation and [the] attendant reduction in ascription."
52. This definition's emphasis on adaptive problems is consistent with Parsons' growing concern with boundary interchanges between and within systems–cultural, social, personal, biological, and external-environmental.

    Smelser's conceptualization of the "components of social action" are closely analogous to Parsons' LIGA categories: Values (L), Norms (G), Forms of Organization (I) and Situational Facilities (A). See *Theory of Collective Behavior*, chapter II.
53. "An Outline of the Social System," p. 38.
54. This is not an exhaustive listing, but rather is intended to specify the important sources of constancy and change in protest systems.
55. *Social Change in the Industrial Revolution*, p. 11.
56. The major defining characteristic of ideology is that the values contained therein have *empirical* referents, compared to "religion"–in which the values have a transcendental referent. This formulation goes beyond the standard definitions in its specification of components, especially in the area of prescription of means (see Parsons, *The Social System*, p. 349; Killian and Turner, *Collective Behavior*, pp. 332-33; Harry C. Bredemeier and Richard M. Stephenson, *The Analysis of Social Systems* [New York: Holt, Rinehart and Winston, 1962], chapter 10; and Smelser, *Theory of Collective Behavior*, p. 8).

57. Killian and Turner make this observation (*Collective Behavior*, pp. 420-21), drawing on Cantril's *The Psychology of Social Movements* (New York: John Wiley and Sons, Inc., 1941).
58. Parsons, "An Outline of the Social System," p. 40.
59. At this point in the development of rationalization theory, it is not possible to identify time priorities *within* the four stages, except in certain cases as noted. It is hoped that more sophisticated models growing from this basic framework will have that capability.
60. Conversations, May 8, 1962 (White) and May 24, 1962 (Parsons).
61. Parsons notes that "Just as a revolutionary movement can and does result in the introduction of permanent change, so also in its residue it often leaves certain unresolved strains which may be the starting points for further dynamic processes." (*The Social System*, pp. 529-30).
62. Coser, interpreting Simmel, states the case: "Outside conflict . . . mobilizes the group's defenses among which is the reaffirmation of their value system against the outside enemy." (*The Functions of Social Conflict*, p. 90). Blumer makes the same point in "Collective Behavior" (p. 215).
63. The conceptualization for this stage is abstracted from widely varying sources:

> Kenneth Boulding — "...Divergent modification...is particularly likely to take place in the early days of the development of an ideology, when it is fighting to differentiate itself sharply from the world around it." (*Conflict and Defense: A General Theory* [New York: Harper Torchbooks, 1962], p. 285).
>
> Talcott Parsons — ". . . Because of the tension involved in the break with the main society . . . the ideological preoccupations of members of ['radical'] movements are likely to be very intense. They have both the interest in convincing themselves and winning proselytes. It is crucially important for them to believe that the aspects of the established society . . . against which they are in revolt, can be defined as illegitimate in terms of a common set of beliefs and values." (*The Social System*, p. 355; see also p. 527 on the "compulsive cognitive distortion" of the host system which may play a role in divergent modification.)
>
> Charles S. Syndor — "Various abolitionists [in the early days of the movement] insisted that the Declaration of Independence was a higher authority than the Constitution and that its statements abrogated any part of the Constitution that seemed to be in conflict. In the last analysis, the abolitionists set up their own ideas of right as the supreme law of the land . . ." (*The Development of Southern Sectionalism: 1819-1948* [Baton Rouge: Louisiana State University Press, 1948], p. 247).

64. "Reciprocal exposure" refers to the fact that media allows the world to see more of the protest system and the protestors to see more of the world—which promotes the growth of both from local to cosmopolitan.
65. The emergence of a universalistic ideology has been, at most points in the history of man, a revolutionary development. It is considered as such in this scheme mainly because the two deepest characteristics of man prevail today as always: *egocentrism* and its group-life extension, *ethnocentrism*. Universalistic ideologies thus seem to arise when man literally "forgets himself," then they engender continuous conflict as man's gratification-seeking nature comes back to the surface.
66. The importance of the dimensions of *appeal* and *intensity* was suggested by Boulding, *Ibid*., pp. 281-82.
67. The appeal also is small because the limited size and resources of the system at this stage make widespread appeals impossible. The ideological content and its appeal resemble that of the ideal-typical sect.
68. Boulding notes this phenomenon when an ideology "cultivates ambitions for political dominance" and is "forced to change its character to appeal to a larger and more middle-class clientele." (*Conflict and Defense*, p. 282).
69. Boulding notes that there seems to be a negative functional relation between appeal and intensity: the greater the appeal, the less the intensity (*Ibid*., p. 281).
70. In fact, the ideology may begin to incorporate religious elements as certain parts of the charismatic ideal become deified (i.e., tied to transcendent referents). The high degree of rationalization of Christian ethics rooted in systematic theology is a good indication that the contents of beliefs systems in Stage IV of this paradigm is not restricted to purely "rational" material.
71. The structural type toward which the system's internal organization knowingly or unknowingly strives is the rational bureaucracy, whose most important characteristics are (a) a division of labor based on functional specialization, (b) a well-defined hierarchy of authority, (c) a precise system of rules governing work and work relationships, (d) emphasis on efficiency, (e) selection and promotion based on technical competence and (f) institutionalized impersonality. Recent assessments of the concept of bureaucracy generally agree on at least these six dimensions or some variant of them. The most comprehensive treatment of the concept is to be found in Peter Blau, *Bureaucracy in Modern Society* (New York: Random House, 1956), especially pp. 28-36, and *The Dynamics of Bureaucracy* (Chicago: University of Chicago Press, 1963). More systematic discussions which incorporate other models in addition to the classical Weberian scheme are found in Eugene Litwak, "Models of Bureaucracy Which Permit Conflict," *AJS* 67, 2 (September, 1961), pp. 177-84, and Richard H. Hall, "The Concept of Bureaucracy: An Empirical Assessment," *AJS* 69, 1 (July, 1963), pp. 32-40. See also the refinements and application of the concept development in Stanley H. Udy, Jr., "'Bureaucracy' and 'Rationality' in Weber's Organization Theory," *ASR* 24, 6 (December, 1959), pp. 791-95, and Udy, "Administrative Rationality, Social Setting and Organizational Development."

72. See Dominant Leadership and Membership Roles below (I.2.b and c).
73. For a more comprehensive and more general treatment of the changing bases of recruitment in innovative systems, see Everett M. Rogers, *Diffusion of Innovations* (New York: The Free Press, 1962), especially chapter XI.
74. A certain number of *degrees of freedom* in the structural sense seems to be a predicator of protest-joining. Most important is that the protestors are *economically independent of the enforcers of Traditional Control.* This concept is elaborated in chapter 8 as applied to the direct action movement.

    Although this study does not focus on membership characteristics *per se*, it is well to note some of the personality dimensions which may predispose recruits at this stage. Killian and Turner find five common traits in their survey of the literature: sense of prestige from innovative isolation, desire for martyrdom, authoritarianism, sense of personal inadequacy, and a tendency toward black-and-white thinking (*Collective Behavior*, pp. 440-41). From my own research and involvement, I suggest that relative economic independence, lack of personal fulfillment and the desire for such fulfillment (usually unconscious) are common to all recruits at the charismatic stage.
75. The goals still may be revolutionary, but a wide enough segment of the class-racial-geographical spectrum is participating (ministers and college professors, for instance) to give the cause a certain acceptance and respectability.
76. The following analysis of leadership role differentiation derives several concepts from Crane Brinton, *The Tasks of Economic History, Supplement VIII* (New York: New York University Press, 1948, quoted in Killian and Turner, *Collective Behavior*, p. 474); Rex Hopper, "The Revolutionary Process: A Frame of Reference for the Study of Revolutionary Movements," *SF* 8, 3 (March 1950), pp. 270-79; and C.W. King, *Social Movement in the United States* (pp. 71-77). See also John P. Roche and Stephen Sachs, "The Bureaucrat and the Enthusiast: An Exploration of the Leadership of Social Movements," *Western Political Science Quarterly* 8, 2 (June, 1955), pp. 248-61.
77. Killian and Turner succinctly place the charismatic leader in the dynamic social context of protest: "The symbol that a leader represents is partly a product of his own personal characteristics, partly a creation of the promoters of the movement, and largely a projection by the followers" (*Collective Behavior*, p. 472).
78. A pressing *external* problem here is the need to furnish ideological explanations for the evermore inquisitive media.
79. "Social control" is used in the broad sense here, referring to the numerous processes such as recruitment, socialization, differentiation, allocation and motivation-to-conformity which combine to produce social cohesion. The categories at this level in the paradigm thus refer to the major object to which integrative appeals are directed.
80. See Parsons, *The Social System*, pp. 521-22.
81. In protest systems, the turn toward authoritarian control usually results from the growing need for *centrally conceived and administered strategy* as the opposition gets smarter. Weber discusses this phenomenon as the period of

"revolutionary dictatorship," with reference to the Gracchi of Rome, the *Capitani del poplo* in the Italian city states, Cromwell in England, and Robespierre and the "Committee of Public Safety" in France (*The Theory of Social and Economic Organization*, pp. 387-89). Parsons points to the legitimizing of coercion in twentieth-century Russian communism as a current manifestation of this principle (*The Social System*, p. 528).

82. A basic paradox of rationalization is illustrated here, as needs for informal personal contact develop in response to the increasingly depersonalized role definitions of the rationalizing system.
83. The major theoretical problem on which this section focuses has been called "succession of goals." The process is treated more fully at the end of this chapter.
84. Sheldon Messinger, "Organizational Transformation: A Case Study of a Declining Social Movement," p. 10. The shift to emphasis on organizational goals may be taken as one measure of emergence of the system as a deviant subculture (*cf.* "success-centrism" as the dominant integrative mechanism in Stage III).
85. Smelser (*Theory of Collective Behavior*, p. 270) defines a "norm-oriented movement" in this way. His distinction between "norm-oriented movements" and "value-oriented movements" (chapters IX and X) is applied at this problem-level to the changes *within* a protest system as it matures.
86. Crane Brinton, *The Anatomy of Revolution* (New York: Vintage Books, 1958), pp. 95-96/
87. Smelser further emphasizes the depth and scope of the "value-oriented" challenge, saying that it ". . . necessarily involves all the components of action; that is, it envisions a reconstitution of values, a redefinition of norms, a reorganization of the motivation of individuals, and a redefinition of situational facilities" (*Theory of Collective Behavior*, p. 313).
88. See Killian and Turner, *Collective Behavior*, p. 481.
89. The emphasis here is on mechanisms and facilities for achievement of external goals, with the assumption that their status at any given time largely determines the efficacy and stability of internal goal-achievement.
90. Adaptive problems are considered the dynamic pivotal point of this analysis for several reasons. First, boundary interchanges—the major analytical unit of change theory—by definition are adaptive processes. Second, changes in economic-technological processes are viewed as the "core" of general social change (see Parsons, *The Social System*, pp. 519-20), for they drastically alter the state of integration and adaptation within and between the host system and subsystems. Further, the effects of economic-technological change on the rest of the system are first articulated at the level of the adaptive imperative. Finally, the total process of societal development may be viewed as a drive toward *increasing the adaptive capacity* of the system (see Parsons, "Evolutionary Universals in Society," p. 339).

    It also should be reiterated that the present analysis focuses on the *internal* effects of rationalizing protest. Thus, the functions of the total system are only important for us as they relate to internal growth and differentiation.

91. External organizational structure should be seen as a complementary process with the development of internal structure (problem I.1, stages I-IV).
92. "A movement needs enemies," write Killian and Turner, ". . . to marshal the determination of its members to overcome the obstacles" (*Collective Behavior*, p. 337). Counter-movements commonly take the form of increasing mobilization of police, military or political power—or mass sentiment through the media–as well as the classical "counter-revolution." The interaction with counter-systems is, from Stage III on, the most important source of change in the protest system. Going back a step further, ". . . the increasing success or failure of the initial movement [is] the most important determinant of changes in the . . . counter-movement" (*Ibid.*, p. 383).
93. Note that solutions to this priority problem are essentially the same as those at level L.2.a (bases of leadership and membership recruitment) since they are interrelated dimensions of the same basic problem.
94. Commenting on the importance of the media in expanding the relevance of a protest movement, C.W. King writes, ". . . mass communication is an instrument capable of revealing and building a far-flung camaraderie between unacquainted individuals seeking surcease from their discontent" (*Social Movements in the United States*, p. 74).
95. This rate-stability often manifests itself as an intersystemic agreement on a timetable for future change.
96. If formal organizations exist at this stage, their adaptive problems with one another are usually resolved through an informal and tacitly agreed-upon division of labor, since no transcendent mediating structure exists.
97. Adaptive mechanisms to external systems are the *point of first contact* between systems and thus the growing edge of development and change. This set of categories describes the changing modes of relationship between protest system and external systems which contribute to the diffusion, absorption and rationalization of innovations at all system levels involved. It should be reiterated that our particular focus here is rationalization *within the protest system*, with rationalization at other levels a necessarily peripheral concern. See Rogers, *Diffusion of Innovations*, and Elihu Katz, Martin L. Levin, and Herbert Hamilton, "Traditions of Research on the Diffusion of Innovations," *ASR* 28, 2 (April, 1963), pp. 237-52.
98. For a more comprehensive treatment of this system of eight adaptive modes outlined here, see Laue, "The Movement, Negro Challenge to The Myth." A similar framework is employed less explicitly in Lewis M. Killian and Charles M. Grigg, *Racial Crisis in America* (Englewood Cliffs, N.J.: Prentice-Hall, 1964).
99. See *Ibid.*; Coleman, *Community Conflict*; and Brinton, *The Anatomy of Revolution* (especially pp. 82-83 and 270-72).
100. It should be reiterated that the categorical sequence here is intended to show the *dominant* mode of adaptation at each stage–not the only mode.
101. The LIGA sequence represents the ". . . order of significance from the point of view of cybernetic control of action processes in the system" (Parsons, "An Outline of the Social System," p. 38).

102. Charles P. Loomis prefers to call this phenomenon "systemic linkage." In a recent synthesis of his theories of social structure and change, he emphasizes the causal importance of systemic linkage (i.e., boundary interchanges, intra- and intersystemic communication, etc.) for social change. See "Social Change and Social Systems," pp. 185-215 in Edward Tiryakian (ed.), *Sociological Theory, Values and Sociocultural Change* (New York: The Free Press of Glencoe, 1963), especially pp. 199-206.
103. Briefly summarized, the reasons for this inevitable drive toward universalism-rationalism in protest systems are: (1) as conflict proceeds, all parties develop more sophisticated means as they discard old techniques which have been outsmarted by the opposition; (2) close and prolonged contact in the game of intergroup conflict brings antagonists to see the dedication and skills of one another and thereby realize the impossibility of total victory for one side; and therefore (3) the antagonists' own best interests lead them to look for *common goals*—the beginning point of the mutuality which leads to democratic inclusivism and rationality.
104. Amitai Etzioni, *Modern Organizations* (Englewood Cliffs, N.J.: Prentice-Hall, 1964), p. 56.
105. *Ibid*., p. 55. Weber discusses the problem of succession mainly in terms of replacing the "personal charismatic leader." He suggests six modes of seeking a replacement, two of which (basing selection on defined criteria of leadership or shamanistic transferral of charisma) are evident throughout this study. See Weber's *The Theory of Social and Economic Organization*, pp. 363-66.
106. "Organizational Transformation: A Case Study of a Declining Social Movement," p. 10 (italics in original). For a more comprehensive treatment of this phenomenon, see Etzioni, *Modern Organizations*, chapter 2, and Blau, *The Dynamics of Bureaucracy*, pp. 237-46.
107. "Revolution" does *not*, as in popular usages, imply the necessity of violent means–although prolonged conflict over values often leads to violence.
108. Killian and Turner, *Collective Behavior*, p. 504.
109. *Ibid*., pp. 504-05. Broom and Selznick note that, in the maturing labor movement in Germany in 1953, ". . . the protests soon shifted from the economic to the political level" (*Introduction to Sociology*, p. 588). See also Heberle, "Observations on the Sociology of Social Movements," p. 350.
110. The concept is not formally defined by its originator, Samuel Stouffer, although he uses it extensively in *The American Soldier* (Princeton, N.J.: Princeton University Press, 1949). Robert Merton, too, uses relative deprivation as an intervening variable without formally defining it (see *Social Theory and Social Structure* [Glencoe, Ill.: The Free Press, 1957], especially pp. 227-36).
111. Moore elaborates this suggestive listing to include economic imperialism, wars, religious imperialism, mass and individual migration, trade, tourism, transported labor, transfers of knowledge and diplomacy (*Social Change*, p. 86).

112. See L.P. Edwards, *The Natural History of Revolutions* (Chicago: University of Chicago Press, 1927).
113. Meadows, "Sequence in Revolution," p. 708.
114. Blumer, "Collective Behavior," p. 203.
115. See Walt W. Rostow, *The Stages of Economic Growth* (Cambridge, England: University Press, 1960), chapter 3.
116. Smelser, *Social Change in the Industrial Revolution*, p. 28, and *Theory of Collective Behavior*, pp. 15-18.
117. David Willer and George K. Zollschan, "Prolegomenon to a Theory of Revolutions," in Zollschan and Hirsch, *Explorations in Social Change*, pp. 125-51.
118. James C. Davies, "Toward a Theory of Revolution," *ASR* 27, 1 (February, 1962), p. 5. Davies' theory is based on his examination of Dorr's Rebellion, the Russian Revolution and the Egyptian Revolution of the mid-twentieth century.
119. Brinton, *The Anatomy of Revolution*, pp. 264-66; Moore, "A Reconsideration of Theories of Social Change," pp. 514-16; Parsons, *The Social System*, pp. 521-23; Smelser, *Social Change in the Industrial Revolution*, p. 15; and A.F.C. Wallace, "Revitalization Movements," *American Anthropologist* 58, 3 (April, 1956), pp. 264-81.
120. Coser, *The Functions of Social Conflict*, pp. 41-48, 157.
121. Development of an innovative elite at this stage is discussed in Coleman, *Community Conflict*, pp. 10-12; Laue, "The Movement, Negro Challenge to The Myth," p. 12; Vladimer Nahirny, "Some Observations on Ideological Groups," *AJS* 67, 4 (January, 1962), pp. 397-405; and Snell Putney and Gladys J. Putney, "Radical Innovations and Prestige," *ASR* 27, 4 (August, 1962), pp. 548-51.

    My conceptualization of this problem is greatly indebted to conversations with Winston White, especially in April and May 1962.
122. Killian and Turner, *Collective Behavior*, p. 447. Conversely, such an either/or situation could strengthen the protest system by eliciting a firm commitment from previously marginal members.
123. Brinton cites additional reasons for the "terror" period of revolutions which have important analogies with protests systems. They include the newness of the machinery of the newly emerged governmental systems, the "acute economic crisis" which follows upheaval in the social system, and the ascendancy of the shrewdest leaders naturally selected "almost in a Darwinian sense" (*The Anatomy of Revolution*, pp. 208-14).
124. Blau's empirical assessment of "bureaucratic conditions which generate . . . favorable attitudes toward change" is instructive here. See *The Dynamics of Bureaucracy*, pp. 246-49.
125. Thomas O'Dea's "Sociological Dilemmas: Five Paradoxes of Institutionalization" (pp. 71-89 in *Sociological Theory, Values and Sociocultural Change*) deals with some complementary problems.
126. Extrapolating to the total system, it may be argued that all of social life is ultimately non-rationalizable. Essentially *insoluble tensions* are inherent in the

nature of men's life in groups. One finds this +/- juxtaposition at every turn in sociological theory. Hegel and Marx get credit for making this clear to the modern mind, but nearly every religion has known that existence (including man's life in social systems) is an eternal struggle between good and evil. Weber's opposition of charisma and bureaucracy is in this tradition. The challenge/response of Toynbee and the sensate/ideational/idealistic fluctuations of Sorokin were early twentieth-century expressions of this principle. Now Parsons and Eisenstadt, two modern sociologists of change, have formulated the principle to aid in the development of general theory:

> Obviously one fundamental feature of . . . institutionalization . . . is the introduction of a continual system of factors of change into the social system (Parsons, *The Social System*, p. 505).

> Our major point is that the institutionalization of any social system—be it political, economic or a system of social stratification or of any collectivity or role—creates in its wake the possibilities for change (Eisenstadt, "Institutionalization and Change," p. 235).

# CHAPTER EIGHT

1. Silone, *Bread and Wine*, p. 142.
2. See chapter 7, pp. 212-13.
3. It is hoped that the theory may stimulate further research to determine its applicability and validity for subsystems and external systems. Space limitations prevent the spelling-out of these implications in the present study.
4. Several psychologists and psychoanalysts have explored the personality dimensions involved. Among published works are four articles by Jacob R. Fishman and Fredric Solomon: "Youth and Social Action, I: Perspectives on the Student Sit-In Movement," *American Journal of Orthopsychiatry* 33, 5 (October, 1963), pp. 872-82; ". . . II: Action and Identity Formation in the First 'Student Sit-In Demonstration,'" presented at the annual meeting of the American Psychiatric Association, May 11, 1962, Toronto, Canada; ". . . III: Nonviolence in the South," presented at the Gandhi Memorial Conference on Youth, Nonviolence and Social Change, November, 1963, Washington, D.C.; and "The Psychological Meaning of Nonviolence in Student Civil Rights Activities," *Psychiatry* 27, 2 (May, 1964), pp. 91-99.
5. Recorded in a pre-demonstration mass meeting at Spelman College, Atlanta, October 18, 1960.
6. One of many examples I met as a researcher (i.e., as a professional discusser and analyst) was a response from SNCC executive Forman when I asked him whether he viewed nonviolence as a situational tactic or as a total way-of-life:

   > Well man, to me this is totally academic at this point because some of the immediate objectives are to change the patterns of segregation

and discrimination. So long as you *do something*, this doesn't make any difference to me.

7. Henry Thomas, D.C. representative to SNCC, August 9, 1960.
8. Words by Candie Anderson Carawan, February, 1960; taught to me by Angeline Butler, Nashville, June, 1960.
9. "The Freedom Trilogy" had become popular throughout the movement by 1961, and Odetta soon revived it for the folk record audience.
10. Taught to me by high school students in the Albany Movement, March, 1962.
11. An old labor song, with new verses by Freedom Rider Jesse Hill written in the Hinds County Jail, and taught to me by members of the Jackson Nonviolent Movement, March 23, 1962. This song remains one of the most popular calls to commitment in many Deep South areas.
12. It will be difficult to keep the data strictly within stages, for in sociohistorical reality there is considerable overlapping. Frequent reference to the master fold-out chart at the end of the book may add clarity to the applied analysis and help overcome the inherent difficulties involved in dealing with general theory at this level of componential specificity.
13. Dunbar, interview, March 9, 1962; and Fleming, interview, April 5, 1962.
14. *The Theory of Social and Economic Organization*, p. 343.
15. The term was coined by W.E.B. DuBois in founding the NAACP for the small percentage of Negroes who had achieved education and social position–and who, it was argued, therefore deserved access to the vices and virtues available to middle class white society. See Langston Hughes, *Fight for Freedom: The Story of the NAACP* (New York: Norton, 1962).
16. For elaboration of this point, see Lomax, *The Negro Revolt*, especially Part II; and Lerone Bennett, *The Negro Mood* (Chicago: Johnson Publishing Co., 1964).
17. James R. Robinson, "Executive Secretary's Report of the 1960 Convention, St. Louis, Mo., June 29 to July 3, 1960," p. 1.
18. My survey of the pre-1960 literature of CORE and the NAACP is not systematic or extensive. It is complemented by my observation that leaders of these groups never were concerned about mechanisms for *maintaining* ideological commitment—only mechanisms for *implementing* the commitment in society.
19. See James H. Laue, "The Changing Character of the Negro Protest," *The Annals of the American Academy of Political and Social Science* 357 (January, 1965), pp. 119-26.
20. In CORE, for instance, a full-time staff of only seven persons ran the national organization before the sit-ins tripled the staff in one year. Although staff roles were formally differentiated (Executive Director, Field Director, Community Relations Director, Editor of Newsletter Field Secretaries and Office Secretary), I know from participant observation that there was much overlapping of functions in actual role performance.

21. From CORE records, conversations with national staff, observations in CORE's national office, 1960, and attendance at CORE national convention, June 29–July 3, 1960.
22. It should be emphasized that this phase of the analysis does *not* refer to the degree of rationality of specific civil rights organizations, but rather to the pre-1960 civil rights effort (it cannot yet be called a "movement") as a whole. One could make a strong argument for a high degree of rationality *within the NAACP* in relation to a specific program—school desegregation—which had involved considerable legal work and long-range planning since the mid-1930s.
23. An example is James T. McCain, who was "discovered" by CORE for a national job while leading local desegregation campaigns in South Carolina.
24. Carl Braden began work with the Southern Conference Educational Fund in the late 1950s–a group for whom his wife had worked for several years. And many board and staff members came to SCEF via old friendships as New Dealers: James Dombrowski, Aubrey Williams, Ella Baker and Clifford Durr, for example.
25. See Hughes, *Fight for Freedom*.
26. See especially, *This is CORE, Cracking the Color Line*, and issues of the *CORElator* (bi-monthly newsletter), all published by the Congress of Racial Equality, New York.
27. "One of the significant features of race relations in the past five years," wrote Killian and Smith in 1960 before the movement began, "has been the emergence of new patterns of Negro leadership in southern communities . . . The desegregation decisions of the U.S. Supreme Court, even without extensive implementation, redefined [the] power situation" (Killian and Smith, "Negro Protest Leaders in a Southern Community," p. 253).
28. Until about 1963, NAACP local chapters were not geared primarily for action at all, but rather served as institutionalized fund-raising mechanisms to support the national staff professionals. Reports of chapter activities in the national magazine, *The Crisis*, during the late 1950s and early 1960s focused on fund-raising drives and pictures of new "Life Members"—mostly elderly women who had contributed at least $500 in their lifetimes.
29. The reading of any issue of *The Crisis* before 1960 substantiates this point.
30. "This is the NAACP," New York: April, 1960. The basic goals have been the same since the NAACP was founded in 1909.
31. See CORE's *Cracking the Color Line*.
32. See p. 90. The 1954 decision ranked third with both Student (38 percent mentioned it) and Adult (30 percent) samples when they were asked, "What do you think were the most important factors in the start and rapid spread of the sit-ins?"
33. Claude Sitton, "Integration: Pace Slows in the South," *New York Times*, May 22, 1960. See also *School Desegregation: The First Six Years* (Atlanta: Southern Regional Council, 1960) and issues of the *Southern School News*, published by the Southern Education Reporting Service, Nashville.
34. NBC Television News, August, 1964.

35. The Stage II categories of the theory provide a framework in which this particular time period may be analyzed, but they also are intended to apply to charismatic periods in this and other movements. Each new upsurge of commitment and high protest motivation in any movement may be viewed as a new level of charismatic breakthrough.
36. Weber, The Sociology of Charismatic Authority" (pp. 245-52 in Gerth and Mills, *From Max Weber*), p. 249.
37. *Cf.* chapter 4.
38. *The Student Voice* 1, 1 (June, 1960), p. 1.
39. Several "unity meetings" involving the NAACP, CORE, SCLC, and SNCC in the summer of 1960 produced statements which defensively made this point. And as late as 1963, the NAACP Youth Council marched on the National Board to demand the right to engage in more direct action programs (Art Sears and Larry Still, "Demand for More Negro Action, Funds, Pushed Groups Closer Together," *Jet* 24, 13, July 18, 1963, p. 20). NAACP Executive Secretary Roy Wilkins "put his body on the line" and was arrested for picketing in Mississippi in 1963.
40. In answer to the open-ended question, "Has your participation in the movement changed your outlook on life?" (*Form 2*, VII.7). No other response category was mentioned by more than three respondents.
41. SNCC Field Secretary, interview, March 24, 1962 (emphasis added).
42. Reported by Constance Curry in a speech to Academic Freedom Conference at Duke University, February, 1962.
43. Quoted in Helen Fuller, "The 'Sit-In' Protest," reprinted from *The New Republic* (April 25 and May 2, 1960) and distributed by the Race Relations Department, Fisk University, Nashville.
44. "Why I Took Part in a Sit-In," *Intercollegian* 77, 12 (October, 1960), p. 4.
45. Quoted in Howard Zinn, *SNCC: The New Abolitionists* (Boston: The Beacon Press, 1964), p. 15.
46. Conversation, Atlanta, October 18, 1960.
47. New York, July 11, 1960, p. 2. My notes from numerous SNCC and CORE meetings in 1960 show a good deal of latent instability manifested in interpersonal and interorganizational antagonisms.
48. The NAACP, for instance, reluctantly approved support of a nationwide boycott against Woolworth's on March 17, 1960—over a month after it had been called for by CORE (AP story, March 18, 1960).
49. Dr. King's statement at the Raleigh Conference spoke of jail as a "badge of honor"; the first issue of *The Student Voice* featured front-cover pictures of bandaged demonstrators; all SNCC chairmen have been arrested a number of times, and Charles McDew (chairman from fall 1961 to summer 1963) had been arrested 26 times in the first two years of the movement.
50. One of numerous examples in my files from the early days of the sit-ins was formulated by Nashville students in February and March of 1960. The "12 Commandments of Nonviolence" included:

    DO show yourself friendly on the counter at all times.

DO sit straight and always face the counter.
DON'T strike back, or curse back if attacked.
DON'T laugh out.
DON'T hold conversations.
DON'T block entrances.

51. Conversations with all of them, summer, 1960.
52. Extensive documentation of this point is contained in my research files and in Zinn, *SNCC: The New Abolitionists*.
53. Cordell Reagon, Diane Nash Bevel, and Tom and Sandra Hayden, all in interviews, March, 1962.
54. *Forms 1* and 2, III.1. Next highest for both Students (46 percent) and Adults (44 percent) was CORE Director James Farmer, who had, less than a year before the interviews, spent two months in Mississippi jails as a Freedom Rider.
55. Compiled from interviews with sit-inners from Alabama, Arkansas, D.C., Florida, Georgia, Kentucky, Louisiana, North Carolina and South Carolina, July and August, 1960. See the Appendix for more details on these exploratory interviews.
56. Ruth Searles and J. Allen Williams, Jr., "Negro College Students' Participation in Sit-Ins," *SF* 40, 3 (March, 1962), pp. 217, 218.
57. *Cf.* footnote 55 above. The other respondent talked of Negro unity, a theme discussed under IV.G.1b in chapter 9.
58. Fuller, "The 'Sit-In' Protest" (no page numbers in reprint).
59. Reported to me by Rev. Wyatt T. Walker, August 9, 1960.
60. Figures compiled from releases of CORE, SRC and my own files.
61. Students threatened demonstrations, but a biracial committee settled the issue before sit-ins could take place.
62. Director of Information, Southern Regional Council, interview, March 20, 1962.
63. I am grateful to Ella Baker, who first suggested the movement/program interpretation.
64. Attendance observations from research notes, October 14-16, 1960; topics from conference program, "Nonviolence and the Achievement of Desegregation."
65. Research notes, Atlanta, April 27-29, 1962.
66. *Forms 1* and 2, II.4. These were the highest response categories for each group.
67. He was referring to the long established latent competition in philosophies, strategies and number of successes between such groups as the NAACP, CORE and SCLC.
68. For a more extensive treatment of the implications of the "research role," see James H. Laue, "The Changing Character of the Negro Protest," especially pp. 123-24, and Laue and Leon M. McCorkle, Jr., "The Association of Southern Women for the Prevention of Lynching: A Commentary on the Role of the 'Moderate.'"

69. I heard SNCC leader Marion Barry condemn the "indifference of the NAACP to the sit-ins" one month after he had participated in the organizational unity meeting in New York (research notes, August 6, 1960).
70. Field report by James T. McCain, supplied through the courtesy of the national CORE office.
71. New York: NAACP, 1960 (emphasis added). Ezell Blair told me later that NAACP officers continually boasted about the "inspiration" Blair and his three Greensboro friends had received from the Oklahoma City sit-ins. "I had never even *heard* of those sit-ins," he complained (conversation, August 11, 1960).
72. Rev. James M. Lawson, Jr., points this out in relation to the organizational problems that arose at the Atlanta SNCC conference in 1960 (conversation, October 14, 1960). Ella Baker had written earlier that ". . . many schools and communities . . . have not provided adequate experience for young Negroes to assume initiative and think and act independently" (*Southern Patriot* 18, 5 [May, 1960], p. 3.
73. From my research files. All three of these documents deal in great detail with SNCC's "autonomy" and its relation to "the movement," "local autonomous groups," "affiliates" and "associates" (other civil rights organizations and fund-raising channels).
74. Conversation with Julian Bond, SNCC office manager, March 5, 1962.
75. Herman Long, Director, Department of Race Relations, Fisk University, interview, February 26, 1962.
76. Howard Zinn suggested this interpretation to me in 1962 (interview, March 14), and has elaborated it in *SNCC: The New Abolitionists*.
77. From my research files and general knowledge of the desegregation process since 1960; Fleming quote from interview, April 5, 1962. The NAACP also experienced leadership changes at local levels in an attempt to keep up with the militant appeal of direct action. In Atlanta, for instance, former student sit-inner James Gibson became Executive Secretary—an appointment which would not have been a remote possibility before 1960.
78. Brooks noted in addition that "canvassing, approaching and contacting" had not been done "systematically" in SNCC until the fall, 1961, takeover. "They did it all in mass meetings before," he said, "but that won't work anymore."
79. From my observations at all conference sessions (October 14-16, 1960), I consider this a reasonable estimate.
80. Lester Carr, instructor in Psychology, Fisk University, and a researcher on the movement (interview, February 25, 1962).
81. *Forms 1* and *2*, I.4.
82. "School Year Ends, But Sit-Ins Continue," *Southern Patriot* 18, 6 (June, 1960), p. 4.
83. Speech to Academic Freedom Conference, Duke University, February, 1962.
84. Twenty-seven percent of the Students and 52 percent of the Adults–*Forms 1* and *2*, VI.1.
85. *Forms 1* and *2*, VI.3.
86. Field Secretary and Director, Mississippi Voting Project (interview, April 8, 1962).

87. "Student Protest Movement Taking Permanent Form," *Southern Patriot* 18, 8 (October, 1960), p. 1.
88. This figure is a composite estimate from Jack Nelson (*Los Angeles Times* southern correspondent, formerly of the *Atlanta Constitution*), W. Haywood Burns (author of *Voices of Negro Protest in America*), and my file of newspaper clippings and agency releases.
89. Cordell Reagon first suggested this point to me, March 27, 1962.
90. I am indebted to Julian Bond of the SNCC office for supplying me with a complete set of releases for that period. The other 11 mailings dealt with reports of demonstrations, announcements of conferences, biographies of SNCC workers, publicity for records, etc. There were many other communiques to various subsystems during this period, including appeals, a formal newsletter, etc.
91. "School Year Ends, But Sit-Ins Continue," *Southern Patriot*, p. 4; and "Students Prefer Jail-Ins to Bail-Outs," *Southern Patriot* 19, 3 (March, 1961), p. 1. Harold Fleming added, "We were bound to have a change in the movement because of the nature of the press in America . . . The same thing would happen if we had a lynching every day.
92. The Student response rate for "Summer, 1961" undoubtedly would have been even higher if I had known about the takeover earlier in the interview period and the Students *knew* I knew. Then they would have felt freer to talk with me about this fairly sensitive subject.
93. Both forms, I.6. Interorganizational conflict was mentioned by 38 percent of the Students (only "lack of mass militant Negro support" was named more often), and 40 percent of the Adults (the highest response category along with "problems of leadership recruitment and training").
94. Both forms, I.8. Eighty-five percent of the Students and 67 percent of the Adults named at least one of the following:

    a. more cooperation (less conflict) among civil rights groups.
    b. merger of civil rights groups.
    c. develop a "master plan" or promote better structuring for cooperative group efforts.

95. This quote and other material are adapted from Laue's "The Changing Character of the Negro Protest." The NAACP's current dues-paying membership is more than 400,000 in 1,600 chapters throughout the United States.
96. Interview, March 16, 1962. This is not true; in most cases, NAACP chapters and other established groups were caught unaware by the first sit-ins in their communities.
97. "Races: Confused Crusade," in *Time* 79, 2 (January 12, 1962), p. 15.
98. Where not specifically footnoted, data and interpretation on CORE (as well as SCLC and SNCC below) come from records of my participation in/and observation of these groups since 1960, and my friendships with national and local leaders.

99. Condensed from the masthead of the *COREIator* and *This is CORE*, both published by CORE, New York City. Much of the material in this section comes from my research files of CORE literature, personal correspondence and participant observation in three national (and numerous local) CORE meetings.
100. A less precise but nevertheless enlightening index of growth and rationalization of CORE was the national CORE telephone bill for December, 1961 and January, 1962, which I happened to see in Jackson in March of 1962. It amounted to more than $5,800—roughly half of the *total* CORE budget of only five years earlier.
101. Pamphlet announcing "CORE Interracial Training Institute, August 14–September 5, 1960: Nonviolence in Theory *and* in Action."
102. I am indebted to Dorothy Miller Zellner, who kept excellent notes on group dynamics for me after I left the Institute on August 28. Emphasis added in portions below.
103. CORE was willing to hold the 1961 national council meeting in a relatively hard-to-reach location to continue to establish itself in the South by strengthening local chapters which had previously shown promise. The other civil rights groups, too, knew that preparing for a national meeting to be held locally is an excellent local recruiting device.
104. Bernard Lafayette and James Bevel, Nashville protest veterans, stayed in Jackson after the Freedom Rides in June 1961, to organize the Jackson Nonviolent Movement. Although CORE Field Secretary Richard Haley urged them to leave because of the tension, he respected their decision to stay and ". . . kept our office going, paid for the telephone and gave us pocket money" (LaFayette, SNCC Field Secretary, interview, February 27, 1962).
105. Marvin Rich, "The Congress of Racial Equality and Its Strategy," *The Annals* . . . 357 (January, 1965), p. 115.
106. *Form 1*, V.1a, and *Form 2*, V.2a. And when the Students were asked to discuss whether there had been ". . . times when organizations have actually held back progress in the movement," CORE was named *fewer* times than any other established civil rights group (*Form 1*, V.3):

| *Organization* | *Students Naming* |
|---|---|
| CORE | 4 (31%) |
| SCLC | 6 (46%) |
| NAACP | 8 (62%) |

107. Seventy-seven percent of the Students and 88 percent of the Adults named King when asked to freely list ". . . the most important leaders in the movement today," compared to 46 percent and 44 percent for CORE's James Farmer (both forms, III.1).
108. Condensed from masthead of the *SCLC Newsletter*.
109. Circulation figures reported in *SCLC Newsletter* VII, 5 (February 1964), p. 3.

110. I attended such a meeting led by Rev. Wyatt Walker in Hartford, Conn., October 13, 1961, and he told me that what I observed was the pattern with every SCLC local and regional initiate.
111. *Jet* magazine reported on King's nationwide post-Birmingham tours in several summer 1963 editions. The June 13 issue (Vol. 24, 8, pp. 54-60) told in a seven-page feature, "50,000 Jam L.A. Ball Park for Biggest Rights Rally" and "Paul Newman Pledges Day's Pay; May Join King." The "suffering appeal" was uppermost, as *Jet* reported, "The masses of people assembled in Wrigley field . . . clutched in their hands small pamphlets with a snarling police dog on the cover. In many of their minds were pictures of other snarling dogs, gnawing viciously at Negroes, or high-velocity fire hoses smashing black men and women against buildings . . ." Later issues headlined "SCLC collects $145,000 in Six-City, Cross-Country Tour" and "Church and Traffic Jammed as Cleveland Hails King"—and pictured Wyatt Walker smilingly holding a money bag while gospel singer Mahalia Jackson shoveled in ". . . $38,245.70 raised at an all-star benefit show she arranged in Chicago."
112. When asked in a 1964 *New York Times* survey, "Which one [of a list of 13 Negro leaders] do you think is doing best for Negroes?" 73 percent named King, 22 percent Wilkins, 21 percent Adam Clayton Powell and eight percent Farmer (Layhmond Robinson, "N.Y. Negroes Blame Their Plight on Whites," August 3, 1964). In organizational terms, 54 percent of my Student sample and 83 percent of the Adults freely named SCLC as an organization that has played "one of the most important parts in the movement" (*Form 1*, V.1 and *Form 2*, V.2a).
113. I am indebted to James R. Wood, former SCLC Public Relations Director, for furnishing me a copy of this report.
114. And, from a different perspective, in Howard Zinn's insightful *SNCC: The New Abolitionists*.
115. SNCC reprint from the *Atlanta Inquirer*, March, 1962. This assessment was true then, but must be qualified in 1965: the "bigger civil rights organizations" have *followed* SNCC to the more dangerous areas.
116. SNCC Constitution adopted at Atlanta conference in April, 1962.
117. From a descriptive pamphlet, *SNCC*, issued in August, 1963.
118. These data are drawn from many sources in my files, including SNCC's "Financial Report, 1960," "Budget, 1961," "Survey: Current Field Work, Summer, 1963," and "Mississippi Summer Project;" "Major Organizations Speaking for Negroes Differ," *Jet* 24, 13 (July 18, 1963), pp. 18-19; and interviews.
119. Council of Federated Organizations, including CORE, SNCC, SCLC, NAACP and various local groups.
120. On November 15, 1961, for instance, Forman wrote to me about SNCC's situation: "We are currently in a financial crisis and hope you will be able to mobilize support for our program [in the Boston area]. At this moment we are practically broke. We have a staff of sixteen people working only for room and board subsistence, not really sure they will receive this each week.

The seriousness of the situation is illustrated by the fact that this week we are only sending $20 to each person instead of the usual $40. We are in dire need of funds simply to establish an efficient operating office—the purchase of office equipment, typewriters, etc."

121. SNCC was attempting to guard against a repeat of the collapse of local leadership in the fall of 1960 and the subsequent demise of the plan for organization of state chapters. "When all those local groups faded," said Julian Bond early in 1962, "they left SNCC with nothing to coordinate."
122. See pp. 56-57 for a more complete listing of characteristics of the sample group.
123. Fifty-two percent of the Adults said the Students were "not too well-versed" in nonviolence, and an additional 29 percent said they were "very poorly versed" (*Form 2*, II.4). A sampling of other comments shows the mixed praise and damnation elicited from Adult informants close to the movement:

> They're professional sufferers and agitators, but they do suffer with a great deal of pleasure and exuberance (Margaret Long).
> They're subjected to losing their lives every day and doing things a lot of other civil rights people wouldn't do (Constance Curry).
> [Student X] would manipulate the Lord if he could! (Will Campbell).
> They threaten to become just another bureaucracy (Lewis Jones).
> They should try 'stay-ins' [in school] for a change (Charles Whittenstein).

There was once a movement called SNCC
Whose work in the sit-ins was quick.
But original sin
On them did sit-in,
And the movement became just a clique (Will Campbell).

124. "After a few months on the front lines," said Tom Hayden, "there were status drives in people who had never had them before."
125. *Form 1*, V.9. On the other hand, 73 percent (19 of 26) of the Adults responded in this pro-King manner. The defensively deviant response of Ruby Hurley of the NAACP is noteworthy, however: "It's too early to tell how Martin's going to fit into the total picture!"
126. Hostility toward King continues to the present in many forms. Refusal of SNCC and the NAACP to participate in the early phases of a dramatization of voting problems in Lowndes County, Alabama, in November, 1965 is one example; after working in the area for many months unnoticed by the media, SNCC especially resented SCLC's much publicized attempt to start an instant campaign on the basis of a few visits by King. Perhaps the classic example of this antagonism has just appeared in print: a SNCC book entitled *Negroes*

*in American History: A Freedom Primer* (by Bobbi and Frank Cieciorka, Atlanta: The Student Voice, Inc., 1965), which is written to cover current Negro protest, but does not even mention the Montgomery bus boycott, A. Philip Randolph, Bayard Rustin, the March on Washington or Martin Luther King, Jr.

127. I have found this sentiment in nearly every SNCC worker with whom I have talked, both during the research period covered by this study and since. Recall the party of SNCC workers I attended in March of 1962, described under *Role Conflict* in chapter 2. "Our friend, Bobby Kennedy" was picked as one of the characters for some cathartic role-playing, along with Bull Connor and other noted racists. "We're with you in spirit, boys," and "Yes, yes, we'll see what we can do" were hilariously appropriate lines for Mr. Kennedy. And there is virtually unanimous sentiment among civil rights leaders as this is submitted (December 1965), that the Justice Department has been grossly negligent in authorizing the use of federal referees to register Deep South Negro voters under the Voting Rights Law of 1965.
128. My files are full of further data on communities, local protest movements, the Negro college, etc., which I see as relevant to the type of analysis being developed here. But the limited scope of this study prevents their use at this time. Hopefully the theory of rationalization may be applied to these kinds of data soon.

## CHAPTER NINE

1. Quoted in Thomas Hayden, "Students and Human Rights: A View From the South," *The Intercollegian* 79, 7 (May, 1962), p. 10.
2. And a national election vote split clearly on the race issue. Only the five Deep South states—where percentage of Negroes is highest and Negro registration lowest—joined Barry Goldwater's home state of Arizona in voting for him for President. "We in the South knew what we were voting about!" boomed Georgia Senator Richard Russell to a statewide white farmers' meeting after the election. "We were voting against the federal force bill!" (WSB Radio, Atlanta, November 16, 1964).
3. Three of the Students (Charles McDew, Charles Sherrod and Robert Zellner) were back in school in 1964 and 1965—but only temporarily, to give them added usefulness when they return to the movement. McDew now works as a community organizer for the United Planning Organization in Washington, D.C., Sherrod alternates between Union Theological Seminary and southwest Georgia, and Zellner is active in Boston-area protests while at Brandeis University. Two of the Adults are in activities making them only slightly less related to the movement than they were before: James Gibson in school and Tim Jenkins in a northern law firm.
4. See Appendix for responses to VI.4 (both forms): "What are some of the things that could be done to make the movement more effective?" Response categories are identical to I.8, and elicited responses are similar.

5. Harold Fleming described cumulative rationalization well:

> The length of time in which spontaneity can be maintained is a great deal shorter now, because there are now a set of procedures for systematically seizing on spontaneous protest and turning it into a program. The logistics are pretty well defined now. They know all of this already—how to make signs, how to set up shifts for picketing, etc.

6. "Administrative Rationality, Social Setting and Organizational Development," pp. 301, 308.
7. The minutes of the SNCC Regional Meeting of March 24, 1962, strike me as a prototypical example. Director James Forman reported on the Greenwich, Conn., "Heads of Organization" meeting earlier that month:

> The subject of tensions between the various organizations [came up]. SNCC apparently is a thorn in the flesh to many of the groups . . . The discussion developed into a discussion between NAACP and the Direct Action Groups. The NAACP approach is so different that Wilkins considers such actions as the sit-ins at the Justice Department idiotic . . .

   To show how complex the hierarchy can be, we note a later comment by Forman: "Later Wilkins privately pledged NAACP's willingness to work with SNCC, and also with SCLC, but made it clear that he would not work with CORE."
8. For example, a 1964 SCLC mailing called "Fiscal Facts" emphasized that "only 8.3% of our total income" in 1963 went for administrative costs—"a ratio which is considered by all agencies as extremely low." The same brochure noted that SCLC's books are audited annually by a C.P.A.
9. In September 1965 (after this prediction was written), SCLC hired Dr. Robert Greene, an educational psychologist at Michigan State, to direct its Education Program.
10. Parsons and Henderson, p. 58 in the introduction to Weber's *The Theory of Social and Economic Organization*.
11. The Leadership Conference on Civil Rights pooled leadership from the Protestant, Catholic and Jewish faiths in America in an all-out drive to pass the Civil Rights Law of 1964. They lobbied, testified before House and Senate committees, organized nationwide pilgrimages to Washington, held prayer vigils, etc. "No less a foe of civil rights than Senator Richard Russell of Georgia," wrote the National Council of Churches' Commission on Religion and Race, "has admitted that the religious forces of the nation, through their vigorous support of the legislation, played the deciding role in this momentous victory" (letter, June 18, 1964, shortly after the Senate voted cloture and assured passage of the Law). No such vigorous formal action was needed for the Voting Rights Law of 1965.

12. Whitney Young commented in July of 1963, "It takes courage to try to be a leader when you haven't been in jail" (*Jet* 24, 12 [July 11, 1963], p. 30). And Andrew Young has been arrested "accidentally" three times (conversation, April 9, 1965).
13. Rustin's recent return to prominence, which began with the March on Washington in 1963, is in sharp contrast to his position only three years earlier when a labor group refused to support the Atlanta SNCC conference if he were invited (see chapter 4). This phenomenon is consistent with the broadening of ideological bases (L.1) and the wide and differentiated bases of leadership recruitment (I.2a and b) of Stage IV.
14. The Ford Foundation is considering a project with major universities aimed at rapidly rationalizing recruitment channels for such volunteers (consultation in New Haven, Conn., January 29-30, 1965).
15. "The Changing Character of the Negro Protest," p. 126.
16. "The Need for a Southern Student Organizing Committee," Gene Guerrero (mimeographed, January, 1965).
17. At a SSOC conference in Atlanta, November 13-15, 1964 (attended by 144 students from 43 southern colleges and universities—SSOC Newsletter 1, III [December, 1964], p. 1), and through discussions and correspondence with Gene Guerrero (chairman) and Sue Thrasher (secretary).
18. Persons like James Peck and Albert Bigelow of CORE, who sailed on the "Voyage of the Golden Rule" into a Pacific nuclear test area, long have been trying to make explicit for student protestors the link between peace and human rights. I observed that there were nearly as many pieces of peace literature on display at the Atlanta SNCC conference in April of 1962 as there was desegregation material. Peace marches have been consciously integrated in recent years, and the arrest of members of the Quebec to Guantanamo peace walkers in Albany late in 1963 has strengthened the relationship between the two causes. The Committee for Nonviolent Action changed the name of its monthly newsletter from *CNVA Bulletin* to *Direct Action for a Nonviolent World* after the Albany arrests.
19. SCEF worker Carl Braden served a year in federal prison in 1960-61 for refusing to testify before a segregationist-inspired southern committee of the House Un-American Activities Committee. He and Anne Braden have helped keep the issue before the other civil rights groups through speeches and publications. At SNCC's April 1962 Atlanta conference (where most participants had not yet heard of "civil liberties"), the Bradens led a workshop on "Civil Liberties and Free Speech as Essential Weapons in the Struggle for Civil Rights." They and others have participated in many such workshops since.
20. CORE's setting up of "community centers" in the Deep South with a library, recreation facilities, classes in sewing and child care, etc., began in 1963, adding a new technique to SNCC's Albany-type organizing efforts. Now such centers are a program of all the civil rights groups.
21. Pp. 1-2. I am grateful to Mr. Jenkins for allowing me to keep a copy of this confidential document, a manuscript entitled only "Re-cap of the Project's Rationale."

22. "Student Political Action, 1960-1963: The View of a Participant" (mimeographed, Students for a Democratic Society), p. 11.
23. Jenkins also clearly foresaw what was to happen in Mississippi once the Mississippi Summer Project of 1964 got under way: "The atrocities likely to accrue from a rural campaign will stimulate the urban people to turn out in indignation" ("Re-cap of the Project's Rationale," p. 6).

    The message of the movement had been heard as of July 28, 1964, when, for the first time in Gallup Polling history, "the racial problem" was named most often when a nationwide sample was asked, "What do you think is the most important problem facing the country today?" Forty-seven percent of the respondents mentioned race, compared to 35 who said "international problems" (*Atlanta Constitution*, July 28, 1964). Since then, race has held the top position in times of racial crisis: in April, 1965 (after Selma), and September, 1965 (after ghetto outbreaks in Los Angeles—"Civil Rights Worries Nation More Than Vietnam," *Jet* 29, 3 [October 28, 1965], p. 8).
24. The range of relevant systems will get even broader as provisions of the 1964 Civil Rights Law are implemented. The equal employment opportunity provisions of Title VII, for instance, covered all businesses employing 100 or more workers as of July 2, 1965, will apply to all with 75 or more in 1966, 50 in 1967 and 25 in 1968 (Public Law 88-352, H.R. 7152, July 2, 1964 [U.S. Government Printing Office], pp. 13-14). And Title VI of the Law provides that *all* federal tax money must be used *only* in nondiscriminatory programs, whether publicly or privately administered.
25. "Minutes of SNCC Regional Meeting—Atlanta, Georgia, March 24, 1962," pp. 2, 3, 4.
26. David Kelsey, "Slipping Segregation: Negroes Win Lowering of More Barriers in South," *The Wall Street Journal* (January 16, 1962).
27. In more general theoretical terms, Weber argues that "the more highly developed the interdependence of different economic units in a monetary economy, the greater the pressure of the everyday needs of the followers of the charismatic movement becomes. The effect of this is to strengthen the tendency to routinization . . ." (*The Theory of Social and Economic Organization*, p. 370).
28. In Gerth and Mills, *From Max Weber*, p. 216.
29. I have applied this sequence to virtually every kind of interaction between separated entities, and find that it has wide relevance. Examples are the change in intense two-person relationships, labor-management relations, community factions over educational matters, and the Christian narrative of suffering and redemption.
30. I first noted this prediction early in 1962—before Birmingham, the summer 1964, ghetto outbreaks, the Mississippi lynchings of 1964, Selma and the four murders associated with the 1965 voter drive in Alabama, and the ghetto outbreaks and 34 deaths in Los Angeles in August of 1965.
31. Martin Luther King, Jr., and SCLC already have initiated an all-out campaign to organize Chicago for protests in the summer of 1966. It will be the first large-scale, long-term effort by a civil rights group to apply direct action

protest techniques to problems of large urban areas in the North; I join SCLC's Andrew Young in predicting that Chicago white leaders will perform on cue as have the Barnetts, Wallaces, Connors and Clarks of the Deep South, and help create a full-blown racial crisis from which concessions will be negotiated.

32. This prediction was made in 1962 also, as was the concluding prediction concerning the politicizing of protest.
33. The best example of law-produced crisis-confrontation-change as this is written is the reluctant willingness of virtually every southern Board of Education to sign the "pledge" to the U.S. Office of Education to submit a plan for immediate desegregation. For further discussion on the institutionalization of moderation in race relations, see Daniel Bell, "Plea for a 'New Phase in Negro Leadership'" (*New York Times Magazine*, May 31, 1964, pp. 11, 28-29, 31), and Laue and McCorkle, "The Association of Southern Women for the Prevention of Lynching . . ."
34. Southern Regional Council release, August 2, 1964.
35. Quoted from the *New York Times* of November 16, 1964, in "The Quiet Revolution," *Four Lights* 24, 10 (December, 1964, published by the U.S. Section of the Women's International League for Peace and Freedom), p. 3. This account omits at least one death—the June 1964 ambush murder of Mississippi NAACP Field Secretary Medgar Evers.
36. Death statistics from Chapnick, "Civil Rights Casualties, 1954-65."

# Bibliography

## BOOKS

Allport, Gordon W., *The Nature of Prejudice*. Garden City, N.Y.: Doubleday Anchor Books, 1958 (original, 1954).

Alpert, Harry, *Emile Durkheim and His Sociology*. New York: Columbia University Press, 1939.

Aptheker, Herbert, *American Negro Slave Revolts*. New York: Columbia University Press, 1943.

_____, *Essays in the History of the American Negro*. New York: International Publishers, 1945.

Bennett, Lerone, *The Negro Mood*. Chicago: Johnson Publishing Company, 1964.

Bernard, Jessie, *American Community Behavior*. New York: Holt, Rinehart and Winston, 1962.

Blau, Peter, *Bureaucracy in Modern Society*. New York: Random House, 1956.

_____, *The Dynamics of Bureaucracy*. Chicago: University of Chicago Press, 1963.

Boulding, Kenneth, *Conflict and Defense: A General Theory*. New York: Harper Torchbooks, 1962.

Brink, William, and Louis Harris, *The Negro Revolution in America*. New York: Simon and Schuster, Inc., 1963.

Brinton, Crane, *The Tasks of Economic History, Supplement VIII*. New York: New York University Press, 1948.

_____, *The Anatomy of Revolution*. New York: Vintage Books, 1958.

Bredemeier, Harry C., and Richard M. Stephenson, *The Analysis of Social Systems*. New York: Holt, Rinehart and Winston, 1962.

Broom, Leonard and Phillip Selznick, *Sociology: A Text with Adapted Readings*. Evanston, Ill.: Row and Peterson, 1958 (second edition).

Burns, W. Haywood, *The Voices of Negro Protest*. London: Oxford University Press, 1963.

Cantril, Hadley, *The Psychology of Social Movements*. New York: John Wiley and Sons, Inc., 1941.

Cieciorka, Bobbi and Frank Cieciorka, *Negroes in American History: A Freedom Primer*. Atlanta: The Student Voice, Inc., 1965.

Coleman, James S., *Community Conflict*. Glencoe, Ill.: The Free Press, 1957.

Coser, Lewis A., *The Functions of Social Conflict*. Glencoe, Ill.: The Free Press, 1956.

Dollard, John, *Caste and Class in a Southern Town*. Garden City, N.Y.: Doubleday Anchor Books, 1949.

Edwards, L.P., *The Natural History of Revolution*. Chicago: University of Chicago Press, 1927.

Elkins, Stanley M., *Slavery: A Problem in American Institutional and Intellectual Life*. Chicago: University of Chicago Press, 1959.
Erikson, Kai T., *Wayward Puritans* (to be published by John A. Wiley in 1966).
Etzioni, Amitai, *Modern Organizations*. Englewood Cliffs, N.J.: Prentice-Hall, 1964.
Fischer, Louis, *Gandhi: His Life and Message for the World*. New York: New American Library (Signet Books), 1954.
Gandhi, Mohandas K., *An Autobiography*. Boston: The Beacon Press, 1957.
Garfinkel, Herbert, *When Negroes March*. Glencoe, Ill.: The Free Press, 1959.
Gerth, Hans, and C. Wright Mills, *From Max Weber: Essays in Sociology*. New York: Oxford University Press, 1958.
Heberle, Rudolf, *Social Movements*. New York: Appleton-Century-Crofts, 1951.
Helper, Hinton Rowan, *Ante-Bellum*. New York: Putnam Capricorn Books, 1960.
Herberg, Will (ed.), *The Writings of Martin Buber*. New York: The World Publishing Co. (Meridian Books), 1956.
Hughes, Langston, *Fight for Freedom: The Story of the NAACP*. New York: Norton, 1962.
Killian, Lewis M., and Ralph Turner, *Collective Behavior*. Englewood Cliffs, N.J.: Prentice-Hall, Inc., 1957.
____, and Charles M. Grigg, *Racial Crisis in America*. Englewood Cliffs, N.J.: Prentice-Hall, 1964.
King, C. Wendell, *Social Movements in the United States*. New York: Random House, 1956.
King, Martin Luther, Jr., *Stride Toward Freedom*. New York: Ballentine Books, 1958.
Kuper, Leo, *Passive Resistance in South Africa*. New Haven: Yale University Press, 1957.
Lasswell, H.D., *Politics*. New York: McGraw Hill, Inc., 1936.
Lewin, Kurt (Gertrud Weiss Lewin, ed.), *Resolving Social Conflicts*. New York: Harper and Brothers, 1948.
Lomax, Louis, *The Negro Revolt*. New York: Harper Bros, Inc., 1962.
Loomis, Charles P., *Social Systems: Essays on Their Persistence and Change*. New York: Van Nostrand, 1960.
MacIver, Robert M., *Social Causation*. Boston: Ginn and Co., 1942.
Martindale, Don, *Social Life and Cultural Change*. Princeton, N.J.: Van Nostrand, 1962.
Merton, Robert, *Social Theory and Social Structure*. Glencoe, Ill.: The Free Press, 1957.
Moore, Wilbert E., *Social Change*. Englewood Cliffs, N.J.: Prentice-Hall, 1963.
Nehru, Jawaharlal, *Toward Freedom*. Boston: The Beacon Press, 1958.
Olmstead, Frederick Law, *Slave States*. New York: Putnam Capricorn Books, 1959.
Parsons, Talcott, *The Structure of Social Action*. Glencoe, Ill.: The Free Press, 1949 (second edition).
____, *The Social System*. Glencoe, Ill.: The Free Press, 1951.
____, and Neil J. Smelser, *Economy and Society*. Glencoe, Ill.: The Free Press, 1956.

_____, and Edward Shils (ed.), *Toward a General Theory of Action*. Cambridge, Mass.: Harvard University Press, 1959.

Peatman, John G., *Introduction to Applied Statistics*. New York: Harper Bros., Inc., 1963.

Peck, James, *Freedom Ride*. New York: Simon and Schuster, Inc., 1962.

Pettigrew, Thomas F., and Ernest Q. Campbell, *Christians in Racial Crisis*. Washington, D.C.: Public Affairs Press, 1959.

Reddick, L.D., *Crusader Without Violence*. New York: Harper Bros., Inc., 1959.

Redfield, Robert, *The Primitive World and Its Transformations*. Ithaca, N.Y.: Cornell University Press, 1953.

Riley, Matilda W., *Sociological Research: A Case Approach*. New York: Harcourt, Brace and World, Inc., 1963.

Rogers, Everett, *Diffusion of Innovations*. New York: The Free Press of Glencoe, 1962.

Rose, Arnold M., *The Negro in America*. Boston: The Beacon Press, 1948.

Rostow, Walt W., *The Stages of Economic Growth*. Cambridge, England: University Press, 1960.

Selltiz, Claire, and Marie Jahoda, Morton Deutsch and Stuart W. Cook, *Research Methods in Social Relations*. New York: Henry Holt and Co., 1960 (revised edition).

Siegel, Sidney, *Nonparametric Statistics for the Behavioral Sciences*. New York: McGraw Hill, 1956.

Silone, Ignazio, *Bread and Wine*. New York: New American Library (Signet Books), 1961 (original, 1937).

Simpson, George, and J. Milton Yinger, *Racial and Cultural Minorities*. New York: Harper and Bros., 1953.

Smelser, Neil J., *Social Change in the Industrial Revolution*. Chicago: University of Chicago Press, 1959.

_____, *Theory of Collective Behavior*. New York: The Free Press of Glencoe, 1963.

Sorokin, Pitirim, *Social and Cultural Dynamics*. Boston: Porter Sargent, Publishers, 1957 (revised edition).

Stouffer, Samuel, *The American Soldier*. Princeton, N.J.: Princeton University Press, 1949.

Sumner, William Graham, *Folkways*. New York: Dover, 1959 (original, 1906).

Syndor, Charles S., *The Development of Southern Sectionalism: 1819-1848*. Baton Rouge: Louisiana State University Press, 1948.

Thompson, Edgar, and Everett Hughes (ed.), *Race: Individual and Collective Behavior*. Glencoe, Ill.: The Free Press, 1958.

Weber, Max, *The Theory of Social and Economic Organizations* (second edition, translated by A.M. Henderson and Talcott Parsons). Glencoe, Ill.: The Free Press, 1947.

Whyte, William Foote, *Street Corner Society*. Chicago: University of Chicago Press, 1955 (second edition).

Williams, Robert, *Negroes with Guns*. New York: Munsell and Marzani, Inc., 1962.

Williams, Robin, *The Reduction of Intergroup Tensions*. New York: Social Science Research Council, Bulletin 57, 1947.

Wilson, James Q., *Negro Politics*. Glencoe, Ill.: The Free Press, 1960.
Woodward, C. Vann, *The Strange Career of Jim Crow*. New York: Oxford University Press (Galaxy Books), 1957.
Zinn, Howard, *SNCC: The New Abolitionists*. Boston: The Beacon Press, 1964.
Znaniecki, Florian, *Cultural Sciences*. Urbana, Ill.: University of Illinois Press, 1952.

## ARTICLES

Becker, Howard, and Blanche Geer, "Problems of Inference and Proof in Participant Observation," *American Sociological Review* 23, 5 (October, 1958), pp. 652-60.
Bell, Daniel, "Plea for a 'New Phase in Negro Leadership.'" *New York Times Magazine*, May 31, 1964, pp. 11, 28-29, 31.
Bertrand, Alvin L., "The Stress-Strain Element of Social Systems." *SF* 42, 1 (October, 1963), pp. 1-9.
Blumer, Herbert, "Social Movements," in Alfred McClung Lee (ed.), *Principles of Sociology*. New York, College Outline Series, 1961.
Bock, Kenneth, "Evolution, Function and Change." *ASR* 28, 2 (April, 1963), pp. 229-37.
Boskoff, Alvin, "Social Change: Major Problems in the Emergence of Theoretical and Research Foci," in Howard Becker and Alvin Boskoff (ed.), *Modern Sociological Theory*. New York: Dryden Press, 1957.
_____, "Functional Theory as a Source of a Theoretical Repertory and Research Tasks in the Study of Social Change," in George K. Zollschan and Walter Hirsch (ed.), *Explorations in Social Change*. New York: Macmillan, 1964.
Brown, Robert McAfee, "The Freedom Riders: A Clergyman's View." Reprinted by CORE from *Amherst College Alumni News* (no date given).
Campbell, Will C., "The Sit-Ins: Passive Resistance or Civil Disobedience?" *Social Action* 27, 5 (January, 1961), pp. 14-18.
"Chain Stores Announce Desegregation." *New York Times*, October 18, 1960.
"Civil Rights Worries Nation More Than Vietnam." *Jet* 29, 3 (October 28, 1965), p. 8.
Cornell, George W., "In Civil Rights the Church is Truly Militant." Associated Press, May 30, 1965.
Cothran, Tilman C., "Negro Leadership in a Crisis Situation." *Phylon* 22, 2 (Summer, 1961), pp. 107-18.
Davies, James C., "Toward a Theory of Revolution." *ASR* 27, 1 (February, 1962), pp. 5-19.
Eisenstadt, S.N., "Institutionalization and Change." *ASR* 29, 2 (April, 1964), pp. 235-47.
Elias, Norbert, "Problems of Involvement and Detachment." *British Journal of Sociology* 7, 3 (September, 1956), pp. 226-52.
"Fifty Thousand Jam L.A. Ball Park for Biggest Rights Rally," "Paul Newman Pledges Day's Pay; May Join King." *Jet* 24, 8 (June 13, 1963), pp. 54-60.

Fishman, Jacob R., and Fredric Solomon, "Youth and Social Action, I: Perspectives on the Student Sit-In Movement," *American Journal of Orthopsychiatry* 33, 5 (October, 1963), pp. 872-82.

_____, "Youth and Social Action, II: Action and Identity Formation in the First 'Student Sit-In Demonstration.'" Toronto, Canada: presented at annual meeting of American Psychiatric Association, May 11, 1962.

_____, "Youth and Social Action, III: Nonviolence in the South." Washington, D.C.: presented at the Gandhi Memorial Conference on Youth, Nonviolence and Social Change, November, 1963.

_____, "The Psychological Meaning of Nonviolence in Student Civil Rights Activities." *Psychiatry* 27, 2 (May, 1964), pp. 91-99.

Fuller, Helen, "The 'Sit-In' Protest." *The New Republic* (April 25 and May 2, 1960 – reprinted by Race Relations Department, Fisk University).

Fullerton, Gary, "New Factories Thing of Past in Little Rock." *Nashville Tennesseean*, May 31, 1959.

Hall, Richard H. "The Concept of Bureaucracy: An Empirical Assessment." *AJS* 69, 1 (July, 1963), pp. 32-40.

Hayden, Thomas, "Students and Human Rights: A View from the South." *The Intercollegian* 79, 7 (May, 1962), pp. 10-13.

Heberle, Rudolf, "Observations on the Sociology of Social Movements." *ASR* 14, 3 (June, 1949), pp. 346-57.

Hopper, Rex, "The Revolutionary Process: A Frame of Reference for the Study of Revolutionary Movements." *SF* 8, 3 (March, 1950), pp. 270-79.

Katz, Elihu, Martin L. Levin, and Herbert Hamilton, "Traditions of Research on the Diffusion of Innovations." *ASR* 28, 2 (April, 1963), pp. 237-52.

Kelsey, David, "Slipping Segregation: Negroes Win Lowering of More Barriers in South." *The Wall Street Journal*, January 16, 1962.

Killian, Lewis M. and C.U. Smith, "Negro Protest Leaders in a Southern Community." *SF* 38, 3 (March, 1960), pp. 253-57.

_____, "Leadership in the Desegregation Crisis," in Muzafer Sherif (ed.), *Intergroup Relations and Leadership*. New York: John Wiley and Sons, 1962.

King, Mae, "Why I took Part in a Sit-In." *The Intercollegian* 77, 12 (October, 1960), pp. 3-5.

Kluckhohn, Florence R., "The Participant Observer Technique in Small Communities." *AJS* 45, 3 (November, 1940), pp. 331-43.

Laue, James H., "The Movement, Negro Challenge to The Myth." *New South* 18, 7-8 (July-August, 1963), pp. 9-17.

_____, "The Changing Character of the Negro Protest." *The Annals of the American Academy of Political and Social Science* 327 (January, 1965), pp. 119-26.

_____, and Leon M. McCorkle, Jr., "The Association of Southern Women for the Prevention of Lynching: A Commentary on the Role of the 'Moderate.'" *Sociological Inquiry* 35, 1 (Winter, 1965), pp. 80-93.

Lewis, Roscoe E., "The Role of Pressure Groups in Maintaining Morale Among Negroes." *Journal of Negro Education* 12, 3 (Summer, 1943), pp. 464-73.

Litwak, Eugene, "Models of Bureaucracy Which Permit Conflict." *AJS* 68, 2 (September, 1961), pp. 177-84.

Lomax, Louis E., "The Kennedys Move in on Dixie." *Harper's Magazine* 224, 1344 (May, 1962), pp. 27-33.

Loomis, Charles P., "Social Change and Social Systems," pp. 185-215 in Edward Tiryakian (ed.), *Sociological Theory, Values and Sociocultural Change*. New York: The Free Press of Glencoe, 1963.

"Major Organizations Speaking for Negroes Differ." *Jet* 24, 13 (July 18, 1963), pp. 18-19.

Meadows, Paul, "Sequence in Revolution." *ASR* 6, 5 (October, 1941), pp. 702-709.

____, "Theses on Social Movements." *SF* 24, 4 (May, 1946), pp. 408-12.

Monohan, T.P., and E.H., "Some Characteristics of American Negro Leaders." *ASR* 21, 4 (August, 1956), pp. 589-96.

Moore, Wilbert E., "The MacIver Lecture: Predicting Discontinuities in Social Change." *ASR* 29, 3 (June, 1964), pp. 331-38.

____, "A Reconsideration of Theories of Social Change." *ASR* 25, 6 (December, 1960), pp. 810-18.

Munch, Peter A., "Empirical Science and Max Weber's *Verstehende Soziologie*." *ASR* 22, 1 (February, 1957), pp. 26-32.

Naess, Arne, "A Systematization of Gandhian Ethics of Conflict Resolution." *Journal of Conflict Resolution* 2, 2 (July, 1958), pp. 140-55.

Nahirny, Vladimer C., "Some Observations on Ideological Groups." *AJS* 67, 4 (January, 1962), pp. 397-405.

"The Need to Speak Out." *Time* 79, 8 (February 23, 1962), p. 74.

O'Dea, Thomas, "Sociological Dilemmas: Five Paradoxes of Institutionalization," pp. 71-89 in Edward Tiryakian (ed.), *Sociological Theory, Values and Sociocultural Change*. New York: The Free Press of Glencoe, 1963.

Parsons, Talcott, "An Outline of the Social System," in *Theories of Society*. New York: The Free Press of Glencoe, 1961.

____, "Evolutionary Universals in Society." *ASR* 29, 3 (June, 1964), pp. 339-57.

Pettigrew, Thomas F., and Richard M. Cramer, "The Demography of Desegregation." *The Journal of Social Issues* 15, 4 (1959), pp. 61-71.

Putney, Snell, and Gladys J. Putney, "Radical Innovation and Prestige." *ASR* 27, 4 (August, 1962), pp. 548-51.

"The Quiet Revolution." *Four Lights* 24, 10 (December, 1964), p. 3 – quoted from the *New York Times* of November 16, 1964.

"Races: Confused Crusade." *Time* 79, 2 (January 12, 1962), p. 15.

Randall, Frank, "The Freedom Riders: A Historian's View." Reprinted by CORE from *Amherst College Alumni News* (no date given).

Rich, Marvin, "The Congress of Racial Equality and Its Strategy." *The Annals of the American Academy of Political and Social Science* 357 (January, 1965), pp. 114-18.

Riesman, David, "Some Observations on the Interviewing Study," in Paul Lazarsfeld and Wagner Thielens, Jr., *The Academic Mind*. Glencoe, Ill.: The Free Press, 1958.

____, "Interviewers, Elites and Academic Freedom." *Social Problems* 6, 2 (Fall, 1958), pp. 115-26.

_____, and Mark Benny, "The Sociology of the Interview," an address delivered to the Midwest Sociological Society, Des Moines, April 22, 1955, and reprinted in *The Midwest Sociologist* (full citation not given in reprint).

_____, "Asking and Answering." *The Journal of Business of the University of Chicago* 29, 4 (October, 1956), pp. 225-36.

Robertson, Nan, untitled series on college youth, *New York Times*. Began May 14, 1962.

Robinson, Layhmond, "N.Y. Negroes Blame Their Plight on Whites." *New York Times*, August 3, 1964.

Roche, John P., and Sachs, Stephen, "The Bureaucrat and the Enthusiast: An Exploration of the Leadership of Social Movements." *Western Political Quarterly* 8, 2 (June, 1955), pp. 248-61.

Searles, Ruth, and J. Allen Williams, Jr., "Negro College Students' Participation in Sit-Ins." *SF* 40, 3 (March, 1962), pp. 215-20.

Sears, Art, and Larry Still, "Demand for More Negro Action, Funds, Pushes Groups Closer Together." *Jet* 24, 13 (July 18, 1963), pp. 18-21.

Simmel, Georg, "On Conflict," pp. 1324-25 in Parsons, *et al*, *Theories of Society*. Glencoe, Ill.: The Free Press, 1961 (from Simmel, *Conflict and the Web of Group Affiliations*. Glencoe, Ill.: The Free Press, 1955, pp. 107-10).

Sitton, Claude, "Integration: Pace Slows in the South." *New York Times*, May 22, 1960.

Thoreau, Henry David, "Civil Disobedience," in *The Writings of Thoreau*. New York: Random House Modern Library, 1950.

Udy, Stanley H., Jr., "'Bureaucracy' and 'Rationality' in Weber's Organization Theory." *ASR* 24, 6 (December, 1959), pp. 791-95.

_____, "Administrative Rationality, Social Setting and Organizational Development." *AJS* 68, 3 (November, 1962), pp. 299-308.

Vander Zanden, James W., "The Non-Violent [sic] Resistance Movement Against Segregation." *AJS* 68, 5 (March, 1963), pp. 544-50.

Wallace, A.F.C., "Revitalization Movements." *American Anthropologist* 58, 3 (April, 1956), pp. 264-81.

Walzer, Michael, "A Cup of Coffee and a Seat." *Dissent* 7, 2 (Spring, 1960), pp. 111-20.

Westin, Alan, "Ride-In." *American Heritage* 13 (August, 1962), pp. 57-64.

Wilber, David, and George K. Zollschan, "Prolegomenon to a Theory of Revolutions," pp. 125-51 in G. Zollschan and Walter Hirsch, *Explorations in Social Change*. New York: Macmillan, 1964.

Wilson, James Q., "The Strategy of Protest: Problems of Negro Civic Action." *Journal of Conflict Resolution* 5, 3 (September, 1961), pp. 291-303.

Wish, Harvey, "American Slave Insurrections Before 1861." *Journal of Negro History* 22, 3 (July, 1937), pp. 299-320.

Zelditch, Morris, Jr., "Some Methodological Problems of Field Studies." *AJS* 67, 5 (March, 1962), pp. 566-76.

# OTHER PUBLICATIONS

Associated Press Releases: March 18, 1960; September 23, 1961; October 17, 1961; and July 3, 1964.

*Atlanta Constitution*: July 28, 1964.

"Bus Integration Ruling Backed, But Many Decry 'Freedom Rides.'" Princeton, N.J.: American Institute of Public Opinion, June 21, 1961.

*Chicago Sun-Times*: July 31, 1961.

"Cities Turning to Committees in Race Issues." *Atlanta Journal-Constitution*, August 23, 1964.

*Christian Science Monitor*: May 23 and 25, 1961.

"CORE Rules for Action." New York: Congress of Racial Equality, no date.

"CORE Interracial Training Institute, August 14 - September 5, 1961: "Nonviolence in Theory *and* in Action." New York: CORE, 1960 (institute held in Miami, Fla.).

*CORElator*, No. 80 (March, 1960–special issue).

*Cracking the Color Line*. New York: CORE, 1959.

Recent issues of *The Crisis* (Monthly publication of the NAACP).

"The Day They Changed Their Minds." New York: NAACP, 1960.

Recent issues of *Direct Action for a Nonviolent World* (formerly *CNVA Bulletin*, published by the Committee for Nonviolent Action).

Dunbar, Leslie W., "The Student Protest Movement, Winter, 1960." Atlanta: Southern Regional Council, 1960.

____, "Reflections on the Latest Reform of the South." Atlanta: Southern Regional Council, 1960.

*Economic and Social Status of the Negro in the United States*. New York: National Urban League, 1961.

"Executive Support of Civil Rights." Atlanta: Southern Regional Council, March 13, 1962.

"First Status Report, Voter Education Project, September 20, 1962" (Confidential). Atlanta: Southern Regional Council.

"Fiscal Facts." Atlanta: SCLC, 1963 (part of a fund-appeal mailing).

Forman, James, "Nonviolence Leader Tells Organization of 'Fill the Jails' Movement in Albany." *New University News* 1, 1 (January, 1962), pp. 1, 5, 7.

"*FREEDOM RIDE, 1961*." New York: CORE (no date—apparently March-April, 1961).

"Freedom Rides." *New South* 17, 7-8 (July-August, 1961, total issue).

"The Freedom Ride, May, 1961." Atlanta: Southern Regional Council, 1961.

"Freedom Ride Costs" ("Memo to CORE Groups and Friends"). New York: CORE, September 28, 1961.

Gaither, Thomas, "Jailed-In." New York: League for Industrial Democracy (Published by CORE), 1961.

Gitlin, Todd, "Student Political Action, 1960-63: The View of a Participant." New York: Students for a Democratic Society, 1964.

Guerrero, Gene, "The Need for a Southern Student Organizing Committee." Nashville: SSOC, January, 1965.
Hayden, Tom, "Revolution in Mississippi." New York: Students for a Democratic Society, 1962.
Henderson, Vivian W., *The Economic Status of Negroes: In the Nation and the South*. Atlanta: Southern Regional Council, 1963.
Kahn, Thomas, "The Political Significance of the Freedom Rides." Prepared for the Liberal Study Group of the National Student Association Congress, August 19-30, 1962, and distributed by the Students for a Democratic Society.
"To Local Chapters and Advisory Committee." New York: CORE release, July, 1961.
"The Meaning of the Sit-Ins." New York: issued by a joint meeting of the National Council of Churches, SNCC, SCLC, CORE and the NAACP, July 11, 1960.
"Memorandum to Affiliated Groups and Friends." New York: CORE, August 5, 1961.
*New York Times*: October 12, 1960, and May 17, 1961.
Price, Margaret (ed.), "The Price We Pay." New York and Atlanta: Anti-Defamation League and Southern Regional Council, 1964.
"Public for Gradual Approach in De-Segregation Attempts." Princeton, N.J.: American Institute of Public Opinion, June 28, 1961.
Public Law 88-352, H.R. 7152, the Civil Rights Act of July 2, 1964. Washington, D.C.: U.S. Government Printing Office.
"Report of the Executive Director to Members and Friends of the Southern Regional Council." Atlanta: October 19, 1959.
Robinson, James R., "Executive Secretary's Report to the 1960 CORE Convention, St. Louis, Mo., June 29 to July 3, 1960."
*St. Paul* (Minn.) *Pioneer Press*: August 3, 1961.
"School Closing Project." Atlanta: SNCC, May, 1961 (release to affiliates and friends).
*School Desegregation: the First Six Years*. Atlanta: Southern Regional Council, 1960.
*SCLC Newsletter* 7, 5 (February, 1964.)
SNCC brochure (untitled). Distributed at the Atlanta, 1960, SNCC Conference.
SNCC "Statement of Purpose." Written by Rev. James M. Lawson, Jr., and reprinted in *The Student Voice* 1, 1 (June, 1960), p. 1.
Reprint on SNCC. Atlanta: *Atlanta Inquirer*, March, 1962.
*SNCC* (a descriptive pamphlet). Atlanta: SNCC, August, 1963.
*Southern Patriot*: 18, 5 (May, 1960); 18, 6 (June, 1960); 18, 8 (October, 1960); 19, 3 (March, 1961); and 20, 1 (January, 1962).
Recent issues of the *Southern School News* (published by the Southern Education Reporting Service, Nashville).
*SSOC Newsletter* 1, III (December, 1964). Published by the Southern Student Organizing Committee, Nashville.
"A Statement on the Research Aims and Methods of the Voter Education Project." Atlanta: Southern Regional Council, February, 1963.
"The Student Protest Movement: A Recapitulation, September, 1961." Atlanta: Southern Regional Council.

*This is CORE*. New York: Congress of Racial Equality (no date).
"This is the NAACP." New York: NAACP, April, 1960.
Westfeldt, Wallace, "Settling a Sit-In." Nashville: Nashville Community Relations Conference, 1961.
Young, Whitney M., Jr., in "Quotes of the Week." *Jet* 24, 12 (July 11, 1963), p. 30.
Zinn, Howard, "Albany." Atlanta: Southern Regional Council, January 8, 1962.

Plus many other news releases and informal publications of the Congress of Racial Equality, Southern Regional Council, Southern Christian Leadership Conference, and Student Nonviolent Coordinating Committee.

## OTHER SOURCES

Albany, Ga., high school students, song session, March, 1962.
Albany, Ga., discussions with numerous white and Negro leaders (including officials of the Retail Merchants Association and the Albany Movement), newsmen, ministers, and others, and examination of newspaper files during research trips to Albany in March and August-September, 1962.
Bellah, Robert N., seminar. Harvard University: September 28, 1961.
Blair, Ezell, discussion. Greensboro, N.C.: August 11, 1960.
Bond, Julian, discussion. Atlanta: March 5, 1962.
Brown, John (chairman of Miami CORE), discussion. Miami, Fla.: August 17, 1960.
Butler, Angeline, discussion. Nashville: June, 1960.
Carey, Gordon, discussion. St. Louis, Mo.: July 1, 1960.
Chapnick, Mary, "Civil Rights Casualties, 1964-65," Washington, D.C.: Community Relations Service, 1965 (unpublished research report).
"Agenda - National Council" (for 1961 CORE Council Meeting). Lexington, Ky., February 10-12, 1961.
Cothran, Tilman C., discussion. Atlanta University: March 13, 1962.
Curry, Constance, speech to Academic Freedom Conference. Duke University: February, 1962.
Farmer, James, speech for Harvard-Radcliffe Liberal Union. Harvard University: October 5, 1961.
Forman, James, letter from Atlanta. November 15, 1961.
Gaither, Thomas, letter from Rock Hill, S.C., Prison Camp, February 5, 1961.
Members of the Jackson Nonviolent Movement, song session. Jackson, Miss.: March 23, 1962.
Agenda for "Special Southern Student Leadership Seminar" (July 30-August 26, 1961, Nashville), furnished by Tim Jenkins.
Jenkins, Tim, "Re-cap of the Project's Rationale" (an unpublished confidential manuscript). March, 1962.
Laue, James H., "The Sit-Ins: A New Decade and a New Generation?" (unpublished paper). Harvard University, 1960.

_____, "Meaning and Marginality" (unpublished paper). Harvard University, May, 1961.
_____, "Race Relations Revolution: The Sit-In Movement" (unpublished paper). Harvard University, 1961.
Lawson, James M., Jr., discussion. Atlanta: October, 1960.
Mays, Benjamin, discussion. Chicago, Ill.: January 16, 1963.
McCain, James T., "Field Report" (from South Carolina). Courtesy of CORE National Office, New York, May, 1960.
"The Meaning of the Sit-Ins," issued after a joint meeting of representatives of the National Council of Churches, NAACP, CORE, SCLC and SNCC (New York: 1960, mimeographed).
Motley, Constance Baker (NAACP lawyer), discussion. Atlanta: September 4, 1962.
NBC Television News broadcast (Huntley-Brinkley), August, 1964.
Letter. New York: National Council of Churches, Commission on Religion and Race, June 18, 1964.
Parsons, Talcott, discussion. Harvard University: May 25, 1962.
Pettigrew, Thomas F., lecture. Harvard University: September 27, 1961.
Reagon, Cordell, discussion. Albany, Ga.: March 27, 1962.
Russell, Senator Richard (D.-Ga.), speech. Quoted on WSB Radio, Atlanta, November 16, 1964.
Sherrod, Charles, (an untitled, unpublished 40-page paper on his experiences in Albany, Ga., from October, 1961, to February, 1962).
Smith, Edwina, discussion. Atlanta: July 3, 1964.
Research notes from attendance at SCLC mass meeting in Hartford, Conn., October 13, 1961.
Southern Regional Council files on the sit-in movement (1960 to present).
Southern Regional Council release. Atlanta: August 2, 1964.
Research notes from conference of the Southern Student Organizing Committee. Atlanta: November 13-15, 1964.
Stembridge, Jane (first SNCC secretary), discussion. Atlanta: October 13, 1960.
Storer, Norman, "Federal Science Policy and the Sociology of Science" (unpublished paper). Harvard University, January, 1962.
"Financial Report, 1960." Atlanta: SNCC, 1960.
Research notes from attendance at SNCC conference on "Nonviolence and the Achievement of Desegregation." Atlanta: October 14-16, 1960.
"Budget, 1961." Atlanta: SNCC, 1961.
"Minutes–SNCC Regional Meeting, March 24, 1962." Atlanta.
"The Student Voice, Albany, Ga., March 26, 1962" (mimeographed by SNCC, no other information given).
"Constitution of the Student Nonviolent Coordinating Committee." Atlanta: SNCC, April, 1962.
Research notes from SNCC conference. Atlanta: April 27-29, 1962.
"Survey: Current Field Work." Atlanta: SNCC, Summer, 1963.
"Mississippi Summer Project." Atlanta: SNCC, April, 1964.
Thomas, Henry, discussion. Atlanta: August 9, 1960.
Walker, Wyatt, discussion. Atlanta: August 9, 1960.

_____, confidential report on "General Program" to the Executive Board of the Southern Christian Leadership Conference. Atlanta: September, 1960.
War Resister's League calendar, 1962. New York.
White, Winston, discussion. Harvard University: May 8, 1962.
Wood, James R., discussion. Atlanta: October 18, 1960.
Young, Andrew J., discussion. Atlanta: July 11, 1964.
Zellner, Dorothy Miller, notes on sessions of CORE Interracial Training Institute. Miami, Fla.: August 28-September 5, 1960).

# About the Author

Promoting social change through creative approaches to conflict has continued to be the focus of author James H. Laue. Since 1987 he has been the Vernon M. and Minnie I. Lynch Professor of Conflict Resolution in the new Center for Analysis and Resolution of Conflict at George Mason University in Faixfax, Virginia. The Center is the first institution to offer the PH.D. in Conflict Resolution, accepting its first class in 1988.

Following his research and participation in the civil rights movement in the early 1960s, Laue held academic appointments at Hollins College and Emory University, and completed his PH.D. in Sociology at Harvard in 1966. From 1965 to 1969 he was a field mediator, researcher, and director of program development for the Community Relations Service of the U.S. Department of Justice, a racial mediation agency established under the 1964 Civil Rights Act. After serving in academic and administrative positions at Harvard Medical School and Washington University, he was affiliated with the University of Missouri-St. Louis from 1975 to 1987, directing the Center for Metropolitan Studies and serving as the first President and Executive Director of the Conflict Clinic, Inc., before moving to George Mason in 1987.

Laue has been active in the growth of the field of conflict resolution as a founding board member of the National Conference on Peacemaking and Conflict Resolution, Vice Chair of the U.S. Peace Academy Commission, and current Co-Chair of the Consortium on Peace Research, Education and Development. He has published widely in the fields of conflict intervention, race relations and social change.

# Index

# The Rationa

## The Rationalization Cycle

| Functional Imperative | Priority Problems | I. Traditional Control |
|---|---|---|
| L: Ideology | 1. Content & Structure | * Particularistic, exclusive (I.2.b) (I.3) |
| | 2. Range of: a. Appeal b. Intensity | Narrow: specific subgroups Latent (I.2.a) (G.2) (A.2.a) |
| | 3. Dominant Maintenance Mechanisms | Ideal-centrism |
| I: Integration | 1. Internal Organizational Structure | Fragmented, undifferentiated |
| | 2. Membership Characteristics: a. Bases of recruitment | (L.2.b) Narrow (A.2.b) |
| | b. Dominant leadership roles | All-purpose professional |
| | c. Dominant membership roles | Nominal supporter (L.1) |
| | 3. Dominant Integrative Mechanisms | Tradition-centrism |
| G: Goal-Attainment | 1. Nature and Structure of Goals: a. Internal b. External | Ideal-centered Ideal-centered |
| | 2. Range of Goals | Situational (L.2.a) (A.2.a) |
| | 3. Dominant Achievement Mechanisms | Localized protests: responding |
| A: Relation to other Systems | 1. External Organizational Structure | Latent, fragmented, situation (G.2) |
| | 2. Relevant Systems: a. Range b. Rate of desired change | Narrow, specific Slow (I.2.a |
| | 3. Dominant Adaptive Mechanisms: a. To subsystems b. To external systems | Latent Competition; challe |

# ...alization of Protest

## : Problem Solutions in Four Stages

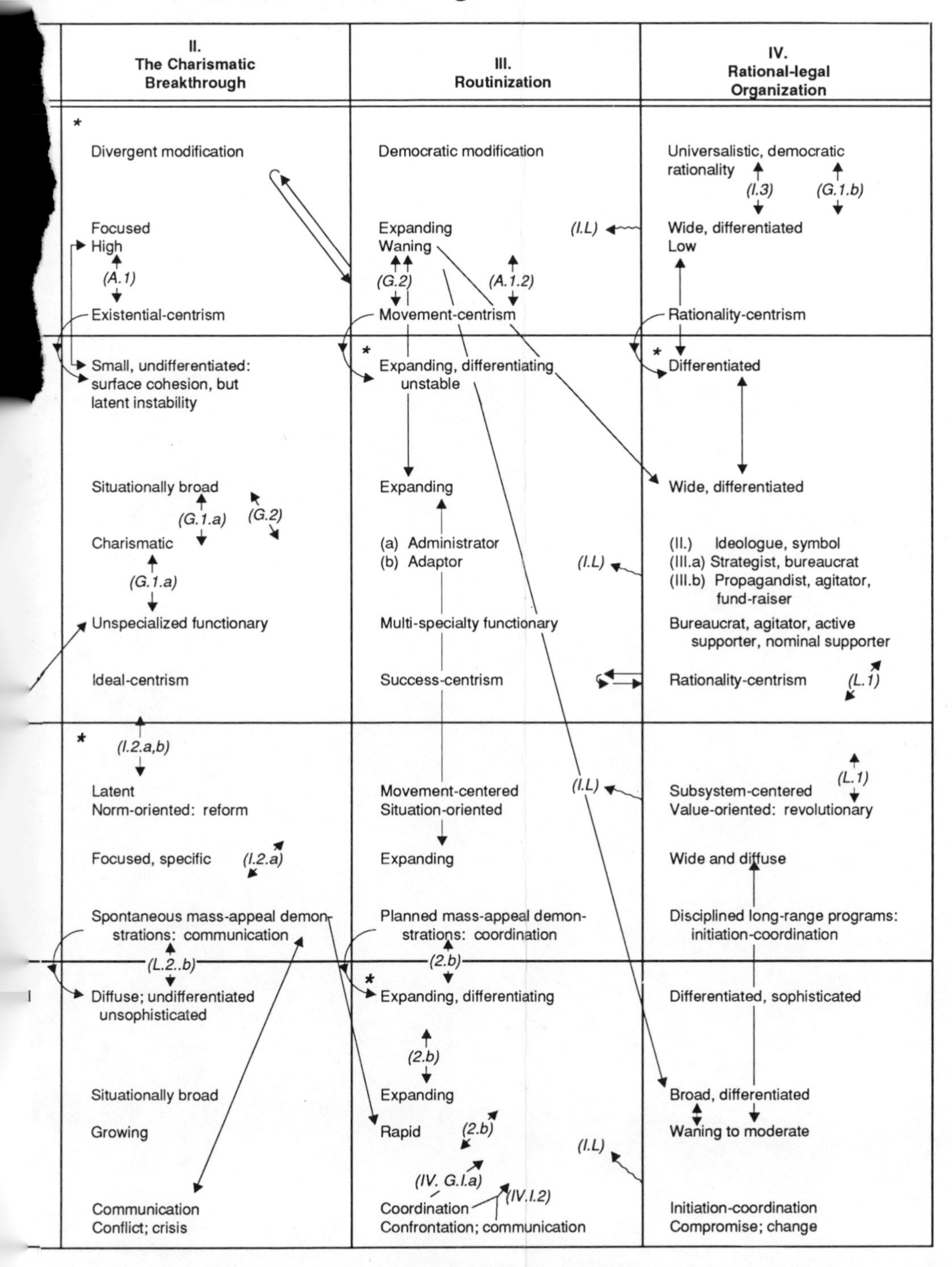

| II. The Charismatic Breakthrough | III. Routinization | IV. Rational-legal Organization |
| --- | --- | --- |
| * Divergent modification | Democratic modification | Universalistic, democratic rationality (I.3) (G.1.b) |
| Focused | Expanding | Wide, differentiated |
| High (A.1) | Waning (G.2) (A.1.2) | Low |
| Existential-centrism | Movement-centrism | Rationality-centrism |
| Small, undifferentiated: surface cohesion, but latent instability | * Expanding, differentiating unstable | * Differentiated |
| Situationally broad (G.1.a) (G.2) | Expanding | Wide, differentiated |
| Charismatic (G.1.a) | (a) Administrator (b) Adaptor (I.L) | (II.) Ideologue, symbol (III.a) Strategist, bureaucrat (III.b) Propagandist, agitator, fund-raiser |
| Unspecialized functionary | Multi-specialty functionary | Bureaucrat, agitator, active supporter, nominal supporter |
| Ideal-centrism | Success-centrism | Rationality-centrism (L.1) |
| * (I.2.a,b) Latent Norm-oriented: reform | Movement-centered Situation-oriented (I.L) | Subsystem-centered Value-oriented: revolutionary (L.1) |
| Focused, specific (I.2.a) | Expanding | Wide and diffuse |
| Spontaneous mass-appeal demonstrations: communication (L.2..b) | Planned mass-appeal demonstrations: coordination (2.b) | Disciplined long-range programs: initiation-coordination |
| Diffuse; undifferentiated unsophisticated | * Expanding, differentiating (2.b) | Differentiated, sophisticated |
| Situationally broad | Expanding | Broad, differentiated |
| Growing | Rapid (2.b) | Waning to moderate |
| Communication Conflict; crisis | (IV. G.I.a) Coordination (IV.I.2) Confrontation; communication (I.L) | Initiation-coordination Compromise; change |

## TITLES IN THE SERIES

# Martin Luther King, Jr. and the Civil Rights Movement

*DAVID J. GARROW, EDITOR*

1-3. *Martin Luther King, Jr.: Civil Rights Leader, Theologian, Orator*, Edited by David J. Garrow

4-6. *We Shall Overcome: The Civil Rights Movement in the United States in the 1950s and 1960s*, Edited by David J. Garrow

7. *The Walking City: The Montgomery Bus Boycott, 1955-1956*, edited by David J. Garrow

8. *Birmingham, Alabama, 1956-1963: The Black Struggle for Civil Rights*, Edited by David J. Garrow

9. *Atlanta, Georgia, 1960-1961: Sit-Ins and Student Activism*, Edited by David J. Garrow

10. *St. Augustine, Florida, 1963-1964: Mass Protest and Racial Violence*, Edited by David J. Garrow

11. *Chicago 1966: Open-Housing Marches, Summit Negotiations and Operation Breadbasket*, Edited by David J. Garrow

12. *At the River I Stand: Memphis, the 1968 Strike, and Martin Luther King*, by Joan Turner Beifuss

13. *The Highlander Folk School: A History of its Major Programs, 1932-1961*, by Aimee Isgrig Horton

14. *Conscience of a Troubled South: The Southern Conference Educational Fund, 1946-1966*, by Irwin Klibaner

15. *Direct Action and Desegregation, 1960-1962: Toward a Theory of the Rationalization of Protest*, by James H. Laue

16. *The Sit-In Movement of 1960*, by Martin Oppenheimer

17. *The Student Nonviolent Coordinating Committee: The Growth of Radicalism in a Civil Rights Organization*, by Emily Stoper

18. *The Social Vision of Martin Luther King, Jr.*, by Ira G. Zepp, Jr.